URBANISM AND EMPIRE IN ROMAN SICILY

Ashley and Peter Larkin Series in Greek and Roman Culture

URBANISM AND EMPIRE IN ROMAN SICILY

LAURA PFUNTNER

UNIVERSITY OF TEXAS PRESS
Austin

Printed in the United States of America
First edition, 2019
First paperback printing, 2025

♾ The paper used in this book meets the minimum requirements of ANSI/NISO Z39.48–1992 (R1997) (Permanence of Paper).

Library of Congress Cataloging-in-Publication Data

Names: Pfuntner, Laura, author.
Title: Urbanism and empire in Roman Sicily / Laura Pfuntner.
Description: First edition. | Austin : University of Texas Press, 2019. | Includes bibliographical references and index.
Identifiers: LCCN 2018007911 | ISBN 978-1-4773-3363-1 (paperback) | ISBN 978-1-4773-1723-5 (library e-book) | ISBN 978-1-4773-1724-2 (nonlibrary e-book)
Subjects: LCSH: Sicily (Italy)—Antiquities. | Sicily (Italy)—History—To 800. | Urbanization—Italy—Sicily—History. | Cities and towns—Italy—Sicily—History. | Rome—Territorial expansion.
Classification: LCC DG55.S5 P47 2019 | DDC 937/.8—dc23
LC record available at https://lccn.loc.gov/2018007911

doi:10.7560/317228

CONTENTS

ACKNOWLEDGMENTS

I first wish to thank Carlos Noreña, who supervised the 2013 dissertation that eventually became this book, and the other members of my committee: Susanna Elm, J. Theodore Peña, and Dylan Sailor. I am also grateful to many colleagues working in (and on) Sicily for their advice and hospitality at various stages, most particularly Carmine Ampolo, Lorenzo Campagna, Roksana Chowaniec, Alessandro Corretti, Ralph Covino, Donatella Erdas, Antonino Facella, Caroline Goodson, Daniele Malfitana, Ferdinando Maurici, Peter Morton, Jonathan Prag, Randall Souza, Emanuele Vaccaro, Stefano Vassallo, and Roger Wilson. I have profited from discussions with Lisa Eberle, Amy Russell, and Michael J. Taylor. Malcolm Bell, Kim Bowes, Rocco Burgio, Enrico Caruso, Francesco Collura, Gioacchino Francesco La Torre, Dieter Mertens, Martin Mohr, Jari Pakkanen, Umberto Spigo, Erik Thorkildsen, Edoardo Tortorici, Alessio Toscano Raffa, Henri Tréziny, and Markus Wolf kindly let me reproduce the site plans that appear in this book.

Ralph Hexter has been an inspiring and generous mentor. I am grateful to my former colleagues at the University of California, Davis, and my current colleagues at Queen's University Belfast for their support in the intermediate and final stages of this project. In addition, I am appreciative of the support I received for my initial research in Sicily from the University of California, Berkeley: the Graduate Group in Ancient History and Mediterranean Archaeology (Nickel fund, 2011), the Department of Classics (Heller fund, 2010, and Corinne Crawford memorial fund, 2012), the Archaeological Research Facility (Stahl Grant, 2012), and the Graduate Division (summer grant, 2012).

I thank Jim Burr, Sarah McGavick, Kathy Lewis, and everyone else at the University of Texas Press. I am also grateful to Alex Walthall and the other anonymous reader, whose suggestions have made this a much better book. Lorraine Berry and Karen Rasmussen deserve thanks for their work on the maps and site plans, as does Deborah Davidson for her careful editorial eye. All of the shortcomings of this book are of course my own.

To LuAnn Kressley, Anne Pfuntner, and Jordan Pfuntner, I owe happy memories of travels in Sicily and so much more. This book is dedicated to them, with all my love.

URBANISM AND EMPIRE IN ROMAN SICILY

INTRODUCTION

This book examines changes in the consistency and nature of urban settlement in Sicily in the seven centuries in which the island formed part of Rome's overseas empire (ca. 250 BC–AD 450). At first glance, this topic may not appear promising for a large-scale study: the textual and archaeological evidence for the Roman period in Sicily is notoriously sparse and problematic, especially compared to the data for other regions of the Roman Empire, such as North Africa, Italy, Gaul, Spain, and Asia Minor. But this evidentiary challenge, I believe, is one of the main reasons historians of the Roman Empire should not ignore places like Sicily.

Scholars risk ignoring important elements of the Roman-era settlement landscape and miss out on the opportunity to understand the complexity of Roman imperial power structures in the provinces (and local responses to them) if they focus only on the provinces and cities where the monumental remains of these power relationships are best preserved and most visible. In other words, the sparse topography of the famously maligned Panopeus in Phocis—whose residents, Pausanias claims, "possess no government offices [*archeia*], no gymnasium, no theater, no agora, no water descending to a fountain" (10.4.1)—may tell a different story about how individual communities adapted to the exigencies of Roman imperial power than the lavish monumental cityscapes of Corinth, Carthage, or Tarraco. But this story is no less valuable for understanding the development of provincial settlement landscapes under the Roman Empire.

In addition, Sicily occupies a unique place in the history of Roman overseas expansion that makes it a valuable case study for the impact of Roman imperialism on settlement in the provinces. Sicily was geographically, ethnically, and culturally diverse and possessed a variety of ever-shifting maritime connections to other Mediterranean regions. But as an island it represented a self-contained geographic unit of administration for the Romans, with clear external borders. Together with the nearby Aegadian (Egadi), Pelagian, and Aeolian archipelagos, as well as the more distant, larger islands of Cossyra (Pantelleria), Gaulos (Gozo), and Melita (Malta), it was administered as a single province after the Second Punic War. Diocletian's reforms of the late third century AD transformed it into an administrative unit of Italia. Throughout its Roman history, Sicily lay at the heart of Rome's Mediterranean empire, between Italy and the Tunisian coast and dividing the eastern and western Mediterranean basins. Sicily's fertile agricultural territories were therefore relatively easily accessible from the Tyrrhenian coast of Italy and from the central North African provinces. The island was also at the center of several major trade routes, including the shipping channels that carried commodities such as grain, olive oil, and wine between the Italian coast and other Mediterranean provinces.

Sicily was also a vital and fully incorporated part of the Roman Empire longer than any other overseas province. The Romans were first involved militarily on the island during the First Punic War against Carthage (264–241 BC). The Roman state (as well as individual Romans) had economic and political interests in Sicily before that war, however, and the island had long been a source of food for the expanding city of Rome. After the incorporation of the entire island as a province following the conclusion of the Sicilian phase of the Second Punic War (ca. 210 BC), Sicily remained under Rome's firm hegemony for the entirety of the imperial period, long after the weakening of Roman power in other areas of the Mediterranean. Arguably, the Roman history of Sicily lasted until the Vandal incursions from Africa in the mid-fifth century severed the island's political and economic connection with Rome. Afterward, western Roman political and economic control was irregular and subject to negotiation, though the island retained links with the Church of Rome, especially through extensive ecclesiastical landholdings.

Even before the Roman conquest, moreover, the communities of Sicily had a long history of urban development. The Greek colonial settlements (*apoikiai*) founded in the early archaic period had expanded and developed into true urban centers, often in control of extensive agricultural territories, by the sixth and fifth centuries BC. These centers possessed the full range of *polis* government, military, economic, religious, and cultural institutions as well as the monumental expressions of these institutions, including temples, perimeter walls, industrial areas, and public buildings and open spaces. Indeed, scholars have argued that the colonial experience of the early archaic period was integral to the emergence of the institutions of the *polis* in Greece.[1]

In the western corner of Sicily, Phoenician settlers established footholds in a number of coastal locations at around the same time as the Greek *apoikiai*. The development of these settlements is not as well known as those of their

Greek counterparts.[2] Nonetheless, communities like Motya show sufficient evidence of political, economic, and religious organization, monumentality, and internal cohesion to be described as true urban centers by the classical period. Additionally, many "native" non-Greek settlements in the mountainous interior of Sicily (the Elymian stronghold of Segesta being the most notorious example) developed into organized and monumentalized urban communities in the archaic and classical periods.[3] They apparently drew on the political, religious, and cultural institutions and the architectural forms of the Greek *apoikiai*, with whom they frequently competed for territory.

All of the island's communities also had long experiences of imperial hegemony, even before the Roman conquest in the third century BC. Beginning in the early fifth century, the competing territorial claims of Carthage and the Greek city-states (especially Syracuse) resulted in wars, forced population movements, and other upheavals across the island. In the early third century Pyrrhus of Epirus and Agathocles and Hieron II of Syracuse made more fleeting attempts to establish political, economic, and military dominance over the island.

The overseas military and administrative apparatus of Rome (the "Roman imperial state") was in its earliest form when it first made its presence felt on the island during the First Punic War.[4] The institutional framework of this imperial state continued to develop in Sicily over the course of the Republic (until ca. 30 BC), undergoing major changes in the reign of Augustus and further evolutions under the Principate (ca. 30 BC–AD 300). The short-term and long-term effects of these changes form the backbone of the analysis of settlement evolution in the following chapters. The impact of Sextus Pompey's occupation of the island in 43 BC and his consequent war with the triumvirs, in which he was decisively defeated at Naulochus in 36 BC, is difficult to trace in the archaeological record. The precise political and economic changes that resulted from this period of instability also remain the subjects of debate.[5] It is clear, however, that Augustus's major post–civil war reform was the imposition of colonies, probably composed of Italian veterans, in six coastal cities (Tauromenium, Syracuse, Catina, Thermae Himeraeae, Tyndaris, and Panormus). This was likely accompanied by grants of land in their territories.[6] As in Italy, Greece, and other urbanized regions of the Mediterranean, the establishment of such colonies—and the interactions (and potential conflicts) between new and existing residents—would have a profound impact on the physical and social fabric of individual Sicilian cities and on the settlement network of the island as a whole.

As in other Mediterranean regions, the Augustan period also saw the establishment of imperial landholdings on Sicily, first by Agrippa, whose lands passed to Augustus after his death, and later by other members of the imperial family.[7] The imperial patrimony at first consisted of lands confiscated from Sextus Pompey's supporters, primarily on the northern and eastern coasts. In addition, Augustus and his successors sanctioned senatorial ownership of Sicilian land, because it was one of the few provinces that senators could visit without restriction.[8] The reign of Augustus also brought large-scale economic changes to the Mediterranean basin that impacted Sicily. Most notably, the post-Actium years saw the incorporation of Egypt into the Roman Empire, providing Rome with a new source for its *annona* grain and thereby (in theory) reducing its dependence on Sicilian production.

The Roman state had played an active role in the development of the essential physical forms of Roman urbanism from at least the third century BC onward, both in the city of Rome itself (by constructing sewer systems, *basilicae*, *porticus*, *macella*, etc.) and in new urban centers (e.g., colonies first in Italy, then in other regions of the Mediterranean). Along the way, in order to accommodate the needs and tastes of its growing population and to facilitate its increasingly complex apparatus of magistrates, legislative bodies, and law courts, the Roman state adopted and modified urban forms that it encountered in other regions, such as the monumental theaters and stoas of Magna Graecia and the Hellenic Eastern Mediterranean.[9] Furthermore, the institutions of the Roman state (for example, the personnel and procedures used to administer justice in the provinces) were shaped through interactions with existing polities, especially in the Hellenic world.[10] So it follows that tracing processes of settlement change in Sicily, which was highly urbanized, had been subject to imperial power before the Roman conquest, and had experienced early iterations of Roman imperialism, can lead to a more nuanced understanding of the influence that Rome had on the territories under its domain (and vice versa).

My approach emphasizes settlement change in Roman Sicily as a complex process that can easily be misunderstood on empirical grounds, as the result of an overreliance on literary sources and on the archaeology of monumental urban centers.[11] I reject the dichotomy between urban and rural settlement and the notion of competition between processes of urbanization and ruralization in the various periods of Sicily's ancient history. Such dichotomies mask the variable range of social, economic, and political functions that urban centers could serve for their rural territories as well as the diversity of nonurban or semiurban settlements that dotted the Sicilian landscape. It is also difficult to distinguish finite territorial and maritime "hinterlands" from individual urban centers at any point in antiquity. Instead, I adopt a flexible definition of urban settlement that takes into account the wide range of roles that cities could play for their inhabitants and the potential for these roles to change over time. Urban centers lay at one end of a spectrum of settlement in the ancient Mediterranean landscape. They are distinguished from other settlements mainly by their density of occupation and by the intensity of the activities taking place within them.

In the following chapters I examine the Roman-era development of individual cities as well as other forms of settlement (see map 1). I argue that the settlement spectrum of Sicily did not exist in a vacuum. The way in which Sicilian settlements got "plugged into" the wider Mediterranean world changed from the Hellenistic period to the Roman Republican era and over the course of the Roman Empire, with significant regional variation. These changes in connectivity reveal the variable roles that cities could play as centers of authority within larger state and imperial systems.

My analysis points to three key developments in the Sicilian settlement landscape in the Roman period. First, as discussed in chapters 1 and 2, between the late Republic and the mid-imperial period, many former *poleis* in Sicily (especially along the southern coast and in the interior) gradually lost their roles as centers of political authority and elite residence and investment. Some remained centers of economic activity, however, at times following movement to more economically integrated sites. Political activity was instead concentrated in a few large coastal cities that had been made colonies by Augustus or later gained colonial status, which are the subject of chapters 3, 4, and 5. These cities were centers of diverse populations and a wide range of economic activities and maintained strong connections with other Mediterranean regions.

Second, as I argue in chapter 6, with the shift of the urban centers of gravity in Sicily to the eastern and western coasts a distinct Romano-Sicilian urbanism emerged. Chapter 7 examines one of the most significant indirect effects of the political, economic, and social changes brought by the Principate: the emergence of new forms of nonurban settlement in Sicily, especially in areas where older urban centers were in crisis or had largely disappeared. The picture that emerges from this study of the Sicilian urban landscape is one of cities not only as passive consumers of wealth and cultural capital but as active connectors of people and resources. This is particularly true in the Roman imperial period, when the psychological, economic, and political barriers to connections among Mediterranean regions were greatly reduced and the incentives for establishing such connections were heightened.

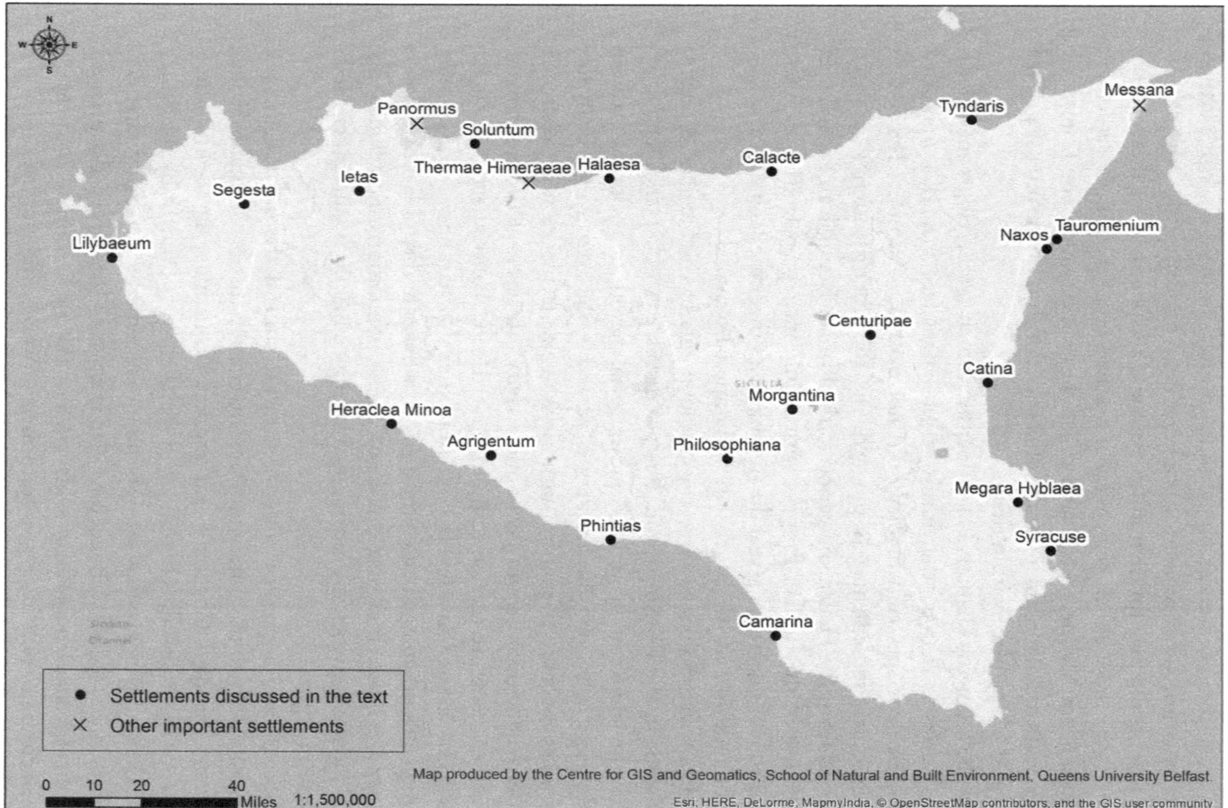

MAP 1.

Sites discussed in the text.

STUDYING THE SETTLEMENT LANDSCAPE OF ROMAN SICILY

Sicily is the archetype of the "noninsular" Mediterranean island: lying approximately midway between the eastern and western ends of the sea and a short distance from the shores of North Africa and Italy, it has served as a stopping point for seafarers since prehistory.[12] Sicily's fertility and climate made it one of the most attractive tesserae in the Mediterranean microregional mosaic (in the phrasing of Franco De Angelis) but also one of the most unstable.[13] Throughout history, periodic influxes of new peoples and the movement of people and resources out of the island have affected settlement patterns and productive regimes as well as the social and political organization, religion, culture, and economy of individual settlements. The nature and extent of change depended on the adaptive decisions of the island's inhabitants as well as the often detrimental economic logic of the newcomers, whether individuals, communities, or states.

With the exception of the prehistoric and protohistoric eras, however, the settlement landscape of ancient Sicily has received little attention.[14] For later periods of antiquity, and especially the period of Roman hegemony over the island, basic but important (and interrelated) questions are usually addressed only indirectly, in the service of elucidating other topics. These questions include why communities formed where and when they did; their relationship with the physical environment; the nature of the structures and institutions that they acquired; the functions that they performed for their members and their definitions of membership; the nature of their relations with each other; and their engagement with the world beyond Sicily (including their responses to imperial interventions).[15]

This subordination of the study of the human landscape has largely been due to the paucity of archaeological evidence for all but the largest settlements and the accompanying lack of a sophisticated theoretical framework for interpreting such evidence. This is rapidly changing, however, as the publication of the results of field surveys conducted across the island has enabled the diachronic study not only of individual settlements but also of networks of settlements across regions.[16] In the following chapters, I incorporate the results of such projects, where available, into my assessment of the development of individual urban landscapes.

The increased availability of archaeological evidence necessitates a reevaluation of the traditional dominance of the ancient literary sources in analyses of the settlement landscape of Roman Sicily. No single ancient author provides a synchronic portrait of Sicily and its settlements under the

Principate, so scholars have instead relied on the few contemporary texts that include descriptions of the province and its cities: Strabo's *Geography*, Pliny the Elder's *Natural History*, and anonymous late imperial collections of land and sea routes (the "Antonine Itinerary" and the "Peutinger Table"), supplemented by the less-detailed geographic works of Pomponius Mela and Ptolemy. Each of these sources, however, presents a unique set of challenges that prevents their synthesis into a coherent account of Sicilian settlement.

The earliest description is by Strabo, who probably completed his *Geography* in the early Tiberian period.[17] In book 6 Strabo briefly describes the location, present condition, and historical vicissitudes of Sicily's cities in a narrative *periplus* (circumnavigation) of the island. Katherine Clarke has characterized Strabo's concern with the transformative periods that shaped the condition and identity of the regions he describes as an innovative aspect of his work. But this makes it a difficult text to use as evidence for Sicilian urban life in the early Principate. Like his Stoic-influenced predecessors Polybius and Posidonius, Strabo views cities as living entities with births and deaths, whose lifecycles are among the principal concerns of the geographer/historian.[18]

In Sicily as well as the rest of the settled world, Strabo's primary interest is in the history of the Greek cities from their mythical foundations to the end of their autonomy as a result of their destruction or abandonment or their absorption into the Roman Empire. Strabo expresses the status of each city only in terms of its own past and its place in the world order established by Rome, giving little attention to relations between individual cities and settlements. As Clarke suggests, Strabo may offer valuable insight into the "social memory" of the regions he describes. But the value of his work as a testimony to the condition of Sicilian cities in the early empire and the general shape of the settlement network is limited.

Pliny, writing under Vespasian and Titus, states that Sicily has sixty-three *urbes aut civitates* (cities or states) and five *coloniae* (*HN* 3.87–91). First he lists the chief geographic features of the coast along with the names of eighteen coastal settlements, which he describes either as *coloniae* (towns containing settlements of Roman citizens, probably veterans) or *oppida* (towns). Next he turns inland and lists fifty ethnicities, beginning with three (the Centuripini, Netini, and Segestani) that possess *latina condicio* (a status probably roughly equivalent to that of a *municipium*). The others are described as *stipendiarii* (subject to Roman taxation).[19]

The first difficulty with Pliny's list, which is generally agreed to be a product of the early Augustan period, is its specific date of composition and the nature of his changes to it. The status of some communities in Pliny does not accord with their self-proclaimed status in the numismatic and epigraphic record. For example, Lilybaeum and Agrigentum are listed as *oppida* but clearly became *municipia* under Augustus. Pliny's source may have been an official list composed after the defeat of Sextus Pompey in 36 BC, probably in connection with Augustus's "settlement" of Sicily in 21 BC. He might not have updated it to reflect subsequent changes to the juridical status of cities.[20]

Problems also arise regarding the condition of Pliny's *oppida*. At least two of the towns in his list, Selinus and Himera, had ceased to exist long before the Augustan period.[21] Such anachronisms give Pliny's account the flavor of a historical geography rather than a contemporary description of Sicily and probably reflect a Hellenistic source.[22] The accuracy of his account of the *stipendiarii* of the interior is even more difficult to assess. As he does with other provinces, Pliny lists the *stipendiarii* in alphabetical order, as Latinized *ethne* rather than toponyms, giving no indication of the communities' locations or systems of government. His description of them as *urbes aut civitates* leaves open the possibility that, at least to Roman eyes, they were not all structured as single *poleis* with an urban center. They could alternatively be groups of communities centered on a single urban center for taxation purposes, as in less-urbanized western provinces and some underurbanized regions of the Greek East.[23] It need not follow that an *ethnos* corresponded to an actual urban center, let alone one in existence in Augustan times. It is therefore unsurprising that scholars have difficulty matching the names in Pliny's list with actual sites. Of the forty-five names in the list, the locations of at least half are unknown or merely conjectured.[24] Additionally, some names are clearly associated with coastal urban centers, despite being classed among the *civitates* of the interior (for example, the Drepanitani and the Erycini, apparently referring to Drepanum and Eryx on the northwestern coast).

Given these difficulties, it is important to remember that Pliny's intention was not to report contemporary conditions precisely and accurately but rather to summarize the Romans' (and particularly Augustus's) organization of Sicily into a tax-producing province.[25] Indeed, Pliny's description of Sicily is broadly reflective of contemporary Roman attitudes to the island. The coastal cities of Sicily are part of a *periplus* like Strabo's, beginning at Messana as a traveler from Rome or Italy would and proceeding south and west along the coast. Conversely, the communities of the interior are differentiated only by their taxation status and are of interest only for their extractive potential and their being part of the Roman Empire. Unlike Strabo, Pliny's geographical description of Sicily is unconcerned with history, instead presenting a catalogue of communities now possessed by Rome according to their status vis-à-vis the Roman state. However, both Strabo and Pliny view Sicily essentially from the perspective of the imperial center of Rome, as a province whose independent history has effectively ceased with its final incorporation into the empire of Augustus and his successors. It was an island at peace, whose geography and history lay open and accessible to those at the center of power.

Much different in scope and nature are the *itineraria* of the later imperial period. The collection of routes known as the Antonine Itinerary (*It. Ant.*), of unknown origin but perhaps intended for use in planning long-distance travel in the Roman Empire, includes several sequential lists of settlements along the major roads of Sicily (usually placed at intervals of a day's travel) as well as maritime routes incorporating the island's ports. The *It. Ant.*, although a complex document on the whole, is relatively straightforward in its presentation of Sicily's land and sea routes. The land routes (86.2–98.1) probably derive from a regional collection of itineraries that was placed between the lists for Corsica and Sardinia and those for Italy.[26] The Sicilian routes begin and end in a half-dozen nodal settlements (all coastal cities) and consist of sequences of settlements (either existing cities or specially appointed *stationes*) that can be matched with the courses of known Roman roads (see map 2). East-west movement is given priority, as most of the routes begin or end in the cities on the eastern and western tips of the island (Messana and Lilybaeum, respectively), which were also the main embarkation points for Italy and Africa.

As with Pliny's list, it is difficult to match toponyms in the *It. Ant.* with actual sites, because many, especially the road stations in the interior, make their first and only appearance in the itineraries themselves. These itineraries were primarily intended for long-distance travelers, to provide information about the most efficient routes and the amenities along them, so they must be used with care as evidence of the Sicilian settlement network in the high and late empire. They are valuable above all as indications of the main routes of land travel and of the cities and settlements thought to offer sufficient accommodation and amenities for travelers.[27] They hint that the compilers conceived of the province primarily as a stopping point on the journey from Italy to North Africa, given the prominence of routes between Messana and Lilybaeum.[28]

Like Pliny and Strabo, the itineraries therefore do not reflect conditions "on the ground" in Sicily but rather Sicily as viewed by outsiders concerned with traversing the province (and perhaps accessing areas of economic interest) as efficiently and easily as possible. Therefore, it is hardly surprising that efforts to smooth over the discrepancies between these sources and match their toponyms with archaeologically known sites are rarely successful. Even when sites can be matched with ancient toponyms, as is the case with most of the coastal cities and a few in the interior, the chronology of their urbani-

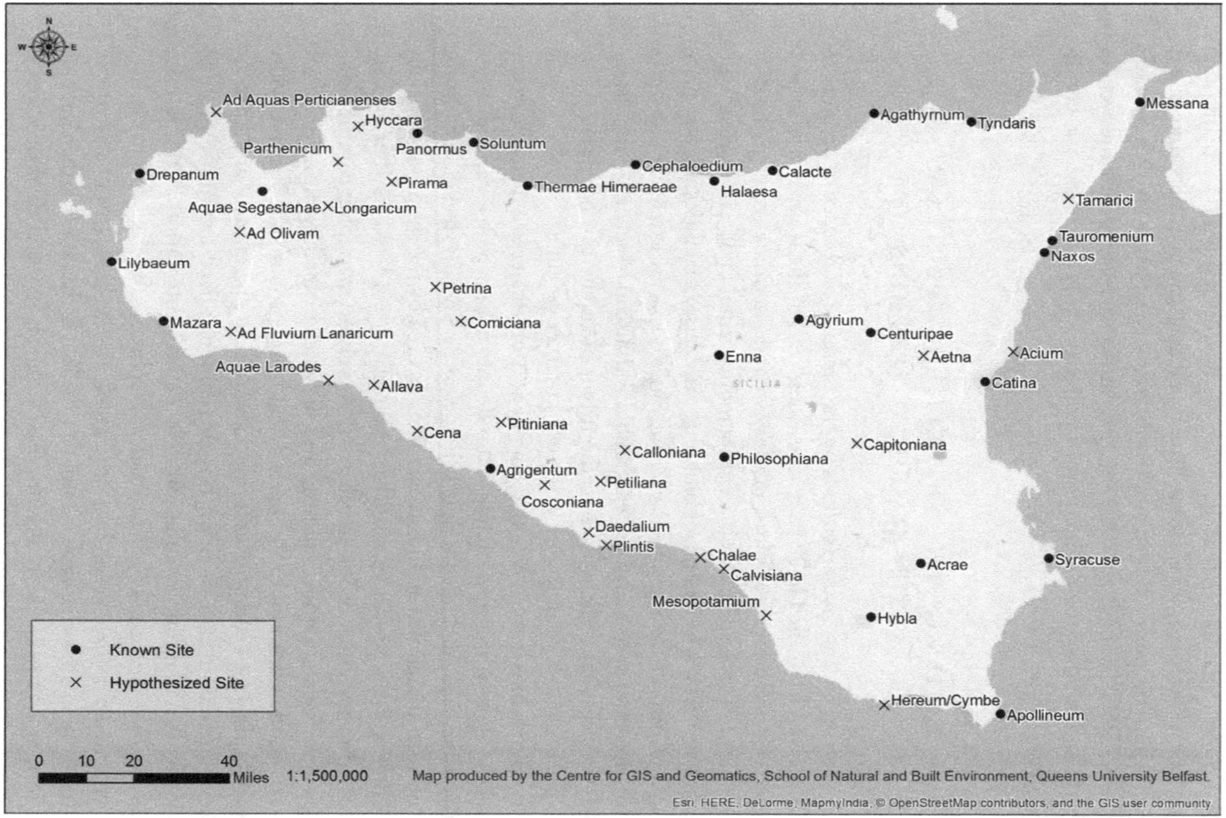

MAP 2.

Sites named in the Sicilian section of the It. Ant.

zation and the nature of their urbanism in the imperial period remain open questions. How, then, how can we study Sicilian settlement networks in the Roman imperial period if we cannot even draw a complete map of the island's cities (let alone its smaller settlements)?[29] And how can we define the Sicilian city if we downplay the distinctions in political status and economic condition made by the literary sources?

CITIES IN THE SETTLEMENT SPECTRUM: GENERAL CONSIDERATIONS

One way of defining Sicilian cities is by the presence or absence of certain criteria derived from the Greek *polis* and widespread in the Roman world: possession of special juridical status (as *coloniae* and *municipia*) accompanied by a constitution and a defined citizenship; monumental public architecture, including temples, administrative buildings, and leisure facilities; regular planning and respect for the street grid and public spaces; extensive but dense habitation; and presence in the epigraphic and historical record.[30] Individual cities' "success" and their place in the urban hierarchy can be measured by the persistence or disappearance of these criteria over time.

For a province like Sicily with a long history of urban settlement, however, a disadvantage of this approach is that it defines urbanism in external Roman rather than in local Sicilian terms. It judges as decline any deviation from the set of institutional and architectural forms favored by the Romans, especially in other western provinces with less extensive urban histories (but also reinforced in the cities of the Greek East). Levels of epigraphic commemoration, monumental public building, and presence in the historical record are indeed good indications of the general health and prominence of cities. More precisely, they are good proxies for the extent of elite investment and, in some cases, imperial interest in cities. But their absence need not imply a lack of civic identity, community cohesion, or economic integration.[31] An exclusive focus on such measures of urban vitality can obscure the city's role in the lives of its nonelite residents as well as its relations with other forms of settlement.

In the following chapters, I employ a flexible definition of urbanism that is not limited to the externally imposed political/juridical roles of cities as centers of government and tribute extraction. But these roles were often espoused and reinforced by the urban community itself (or more precisely by its elite) through the construction of public buildings, monuments, and luxurious houses. Under the Roman Empire, these roles also implicated the entire urban population. Cities served as nodes for the collection, marketing, and export of raw materials produced in their agricultural hinterlands through trade or state extraction of tax and as centers of specialized production: the transformation of high-volume, low-cost commodities into low-volume, high-cost goods (e.g., wool into cloth), and their sale, often for cash.[32]

Although the elite had the most visible impact on urban space, the persistence of urban life also relied on the willingness of the whole community to live in close proximity; to form associations for worship and economic and social advancement; to continue to produce, consume, and exchange goods from within and outside the city; to use its public spaces; and to provide the labor to maintain and enhance its public buildings. At various times in its history, the external and elite definitions of a city (as a center of governance, consumption, and social display) and its internal, subelite definitions (as a center of population and communal activities such as exchange and worship) can cohere or exist in opposition. The political, social, economic, and cultural authority of the city's elite rests on the incentives or compulsions that it can offer to the rest of the population to reside there and is constantly being negotiated. Cities often appear at their "healthiest" when the terms of this implicit social contract are kept and when there is general consensus and cooperation between social strata: infrastructure is maintained, residences are inhabited and rents are paid, goods are produced and exchanged, and wages are available. Urban life is therefore attractive to both elites and nonelites. This consensus is endangered, however, when members of the elite lose their incentive to live in cities, whether due to loss of political power or changing cultural values. Nonelite residents can then choose not to reside in a city if the costs outweigh the benefits and if they are not compelled to do so (for example, if infrastructure has decayed or if opportunities for employment decrease). They can also alter the physical spaces created by the urban elite by refusing to use them for their intended purpose (e.g., not using planned marketplaces for trade) and can create or adapt other spaces for their own purposes.

Moreover, the cities and towns of the ancient Mediterranean are better seen as "arenas" or "addresses" that concentrate wider social and ecological processes than as distinct, independent entities that actively drive historical change.[33] Cities and towns are only one part of the settlement spectrum, distinguished from other forms of settlement by their political privilege, size of population, physical extent, level of monumentality, or the number and scope of their functions.[34] In other words, the city is only one particular politically, economically, and socially constructed form of community, defined according to "what each age takes it to be," whereas the process of urbanization can result in numerous forms of agglomerated settlement.[35]

Cities and towns can share economic, social, and defensive functions with a range of settlement types. "Forts" or "outposts" (*phrouria*) can share or take over the defensive functions of cities in times of unrest and then disappear when defense is no longer a priority. Rural farmsteads, villas, villages, and hamlets can share the economic functions of cities as centers of agricultural storage, processing, and exchange. Likewise, all of these settlement types can, to varying extents, share the social and demographic roles of cities as centers of population (both permanent and temporary). Indeed, the very notion of the Greek *polis* (and the Latin *civitas*) implies an urban center (*astu*) with a territory (*chora*) containing dependent or subsidiary settlements (*komai*). It is impossible to define any Sicilian city's territory or recognize every settlement contained within it. Definitions of territory are in any case fluid: a city's boundaries can shift over time in response to changing internal and external circumstances. Nonetheless, as the following chapters show, the relations between cities and other forms of settlement, and between nonurban settlements themselves, are becoming clearer thanks to the proliferation of field survey projects in Sicily.

Just as a city can share or cede functions to other types of settlement, so its "urbanism" and even its physical location can fluctuate over time as a result of internal as well as external political and economic changes. These can include the presence or absence of a militarily, politically, and economically dominant power such as the Roman imperial state.[36] The intervention of an outside power can result in visible and often traumatic changes to the fabric of individual cities, through deliberate destruction of structures, erection of new ones, or transfer of population or by more indirect means, such as bestowing or withholding political or economic favor. The political history of Sicily can be written as a series of such interventions by powers originating within and beyond the island, beginning with the territorial expansion of the archaic Greek colonies into the interior and western part of the island. In the classical and Hellenistic periods, the leaders of Syracuse sought to extend the territory and influence of their city while Carthage continued to exert economic and military influence in western Sicily, until the entire island was finally incorporated into the nascent Roman overseas empire.

In addition, incorporation into a larger political entity, whether a territorial state or an overseas empire, can redefine the fundamental roles of cities in their societies as well as their relations with other forms of settlement. The impact of the Roman state on provincial settlement landscapes is the subject of extensive scholarship. Its fundamental premise often is that Rome's impact was largely indirect and was based above all on the extractive demands of the Roman core (i.e., the exploding population of the city of Rome itself) and periphery (the militarized frontiers). This view owes much to Keith Hopkins's influential "taxes and trade" model. Recent works have emphasized the complexity of Rome's cultural impact on the territories brought into its overseas empire in the last three centuries BC. Terms like "convergence," "interplay," and "entanglement" have been proposed as alternatives to the asymmetrical concept of "Romanization," which, in its crudest form, privileges Roman traditions over local ones in models of cultural change.[37]

Just as state power itself is never static, however, the extent of its impact on a particular region can be periodic and can fluctuate over time. The century encompassing the final years of the Republic and the reigns of Augustus and his immediate successors (ca. 50 BC–AD 50) has been interpreted as a key formative period not only in Roman political history but also in the cultures, economies, and societies of the Roman provinces and particularly in the development of urban culture across the empire.[38] The absence or disappearance of an outside power, which was felt most acutely in the Mediterranean core of Rome's empire only in the fifth and sixth centuries AD, can have an equally profound effect on cities even if it does not inevitably lead to their decline or disappearance.

The following chapters do not in general ascribe changes in the urban fabric of individual cities and in the settlement network as a whole to single and finite historical events like the war between the triumvirs and Sextus Pompey (38–36 BC) and the subsequent establishment of veteran colonies and imperial landholdings on the island. Nonetheless, they focus on the Principate (ca. 30 BC–AD 300) as a period of profound change for the settlement landscape of Sicily. The first two chapters assess the course and causes of a process that has been described in extreme terms as the decline of urban civilization in Sicily under Roman rule.[39] It is generally agreed to have resulted in a reduction in the number of urban settlements and in the population and wealth of the remaining cities. In some cases this process of abandonment appears to be relatively abrupt and quick. In others it is more gradual, with different buildings or areas of settlement going out of use at different times. Therefore, it is important first to establish a methodology for determining if, when, and how an urban settlement was abandoned. That requires a closer analysis of what is meant, especially archaeologically, by the notion of urban "decline."

TRACING DEURBANIZATION IN THE ARCHAEOLOGICAL RECORD

The most direct evidence for the abandonment of an urban settlement is the site-wide, contemporaneous destruction or collapse of its buildings and the failure to rebuild on the same site soon after the destruction. However, such occurrences are rare in the archaeological record.[40] Even in the best-known instance of sudden and permanent settlement abandonment in the Roman world, the destruction of Pompeii and nearby settlements by the eruption of Vesuvius in AD 79, the pace of abandonment is unclear. The earthquake of AD 62 had already caused extensive damage to urban infrastructure, and looting of the site of Pompeii continued in antiquity even after its burial.

All other evidence for urban abandonment or decline is indirect or proximate. In the context of the European Early Middle Ages, Chris Wickham has characterized such evidence as the "weakening of material forms" in the city.[41] Such archaeologically observable processes as public spaces and buildings that fall into disuse or disrepair, lack of new construction, absence or relative rarity of new forms of datable material culture (such as coins and ceramics), failure to adopt new building technologies and architectural styles and/or the return to simpler construction methods and materials, and contraction or fragmentation of occupation on a site may well be indications of a larger process of desertion.

The decay or collapse of public buildings and infrastructure such as streets, sewer systems, or fortifications due to lack of maintenance is commonly cited as evidence of urban decline, particularly in late antique and early medieval cities. A related development is the decay or collapse of private residences, particularly the luxury townhouses of the urban elite, and the subdivision of houses and/or public buildings into smaller, poorer dwellings or their reappropriation as workshops or agricultural processing facilities. Yet the dating of the abandonment and collapse of individual buildings is far from straightforward and can rarely be determined with greater precision than a span of decades. Stratigraphically, occupation and abandonment are essentially nonevents characterized by artifactual voids, as a building's surfaces are usually kept clean while it is in use. Also, abandonment may not be intended as permanent, so buildings may be maintained even after they are no longer in use. Therefore, the earliest deposits created by structural collapse or by the use of a building as a waste ground may occur years or decades after abandonment. It is also rare that all of the buildings in a single urban settlement are abandoned, demolished, and fail to be replaced at the same time and at the same rate. Abandonment and collapse of structures more often occurs over a longer period (perhaps as long as a half-century in the case of the Roman town of Verulamium in southern England) and does not affect all parts of a settlement at the same pace and in the same way.[42]

Even if such developments can be traced across a whole settlement with chronological confidence, they are more revealing of the level of elite investment in urban infrastructure, and the political and social priorities behind such investment, than of the actual population level of a city: in other words, a city's "urbanism" rather than its "urbanization." Temples, bath houses, theaters, amphitheaters, market buildings, administrative offices (*basilicae, curiae, porticus*), and luxury townhouses are often erected in enduring materials such as stone or brick and centered on the open public space of the forum. These grand public and private edifices and technologically advanced infrastructure projects such as paved streets and water supply and sewage systems are the most visible signs of elite investment in the city as a locus of social, economic, and political power in the early and high Empire. When they decay and disappear, so does the main body of archaeological evidence for the presence of an urban elite.

However, the absence of such structures should not necessarily be interpreted as the absence of an urban elite, much less the absence of nonelite strata within a city. These structures were the most visible archaeologically and were long associated with the high point of Greco-Roman urban civilization. Earlier generations of excavators often paid more attention to them than to the structures that took their place, which in many regions were built in more perishable materials such as wood.[43] Only with careful excavation can these subsequent structures be traced, and such thorough investigation can rarely be extended to a whole settlement. Nonetheless, if the apparent decline of elite investment in a city proves to be not just an accident of preservation, it is important to ask why this occurred and what its consequences were for the roles that the city played in the lives of all of its inhabitants.

A related but even more problematic indication of urban decline is the failure of civic authorities to employ new architectural styles, construction methods, and materials. They may instead transition from using expensive materials and complex methods to using simpler, cheaper ones. Like the abandonment and decay of monuments and infrastructure, however, these developments say more about the level of elite investment and the changing nature of elite taste, as well as a city's integration into wider social and economic networks, than about the quality of life there. The availability of materials such as bricks and colored marbles or of trained architects, mosaicists, masons, and other skilled workers may not be consistent across all regions and periods. As in the case of the processes of elite disinvestment and material impoverishment that are often blamed for the decay of urban landscapes in late antiquity, the reasons for these variations in access to technologies and materials must be sought beyond simple explanations of decline.

One way to establish a broad chronology of a site's abandonment is according to the latest datable forms of material culture scattered on the surface or deposited within excavated structures. For the Roman period, this material primarily consists of coins and datable ceramics such as imported transport amphorae and high-end tablewares (mainly Italian and African red slip wares). This method can be unreliable because of the various ways in which ceramics can enter the archaeological record. The chronological gap between a vessel's creation and its deposition in an archaeological context is rarely easy to determine. It can be as short as a few minutes or as long as several decades, depending on the vessel's durability, how long it is in primary use, and whether all or part of it is subsequently modified and reused or recycled instead of discarded.[44] After a vessel is finally discarded, disturbances of its depositional context may follow, ranging from later scavenging to the dispersal and mixture of sherds through plowing. Furthermore, the relationship between abandonment processes and material-cultural deposition is not straightforward. The accumulation of datable material like discarded ceramics within a structure may follow its abandonment, whereas an absence of material can be a sign of occupation and upkeep.

Even when datable materials come from reliable contexts across a city, their presence points more directly to the city's integration into wider systems (such as long-distance exchange networks or a monetized economy) than to its level of occupation. The absence or relative rarity of such material in a certain period is therefore more indicative of a city's reduced access to widespread, well-known datable forms of material culture than of its state of habitation. It may also reflect its reliance on more chronologically and spatially restricted and thus less easily datable forms, such as locally produced amphorae or tablewares. Additionally, an apparent absence of material from a particular period on a site may be the result of excavator bias, such as the inconsistent preservation and publication of late antique material from excavations of "classical" urban settlements. Another potential bias may occur in the recovery of ceramics, particularly in field surveys. More visible forms such as the glossy, bright red imported tablewares of the early and high Empire may be favored over less conspicuous forms, often from earlier (Hellenistic) or later (early medieval) periods.

Finally, the contraction or fragmentation of settlement deduced from the abandonment of certain sectors of the city (such as its residential districts or forum) is often used as evidence of urban decline. While contraction and fragmentation can be indications of a falling population and lower levels of prosperity among the remaining inhabitants, the interpretation of such processes can be difficult if the whole settlement has not been excavated. Just as settlement boundaries can shift over time, so too an urban settlement's center of gravity can shift according to the needs of the community and the priorities of its elite. This process is well attested in the cities of the late and post-Roman Western Mediterranean, in which the forum as the traditional locus of city government and elite benefaction was frequently replaced by "islands" of monumental activity, especially around church buildings and often on the edges of the classical city center.[45] These can be difficult to detect, especially if excavators concentrate on the city center and the monuments of the high periods of Greco-Roman urbanism.

The interpretive challenge of projecting evidence for decline or abandonment from one part of a settlement to the whole site, especially when the extent of settlement is unknown, can contribute to the difficulty of determining the nature and extent of a particular abandonment episode. Ethnoarchaeological work on modern agricultural communities has emphasized abandonment as a normal and not necessarily permanent process. It can occur on a continuum, from the disuse of structures and areas within settlements to the abandonment of whole regional settlement networks. This work has distinguished two often-overlapping types of settlement stability: locational (spatial) and occupational (temporal). Locational stability refers to the degree to which settlements are continuously or repeatedly located in the same places, while occupational stability refers to how long an occupation continues without interruption at a given location.[46]

A high number of settlements in a particular region that exhibit short-term locational and/or occupational instability (such as temporary pastoral stations that are rebuilt in different locations every year) can skew the archaeological record, giving the impression of a greater number of sites than were ever actually occupied during a given period. Such potential short-term instability would not have as pronounced an impact on the archaeology of cities, which possess a more or less permanent population and a stable range of economic and political functions. But it is a challenge for the interpretation of such settlements as agricultural villages or hilltop forts. Their existence is dependent on particular communal needs regarding agricultural production and defense, so their presence in the landscape can therefore be more fleeting.

The difficulty of establishing a firm chronology of urban decline and abandonment on individual sites makes the task of determining the broader causes of settlement change all the more challenging. Obvious questions arise from the observation of the abandonment of an individual settlement or multiple settlements in a region. Did a discrete event cause such change? If so, how much time elapsed between the event and the actual abandonment? Studies of the Roman provinces have tended to attribute "negative" changes like destruction and abandonment to events in the historical record, primarily wars and natural disasters. Although such occurrences could cause destruction to cities that resulted in their temporary or permanent abandonment, the tendency to connect destructions observed in the archaeological record to known events can lead to a circularity of argument. Reinforcement of the historical record becomes both the primary goal and the end result of excavation.[47]

Archaeologists and anthropologists have turned to other academic disciplines for interpretive frameworks for the processes of settlement change that they have observed in ancient and modern societies. For example, Colin Renfrew and Tim Poston, in their application of mathematical catastrophe theory to the archaeology of settlement change, point out that swift and dramatic shifts in settlement size and location can actually be the result of long-term processes rather than a reaction to a sudden, exogenous event.[48] For example, the shift from nucleated to dispersed settlement (of which urban abandonment can be a symptom) or from settlement on hilltops to valley locations may be caused by processes such as the intensification of agricultural production and the increase in population density. The danger in associating dramatic changes in settlement patterns with contemporaneous events such as natural disasters, plague, or warfare is that these events more often trigger than actually cause change.[49]

Similarly, the application of the insights of settlement ecology (the study of the relationship between human settlement, productive regimes and the political and social institutions that govern them, and the environment) to archaeology has led to the reinterpretation of settlement abandonment as a normal and potentially positive process that need not imply decline. Communities may choose to abandon a settlement site as a temporary measure prompted by the instability of the social and physical environment, which makes it wise to maintain flexibility in the structure and function of settlements.[50] Abandonment, whether temporary or permanent, can also be one of a range of responses to economic, social, or political pressure on a community from the outside, as Emily Mackil has shown for Greek *poleis* of the classical and Hellenistic periods.[51]

Nonetheless, the complete and permanent abandonment of a settlement, or the widespread abandonment of one type of settlement in a region, is a relatively rare occurrence and can be the result of broader social, political, and economic changes rather than simply a community's response to its changing physical environment. In such cases, and particularly in highly integrated societies, system-wide as well as local explanations for settlement change should be investigated.[52] Chapter 1 examines the causes and consequences of the widespread abandonment of urban settlement on the southern coast and in the interior in the late Republic and early Principate (ca. 50 BC–

AD 50). On the basis of the methodology outlined above, it emphasizes the role of the long-term processes of declining civic authority and shifting commercial networks in bringing about the "weakening of material forms" in the city, although events like fires, sieges, and earthquakes could trigger permanent abandonment.

ONE

URBAN ABANDONMENT IN THE LATE REPUBLIC AND EARLY PRINCIPATE (CA. 50 BC–AD 50)

The focus of this chapter is the Sicilian cities in which the process of deurbanization reached its climax between the mid-first century BC and the mid-first century AD. The first few decades of this period were eventful for Sicily. Following Sextus Pompey's occupation and war with the triumvirs (43–36 BC), the province was brought firmly into the Augustan empire, and the *princeps* himself visited the island again in 21 BC to "settle affairs" there.[1] More broadly, this also was the key century for the development of a distinctly Roman urbanism, in which the consolidation of the Roman Mediterranean empire led to a general atmosphere of economic prosperity, increased exchange, and political participation among provincial elites. This in turn led to the emergence of new cities (or the renovation and reshaping of older ones) as centers of political, economic, social, religious, and cultural life in the provinces. The Principate of Augustus (27 BC–AD 14) saw the development of a rhetoric of "restoration" and "renovation" of urban centers (beginning with Rome itself and extending out to the cities of the empire) that was adopted by successive emperors and trickled down the social scale to provincial and local elites.[2]

In this context of actual and rhetorical urban growth and renovation in the empire, the disappearance of ancient urban centers in Sicily, as visible in the archaeological record, is worthy of exploration. The deterioration of the urban built environment, potentially accompanied by a decrease in population, particularly among the ancient urbanized hilltop centers of the interior, has long been a focus of research on the Roman imperial period in Sicily.[3] However, it is usually taken as an explanation for wider changes in the settlement landscape rather than as a phenomenon that itself needs explanation. A certain circularity of argument can ensue, in which the general "decline of hill towns" in Sicily is cited as a reason for the material impoverishment or disintegration of individual centers. There has been little interest in tracing the potentially varying paces and processes by which urban centers ceased to be "urban" in the archaeological record (to modern scholars), to contemporary Roman observers like Strabo and Pliny, and in the eyes of their current and former inhabitants.

This chapter presents a series of case studies of urban settlements that appear to have undergone abandonment on a settlement-wide scale starting in the middle decades of the first century BC on the basis of archaeological and historical evidence. Although several other Sicilian settlements show signs of contraction and abandonment in this period,[4] the highly variable extent and quality of the archaeological research conducted in these settlements make a precise chronological and quantitative analysis of these phenomena difficult, if not impossible. The cities under examination in this chapter are notable for the extent of archaeological excavation and research there in the past three decades; at least at Morgantina and Ietas (Monte Iato), this research will continue for the foreseeable future. Unlike many other sites in Sicily that show signs of "decline," the research on these cities has for the most part been published in a thorough and timely manner, and excavators have paid particular attention to processes of urban contraction and abandonment. The case studies of this chapter are also geographically diverse. Their settlement histories therefore reflect the broad shifts in the Sicilian urban landscape that resulted from island-wide political and economic changes, while also illustrating the impact of more localized developments.

The order of the case studies is broadly chronological. Each describes and analyzes the pace and extent of settlement abandonment as revealed in the published archaeological record with a critical eye toward the interpretation of this record, in accordance with the principles outlined in the introduction. The six urban centers share a number of traits. All occupied elevated positions on coastal promontories, hillsides, or bluffs or on mountain ridges and summits in the interior. Heraclea Minoa, Phintias, and Camarina are located on the southern and southeastern coasts and are situated on low hills above or near river mouths. Calacte is on a high hill on the northern coast, overlooking a harbor. Ietas is a hilltop settlement in the western interior, and Morgantina occupies a long ridge in the east-central interior.

All of the urban centers had lengthy and eventful histories of settlement by the mid-first century BC. Their location in highly visible but readily defendable places is easily explained by the military, political, and economic priorities of their founders. Four emerged in the archaic period, as Greek or Phoenician colonies and subcolonies (Heraclea Minoa and Camarina) or as fortified indigenous centers that adopted monumental and institutional aspects of Greek *poleis* (Ietas and probably Morgantina). Calacte was founded in the fifth century by Ducetius, while Phintias was established by the eponymous tyrant of Akragas around 282 BC. By the end of the third century all of them (with the possible exception of Calacte) possessed a defensive wall circuit. Most had experienced at least one abandonment episode or settlement shift in the centuries preceding the Roman Empire.

The economic base of each settlement was agricultural, with the urban center serving as a processing, storage, and marketing center for the products of a rural hinterland and, in the case of the coastal centers, also as a point of embarkation and importation. Storage facilities from various periods have been excavated at Morgantina, Camarina, and Calacte, while a market structure (*macellum*) has been identified at Morgantina. These storage and redistributive activities could be accompanied by artisanal activity within or just outside the urban center, most visibly in the form of ceramic production (as at Morgantina, Camarina, and Calacte).

However, the differences between the settlements are also considerable: they are found on the northern and southern coasts and in the East and West. Ietas lay within or at the edge of the Carthaginian *eparchia* established in the late fifth century in the western half of the island, while Morgantina and Camarina were long under the control or influence of Syracuse, and Heraclea Minoa and Phintias fell into the border zone between "Punic" and "Greek" Sicily. The cities' early relations with Rome also diverged: Morgantina and Camarina were subject to violent destruction in the course of the Punic Wars, whereas Calacte played only a minor role in Rome's conquest and arrangement of the Sicilian *provincia*.

Despite these differences, all of these cities underwent processes of abandonment between ca. 50 BC and AD 50. In some cases these abandonments can be linked to local climatic and environmental factors, such as water scarcity and coastal erosion. Long-term processes of political and economic change that culminated in the Principate of Augustus—namely, the decline in the efficacy of *polis* government and shifts in Sicily's economic position in Rome's empire—also played a significant role in the disintegration and depopulation of each city.

HERACLEA MINOA

Heraclea Minoa was founded in the mid-sixth century BC as a subcolony of Selinus in order to check the westward expansion of Akragas (Roman Agrigentum) along the southern coast. The ancient city center, located on a promontory above the mouth of the Platani, and its hinterland have been uninhabited since antiquity and largely undisturbed except by agricultural

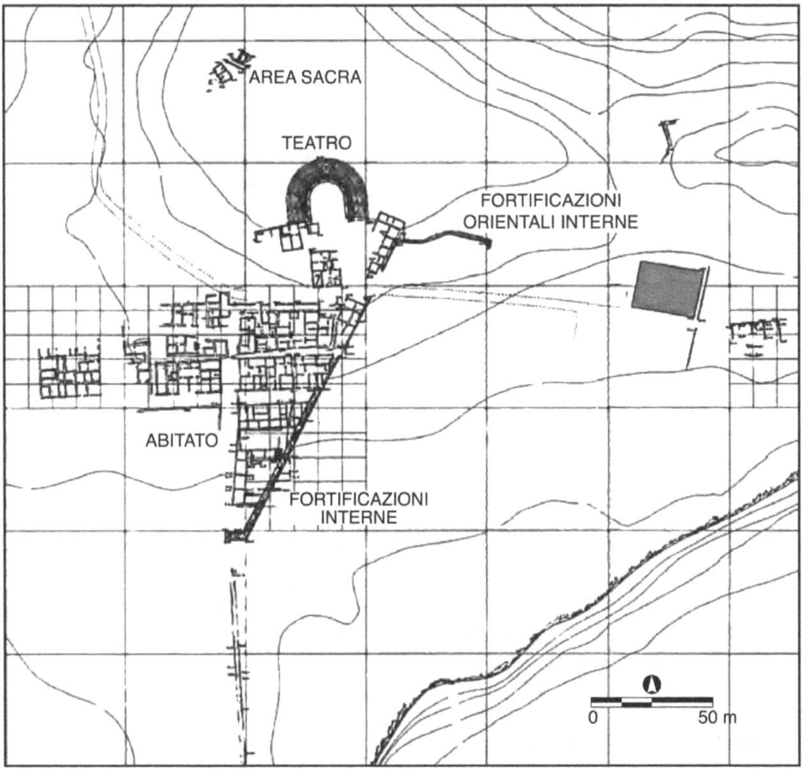

FIGURE 1.1.
Plan of Heraclea Minoa (De Miro 2014, reproduced with permission of Fabrizio Serra Editore, with modifications by K. Rasmussen).

activity. Excavations of the city center in the 1950s–1970s uncovered a theater built into the hillside overlooking the sea, sections of a wall circuit, and a series of residential blocks within a regular street plan that sloped south from the theater toward the sea (see figure 1.1). More limited campaigns in the last three decades have focused on further articulating the layout of this residential area.[5]

The excavated remains of the city center date largely to the mid-fourth century BC through the mid-first century BC; little evidence of the archaic and classical-era settlement has been found beyond the extramural necropolises. The focal point of the Hellenistic city (fourth and third centuries BC) was the theater. The open space immediately south of the theater perhaps served as the agora. The first phase of occupation of the residential blocks to the south and west of the theater (Blocchi 4–15) broadly dates to the late fourth and third centuries. The three houses in the only city block whose early phase is completely legible, Blocco 8, share a simple plan of rooms arranged around a central open courtyard that is found in townhouses across the Hellenistic Mediterranean.

The urban center underwent at least two phases of destruction and contraction, followed by significant rebuilding, in the Hellenistic and Roman Republican periods. In the course of the third century a new section of the city wall was constructed, reusing elements from earlier structures (including an altar and inscriptions). This wall marked the new eastern limit of the city and was built directly over residences from the late fourth- or early third-century phase. Although this wall indicates the contraction of the city's inhabited area to the western portion of the coastal promontory, the reasons for its construction are unclear; most likely, it was built following a natural disaster (such as an earthquake or tsunami) that caused a landslide. Moreover, the wall's third-century date can only be inferred from its stratigraphic relationship to the preexisting theater, the residences it was superimposed upon, and the structures that were later built onto it.

Construction and habitation continued in the residential quarter in the third and early second century BC. In the second half of the second century BC, however, the city underwent a major phase of rebuilding that the excavators connected to the servile wars and the resettlement of displaced locals (perhaps supplemented with Roman and Italian colonists) by the consul Rupilius in 132/131 BC (Cic., II *Verr.* 2.15). The houses in the residential area south of the theater from the late fourth and third centuries show signs of destruction and reconstruction or reuse in the course of the second century. For example, one house in Blocco 8 was divided into two independent sections, with the rooms south of the central courtyard that opened onto the street operating as shops and the rooms in the northern half of the house serving as a residential area. The heart of this second- and first-century house was a room that had been redecorated with an altar and niche (*lararium*), a paved floor, and First-Style wall paintings.

While this new phase of settlement largely respected the plan of the fourth- and third-century city, some dramatic alterations to the urban fabric are visible, such as the construction of a block of residences and shops in the previously open space immediately south of the theater. In addition, the renovation of the eastern perimeter wall in the second century, perhaps in the context of the First Servile War, obstructed the drainage channel of the theater, implying that this building had fallen into disuse. Sediment had begun to accumulate on the floor of the orchestra as early as the third century and continued to accumulate in the first half of the second century.

Occupation of the city center persisted into the first century BC, both in the old residential area and, for the first time, in the area of the theater itself. At least two groups of buildings were built against the eastern and western *analemmata* of the theater, with one of these agglomerations (Blocco 1, on the eastern *analemma*) also incorporating the now-dismantled and abandoned eastern fortification wall. The thick sedimentation layer beneath these buildings indicates a long span of time between the abandonment of the theater and their construction. A large number of Dressel 1A transport amphorae were found in one of the rooms in Blocco 1, indicating that it may have functioned partly as a ceramic workshop. Further evidence for artisanal activity (stoneworking) comes from Casa B of Blocco 4, in the new residential area south of the theater.

Despite the reduced size of the city in the second and first centuries BC, the incorporation of commercial and production spaces into the residential quarters as well as the large numbers of imported Rhodian, Greco-Italic, and early Dressel forms of transport amphorae point to a vibrant urban economy that was perhaps centered on the exchange of grain from the hinterland for imported wine, especially from Italy. The city also appears populous and active in Cicero's Second Verrine Oration: Cicero stayed there during his investigations (5.129), and the city contributed a ship to Verres's antipirate campaign (5.86).

Occupation of the city appears to have ceased in the third quarter of the first century BC. There is no evidence of a single, violent site-wide destructive event, but some structures, such as the supposed ceramic workshop in Blocco 1 (where large numbers of Dressel 1A amphorae were left in place), may have been abandoned relatively hastily. Other structures, such as the houses in Blocco 8, appear to have fallen into ruin by the late first century BC. Early Italian sigillata, which reached other sites in Sicily around 25 BC, is absent from the latest occupation and destruction strata in Heraclea. This absence led excavators to conclude that the settlement was abandoned by the beginning of Augustus's reign, perhaps in connection with the economic and political upheavals of the Roman civil wars. The city is also absent from Pliny's list of Sicilian *civitates*.

Field surveys conducted in the hinterland of the city complement this picture of an urban center in decline with evidence for a decrease in the number of farms in the first century BC. The few farm sites that remained, however, appear to have increased in size over the course of the Principate, apparently growing into villas and estate centers.[6] Excavations in the plain near the old city center in the early 1990s revealed a basilica and cemetery used in the fourth century AD and a nearby settlement with evidence of occupation in the late Republican period and in the third century AD. The development of this settlement/funerary complex may be linked to that of the coastal road connecting the late antique dioceses of Agrigento and Triocala.[7]

Even though the history of the urban center of Heraclea Minoa is fragmentary, it points to the long, drawn-out form that civic disintegration could take and to the difficulty of ascribing this process to single causes or events. The diagnostic ceramic materials found in the use, destruction, and abandonment strata of the fourth/third century phase—primarily Campana A and C black-glaze wares—had long periods of production and distribution in Sicily and are similar to the materials found in the use and destruction strata of the second-century phase. Therefore, it is difficult to assign firm dates (or even time frames) to the changes observed in the city's topography. Consequently, the impact of the servile wars and the Rupilian settlement on the built environment may be overstated, because they are the main documented events in Heraclea's Republican-era history. Nonetheless, it is clear that the community's financial means and political and economic priorities shifted over time from the maintenance of public buildings and spaces such as the theater, street network, and wall circuit to the construction of small houses, storage facilities, and production units.

The diminution of settlement in the hinterland of Heraclea Minoa paralleled the abandonment of the city as early as the mid-first century BC. The decline of the population of the urban center would have reduced its pull on its hinterland as a market for agricultural products, damaging the livelihoods of small-scale farmers in particular. The consolidation of rural settlement into larger estates was a later and gradual process, and these estates seem to have coalesced along the coastal road network rather than around the urban center and harbor of Heraclea. Finally, the persistent threat of coastal erosion and slippage may have reduced the appeal of settlement in the urban center, especially as the community lost the financial and organizational means to cope with such environmental challenges. The site also receives little rainfall, so the difficulty of obtaining water (an even more acute challenge in other Sicilian cities, as discussed below) may also have discouraged settlement in periods of economic hardship.

The case of Heraclea Minoa also shows the difficulty of dating the final abandonment of an urban settlement with precision, as the end of occupation and economic activity at the site is inferred from the absence of ceramics and other datable materials after the early Augustan period. The lack of such datable, portable items as Arretine ware (the dominant fineware of the western Mediterranean of the early and mid-Augustan period) points more directly to Heraclea's lack of economic integration than to its abandonment.

However, we can gain further insight into the factors that contributed to the end of urban settlement at Heraclea by examining Phintias, another city on the southern coast that experienced a similar trajectory of abandonment in the mid-to-late first century BC.

PHINTIAS (LICATA)

Phintias, tyrant of Akragas, founded an eponymous city for the displaced residents of Gela in 282 BC at the mouth of the River Salso on the southern coast, on the outskirts of modern Licata. Excavations since the 1980s have confirmed the existence of a large, planned Hellenistic settlement on Monte S. Angelo, at the eastern end of a range of hills (the so-called Montagna di Licata) overlooking the sea and river mouth.[8] Small sanctuaries and settlements dotted the Montagna di Licata and the coastal plain surrounding it by the archaic period, but the first evidence of occupation on Monte S. Angelo itself comes from the mid-fourth century BC, in the form of ceramics and other datable materials found in secondary contexts related to later terracing. Although its exact form and location are unknown, the earliest settlement may have been a *phrourion* on the summit that formed part of a network of short-lived fortified hilltops at the bounds of the Agrigentine domain.

Phintias itself, though founded on largely virgin ground, lay in an area of major strategic significance in the century or so preceding the First Punic War, at the eastern bounds of Agrigentine political influence and in the broad and fluid border zone between Greek and Carthaginian hegemony in Sicily. The area around the mouth of the Salso was also a battle zone in the First and Second Punic Wars, although it is not known if Phintias took an active role in these conflicts.[9] Only small sectors of the settlement have been excavated, so the extent and layout of the urban center remain unclear. Nonetheless, Phintias offers a valuable chronological and geographical comparandum for the abandonment processes observed farther up the southern coast in Heraclea.

Besides some limited exploration of the summit and the scant remains of the city's necropolis, excavations in the last three decades have largely focused on residential quarters laid out on the southern and northeastern slopes of Monte S. Angelo, similar to the regular urban plan at Heraclea and with houses of similar size and design. Through the 2014 season, excavators had identified six rectangular *insulae* containing houses and shops and had fully or partially excavated remains of sixteen similarly sized houses, most of which were oriented around a central courtyard (see figure 1.2).[10] This residential area underwent two main building phases, first in the period immedi-

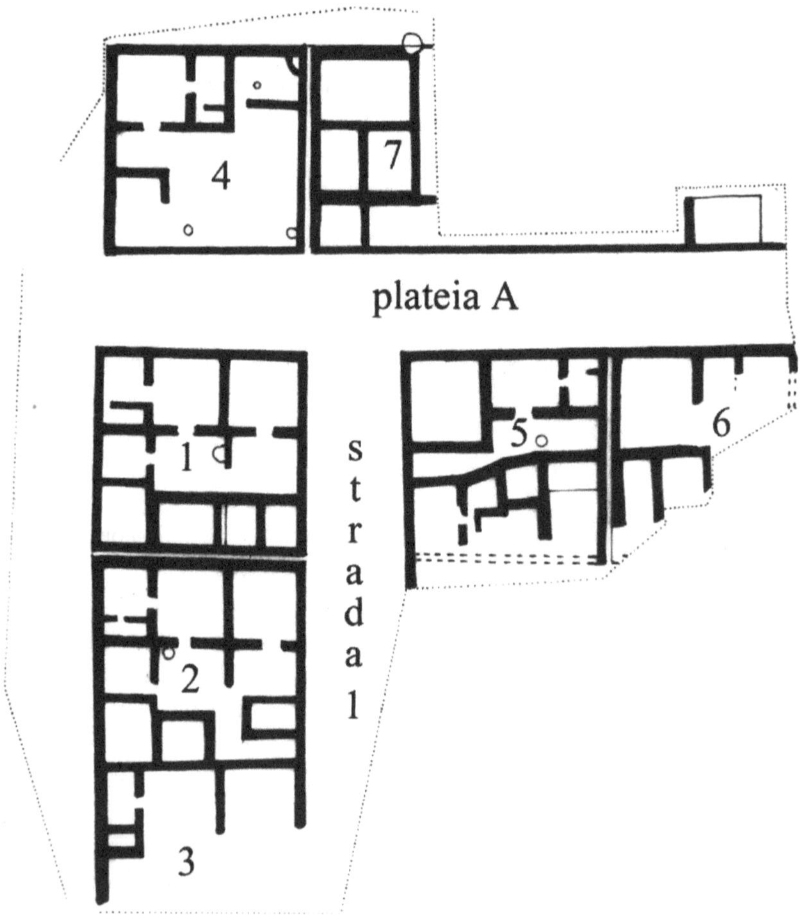

FIGURE 1.2.
Phintias: plan of an excavated residential area (2000–2006) (A. Toscano Raffa/G. F. La Torre).

ately after the foundation of the city and then in the decades after the Second Punic War. The articulation of the urban plan and the construction of its residential quarters have been dated to the late third century or early second century BC; the excavated houses show signs of continuous occupation for over a century thereafter.

The scale and ambition of the urban plan, which required the terracing of the steep slope of Monte S. Angelo, point to the settlement's prosperity in the early second century BC, probably thanks to its rich agricultural hinterland and its role as an embarkation point for its produce to Rome. However, the houses within this plan are relatively modest in size (most are around 200 m^2). The lack of significant renovation to these houses in subsequent decades also suggests that Phintias's prosperity was relatively short-lived.

Nothing is yet known of the public and religious edifices of Phintias, but a Greek inscription found in the residential area sheds important light on its public institutions and activities.[11] This inscription commemorates two men, Nemenios and Theodoros, tasked with oversight (*epimeleia*) of an unknown construction project (*dome*)—perhaps a wall (*teichos* or *toichos*). Although it is not clear if Nemenios and Theodoros held magistracies associated with their *epimeleia*, they oversaw a project of some importance that was financed in a public context, either with civic funds or through private benefaction. The inscription has been dated paleographically to the late third or early second century BC, broadly corresponding to the period in which the excavated residential quarters were planned and constructed. Other inscriptions not from the site—including a decree of the *damos* of the Geloi found on Kos and dated to 242 BC (*SEG* 12.380) and one of the Entella tablets recording the *boetheia* between Entella and the Geloi during the First Punic War—point to a strong Hellenic (and anti-Carthaginian) civic identity still linked to the destroyed metropolis. They also suggest active intra- and extra-Sicilian diplomacy in the first generations following Phintias's foundation.[12]

The abandonment and decay of the residential quarter on Monte S. Angelo has been dated to 40–30 BC from materials found in the collapse layers of the excavated houses, including black gloss wares, presigillata, Italic Dressel 1A-C and Dressel 2–4 amphorae, and lamps. As with Heraclea Minoa, excavators also cited the absence of early Italian sigillata in support of this abandonment date. The immediate causes of the abandonment of the residential area are not apparent, but there are no signs of violent destruction (such as evidence of fire). Excavators noted that the strata immediately below the collapse layers in the houses were largely devoid of metal and glass objects and coins, suggesting that inhabitants had time to remove valuables before abandoning their houses. In addition, the houses were subject to spoliation in the period immediately following their abandonment. This suggests that construction continued in other sectors of the city, perhaps lower on the slopes of Monte S. Angelo, around the port. Phintias is included in Pliny's list of Sicilian *stipendiarii*, but there is so far no archaeological evidence for occupation on Monte S. Angelo beyond the late Republican and early Augustan periods. With the decline of the urban center of Phintias, settlement may have shifted to the coastal plain below, which may be the *refugium* of Plintis included in the *It. Ant.*'s maritime route along the south coast. Although the existence of the modern city of Licata prevents archaeological exploration at the foot of Monte S. Angelo, the surrounding area is dotted with rural settlements occupied from the imperial era through late antiquity.[13]

In contrast to Heraclea, the history of Phintias in the post–Punic War period is "eventless" in the literary record. Cicero notes its prosperity and commercial importance, particularly for the *deportatio ad aquam* of grain from the interior (II *Verr.* 3.192). There is no indication that it suffered directly in any of the military upheavals of the second and first centuries BC. Therefore, we may infer that the causes of its obsolescence—whether accompanied by the complete abandonment of the old urban center, the contraction of settlement, or the shift of settlement to a location closer to the river mouth—were primarily economic. The period of abandonment of the excavated residential district (ca. 40–30 BC) is suggestive, because it coincides with Sextus Pompey's presence in Sicily, his defeat by Octavian, and Sicily's subsequent reincorporation into the Roman Empire. The excavators have proposed Sextus Pompey's blockade of the Sicilian grain supply to Rome and Octavian's subsequent inattention to rebuilding the southern coast of the island as the most immediate causes of the city's decline. Phintias (along with Heraclea Minoa) also may already have suffered economically and politically from the reemergence of Agrigentum and its port in the late second century BC, just as these two cities had stood to benefit from their former hegemon's defeat in the Second Punic War.[14]

It is also significant that there is no evidence of occupation on Monte S. Angelo before the mid-fourth century BC despite the site's clear strategic significance and that no rebuilding occurred over the ruins of ancient Phintias before the construction of a medieval tower on the summit. The excavators attribute this lack of preceding and subsequent occupation to the lack of freshwater springs on the hill. The absence of an immediate water source was especially problematic because the River Salso is brackish, as its name suggests, and the site receives little rain (on average, under 500 mm per year). Excavations of the residential quarters of Phintias have revealed that the supply of water was a major concern: all the excavated houses possessed at least one large cistern for domestic use, and the water used in the kitchens and bathrooms of these houses was sometimes collected for reuse.[15]

For both Phintias and Heraclea Minoa, we can posit that no single event directly caused the city's abandonment. Rather, we can hypothesize a range of economic, political, and environmental causes that coalesced around the mid-first century BC and precipitated the swift (though not sudden) abandonment of the urban center (or significant swaths of it) within a generation. The renaissance of Agrigentum as the hegemonic port city of the southern coast toward the end of the second century BC (explored further in chapter 3) provided economic competition for both cities. Sextus Pompey's occupation of Sicily from 43 to 36 BC and blockade of Rome's grain supply would have caused further economic damage that Octavian did nothing to directly alleviate in subsequent decades. In fact, as chapter 4 emphasizes, the first emperor focused his attention primarily on the northeastern corner of Sicily. Even if pockets of settlement persisted at each site or shifted to nearby coastal landings, significant environmental challenges such as coastal erosion at Heraclea Minoa and the scarcity of fresh water at Phintias may have discouraged settlement in the former urban centers. Furthermore, in the peaceful conditions that followed the establishment of the Principate, fortified settlements on hilltops or coastal promontories no longer held the same strategic significance that they had in previous centuries. Unlike Heraclea Minoa and Phintias, Morgantina lay deep in the interior, was more closely tied to Syracuse throughout its history, and suffered more dramatically in the periodic warfare that followed Rome's provincialization of Sicily, but we can trace broadly similar developments in its urban fabric.

MORGANTINA

The urban center of Morgantina, a settlement of indigenous origin that came under the cultural influence of the eastern Sicilian *apoikiai* (especially Syracuse) relatively early in its history, extended along the long, low ridge of Serra Orlando on the western edge of the plain of Catania. The site was discovered and identified in the 1950s and has been the subject of archaeological research ever since. These extensive excavations have not yet uncovered the full extent of the ancient settlement but have brought to light public and residential areas situated upon the hillocks that dot the ridge and in the valleys between (see figure 1.3). In addition, the Roman-era material culture of the site has been extensively studied and published.[16] For these reasons Morgantina is one of the most important sites for understanding processes of urban abandonment in early imperial Sicily.

The excavations indicate that the city experienced its monumental heyday in the second and third quarters of the third century BC, when it was under the hegemony of the Syracusan Hieron II.[17] In this period the ridge was fortified. The agora was embellished with a theater, sanctuaries, a council chamber (*bouleuterion*), the "Great Steps" (perhaps an *ekklesiasterion*), fountains and fountain houses, shops, granaries, and stoas.[18] In addition, occupation and

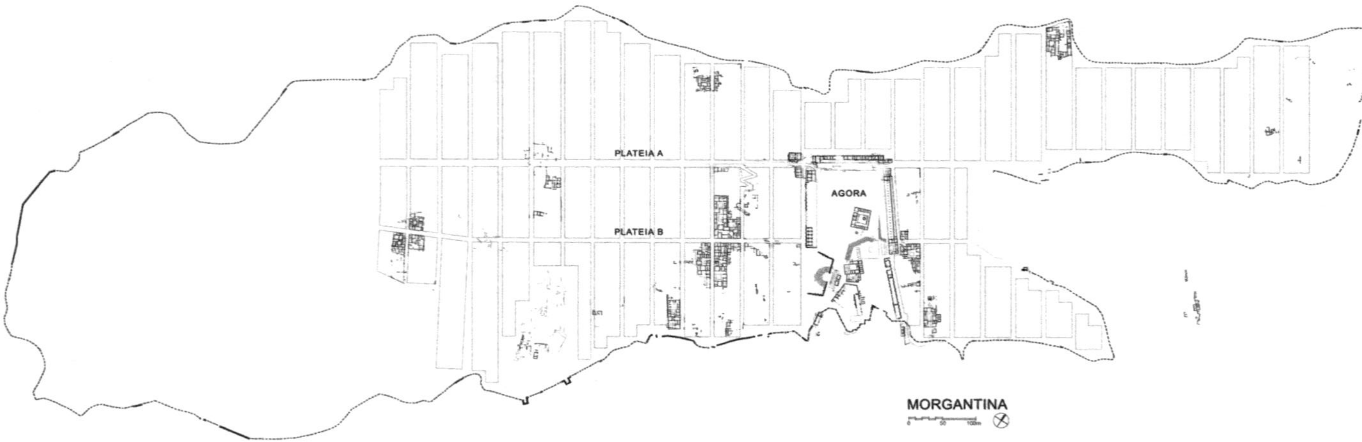

FIGURE 1.3.

Plan of Morgantina (E. Thorkildsen/American Excavations at Morgantina).

FIGURE 1.4.
Morgantina: macellum *(author photo).*

productive activity increased in the city's territory, perhaps reflecting, along with the monumental granaries in the agora, an intensification of grain production in the region to meet the tithe demands of Syracuse.[19]

The agora entered a new phase of use after the Second Punic War. In 211/210 BC Morgantina was besieged and captured by the Romans, who deported its former population and resettled it with Spanish mercenaries (Hispani) (Livy 26.21.14–17). The cityscape bears signs of extensive destruction at the end of the third century.[20] Many structures in and around the agora were not reused or rebuilt later, and the city's fortifications fell out of use. For example, the row of shops at the southern end of the agora, below the West Granary, was abandoned not long after the Roman sack; the complete vessels found in some rooms appear to have been on sale at the time of the city's capture. Although there are signs of brief reuse in the late third century, the ground level of the southern agora had risen by the second century; the shops were no longer in view.[21]

A new *macellum* was constructed in the open space of the agora, however, along with a *temenos* adjoining the theater (see figure 1.4).[22] This *macellum*, like similar structures in Italy, was probably used primarily as a victuals market, given the large numbers of coins and animal bones found in it. Several older structures, including the stoas lining the agora, were rebuilt or modified in the course of the second century. The public water collection and distribution system was also maintained.[23] The city hosted a prosperous pottery industry in the agora (including in a section of the East Granary), in parts of the old fortifications, and in private houses. The Morgantina pottery workshops produced black gloss wares (mainly Campana C) and then thin-walled wares and red gloss "pre-sigillata" throughout the second century and into the first century BC.[24] Although Diodorus claims that the town was at the center of the two servile wars of the second century (cf. 34/35.2.3), the agora and the rest of the city bear little trace of these events.

The development of the residential areas parallels that of the agora. These areas were laid out on a grid on the hills immediately east and west of the agora, in *insulae* of various sizes. Lavish large dwellings such as the House of the Doric Capital, the House of the Arched Cistern, and the House of the Official attest to the city's prosperity in the third century and to the presence of a residential elite. Some of the houses on the East Hill were not reoccupied after the siege of 211, however, and many of the large third-century residences on the West Hill were subdivided into smaller, less ornate dwellings in the second and first centuries BC.[25]

The implications of the Roman siege and takeover of Morgantina for settlement in the city's hinterland are more ambiguous.[26] The territory shows a significant drop in site numbers and in the numbers and densities of artifacts within sites, pointing to a decrease in rural population that mirrors the likely demographic decline in the urban center itself after the Roman conquest. Furthermore, the concentration of the remaining larger sites along waterways and overland transportation routes may indicate that these rural centers took on more significant roles in the collection, processing, and distribution of the region's agricultural produce (still mainly grain, perhaps supplemented by wine and olive oil) as economic activity in the urban center shifted toward pottery production.

The excavators of Morgantina and the interpreters of its material culture are in broad agreement that the city's post-Hieronian history was punctuated by two distinct and dramatic destructions that were followed by periods of cleaning, rebuilding and reuse of existing structures, and limited new construction in the urban center. These destructions left traces in the archaeological record in closed and datable contexts such as fires and structural collapses as well as cistern fills and dumps of refuse from subsequent cleanup and reconstruction activities.

The first destruction accompanied the Roman siege of 211/210 and was followed in the late third and second centuries by cleanup and rebuilding in the agora and residential quarters. The nature, extent, and cause of the second destruction are less certain. Early excavation reports include scattered notices of destruction and abandonment across the city dated broadly to the mid-first century BC.[27] Shelley Stone has analyzed the latest datable ceramic and numismatic material from structures with evidence of violent destruction in this period. He has also studied the ceramic materials and coins from the unified deposits scattered throughout the city, such as closed domestic cisterns, that were presumably created during later cleanup efforts, when they were filled with materials from the destruction event. Stone dates the destruction of the city evidenced by these materials to ca. 35 BC and attributes it to the punitive actions of Octavian against the cities of Sicily in the aftermath of the war with Sextus Pompey.[28]

This mid- to late first-century BC destruction event was followed a few decades later by modest, limited reconstruction and resettlement that continued at least until the second quarter of the first century AD. Some houses in the western residential area were cleared out and reoccupied by the last decade of the first century BC, while there are scattered indications of cult and commercial activity recommencing in the agora around the same time, especially in the shops built over older structures (including the *bouleuterion*) in the northwestern corner.[29] The primary datable materials for this final phase of settlement are imported Arretine ware and other forms of Italian sigillata (especially of the late Augustan and Tiberian periods) along with a few Sicilian imitations and Roman bronze coins issued under Augustus and Tiberius. Some areas of the city show signs of fire and structural collapse in the early first century AD. Life appears to have petered out on the site by mid-century.[30] The absence of activity has been inferred from the dearth of datable material culture after the middle Julio-Claudian period. The latest pottery found in context is of Tiberian or Claudian date, while the latest coin is an issue of Claudius found in the agora.[31]

The main drawback to this interpretation of the material record is its tendency to periodize the history of Morgantina into distinct political and cultural phases of development, punctuated by finite destruction and abandonment episodes that can be matched to historical events: the "Hieronian" phase, which was ended by the Roman siege of 211 BC; the "Roman" or "Hispani" phase that followed until the destruction of ca. 35 BC; and finally the "village" phase of ca. 5 BC until the mid-first century AD. This periodization is natural, since violent events like fire and structural collapse are more visible and more easily datable than long-term, continuous processes such as the occupation of a house, the use of a shop, or the dumping of garbage in a waste heap. However, it may not accurately reflect change through the whole urban space of Morgantina. The emphasis on destruction and rebuilding—and particularly on the 211/210 BC and ca. 35 BC "breaks"—may actually mask continuities, or different types and paces of change, in the use of urban space.[32]

The evidence for such breaks can be challenged. For example, the apparent two- or three-decade gap in coin finds and datable ceramics after ca. 35 BC may not indicate a period of abandonment. This gap, which is better characterized as a preponderance of coins from 43–36 BC over those from ca. 36 to 7 BC, could have other explanations. Perhaps the city had a greater military presence, and hence a greater circulation of coinage, during the civil war than in the period immediately after. Or coins issued under the authority of Sextus Pompey, which constitute the majority of coin finds from the period 45–36 BC, may have been casually or deliberately discarded in greater quantities than later imperial issues because they were no longer "legal tender."[33] Also, the date ranges for the latest pottery recovered from the site—Arretine and other Italian sigillata—are indications of the period of their production rather than of their primary use and deposition. The absence of later forms of these wares more directly indicates the end of the importation of common finewares to the site (and hence its economic isolation) than the precise time of abandonment.

Too much attention to buildings that were violently destroyed risks overlooking the urban structures, activities, and institutions for which dramatic ruptures are not apparent or for which different periodizations are possible. For example, the community of Morgantina encountered various environmental stresses throughout its history, from scarcity of rainfall to instability of terrain.[34] An examination of the town's domestic and public water supply reveals a persistent concern for and efforts to maintain this resource throughout the town's history. The main water sources were springs located throughout Serra Orlando, domestic wells and cisterns, and a large (presumably public) reservoir located on Papa Hill west of the settlement; water was supplied to public and residential areas through a network of terracotta and lead pipes. The pipes that supplied domestic cisterns in the western quarter were aligned with the urban grid, and some were maintained into the early first century AD.[35] Fountains or basins for drinking water were installed in most parts of the agora, in public buildings, and in residential areas.[36]

The history of the fountain house in the northeastern corner of the agora illustrates the continuous effort to maintain the city's water supply (see figure 1.5). This fountain, which was constructed in the mid-third century in front of a spring rising from the East Hill, underwent three subsequent remodelings in its two centuries of use.[37] In the fountain's original design, a closed, inter-

FIGURE 1.5.
Morgantina: agora fountain house (author photo).

nal basin captured and held spring water as well as runoff from the roof of the neighboring East Stoa, perhaps for consumption by residents of the East Hill. A separate, wide external basin whose contents were exposed to dust and wind and therefore less potable provided water for commercial and industrial activities in the agora. The depletion of the spring that fed the fountain by the late third century led to the first modification: the reduction of the intake capacity of the external basin. Further modifications followed around 170 BC, when the exhaustion of the original spring necessitated the construct of new intake systems to channel water from another spring on the East Hill to the external basin and from a spring at the northwest corner of the agora to both basins. The capacity of the fountain was further reduced when the second spring on the East Hill dried up around a century later. The internal basin was completely filled at this point, and an *aediculum* was constructed above it. The external basin remained in use, though it was no longer covered. It continued to be supplied by runoff from the East Stoa and by the spring water brought in underground channels from the other side of the agora. The fountain house remained in use until the early first century AD, when the *aediculum* collapsed and the external basin began to be filled with waste.

By keeping in mind the continuity of community priorities indicated by the provision of water and rejecting the frameworks of "rupture" and "decay" for interpreting the material record, we can better evaluate the nature of post-Punic War occupation at Morgantina. The second century and early first-century BC settlement, although smaller, remained an active civic entity with a strong commercial and industrial aspect. This is shown by the minting of coins of the HISPANORUM series into the early first century BC,[38] the construction of the theater *temenos* and the *macellum* in the agora (though without respecting the old urban plan), the subdivision of some houses in the western residential quarter into shops and workshops, and the construction of large kilns in former public buildings.

These kilns were not "squatter" workshops in the ruins of the third-century city. Rather, the potteries in the agora, as well as the "Great Kiln" built into the old city wall, operated under some degree of civic control and produced on a large scale in aggregate, even if they operated as individual production units.[39] Despite the geographic and climatic disadvantages of the site for pottery production—the lack of an abundant, regular water supply and clay deposits in the immediate vicinity—the potters were able to gather raw materials from sources both near and far (most likely clay from the valleys around Serra Orlando but also volcanic sands from the eastern coast). They produced construction materials (bricks, roof tiles, pipes) and fashionable tablewares (mainly Campana C vessels).[40]

The pottery industry shows the continued pull of the urban center in the second and first centuries as a place of safety and legal protections, where order was maintained and labor and raw materials, as well as knowledge of current production techniques, were accessible. From the city center, ceramic products could be distributed efficiently and profitably, perhaps to civic authorities as well as to households. The city's role in grain production may also have facilitated the pottery industry, with ceramics distributed along the same overland routes (and perhaps as parts of the same cargo) as grain; a similarly symbiotic relationship between pottery and grain production probably arose at Centuripae (see chapter 5). The continual efforts to maintain the town's public water supply into the early first century BC—and especially the supply of nonpotable water from the agora fountain house—could also be connected to the demands of the pottery industry and more generally to the economic life of the agora, including the selling and butchering of livestock through the *macellum*. The *macellum* itself was integrated into the town's water supply, with the basin in the northeast corner of its courtyard receiving water drained from the agora fountain house.[41]

The city center shows fewer signs of industrial activity in its final phase of occupation. All of the urban potteries were abandoned by the third quarter of the first century BC.[42] Instead the city's space was mainly used for commercial and residential purposes, with little indication of any civic authority guiding its organization. Structures were built and maintained on an apparently ad hoc basis, through individual rather than community initiative. The public water supply from the agora fountain house had ceased by the early first century AD, and it is difficult to determine if the pipes that supplied houses in the western residential quarter were maintained through individual or communal effort.[43] The concentration of activity in the areas of the city closest to a reliable source of surface water, the North Stoa and the northwestern corner of the agora, may indicate the absence of wide and regular distribution of water.[44]

The last period of settlement also saw the dumping of waste in obsolete public buildings and abandoned houses and the quarrying of materials from them.[45] New buildings, such as the succession of shops built in the northwestern corner of the agora, were generally constructed using material from nearby abandoned or collapsed structures. Alterations to domestic spaces were also largely accomplished with reused construction materials.[46] These are not necessarily signs of "slum conditions" in the latest phases of occupation, as the pilfering of materials from earlier structures and the dumping of waste in disused areas were also a feature of the second-century rebuilding efforts. However, in contrast to the second century, there is little evidence of the production of new goods and services in the city center alongside these later reclamation efforts and no sign that they were organized at a higher level than individual initiative. Indeed, it seems that the late inhabitants of Morgantina deemed the reclamation of older building materials a more efficient use of time, labor, and resources than the production on site or importation of such materials—a potential indication of the growing economic isolation of the site despite the continuing (though significantly reduced) circulation of coins and imported ceramics.

In conclusion, the shifts in the urban economy of Morgantina in the Hellenistic and Roman periods reflect the city's degree of integration into economic and political networks and its role within these networks. The monumental granaries in the agora trumpeted the dominance of grain storage and marketing in the third century BC; these structures were linked to the city's possession of a rich agricultural hinterland and its role in converting the produce of this hinterland into the Hieronian grain tithe. Marketing activities in the agora continued in the second century BC, though not necessarily in the same places as before. Indeed, the construction of a specialized market facility (*macellum*) suggests that civic authorities prioritized these activities.

The conversion or subdivision of some of the large public structures of the agora, including those previously used for grain storage, into ceramic production facilities reflects the changing role of Morgantina as a regional production and marketing center in the Roman Republican period. The influx of ceramics from eastern Sicily and the wider Mediterranean and the creation of imitation wares in Morgantina itself point to the continued integration of the city into regional and extraregional commercial circuits. In addition, as the construction of new public and religious edifices and the continued occupation and embellishment of the large residences on the western hill show, the urban center continued to house an active local elite.

By the late first century BC, however, the pottery industry of Morgantina had ceased. Imported Arretine wares and other Italian sigillata came to dominate the ceramic assemblage, although the connection of these developments to wider events in Sicily is not clear. They may not be only the result of the destruction of ca. 35 BC. Indeed, recent hydrogeological research suggests that the steady diminution in the settlement's water supply from the second half of the sixth century BC onward, which became problematic as the city reached its greatest physical and demographic extent in the mid-third century, was a more significant factor in the decision to abandon the site than the political changes of the second and first centuries BC.[47] Even if the city was not thoroughly and deliberately destroyed at some point in the third quarter of the first century BC, the increasing difficulty of obtaining water at the site, as evidenced by the diminished capacity of the agora fountain complex, would have made the occurrence of isolated fires more likely, their impact more devastating, and the production of ceramics in the city center therefore less appealing.

The end of the civil war and the transition to the Principate (and the Pax Romana) also would have rendered the defensive advantages of a hilltop urban center less compelling for potters. Finally, the growing competition posed by exports from Italy would have rendered local ceramic production even less profitable. The large quantities of pottery produced in Morgantina or imported in the early and mid-first century BC and found discarded in later dumps show that even finewares were a relatively low-priced, easily available commodity to the later inhabitants of the site. They found it more economically viable to rely on imports than to produce ceramics on site.

By the early Julio-Claudian period the main routes of commerce in the south-central Sicilian interior had shifted along with the main locations of production, away from centers like Morgantina that possessed more ecological disadvantages than advantages for potential occupants. Little is known of rural settlement in the territory of Morgantina in the early imperial period.[48] It is possible that the *statio* of Philosophiana (discussed in chapter 7), which arose along the internal route between the southern and eastern coasts during the latest phase of life at Morgantina, and the villa at Piazza Armerina, which emerged in the high imperial period, assumed the economic activities (if not the entire population) that had previously concentrated in the urban center of Morgantina.[49]

CAMARINA

Camarina/Kamarina was a subcolony of Syracuse established in the early sixth century BC on a coastal promontory between the Hipparis (modern Ippari) and Oanis (modern Rifriscolaro) Rivers 27 km southeast of Gela. The site, like Heraclea Minoa and Morgantina, was not resettled after antiquity. It first attracted the attention of excavators in the late nineteenth century; excavations resumed in 1958 and have continued periodically.[50]

Following a period of abandonment, probably prompted by the Carthaginian conquest in 405 BC, the city was refounded by the Syracusan leader Timoleon (ca. 339 BC). This refoundation saw the expansion and monumentalization of the city and great demographic growth, as indicated by the expansion of the necropolises. Intramural settlement spread west in a series of new *insulae* (see figure 1.6). The double agora (divided into the *agorà di levante* and *agorà di ponente*) also took shape along one side of the main thoroughfare (Plateia B) in the southeastern sector, in the area closest to the sea and to the port and canal at the mouth of the Hipparis.[51]

The city suffered attacks by the Mamertines in the 270s BC that prompted repairs and improvements to the perimeter defensive wall. Although the city was taken over and its population dispersed by the Romans after a siege in 258 BC (Polyb. 1.24; Diod. Sic. 23.9), the excavation of its public and residential areas has confirmed that it continued to be inhabited (and to thrive) thereafter. There are no archaeological indications of a violent destruction. The period after 258 BC saw a restructuring of the urban space, with a reorientation of the double agora toward commerce, and the construction of large houses and workshops (including pottery kilns) in nearby *insulae*. Plateia B was partly redirected in order to accommodate the changing use of space in the agora and the encroachment of houses and workshops onto the previous street surface. Four narrow rectangular buildings—probably granaries—were built in the open space of the *agorà di ponente* and over the disused North

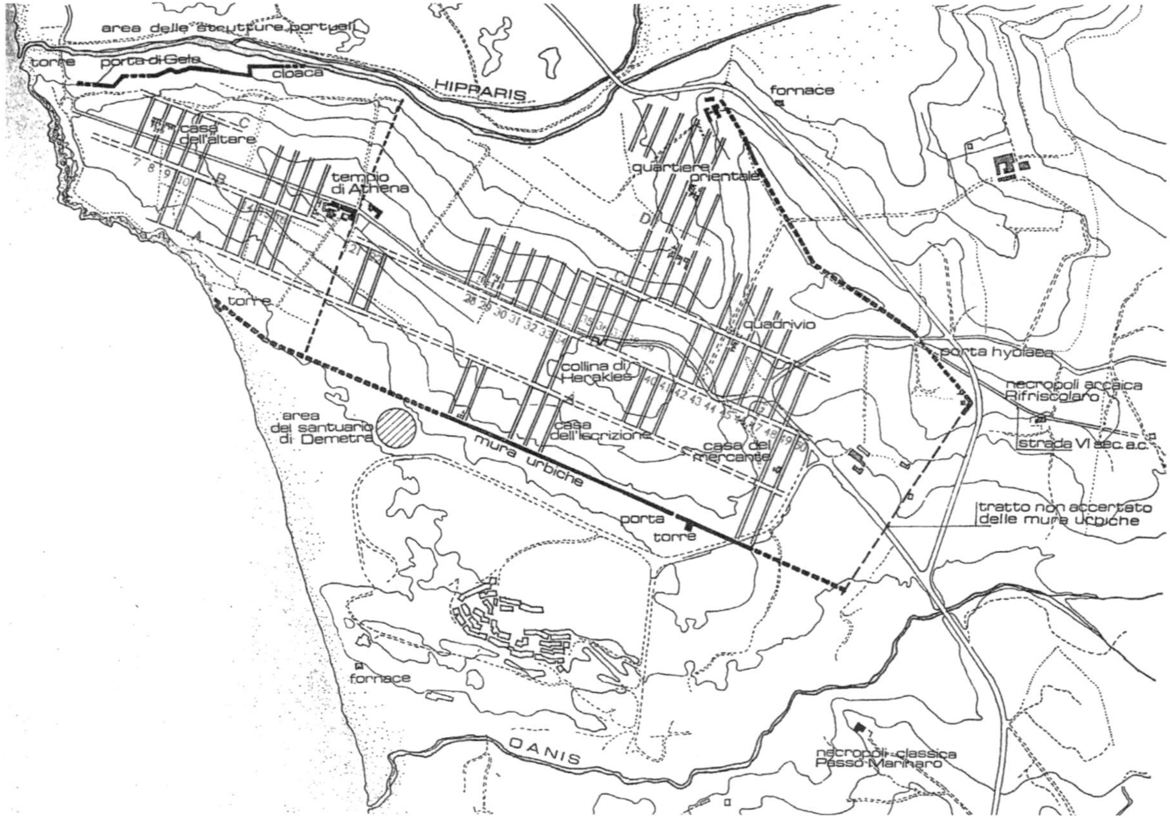

FIGURE 1.6.

Plan of Camarina (Pelagatti et al. 1976, reproduced with permission of Bollettino d'Arte*).*

Stoa.[52] These structures follow the new course of Plateia B and thus must postdate 258. A kiln was built into a room at the eastern end of the northeastern granary, a development paralleled in the East Granary at Morgantina.[53]

Rhodian and Dressel 1 wine transport amphorae found in the agora attest to the city's continued commercial vitality in the late third and second centuries BC.[54] Most of the coins from the agora excavations are from the third century, and issues of Hieron predominate. Indeed, in the agora assemblage it is difficult to detect any break in the circulation of coinage in the city corresponding to the events of 258.[55]

Camarina also possesses an extensive (for Sicily) epigraphic record related to the organization and activities of the *polis* in the Hellenistic and Roman Republican periods. An *asylia* decree issued by the city in 242 BC found on Kos (*SEG* 12.379), the city's inclusion in the Delphic *theorodokoi* list, and a decree of the Delphic Amphiktyony in honor of a citizen of the city all attest to Camarina's attempts to maintain international prestige.[56] In addition, a series of inscribed lead contracts of house and land sales, some of which securely postdate 258, reveal a well-organized, fertile *chora* that was parceled into small landholdings.[57] These records hint at a countryside dominated by a prosperous, *polis*-based class of landholders or owners and an urban center full of economic activity based in workshop-residences, including the production of pottery, wine, and olive oil.

The evidence for the city's economic and political organization and its demographics is less certain after the second century BC, resulting in part from the postantique plundering of building materials from more recent strata of occupation. At the very least, the drop-off in coin finds from the second century BC indicates a reduction of commercial activity in public areas like the agora.[58] The latest improvements to the large houses constructed around the agora after 258, such as the Casa dell'Altare, date to the first century BC, pointing to the emigration of the city's elite thereafter.[59] Finds of Campana C (probably produced in Syracuse or Morgantina), presigillata, and Arretine ware attest to activity in the urban center through the Augustan period. The city is also included among Pliny's Sicilian *oppida*, though its precise juridical status in the late Republic and early Principate is uncertain.

The sharp decrease in numismatic and ceramic evidence after the mid-first century AD may signal an abandonment of the old city center or a shift of activity away from the agora.[60] One excavator hypothesizes that economic activity shifted to the area of the port (a view supported by the numerous imperial-era wrecks in the bay of Camarina discussed below) and was conducted on a "suburban" level.[61] Such a shift in site to accommodate changing economic and commercial networks was also a feature of the abandonment of

Phintias as well as of cities on the northern coast (including Calacte, probably Soluntum, and Halaesa) and was key to the transformation of the settlement landscape of Roman imperial Sicily.

Like Morgantina and much of the rest of southeastern Sicily, Camarina was under the political and economic hegemony of Syracuse for much of its classical and Hellenistic history.[62] While Morgantina served as a key node in the collection and storage of tithe grain for Hieronian Syracuse and later for the Roman Republic, the port of Camarina likely served as a center for the embarkation of this grain and of other agricultural products of the southeastern interior. Several scholars have noted parallels in the urban development of Morgantina and Camarina in the late third and second centuries BC.[63] Most significantly, both cities experienced a shift in the use of public spaces away from political/administrative functions and toward commercial purposes. This commercialization of agora space was perhaps related to the end of the effective political autonomy of these centers under the dominance first of Syracuse and then of Rome and also to their roles in state extractive activities and in commerce (such as pottery production) that piggybacked on these exactions. After a Roman siege in both cities—in 258 BC in Camarina and in 210 BC in Morgantina—the agora was rebuilt with new production, storage, and marketing facilities, along with the residential quarters, sometimes with workshops connected to houses with luxurious display rooms.

Camarina also shared with Morgantina, Phintias, and Heraclea Minoa certain environmental challenges to the integrity of its urban space: the scarcity of water at the site and the erosion of the coastal promontory on which it was situated.[64] The classical urban plan aimed to mitigate the effects of erosion, with *stenopoi* discharging water outside the city walls. A public fountain complex excavated in the agora is similar in chronology and appearance to the fountain house in the northeastern corner of the Morgantina agora and seems to have replaced a series of nearby wells. However, civic authorities appear to have been more concerned with protecting the urban center against landslides and erosion than with furnishing a regular supply of water, which mainly came from cisterns within residences as well as from a few scattered wells.

After the end of substantial urban settlement at Camarina by the mid-first century AD, activity probably persisted in a nearby suburban maritime port-of-call. Shipwrecks found in the bay of Camarina and to the southeast attest to the large-scale movement along this stretch of coast of high-value items (such as fine marble columns) as well as oil, fish products, and other commodities, as part of the commerce of Sicily, Rome, North Africa, and Spain in the high and late empire.[65] As with other points on the southeastern coast, such as Mesopotamium (probably at the mouth of the Dirillo) and Caucana (perhaps the extensive Byzantine settlement excavated near Punta Secca), the mouth of the Hipparis and the sandy beach below ancient Camarina may have served as a landing point (*plaga*, in the terminology of the *It. Ant.*) for small-scale commerce in the Principate and especially in late antiquity.

No formal field surveys have been undertaken in the territory of Camarina. Research elsewhere on the southeastern coast and in the Hyblean plateau, however, has indicated a shift in coastal settlement away from ancient urban centers (some, like Camarina, in rather precarious hillside locations) to smaller, more easily accessible coastal landings, some of which, like Caucana, grew in size and monumentality in late antiquity.[66] The rural landscape of smallholdings owned and/or managed by farmers (*aratores*) resident in ancient urban centers appears to have disappeared in the early imperial period, concomitantly with the abandonment of *poleis* like Camarina. After this caesura, rural settlement concentrated in farms, villas, and villages in the high plain with access to land routes that linked them to the urban centers of the eastern coast.[67] Excavated settlements in the territory of Camarina like the luxury villa at Giarratana, the neighboring *villa rustica* or village (*vicus*) at Margi, and the recently discovered *vicus* at Piombo are all in locations of great agricultural potential and all of substantial size and architectural pretension. They point to the refocusing of economic activity (and perhaps elite social life) to inland rural centers in the high and late empire.[68]

IETAS (MONTE IATO)

Annual fieldwork conducted since 1971 on the summit of Monte Iato, a long ridge in the mountainous interior southwest of Palermo, has revealed the extensive remains of ancient Iaitas/Ietas (see figure 1.7). The chronology of the settlement's development in the fourth and third centuries is controversial. It seems to have prospered in the period after the Punic Wars, however, and its monumental infrastructure underwent extensive improvements that continued into the second century BC.[69] By the first century BC Ietas was equipped with a street system, a theater, and a paved agora. This agora was flanked by stoas, temples, and two *bouleuteria* (the larger supplanted the smaller in the late second century BC) and was surrounded by residential and commercial areas.

Major public building projects ceased by the late first century BC or early first century AD, with some work left unfinished, including modifications to the theater's stage (*scaena*) that had been in progress since the early first century BC.[70] Many structures, including the *bouleuterion*, the temple of Aphro-

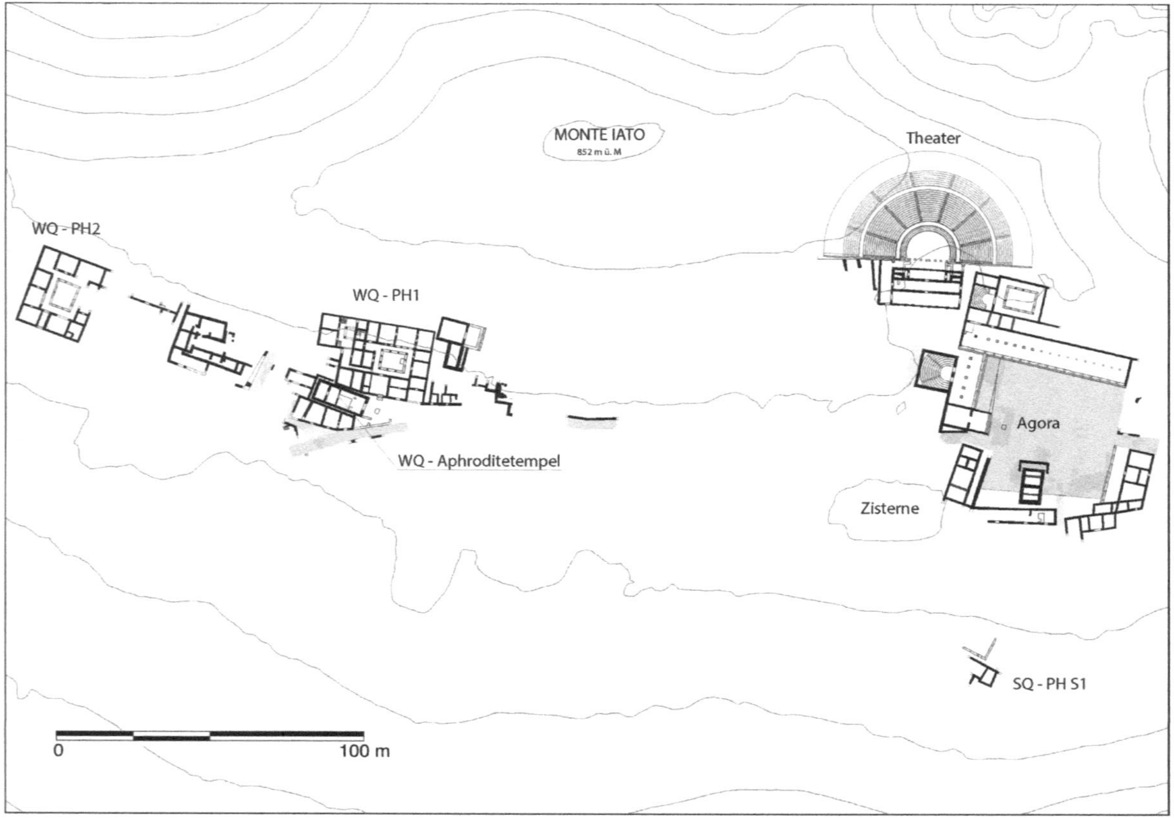

FIGURE 1.7.

Plan of Ietas (© M. Mohr/Zürcher Ietas-Grabung, with modifications by K. Rasmussen).

dite, the theater, and "peristyle house 1," fell into disuse or were destroyed (perhaps by an earthquake) between the mid-first century BC and the mid-first century AD. Occupation of the town continued, however, with buildings in the agora adapted into housing and material from older collapsed structures reused in new residences. Imported ceramics are plentiful. The site is one of the richest in Sicily in Arretine ware, and African terra sigillata proliferated from the late first century AD. It is difficult to ascertain when the site was finally abandoned. Although several structures collapsed by the mid-fifth century, coins and ceramics from the Byzantine period (sixth–eighth centuries AD) have been found sporadically.

Ietas was implicated in none of the historical "ruptures" that characterize the material records of Morgantina and Heraclea Minoa. Its abandonment was piecemeal: some structures were in disuse by the middle or end of the first century BC (such as the *bouleuterion* and wall circuit),[71] while the abandonment of other structures dates to the Augustan or Julio-Claudian period. Some of these abandonments may have been the result of destruction by earthquake and/or fire, such as peristyle house 1 and the structures around it. Elsewhere in the city abandonment was the result of long-term neglect.[72] Construction work on the theater ceased in the Augustan period. After its drainage channel was blocked, the orchestra filled with sediment. The main street leading to the agora was covered by a thick layer of earth in the mid-second century AD, indicating a lack of maintenance, if not disuse, by that period. Over the course of the Principate, structures in the agora, including the second *bouleuterion*, some of the porticoes, and the podium temple, gradually deteriorated and collapsed.[73]

However, occupation continued in the agora, around the theater, and in other areas of the urban center at least until the fifth century AD.[74] The theater's stage building had a secondary use phase in the first century AD and collapsed only several centuries later. In addition, the initial destruction episode of peristyle house 1 was followed soon after by temporary resettlement and reuse.[75] Most notably, the occupant of a residence built in the western portico of the agora in late antiquity left behind a substantial collection of bronze and clay vessels.[76]

Thus signs of reuse, renovation, and adaptation are found amid the gradual destruction, collapse, and decay of the monumental infrastructure after the mid-first century BC. In addition, large amounts of coinage circulated on the site in the second quarter of the first century AD and more sporadically thereafter. Sicilian issues as well as imperial issues of Augustus through Claudius are plentiful in the destruction layers related to the abandonments of the first century AD. Augustan and Tiberian issues from Panormus dominate, hardly surprising given that city's proximity and its status as the only (known) Sicilian mint that continued in operation under Tiberius.[77]

The large quantities of Italian sigillata, as well as coins and transport amphorae from Spain and Italy, found in the destruction layers of peristyle house 1 attest to the intensity of the site's connection to the outside world—especially western and northern Sicilian ports and, through them, Italy—in the mid-first century AD. This assemblage also shows the growing dominance of imported ceramics over local productions, as seen also in the latest settlement at Morgantina.[78] In contrast to Morgantina, however, imports continued to reach Ietas into late antiquity. Plentiful fragments of African lamps and tablewares mark the middle- and late-imperial use and destruction phases of the city's buildings. In addition, the domestic assemblage from the late antique residence in the western portico that was buried when the portico collapsed around the mid-fifth century hints at the (not unsubstantial) means of Ietas's last ancient residents as well as the settlement's varied connections with its neighborhood and with the wider Mediterranean world. This assemblage included two bronze vases, transport amphorae (*spatheia*) from North Africa, African lamps, other locally made vessels, and a fragment of a glass cup.[79]

Although Ietas was abandoned gradually, with scattered residential and economic activity continuing into late antiquity, key points of transition occurred in its settlement history. Roman involvement has been perceived in the development of the agora in the middle and late second century BC.[80] These interventions, perhaps related to a civic reorganization in the context of the servile wars, included the construction of the west portico, the second *bouleuterion*, and the agora podium temple as well as the addition of a tribunal to the north portico, turning it into a basilica. They appear to stem from the initiative of Roman administrators or perhaps "philo-Roman" local elites: a fragmentary Latin inscription referring to the *gens* Hostilia ("CN HOST") found in the area of the north portico is probably associated with the construction of the tribunal.[81] The tiles from the roof of the west portico are also stamped in Latin.

Alterations to the urban fabric after this period seem mainly to be private or small-group efforts, as at Morgantina, rather than initiatives led by civic authorities. The abandonment of the *bouleuterion*, the end of construction work on the theater, and the general lack of maintenance of the monumental infrastructure point to the financial weakening of civic authorities and perhaps to the complete obsolescence of the *polis* government. Public epigraphy, while not common at Ietas, also appears to end in the first century BC.[82] Little positive evidence indicates the persistence of any sort of civic administration after the late first century BC.[83] The most active spaces of the early first century AD are the residences, shops, and workshops around the agora.[84]

Whatever their cause(s), the destruction events of the first century AD struck a decisive blow to the urban fabric. Most productive and commercial activities ceased at that point, followed only by scattered occupation of the agora and theater. As in Morgantina, the conspicuous reuse of older building materials in the renovations to these structures, including architectural decor, monumental inscriptions, and stamped roof tiles produced in the second and first centuries BC (some under the auspices of the civic government), further points to the absence of a central authority to oversee the production of construction materials and the construction activities themselves.[85] The reuse of older building materials also indicates a lack of production facilities, such as tile and brick kilns, in the vicinity of the settlement.

In conclusion, at Ietas the gradual disappearance of permanent inhabitants of means with an interest in public and private prestige display (a "local elite") and civic authority culminated in the early and mid-first century AD.[86] However, survey in the area around Ietas has indicated that this civic disintegration did not mean a general decline in population levels. To the contrary, rural settlement appears to peak in the mid-first century AD and level off thereafter.[87] The persistence of settlement at a suburban level on Monte Iato indicates that the location remained accessible and desirable to a small transient agricultural or pastoral community, probably because of the easy availability of building materials. As a result of the continued connectivity of the western interior with Panormus and other coastal cities, the later inhabitants had access to imported goods and could find outlets for their own produce.

CALACTE (CARONIA)

The site of the *polis* of Calacte/Kale Akte (or Caleacte), founded in the mid-fifth century BC by the Sicel leader Ducetius, is covered by modern Caronia, a hillside town overlooking the Tyrrhenian Sea almost midway between Palermo and Messina. The presence of the modern town has limited archaeological work in the urban center of Calacte to a few excavations around the edges of the city. Research has instead focused on the harbor settlement of Marina di Caronia at the foot of the hill. Calacte is unique and valuable as a case study because it presents substantial remains of a coastal and hilltop settlement, but knowledge of the extent and chronology of settlement at both sites is still far from complete (see figure 1.8).

The ancient settlement on the summit and steep slopes of the hill dates

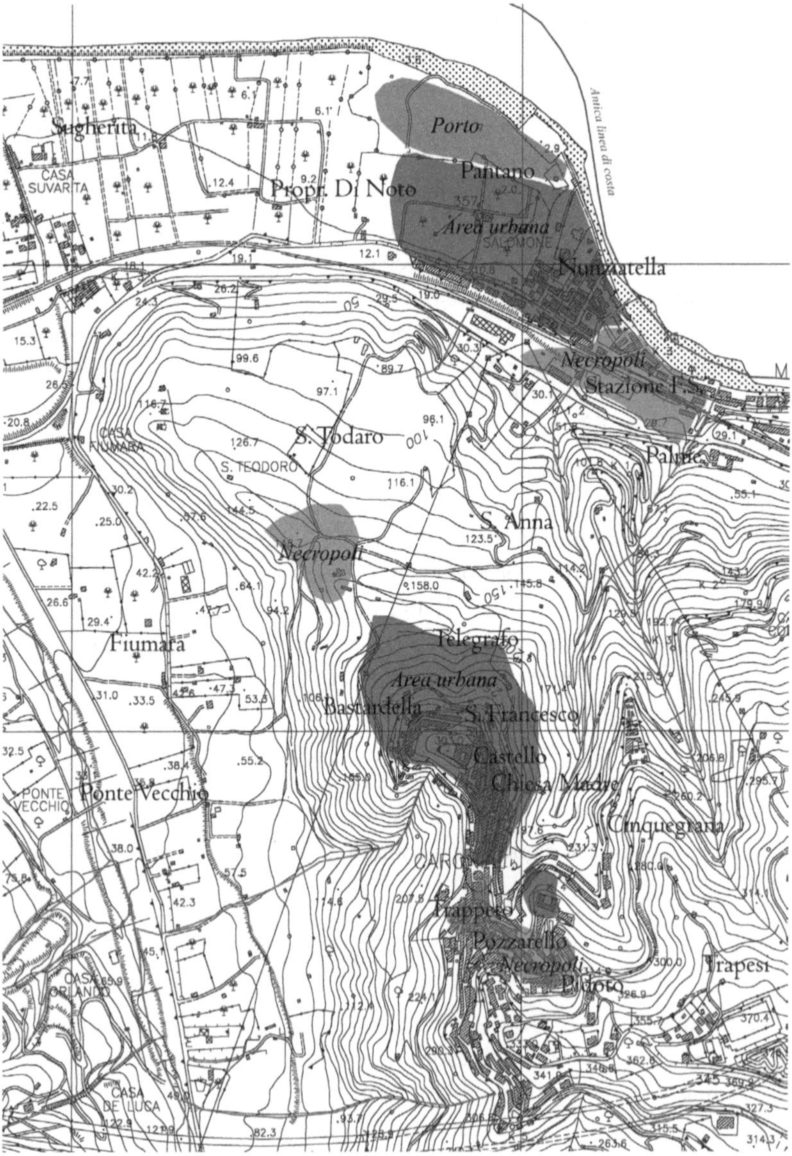

FIGURE 1.8.

Caronia: hilltop and coastal settlement areas (Collura 2016, reproduced with permission of BAR Publishing, www.barpublishing.com).

mainly from the late fourth century BC to the first century AD.[88] Although little is known of this settlement's public spaces, a recently discovered Greek honorific decree alluding to a sanctuary of Apollo and to three legislative bodies (*boule*, *halia*, *synkletos*) points to an active civic life in the Hellenistic/Republican period.[89] The *polis* also joined with three other cities in honoring the naval commander Caninius Niger, perhaps for victories against pirates, in an early first-century BC inscription found in the agora of Halaesa (discussed in chapter 2).[90] In addition, the settlement received large quantities of Italian sigillata, probably imported directly from the Tyrrhenian coast of Italy, beginning in the late first century BC.[91]

The hillside settlement was mostly abandoned by the late first century AD, perhaps as the result of earthquake damage. The population then appears to have shifted to an existing port settlement a few kilometers away at Marina di Caronia. There excavators uncovered the remains of several buildings associated with the port, including a probable warehouse (*horreum*) and shops.[92] These structures, in place since the Hellenistic period, were also destroyed in the mid-to-late first century AD, though new structures were built on their remains by the end of the second century. These later structures were destroyed in the third quarter of the fourth century, perhaps as a result of another earthquake. Nonetheless, ceramics (including numerous transport amphorae) attest to continued commercial activity in the area in the fifth century.

Seismic activity and landslides have had a significant impact on the settlement history of the hilltop and Marina sites from antiquity to the present day.[93] Although the destruction of the ancient hilltop site by earthquake is only speculated, the walls of the possible *horreum* at Marina and surrounding structures were certainly brought down by a strong force or blow, an event dated by ceramics to ca. AD 30–70 and linked by excavators to the earthquake(s) in the region that Pliny the Elder records (*HN* 2.206). The choice to rebuild on a substantial organized scale at Marina after such a destructive event indicates the great economic potential and hence desirability of easily accessible coastal locales in Roman imperial Sicily, especially compared to more isolated hilltops whose defensive potential was no longer a significant consideration. The ceramic assemblage from the Marina site, as studied by Adam Lindhagen, shows the strong ties that even such a small coastal center could have with the outside world, especially if it had a commodity to offer for export: wine. The settlement was engaged in the production and distribution of wine from the early third century BC until the late fifth century AD, with special intensity from the first century AD and with no apparent chronological breaks. These processes can be traced by the presence of locally produced amphorae, beginning with small MGS V types in the late fourth/early third century BC, followed by Dressel 2–4s by the first century AD, and so on.[94] The settlement also imported substantial quantities of foodstuffs, cookwares, and tablewares from around the Mediterranean until the fifth century.[95] In addition, the site participated in local and regional commerce in ceramics and staples. The large quantities of tuna bones found on the site may indicate local production of fish products.[96]

Furthermore, the history of settlement at Caronia and Marina di Caronia highlights the potential separation of the political from the economic roles of the city. Calacte's political identity seems to have ceased with the end of settlement at the hilltop site, while economic activity continued independently at the Marina site. The apparently synchronic development of the hilltop and harbor site in the Hellenistic period, and the continued economic integration of the harbor site and its production and distribution facilities during the imperial period, also warns against drawing too strong a distinction between "city" and "countryside" or "urban" and "rural" settlement. While the settlement at Marina was not a true *polis*, it shared and eventually took over the economic functions of the hillside urban center.

No significant survey work has been done in the territory around Calacte. Little is known of rural settlement patterns, though the structures brought to light by the landslide of 2010 (including large numbers of *dolia*) suggest the intensive cultivation of the area around the hilltop site from the late Hellenistic period through late antiquity. Extensive forests as well as good sources of fresh water and clay are found in the *chora* of the ancient city. These resources would have facilitated the production of ceramics at rural (and potentially urban and suburban) locations.[97]

The *polis* and its harbor site were also well situated for exchange both by sea and by land: the main coastal route between Messana and Lilybaeum traversed the territory. Therefore, local agricultural producers and processors were in a good position to participate in prevailing Mediterranean commercial trends, such as the opening of the Roman wine market to imports. In addition, foodstuffs not produced on a significant scale in the area, such as olive oil, could easily be imported from abroad. Thus Calacte and its rural territory had a more flexible economy than, for example, Morgantina. Morgantina served as a regional processing and marketing center for grain and other local and regional productions, such as ceramics. Its settlement vicissitudes thus were more directly tied to the nature and direction of state exactions.[98]

Finally, although Calacte, along with much of the rest of Sicily, was subject to strong occasional seismic activity (as well as landslides of varying severity), its inhabitants faced fewer regular ecological challenges than the residents of other cities examined in this chapter. The northeastern coast of Sicily receives more consistent rainfall than other areas, and the forests of the Nebrodi range provide plentiful fuel. The pottery kilns around the Marina di Caronia settlement could probably produce amphorae for exporting wine more consistently, securely, and for longer than the pottery kilns of Morgantina, where water and fuel supplies were less reliable. After the abandonment of the hilltop site, the economic importance of the settlement at Marina di Caronia appears to have persisted far longer than the civic identity of the *polis* of Calacte. This development was paralleled at other settlements along the Tyrrhenian coast, including Halaesa, which is examined in chapter 2.

ANALYSIS: THE CAUSES AND CONSEQUENCES OF DEURBANIZATION

The prolonged and ambiguous course of deurbanization in the cities examined in this chapter points to the importance of long-term processes in bringing about the "weakening of material forms" in the city, although such specific events as fires, sieges, and earthquakes could act as triggers to abandonment episodes. The most significant process at work in Sicilian urban centers in the late Republic and early Principate is the decline of civic authority: the reduction of the efficacy of formal city government. The symptoms of this decline that are visible in the urban archaeological record include weakened control over the organization of social and economic life, the shape and integrity of public spaces, and community resources such as water and building materials.

This decline of civic authority requires further explanation. In Roman Republican Sicily, the ancient nexus of *polis* citizenship, ownership of land in the *chora*, and residence in the urban center persisted and was a driving factor behind the development of many cities. The tablets from Camarina recording land sales and other transactions are evidence for the role of the *polis* in the organization of its agricultural hinterland in the Hellenistic and Republican periods.[99] In Ietas, and in Camarina and Phintias to a less visible extent, the topography was transformed mainly through the efforts of local elites, with the occasional intervention of Roman authorities.

The sponsorship of monumental public buildings and the construction of houses with luxurious reception rooms were elements of the self-representation of local notables who thrived under the economic regime of the Roman province and aimed to gain individual and community prestige and privileges through their participation in city government and their interactions with Roman authorities.[100] Even Morgantina, a city upended by warfare and population displacement at the end of the third century, reveals indications of rebuilding and renewed prosperity under the new Roman regime in the second century.[101] Although Heraclea Minoa may have been adversely affected by the servile wars of the second half of the second century BC, the fine paved floors, painted walls, and household shrines (*lararia*) added to several houses reflect their owners' relative affluence and cultural and social links with Italy.

The cities discussed in this chapter were all affected by the political, economic, and social changes of the end of the Republic and the first decades of the Principate (ca. 50 BC–AD 50). Even before that time, however, some cities experienced a reduction in activity, especially those on the southern coast (Heraclea Minoa, Phintias, Camarina). By the early third century BC several prominent *poleis* on this coast, including Gela and Selinus, had become casualties of war. In the relatively peaceful decades after the Second Punic War, moreover, the south coast was gradually bypassed by Mediterranean commercial networks that were increasingly focused on the expanding market of Rome: between the North African and Campanian coasts and between Italy and the Eastern Mediterranean. With the final collapse of the Carthaginian state after the Third Punic War and the incorporation of North Africa into the Roman overseas tributary empire by the mid-first century BC, the metropolis of Rome surpassed Carthage as the key node in these networks. (In late antiquity, the breakdown of these Rome-centered networks and the disintegration of Roman political control had the opposite effect, facilitating the revival of direct economic links between the southern coast of Sicily and Africa, as discussed in chapter 7.) Although cities like Phintias and Heraclea Minoa initially may have been able to take advantage of the opening of Rome to Sicilian grain, in the first century BC they faced the revival of Agrigentum and its port as a commercial competitor. They were further challenged by the events of the civil war, which cut off access to Rome's grain market.

The concomitant abandonment of Heraclea Minoa and many of the farms of its hinterland in the third quarter of the first century BC and the lack of Augustan-era ceramics or imported amphorae in the city itself point to primarily economic reasons for the city's decline, although it may have been hastened by coastal erosion and by events like the servile wars. Farther east, Camarina prospered in the third century under the auspices of Hieron's Syracusan kingdom, when its agora was the center of commercial and artisanal activity. This activity dropped off in the second century BC, however, perhaps in connection with the end of Syracusan autonomy, and was sharply curtailed after the middle of the first century BC.

The civil war between the triumvirs and Sextus Pompey, the political, economic, and social transformations brought by the transition to the Principate, and seismic activity in parts of Sicily all contributed to the permanent abandonment of some urban centers and a significant reduction in activity in others. The early reign of Augustus saw the demilitarization of Sicily and its urban centers, punitive redistributions of civic land, the displacement of urban populations, and the beginning of imperial landholding. Though significant in altering the political, economic, and social landscape of Sicily, none of these measures individually led directly to deurbanization. In fact, as discussed in chapters 3, 4, and 5, some of the cities most directly affected by the civil war and its aftermath, such as Tauromenium and Lilybaeum, actually thrived under the Principate.

The growth of *latifundia* (large estates under absentee ownership) may have accompanied or followed shortly after the economic decline of cities along the south coast and in the interior. Although little can be said at present about the extent of such estates or their mode of agricultural production, in some areas they do appear to have fostered the development of alternatives to the *poleis* that underwent contraction or abandonment in the late Republic and early Empire. These settlements become particularly visible in the high and late Empire. They are usually located along primary or secondary inland transportation routes and seem to have served as the residential bases of the agricultural labor force and as centers for the collection and processing of agricultural produce. Some, such as Campanaio di Montallegro in the hinterland of Heraclea Minoa, could hardly be described as more than agricultural villages. Others, such as Philosophiana (discussed in chapter 7), reached a significant level of organization and monumentality, with *domus*, communal structures like public baths, and eventually a small church.

The Pax Romana imposed by Octavian/Augustus in the years after his victory in the civil war also does not appear to be a significant direct cause of urban abandonment. Relatively low-lying coastal settlements as well as hilltop centers originally founded for defensive purposes were abandoned in the early imperial period. One hilltop center, Ietas, persisted in occupation well into the Principate. Defensive considerations were not totally irrelevant in this period. In spite of imperial rhetoric, Sicilians of the early first century AD could not be certain that they were living in an era of unending peace and prosperity, particularly given their island's history of piracy and brigandage. Nor did hilltop locations immediately become economically disadvantageous with the transition to the Principate. After all, many hilltop settlements across the island, including Ietas and Calacte, had remained vital political and economic centers in earlier prolonged periods of peace under the Romans.

However, we have seen that most of the urban sites examined in this chapter faced persistent threats of water scarcity, landslides, coastal erosion, and other environmental challenges throughout their histories. Rather than positing a general decline in hilltop settlements in the early Principate, we may instead hypothesize that the complex economic and political changes that the Sicilian urban system underwent in the civil war period and the Augustan era made the effort and expense of maintaining the infrastructure (e.g., supplying water and preventing erosion) at certain challenging sites undesirable or unfeasible, especially if these sites were no longer integrated into extraregional commercial networks.

Most significantly for the urban landscape, the early reign of Augustus saw the transformation of the system by which Sicilian cities and their ruling elites acquired and maintained political and social prestige. Under the Republic, *polis* governments remained responsible for the administration of their territory, including many aspects of the assessment and collection of tax owed to Rome, as well as the regulation of political and economic activity and the maintenance of order in the urban center.[102] The status and privileges of a city were negotiated with Roman military and provincial authorities by its ruling class and were often maintained through social links between individual Sicilian notables and members of the Roman senatorial class. Some cities had negotiated favorable relationships with Rome. Segesta, Centuripae, Halicyae, and Halaesa acquired the status of *civitas immunis ac libera* (Cic., II *Verr.* 2.166). Formal treaties governed relations between Rome and the cities of Messana and Tauromenium (*civitates foederatae*: Cic., II *Verr.* 3.13).[103]

In this somewhat ad hoc system, statuses were revocable and changeable, based partly on the perceived strategic needs of the Roman administration and partly on the efforts of Sicilian local elites. It is difficult to link the proclaimed status of individual cities to a defined and consistent set of obligations and privileges.[104] In the majority of cities that did not have special political and taxation status in the Republican period (the *civitates decumanae* of Cicero, including all of the cities in this chapter), individuals and groups could still negotiate directly with Roman authorities for personal and community privileges such as Roman citizenship, a reduced tax burden, or the return of plundered property.[105] This system of provincial administration fostered links between Sicilian notables and the Roman senatorial elite and left room for autonomy and independent action among Sicilian cities. It worked well for both ruler and ruled in the slave and pirate conflicts of the second and early first centuries, when Sicilian cities acted in collaboration with Roman authorities, but not in the civil war, when many cities supported (or at least acquiesced in the rule of) the losing Roman side.

The Augustan reforms of the post–civil war decades ended the potential for individual and collective action by Sicilian cities against the Roman state by shifting to a system of political privilege based on the limited bestowal of municipal and colonial status. The shift began with the establishment of Roman *coloniae* in a half-dozen coastal cities populated by a landholding ruling class of Roman citizens. This privileged group of cities was consolidated, with only limited expansion, over the course of the Principate. In this system, a city's strategic importance and economic potential—and especially its ability to export goods from its agricultural hinterland—were more consequential than its earlier relations with Rome, as the concentration of cities with Roman status on the western, northern, and eastern coasts suggests.[106] For Lilybaeum and Agrigentum, the bestowal of municipal status was a confirmation of their economic vitality and strategic importance, and perhaps a concession to their ruling class, rather than a reward for services rendered to Rome (see chapter 3).

Most other urban centers, including those examined in this chapter, lost political authority to the cities that were most integrated into the Roman system as *municipia* or *coloniae*. With this removal of authority came the loss of elite beneficence and the obsolescence of civic governance and cohesion, seen in the lack of maintenance of public spaces and the gradual decay of public buildings. Amid the general deterioration of the agora of Ietas, for example, the larger *bouleuterion* that had been constructed in the second half of the second century BC fell into disrepair after only a century of use and was thereafter partly dismantled. Its entrance was sealed before the portico in front of it collapsed in the late first or early second century AD.[107]

This decline of civic authority also meant the disappearance of cities from history. When a city lost its role as a center for social, political, and cultural display and promotion, it also no longer functioned as a space for the public commemoration of collective or individual acts, such as the passage of a decree or the construction of a building. Hence no further impetus for the epigraphic habit remained. Ietas appears to be the only city in this chapter to have transitioned to the practice of inscribing public documents and dedications in Latin, though only briefly and to a limited extent, in contrast to the relatively rich Latin epigraphic records of cities like Syracuse, Catina, Thermae, and Lilybaeum. The decline of effective city government also meant the end of a community's relations with the center of power and its appearance in Roman annals. Apart from the early imperial geographical texts of Strabo and Pliny, none of the cities examined in this chapter appears in Roman literature after the time of Cicero.

Political obsolescence and the disappearance of the local elite did not necessarily imply the end of all economic activity within urban centers, as is apparent in early imperial Ietas and in post-35 BC Morgantina. There imported ceramics and other items of material culture, including coins, continued to circulate long after the cessation of significant building activity. High-level economic activity does appear to have ended, however, along with the role of the *polis* in organizing it. Along with the cessation of significant building activity, the public provision of resources such as water and the maintenance of public spaces (and the marshaling of labor that these implied) as well as civic authorities' production and acquisition of stone and ceramic building materials came to an end. The production of pottery was not resumed in post–35 BC Morgantina, and building materials were mostly quarried from earlier structures. At Ietas older construction materials, such as the roof tiles bearing the initials of Hellenistic magistrates that originally covered the theater stage building and the stoas of the agora, were used in the late imperial structures that dotted the urban center. These developments stand in contrast to the Roman Republican phases of Camarina and Morgantina, where civic authorities were fully engaged in monumentalizing economic activity in the urban center.

After the collapse of civic authority (the political, social, and economic institutions of the *polis*) it is difficult to see where authority was located in "declining" or "abandoned" urban centers like Morgantina and Ietas that show signs of later occupation. Individuals or small groups appear responsible for the continued activity on these sites, including the construction of residences and low-scale economic activity. Activity after the mid-first century BC at Ietas seems to be concentrated in the residential areas. Most notably, peristyle house 1 was reoccupied (perhaps by more than one household) after its initial destruction, and small shops, workshops, and residences were constructed in the surrounding area. Spaces in and around the theater were also transformed into small residences, while part of one of the porticoes of the agora was later adapted into a three-room dwelling. The apparent lack of control over the organization of settlement in the last phases of life of Morgantina and Ietas, and lack of any indication of a hierarchy of residents, may hint that the reoccupation of these sites was voluntary and not forced or overseen by an authority such as a landowner. Although it is almost impossible to determine from the material record, the later occupation of these sites may have been temporary or seasonal in nature, perhaps involving pastoralists or other transient groups of rural laborers attracted by the plentiful supplies of building material and the numerous structures still standing.

CONCLUSION

The case studies of this chapter support the concept of the city as a fluid and dynamic settlement form. Sicilian urbanism was a political and economic phenomenon whose parameters changed with the incorporation of the island into the Roman Empire of Augustus. In many parts of Sicily the monumental urban center whose institutions had evolved in the classical and Hellenistic periods (in some cases enduring violence and dislocation) and had continued to function under the Roman Republic no longer played an active role in political, social, cultural, and economic life under the Principate. This change had significant consequences for the island's settlement landscape. Even in areas where the city remained an integral part of the settlement landscape, its roles in local, regional, and extraregional networks evolved under the Principate. Chapter 2 continues the analysis of the variable processes of deurbanization in Sicily by examining three cities where occupation and urban life continued for much but not all of the Principate. It focuses on the consequences of shifting Mediterranean economic currents and of the new power relations established by the post–civil war settlement, while also taking into account more localized historical and geographical influences on urban development.

TWO

URBAN ABANDONMENT IN THE HIGH EMPIRE (CA. AD 50–250)

Like the cities examined in chapter 1, the northern Sicilian towns considered in this chapter (Soluntum, Segesta, and Halaesa) were abandoned in the imperial period. In these communities, however, abandonment processes began after the Augustan era and were more drawn out, extending into the second century AD and beyond. All three cities were located on hilltops at varying distances from the Tyrrhenian coast, with Segesta the furthest inland. They had different ethnic origins: Segesta was an Elymian foundation, Soluntum began as a Phoenician colony, and Halaesa was founded as a subcolony of Herbita in Sicel territory. The communities also had different statuses vis-à-vis Rome under the Republic: Halaesa and Segesta were *civitates immunes ac liberae*, while Soluntum was an unprivileged *civitas stipendiaria*. Their varying development under the Principate further elucidates the complex political, environmental, and economic forces that could contribute to deurbanization.

SOLUNTUM

The promontory of Monte Catalfano east of Palermo and the bay below it were the sites of the Phoenician/Punic colony of Solous and its successor settlement, known to the Romans as Soluntum. Monte Catalfano was first explored sporadically in the nineteenth century, as scholars sought evidence for the city mentioned by Thucydides (6.2.6). Modern excavations have revealed that Thucydides's Punic *emporion* was first situated on the coast, around the harbor of Solanto, but that in the mid- or late fourth century BC the settlement shifted a few kilometers west, to the summit and eastern slope of Monte Catalfano. The public and residential areas of the Hellenistic city on Monte Catalfano have been excavated since the 1950s, though the results have not been fully published (see figure 2.1).[1]

The question that has long dominated discussion of Soluntum is the date of its regular urban plan and the major public monuments (agora, theater, odeum/*bouleuterion*, gymnasium, and temples) built on a series of terraces on the hillside. Does their construction predate or postdate the Roman conquest of western Sicily in the mid-third century BC? Although debate continues (as it does for the urban plans of Ietas and Segesta), scholarly opinion has generally shifted in favor of a postconquest date for the construction of these buildings and of the city's elite residences.[2]

The agora was situated at the northern end of the town's primary paved thoroughfare, the Via dell'Agorà. The grid plan extended both east and west of the Via dell'Agorà, but the main excavated residential areas lie on its western side, along the streets and alleys branching off from it, many of which are stepped in order to accommodate the slope of Monte Catalfano. On the terrace directly above and west of the agora are the city's other major pub-

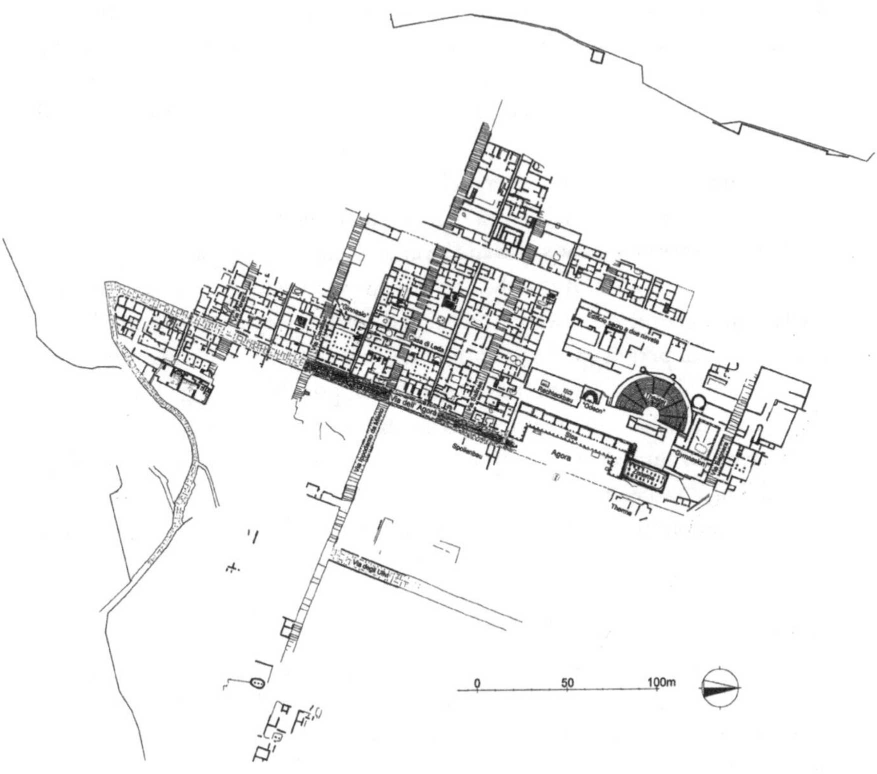

FIGURE 2.1.
Plan of Soluntum (Wolf 2014).

lic buildings, including the theater, an odeum or *bouleuterion*, and a cult precinct.

Based on a detailed examination of the excavated structures in the city center, Markus Wolf has recently hypothesized three main phases of urban development. The earliest public buildings, such as the theater and the odeum/*bouleuterion* (the assembly spaces for the city's political organs), were constructed in the early second century BC. He dates the main phase of monumental construction to the mid-second century BC. This phase saw the erection in the agora of a U-shaped stoa opening onto a paved plaza and adjoining a large public cistern and the construction of the gymnasium and the rectangular sacred complex on the theater terrace.[3] Honorific Greek inscriptions placed in one of the stoa's nine exedras and in the pavement of the Via dell'Agorà point to the key role that members of the local elite played in euergetism and public life in this period of prosperity.[4]

The early imperial city has been the focus of less research, but it is clear that construction activity and occupation continued in the first and second centuries AD. Two bath buildings, one on the southern end of the Via dell'Agorà and the other northeast of the agora plaza, remained in use in the first century AD.[5] The older buildings in the agora also continued to be used and modified: for example, two statue bases were placed in front of one of the stoa's exedras.[6] In addition, several elite houses continued to be renovated.[7] The complex on the Via dell'Agorà that was identified (probably erroneously) as a "Punic" sacred area was also in use at least until the second century AD.[8] The space in and around the theater, which was no longer functional after the late first century BC, was appropriated for housing and other buildings in the imperial period (perhaps in the mid-first century AD); these structures partly reused materials from the theater. Later, possibly during a late antique reoccupation, kilns were constructed in the theater's upper *cavea*.[9] Excavations have also turned up large quantities of Italian and African terra sigillata from the first and early second centuries AD.[10]

The abandonment of the city has been inferred from the lack of material culture and significant building work after the second century AD. The only Latin inscription from the city, a dedication by the *res publica Soluntinorum* to the wife of Caracalla (*CIL* 10.7336), dates to the first decade of the third century and is the latest evidence of the operation of its government. However, the city is mentioned in the *It. Ant.* and in an imperial edict of AD 440, prompting the hypothesis that settlement shifted back to the bay in late antiquity. Third-century African transport amphorae and other ceramics from the fourth through sixth centuries found in the area of Solanto support this hypothesis.[11]

The pace of abandonment of the urban center appears to have been gradual and voluntary, not precipitated by a single event. Some structures, such as the theater, seem to have had a short operational life in which they were maintained by civic authorities for their original purpose (perhaps only for a single century in the case of the theater). Other structures, however, such as certain elite residences, the stoa, and the baths, had multiple phases of use extending into the first and second centuries AD. In addition to the minor modifications to the stoa and agora plaza, the fragments of a statue possibly of Agrippina Maior that was later broken up and reused as building material illustrate the continuing importance of the agora in public life as well as the integration of the city (and its elite) into the political order of the early Principate.[12] But by the third century AD, when parts of the stoa were collapsing, sections of its ceilings were propped up on makeshift pilasters assembled from spoliated materials, such as a seat from the odeum.[13] The entrance to the agora plaza from the Via dell'Agorà was blocked off, and the ruins of the stoa appear to have been used as stables.[14]

There is little positive evidence for the abandonment of the site. Indeed, as it shows no signs of violent destruction and was probably abandoned gradually, it is likely that its last inhabitants took their possessions with them, presumably leaving behind only broken or old items not worth carrying. Nonetheless, the gradual shrinkage of the urban settlement and its population, the weakening of civic authority, and the disinvestment of the local elite in urban infrastructure in the imperial period—in contrast to the growth and prosperity the city experienced under the Republic—can be hypothesized. The evidence includes the disuse and spoliation of the theater and other public buildings as well as the history of occupation of the elite residences lining the main city street and its side streets. The latest decorative elements of many of these houses date to the Augustan period or slightly later. Though some houses continued in occupation thereafter, few changes or renovations to their decor and layout are apparent.[15] On the other hand, the singular and enigmatic Latin dedication of the *res publica Soluntinorum* to Fulvia Plautilla (AD 202–205) hints at the persistence of a city government, at least nominally, beyond substantial occupation at the site itself.

One reason for the voluntary abandonment of Soluntum may have been the attractive pull of other coastal centers directly west and east, respectively, of Monte Catalfano: Thermae Himeraeae and Panormus. These cities quickly emerged as two of the main economic and political centers of Sicily in the imperial period and may have attracted the urban residential elite, their economic and political activities, and their wealth away from Soluntum. The site of Soluntum also had the disadvantage of lacking a regular groundwater supply. Throughout its history the community had relied on collected rainwater, as the numerous domestic cisterns and the enormous public cistern at the northern edge of the agora illustrate.[16] Although economic activity may have shifted from the hillside to the harbor at the bay of Solanto contemporaneously with or shortly after the end of the urban community at Soluntum (similar to the earlier shift observed at Calacte), it is difficult to draw firm conclusions about the last years of the city based on the currently available evidence.

SEGESTA

The Elymian city of Segesta, situated on Monte Barbaro in the northwestern interior, is famous for its splendid fifth-century BC Doric temple and well-preserved Hellenistic theater. However, the site has only been the subject of systematic archaeological research since 1987. Excavations have focused on the summit and slopes of Monte Barbaro, which preserve remains of the ancient city's main public and residential areas as well as two wall circuits (see figure 2.2). Thanks to the extensive and well-published program of excavation in Segesta's urban center (where no modern settlement obscures ancient and medieval structures) and field survey in its territory, Roman-era uses of urban space and processes of abandonment are clearly visible and can be analyzed alongside patterns of rural settlement.

Excavations have revealed an extensive settlement whose greatest prosperity came in the two centuries after the Roman conquest in the First Punic War. At that time Segesta was favored as a *civitas immunis ac libera*, likely meaning that its citizens were exempt from paying tithe to Rome on their grain harvests (Cic., II *Verr.* 3.13 and 3.92–93).[17] During this period—and with particular intensification in the late second century—the main public and residential areas took shape on a series of terraces that followed the contours of Monte Barbaro, centered on a northern and southern acropolis.[18] A theater was built into the northern slope, while public structures, including a *bouleuterion* and a paved agora surrounded by stoas, were constructed on the north acropolis and in the saddle separating it from the south acropolis. Greek inscriptions attest to the role of the local elite in financing the construction and maintenance of these structures.[19]

The south acropolis and the northern and western sides of the north acropolis appear to have been primarily residential. Their finest houses, such as the Casa del Navarca, were built contemporaneously with the main public areas in the late third and second centuries BC.[20] The main wall circuit

FIGURE 2.2.
Monte Barbaro (author photo).

and gate (the Porta di Valle system) fell out of use by the second half of the third century, an indication that defense was no longer at the top of the civic agenda.[21]

Excavated ceramics indicate that Hellenistic Segesta was enmeshed in Mediterranean commercial networks and played a role in the local and regional distribution of olive oil and wine. The assemblage includes numerous Rhodian stamped amphorae, particularly from the first half of the second century BC, but is dominated by Punic and Greco-Italic forms. This indicates that the site participated in the commerce in Italian wine and African oil, particularly after the First Punic War and the integration of western Sicily into Rome's overseas empire.[22] Some of the Punic amphorae, however, were produced in western Sicily for the circulation of local goods like olive oil.[23]

Field surveys in the territory surrounding the urban center on Monte Barbaro have indicated dense rural settlement from the late fourth century until the second century BC, with a high concentration in the "suburban" zone around Segesta.[24] The sites of settlement appear to be mostly single-family homesteads, indicating an agricultural system based on small and medium-sized farms. However, larger agricultural/pastoral villages were detected in territory more distant from Segesta, especially along the main riverine transport routes. As with the ceramic assemblage from the urban center, the numerous Punic amphorae found at rural sites attest to commercial exchange (especially the importation of African olive oil) in the urban hinterland, while the large numbers of Greco-Italic amphorae attest to the wide diffusion of Italian wine alongside local products.

After its prosperous years under the Roman Republic, Segesta emerged largely unscathed from the Roman civil wars, though the partial reuse of the Porta di Valle wall circuit and the construction of a new circuit higher up the slopes of Monte Barbaro may be related to military activities in the vicinity of the city in the first century BC.[25] Segesta is included among the *civitates latinae condicionis* in Pliny's Augustan-era list, along with Netum and Centuripae. The first-century AD civic body referred to itself as a *municipium* (*AE* 1945.64). Although the early imperial phases of the forum area are difficult to untangle due to later spoliation and rebuilding, it appears that building and renovation work continued there until the early second century AD (see figure 2.3).[26]

One of the most important recent discoveries is the monumental complex located southwest of the Hellenistic agora. This "triangular forum" was created in the late first century BC or early first century AD by the paving of the area in front of a late second century BC stoa and the construction of a *tholos* in the middle of the resulting plaza (see figure 2.4).[27] This portico-*tholos* complex probably functioned as a *macellum*;[28] it may be related to the presence of Roman or Italian merchants in the town. In the agora itself, late Republican or early imperial alterations have been detected on the western side, where a small temple on a low podium was constructed in front of a building identified as a cryptoporticus.[29] The numerous fragments of honorific statues and bases found in the agora confirm that it remained the primary location for the commemoration of benefactions.

The settlement also continued to participate in exchange networks. The early and mid-imperial use layers of the forum have produced large quantities of imported ceramics, particularly Italian transport amphorae and terra sigillata mixed with eastern and early African sigillata.[30] Kilns in or near the urban center also continued to produce imitations of popular imported cookwares and kitchenwares from Campania, Pantelleria, northeastern Sicily, and Africa in the first centuries BC and AD.[31]

Settlement contraction appears to have begun in the mid-first century BC, when the upper perimeter wall was constructed over a Hellenistic residential area. The lower perimeter wall (the Porta di Valle system) fell into disuse again in the late first century AD, when its main gate, now *extra moenia*, was trans-

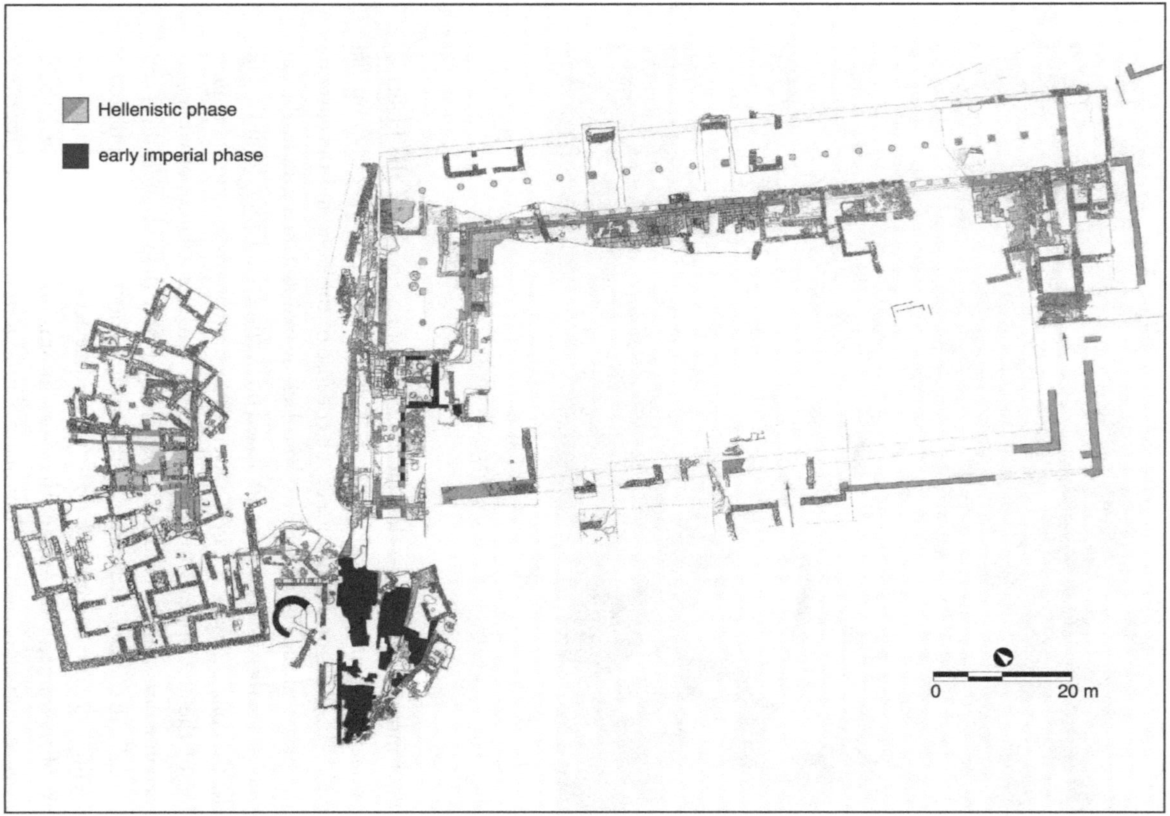

FIGURE 2.3.
The agora of Segesta (2015 plan: C. Ampolo/M. C. Parra/C. Cassanelli; with modifications by K. Rasmussen).

FIGURE 2.4.
Segesta: tholos *in the "triangular forum" (author photo).*

formed into an olive-processing facility.[32] The fine houses of the Hellenistic residential quarters also show signs of abandonment in the early imperial period.[33] In the agora/forum itself, the collapse of the stoas and the covering of the paved surface with detritus from lack of maintenance date to the late second and early third centuries AD, based on ceramics and coins found in and under the collapse layers and in the layers of accumulated sediment.[34] Frequentation of the area appears to cease soon afterward: datable imported ceramics become rare, and no coins have been found later than the mid-third century AD.[35] All this evidence points to the abandonment of the main public and residential areas on Monte Barbaro by the middle decades of the third century. Some of the ruined structures of the agora/forum subsequently show signs of sporadic occupation, such as burnt material produced by temporary hearths.[36]

Field survey in the territory of Segesta has indicated a reduction in the number of small dispersed rural settlements beginning in the late Republic (first century BC) and continuing into the early imperial period.[37] This may reflect a change in the organization of landholding and agricultural production—perhaps a concentration of land into fewer hands—rather than a demographic decline. While fewer sites remained in occupation at the periphery of Segesta's territory in the late Republic, the "suburban" zone around the city was also largely abandoned by the first century AD, indicating that the urban core exerted only a limited pull as a processing and marketing center and as a place of residence for agriculturalists.

As the number of scattered small rural sites continued to decline in the second and third centuries, while the number of medium-sized farmsteads and hamlets remained relatively stable, a concomitant agglomeration of settlement into larger villages occurred. These villages tended to be open and accessible, located in river valleys and near transport routes rather than on hilltops. The most archaeologically prominent is Aquae Segestanae, a three-hectare settlement that arose in the first century AD and reached its greatest extent in the fifth and sixth centuries. Imported African tablewares and kitchenwares are conspicuous on the rural sites of the high Empire, though African, Spanish, and Eastern Mediterranean transport amphorae are rare. This indicates that African household ceramics flooded the market here as elsewhere in Sicily but that the settlements did not import staples like olive oil, wine, grain, fruit, and fish products, perhaps because they were self-sufficient, had access to local or regional sources, or even exported some of these products.[38]

After a gap in occupation of the urban center, there are signs of resettlement in the fifth century.[39] The remains of Hellenistic and Roman-era buildings were used for new structures and for burials. Although the extent of the late antique settlement is unclear, it seems that the inhabitants had a fairly high standard of living. The site has produced coins and imported ceramics from the fifth through seventh centuries, while a Latin funerary inscription from AD 524 indicates some level of literacy within the settlement.[40] The structures of this village settlement have produced evidence of ironworking as well as cooking vessels and animal bones that indicate a high level of meat consumption. This suggests that the village on the ruins of Segesta hosted pastoralists and thus played an economic role complementary to that of contemporary lowland agricultural settlements such as Aquae Segestanae.[41]

The settlement history of Segesta from the late Republic through the high Empire offers parallels with other western Sicilian cities. As with Ietas, the material cultural assemblage of Segesta provides evidence for continued integration into Mediterranean commercial circuits in the first and second centuries AD, even as the public infrastructure decayed. In Segesta late second-century and early third-century African cookwares and finewares are present in the latest use strata as well as in the collapse layers of public buildings. As at Soluntum, the settlement shows no signs of a sudden abandonment precipitated by violent destruction. Instead, abandonment (at least for a century or so) is inferred from the diminution of material culture after the collapse and abandonment of the main public and residential areas.

Thanks to the discovery of several monumental public inscriptions at Segesta, the presence of members of the local elite and their impact on the urban fabric in the late Republic and early Principate can be traced to a greater extent than in any of the cities examined so far. These inscriptions shed light on families, some likely of Elymian origin, with deep roots in Segesta but with ties to Rome and Italy. In the late Republic and under Augustus, these elite families continued the Hellenistic tradition of euergetism in their home city, modifying the civic center to incorporate new Roman-style monuments and using hybrid Greek and Roman epigraphic means of self-presentation.

Because of the singularity of the language and workmanship of these inscriptions, as well as their frequent reuse in later building contexts, most of them (and the monuments they refer to) can be dated only broadly between the mid-first century BC and the late first century AD. It is consequently difficult to link the changes in the urban fabric they describe to specific events, such as the Roman civil wars, the Augustan settlement of Sicily, and the Vespasianic grants of land in the territory of Segesta to veterans and members of the imperial household.[42] By the Julio-Claudian period, however, owing to the economic and political changes that Sicily had undergone in the late Republic and the Augustan era (from whose direst effects Segesta was insulated though not completely immune), local elite families seem to have been of increasingly reduced means and socially, politically, and economically isolated. By the early second century they appear unable to maintain the monumental infrastructure of the urban center.

Families of beneficent local notables can be traced in the Greek inscriptions of Segesta from the Hellenistic period into the first century BC. Of the twenty or so names in the city's onomastic corpus, most are common, well-attested Greek names (Dionysios, Herakleios, Diodoros, etc.). A few appear to be of Italian origin (Dekios/Dekkios), while several are attested only in Elymian cities (Apellichos, Aleidas, Bibakos, Dossis, Minyra), and one (Tittelos) is found only at Segesta. The individuals named in inscriptions—all male, with the exception of a few female relatives of benefactors and one priestess—hold a range of magistracies and other civic and sacred offices that are widely attested in the Hellenistic Greek world, such as gymnasiarch, *agoranomos*, *hierothytas* (probably the eponymous magistrate), *hieromnamon*, and *hierophylax*. Inscriptions also attest to a body of *presbeis*.[43] In the first century BC families of Roman citizens (including the *gentes* Julia, Junia, Sempronia, and Caecilia) appear among the civic benefactors. At least one of these Roman citizens, Lucius Caecilius, son of Aulus, took a double cognomen: the first, Martiales, is widespread in the Roman world, and the second, Apetaius, is an apparent Latinization of the Greek Aretaios.[44]

The transition to the (apparently exclusive) use of Latin in public inscriptions occurred relatively early in Segesta, by the early Augustan period. Romanized magistracies, including those typically found in Italian and provincial *municipia* (e.g., duumvir and triumvir), reflect the city's evolving government. The inscriptions show an imperfect knowledge of Latin and perhaps reflect efforts to adapt Roman epigraphic conventions to the familiar language of Hellenistic civic euergetism.[45] One notable early imperial inscription reused in a medieval context reads thus: *L(ucio) Iulio C(aii) f(ilio) Agrippae / euergetae / hic plateam a Sosia / usque ad fanum*. The individual commemorated, Lucius Julius Agrippa, is clearly a Roman citizen, with his family's grant made in the triumviral or Augustan era.[46] He is honored as a *euergeta*, a transliteration of the Greek εὐεργέτης, for his sponsorship of the paving of a street (*platea*, from the Greek πλατεῖα) from an unknown quarter of the city (*a Sosia*) to an extramural sanctuary (*ad fanum*). The dedication shows an uncertain knowledge of Latin: most egregiously, the stone carver almost ran out of space for the final letter of the third line.

The paved triangular forum southwest of the Hellenistic agora, and perhaps also the *macellum* complex of the late first century BC or early first century AD, was the work of two Romanized local notables, Marcus Onasus and Marcus Sopolis, who were commemorated in an inscription on a series of paving stones in the center of the plaza, stretching across most of the plaza's length and legible to anyone approaching from the west.[47] These men had deep ancestral links to Segesta and possessed considerable wealth and social connections: a Sopolis is mentioned in an earlier Greek inscription commemorating renovations to the theater, while an Onasus makes an appearance in Cicero's Second Verrine Oration (5.120). The family owned tile kilns near Parthenicum on the northwestern coast.[48] The Roman/Italian architectural roots of the *macellum* complex have been noted frequently, and the structure has been linked to the presence of Roman and Italian merchants in the city. Its construction also points to the articulation of a distinct "commercial" public space apart from the "civic"/"cultic" space of the main agora/forum, as seen also in the second-century rebuilding of the agora of Morgantina and in the Roman Republican phases of the agora of Camarina.

An inscription on the highest step of the early imperial podium temple in the forum reads as follows: *L(ucius) Caecilius A(uli) f(ilius) Martiales / Apetaius praefectus / deos forenses reposuit templum / que eis sua pequnia adornavit*.[49] The exact temporal relation of the inscription to the building phases of this area of the forum is unclear. The dedication, like the Sosia inscription, shows an imperfect knowledge of Latin. It indicates that the benefactor Martiales restored statues of gods to the agora/forum, probably to the podium temple itself, perhaps after some sort of destruction or damage.[50] The stone carrying the inscription was reused from an earlier, unidentified structure, however, so the text's date and original context are uncertain. Despite these uncertainties, the inscription and the work on the area around it provide tentative evidence of a late building project in the forum that attempted to restore the integrity of some of its monuments, partly with reused materials from earlier structures.[51]

These scattered indications of public beneficence provide glimpses of the character and chronology of the urban development of late Republican and early imperial Segesta. First, an effort appears to have been made to update the space of the agora and recharacterize it as a forum, perhaps beginning in the mid-first century BC, through the construction of the paved triangular forum and *macellum* complex and the addition of the podium temple to the agora. The late first century and early second century AD saw limited, somewhat improvisational efforts to restore the forum and shore up its substructure using building materials stripped from earlier, presumably disused structures as well as statue bases and monumental inscriptions as recent as the Augustan period. When faced with limited means and materials for public works, the civic authorities of Segesta perhaps prioritized maintaining the spatial and structural integrity of the forum itself over preserving monuments of the city's past.[52]

There is also little indication of the involvement of social and political strata above the local elite in shaping the urban landscape of Segesta. The monuments of the late Republic and early Empire may have drawn inspiration from Roman models, with evidence of the imperial cult in the city by the Julio-Claudian period.[53] But the projects attested in inscriptions were local in scope (limited to the urban center of Segesta), were intended for a local audience, and were executed by a purely local elite. For example, the street-paving project of L. Julius Agrippa is described solely in terms of the city's topography: the location and identity of the Sosia and *fanum* that mark the origin and destination of the street would have been familiar to locals but perhaps as mysterious to outsiders as they are to modern scholars.

In this respect Segesta contrasts with cities like Lilybaeum, where (as discussed in chapter 3) inscriptions attest to a similar range of euergetistic activities (paving of streets, restoration of temples) but also to the introduction of new imperial monuments (e.g., aqueducts and amphitheaters). In Lilybaeum and two other western Sicilian cities, Panormus and Thermae Himeraeae, a fully fledged Latin epigraphic culture developed over the course of the Principate. Inscriptions commemorate the presence of a broader provincial elite and the occasional beneficence of the imperial family. This contrast points to the nexus involving a city's economic integration, its political and social prestige, and the development of its urban fabric in the imperial period.

HALAESA

Halaesa is situated on the eastern slope of a hill that rises steeply above the Tyrrhenian coast between the mouths of two seasonal rivers, the Tusa and Cicera, some 90 km east of Palermo. Although antiquarians knew of the site by the sixteenth century, extensive excavation in the urban center only began in the 1940s. These excavations focused on the agora/forum and its surroundings, with the result that many inscriptions, statuary, and architectural pieces were found in or close to their original context (see figure 2.5). Survey in the surrounding territory has accompanied excavation in the urban center.

Halaesa was founded within Sicel territory in 403 BC by Archonides of Herbita and settled by part of the population of that town. In the Timoleonic period the town began minting coins on behalf of an eponymous *symmachikon*, probably consisting of nearby Sicel centers on the coast and in the interior, including the mother city of Herbita. The city stopped minting after it fell under Carthaginian dominion.[54] Little else is known of the early history or topography of Halaesa, though its first wall circuit was probably constructed in the fourth century BC.[55] The city next appears in historical sources in the campaign of Hieron against the Mamertines. Early in the First Punic War it was the first Sicilian city to go over to the Romans (Diod. Sic. 23.4.1) and was made a *civitas immunis ac libera*. This status, coupled with the city's position as a major port along the Tyrrhenian coast, helps to explain its rapid development and its patronage links with members of the Roman elite in the following centuries. Almost all of the visible urban fabric dates, in its original form, to the period after the Second Punic War. Like other urban centers on or near the northern coast, including Soluntum, Segesta, and Ietas, the main phase of monumentalization of Halaesa followed the city's incorporation into the Roman Empire and was probably motivated by the growing economic power, social connections, and political ambitions of the town's elite.

The urban center was laid out on an extensive grid within the wall circuit, beginning approximately 160 meters above sea level and sloping up to the acropolis (240 meters above sea level). The streets were paved in local stone and consisted of long *cardines* running south to north parallel to the ridge, with the main *cardo* originating at the south gate (the main entrance to the

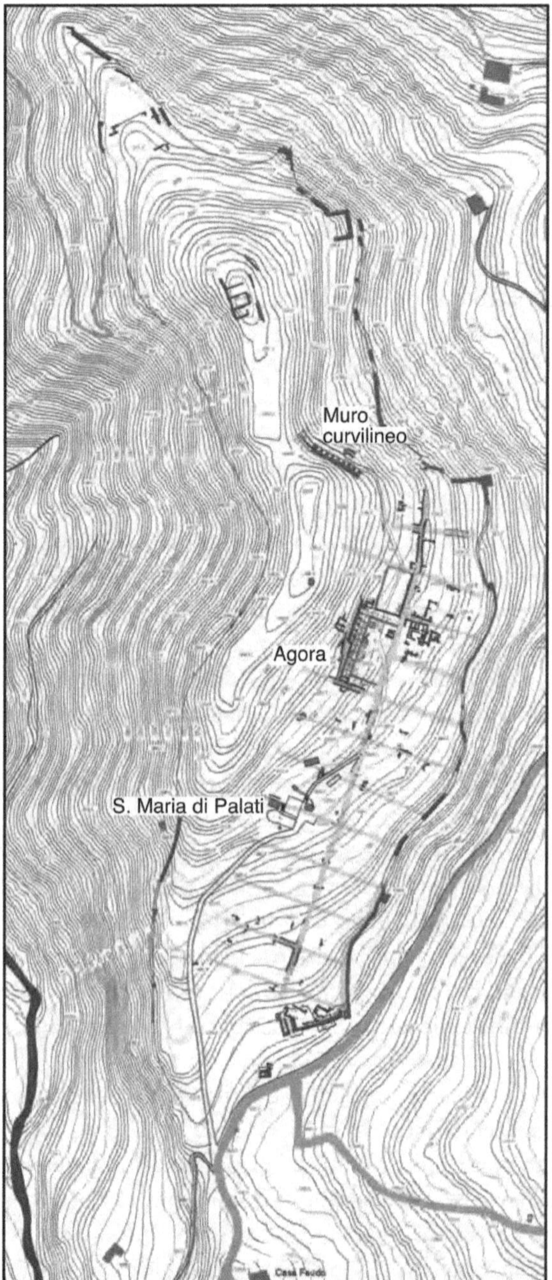

FIGURE 2.5.

Plan of Halaesa (R. Burgio, with modifications by K. Rasmussen).

FIGURE 2.6.
Halaesa: stoa (author photo).

city) and perpendicular *decumani* mostly laid out on terraces. Like the residential districts of Hellenistic Morgantina, the street network of Halaesa was designed to accommodate the steep slope and to mitigate the forces of erosion, with a sophisticated and extensive drainage system of pipes installed below the paved surface.[56]

The agora was located on two terraces above and below the *cardo maximus*, though only the upper terrace has been excavated. The upper agora was paved with terracotta tiles bearing monogrammed stamps, suggesting that they were purpose-made by public workshops.[57] At the end of the second century BC a monumental *pi*-shaped stoa was built on the agora's western side (see figure 2.6).[58] This stoa consisted of a portico faced by an external colonnade of brick columns and divided by a smaller internal colonnade. Behind this portico was a series of rectangular, possibly two-storied rooms with wide thresholds that the excavators called *tabernae* and *sacella*, some of which were built into the slope of the hill.

The agora, and particularly the western stoa, was a prime space for elite display. Most of the public inscriptions from the site, all of which date to the third century BC or later, were found in or near the stoa.[59] These inscriptions attest to an active local elite that held a typical range of Hellenistic Greek magistracies (*agoranomos*, etc.) and performed acts of euergetism in their city. For example, members of the Lapiron/Laphiro family are honored as benefactors in Greek inscriptions of the second and/or first centuries BC.[60] Elite families were also active in religious life and especially in the main civic cult of Apollo, as evidenced by two bronze tablets bearing a Greek inscription honoring a benefactor that were found in a house near the agora (*SEG* 59.1100).[61]

Inscriptions and historical sources also indicate a substantial early Italian/Roman presence in the city: individuals and families probably attracted as much by commercial opportunities in the urban center itself as by the availability of fertile agricultural and pastoral land in its hinterland. The main evidence for this element of the population is epigraphic. A third or early second century BC tufa block now in Palermo but probably from Halaesa bears a Latin dedication to Apollo by L. Carnius, likely a Roman citizen of Etruscan origins (*CIL* 10.7265). A lost dedication to L. Cornelius Scipio (probably the future Asiaticus, praetor in 193 BC) was made by Italicei who were perhaps *negotiatores* or *aratores* resident in Halaesa (*CIL* 10.7459). In addition, the names of some Halaesans betray Italian origins, such as the M. Aemilius who served as *agoranomos* and made a Greek dedication in the agora, whose father has the Oscan name Kipos.[62] One of the Halaesans whom Cicero mentions in the Second Verrine Oration is named Aeneas (3.170). The hero Halaesus, who appears in books 7 and 10 of the *Aeneid*, leads troops from northern Campania, another hint of the links between Halaesa and central Italy.[63]

Halaesa's privileged Roman status, its favorable position for participation in central Mediterranean commerce, the agricultural potential of its territory, and its early population of Romans and Italians all contributed to the development of links of patronage between the city's ruling elite and the Roman senatorial class. These links led to grants of citizenship and other benefits. For example, Cicero mentions the Lap(h)irones, the same family recorded in honorific inscriptions in the agora, in the context of Verres's abuse of Q. Caecilius Dio, who had received Roman citizenship from Q. Metellus and had ties of guest-friendship to M. Lucullus (II *Verr.* 2.19–24). In a letter of 46/45 BC Cicero recommends two Halaesans, M. Clodius Arcagathus and C. Clodius Philo, to the proconsul of Sicily as his *familiares* and *hospites*—relationships formed during his quaestorship in 75 BC or his subsequent visits to the island (*Ad fam.* 13.32). These men probably owed their enfranchisement to C. Claudius Marcellus, during his governorship of 79 BC. On the other side, Roman elite families had enduring links of patronage and service as well as economic interests in Halaesa and other northern cities. Caninius Niger was honored in an early first century BC Greek inscription found in the agora for his leadership of a contingent of ships from Halaesa and nearby towns.[64] Though little else is known of this man, he belonged to a *gens* that produced a praetor of Sicily (C. Caninius Rebilus, 171 BC) and is attested in inscriptions and coins from Thermae Himeraeae, Cephaloedium, and other northern Sicilian cities.[65]

One consequence of the city's ties to Rome and its increasingly heterogeneous ruling elite was that it turned to the Roman senate in 95 BC to reorganize its government, an event described by Cicero a few decades later (II *Verr.* 2.122).[66] As Cicero recounts, because of an internal dispute regarding vacancies on Halaesa's council, perhaps prompted by the desire of the new Italian/Roman population for inclusion, the praetor C. Claudius Pulcher, with help from the Metelli (long-standing patrons of Sicily), provided new regulations on the age of candidates, their occupations, and their property qualifications.

In addition to (and enmeshed with) its links to Rome and Italy, Halaesa had enduring links with nearby cities of the coast and interior. The Sicel *symmachia* could no longer function as an autonomous entity under the Romans. But the defensive considerations behind its formation in the classical period were carried on in the military role that the group played, along with other cities, within the *provincia* of Sicily. The Caninius Niger inscription commemorates an otherwise unknown victory of a fleet of ships from Halaesa, Kale Akte (Calacte), Amestratos, and Herbita. In addition, a *cippus* from the Halaesa agora (*IG* 14.355) was dedicated by Halaesan soldiers to Heraclios, the commander (*chiliarch*) of the military garrison at Eryx—another defensive effort undertaken collectively by the cities of northern and western Sicily under the auspices of Rome.[67]

Halaesa certainly eclipsed its mother city, Herbita, by the Republican period. It exercised an increasingly hegemonic role in its region that was linked to the political and economic advantages that it gained under Roman rule. In addition to its exemption from the *decima*, according to Cicero, Halaesa was one of the chief ports on the north coast for the *deportatio ad aquam* of grain produced in the interior as well as a collection point for export taxes (*portoria*) (II *Verr.* 2.185). Indeed, Cicero implies that the city's economic strength made it a particular target of Verres's abuses. In support of such literary attestations of the city's economic links to Italy, excavations in the city center have produced large quantities of Italian imports, including early terra sigillata, lamps, and transport amphorae.[68]

Halaesa's political fortunes in the civil war period and its immediate aftermath are difficult to trace. Pliny, probably working from an early Augustan-era source document, includes it among the *stipendiarii* of the province. However, coins and inscriptions such as *CIL* 10.7458, a lost dedication to Augustus (ca. 12 BC–AD 14), indicate that the city became (or regained its status as) a *municipium*, likely because of its economic hegemony in the region and its connections with Rome. The city was among the early adopters of the imperial cult in Sicily, with numismatic evidence for the veneration of Augustus even during his lifetime.[69]

Ceramics found in the urban center, including Italian sigillata and lamps, point to the city's continuing economic links with Italy in the early Empire.[70] In addition, Italian elements of the population, some probably of long duration, are present in early-imperial and mid-imperial inscriptions. The gentilician and tribal affiliation of M. Limbricius Rufus, of the tribe Falerna, suggest origins in Campania, probably in a *gens* from Puteoli active in overseas commerce (*CIL* 10.7460). His wife, Helvia Arura, also bears a family name common in Campania and elsewhere (including Sardinia) but not otherwise attested in Sicily. In the public sphere, an L. Naevius Firminus Manilianus is honored in a Latin inscription from the agora.[71] He belonged to a *gens* (Naevius) that is widespread in the late Republic in Campania and Delos but not in Sicily, suggesting Italian origins (perhaps distant) for this individual.[72]

Under the early Empire, Halaesa continued to exercise a hegemonic regional role. Herbita, Calacte, and Amestratus, the cities that had supplied ships to the force of Caninius Niger in the early first century BC, faded into obscurity. One indication of the city's regional economic power comes from its coin assemblage. Halaesa was one of the few Sicilian cities to continue to mint coins under Augustus, probably in order to facilitate daily commerce within the region.[73] In fact, 45 percent of the 198 excavated coins dating from the Second Punic War to the reign of Tiberius (when municipal issues ceased) came from the mint of Halaesa itself, an indication of the town's economic strength and monetary independence.[74]

Public building projects in the early and high imperial period largely consisted of the adaptation of existing public spaces, rather than the creation of new ones: primarily the transformation of the Hellenistic agora into a Roman forum. The western stoa developed with a growing distinction between cultic/honorific space and commercial space that is reminiscent of the "forumization" of the agora of Segesta in the early first century AD. The relatively unadorned rooms designated *tabernae* I and VIII appear to have functioned as shops or storage spaces. The more lavishly decorated rooms (designated *sacella*) were intended for honorific or cult purposes: all have paved floors (most in marble) and contain altars, niches, and/or bases for statues. The most distinctive is *sacellum* III, the third room from the stoa's northern end.[75] Its walls are faced in white and gray marble and its floor is paved in colored marbles imported from Italy, Africa, and Asia Minor. In front of its back wall is a rectangular statue base partly faced in marble. The space in front of the *sacellum* is paved in white marble with gray marble trim and contains a pedestal statue base also faced in marble. Based on the inscriptions found in the vicinity and the lavishness of the decor, excavators have hypothesized that *sacellum* III was dedicated to the imperial cult.

In conjunction with the conversion of the *sacella* into cult and display spaces, the paved open space of the agora (particularly in front of the stoa) became cluttered with statue bases, fountains, and exedras.[76] Most prominently, a large base in *opus reticulatum*, originally faced in white marble with a white marble cornice, was placed outside the northwestern corner of the portico in alignment with *sacellum* III: perhaps a tribunal for orators or the base of an equestrian statue. Immediately south of this podium is a line of four statue bases of various dimensions aligned with the *sacella* of the western stoa; another five bases were placed elsewhere in the agora plaza.

Excavations in the part of the western stoa converted into a lime kiln in late antiquity uncovered sculpture that once adorned the *sacella* and the open space of the agora.[77] Two statues of Ceres probably came from neighboring *sacella*. The base of one, from the late Antonine period, is inscribed with the name of its dedicator, a *sevir*.[78] These images of Ceres evoke the fertility of the hinterland of Halaesa and the beneficence brought by the imperial order. A damaged male portrait head was also found in the agora, originally belonging to a togate figure but recarved in the fourth century AD. A more complete statue of an Antonine-era magistrate, the so-called Claudius Pulcher, was recovered from the site by antiquarians. This statue, which was perhaps imported from Asia Minor, depicts a Roman citizen of senatorial rank who holds symbols of his cultural and political attainment and wears the beard of an intellectual. He is a good citizen, possessed of *paideia*, who has embarked on a public career as a member of the imperial elite: a Roman, but also a cultivated man of the *polis*.

To summarize, the agora/forum continued to be a space for civic commemoration and elite self-display in the imperial period, but even more conspicuously than under the Republic. With Halaesa's full incorporation into the Roman imperial order, granted by Augustus in the form of its municipal status, the community needed spaces in which to celebrate this inclusion (and the benefits it brought) and to show its loyalty to the ruling power (the emperor). The city's continued wealth and connectivity found expression in the range of building materials (such as colored marbles) and techniques (like *opus reticulatum*) that were deployed to fulfill this need for self-promotion and

FIGURE 2.7.
Halaesa: columbarium (author photo).

civic benefaction. This access to materials from the wider Roman Empire (and the prestige associated with them) is seen also in the epigraphic record, in the switch from local stone to marble for public inscriptions.

Parallel efforts at self-promotion are visible in the monumental tombs built in the southern necropolis in the high imperial period: most conspicuously, the columbarium near the southeastern gate and the complex of tombs surrounding it (see figure 2.7).[79] This square monument in *opus reticulatum*, with a single entrance and niches inside to hold ash containers, was constructed in the mid-second century AD, probably for the use of a *paterfamilias* and his immediate family. Surrounding this structure were at least sixteen tombs, probably of members of the same family, from the second to the fourth century AD. The columbarium is unique in Halaesa and has few parallels in western Sicily, though similar structures have been found further east at Tyndaris, Tauromenium, and Catina (see chapters 4 and 5). However, the form is quite common in central Italy, a further indication of the continued Italian and Roman cultural influence on Halaesa.

The rural landscape of Halaesa has received considerable attention because of the Tabula Halaesina, a large marble Greek inscription in two columns found on the site but lost in the seventeenth century, though its text was preserved in two transcriptions. The tabula dates approximately to the Republican period, no earlier than the mid-third century BC and no later than the first century BC (*IG* 14.352).[80] It concerns the leasing of land by an unnamed entity (either the *polis* of Halaesa or its main civic cult of Apollo) in dozens of small parcels (*klaroi* or *daithmoi*) separated by natural and constructed features (streams, hedges, fences, canals, roads, etc.). Its closest Sicilian parallel is the financial registers from Hellenistic Tauromenium, which also record the leasing of civic land (see chapter 4).

The tabula lists plots of land by serial number along with the city district in which they are located and provides a short description of each plot.[81] It yields little concrete information about the organization of the territory of Halaesa (such as the proportion of land under civic, private, or sacred administration or the proportion of land in the hands of smallholders) or about the circumstances that prompted its creation. Nonetheless, the lot descriptions suggest a well-organized, fertile landscape in which mixed farming was practiced, with the potential for forestry and pastoralism in some areas. For example, the tabula mentions fruit trees, olive trees dividing fields, a structure (possibly an olive press: *eliaokomion*) on a property where tanning was prohibited (col. I, ll. 69–71), and a managed woodland (*megalos drymos*) (col. I, ll. 67–68). It also refers to an aqueduct (*ocheton*) (col. I, l. 7), canals or ditches (*skaphiai*), troughs (*pyaloi*), springs, and even a bathhouse, indicating that the distribution of water was highly controlled for use in irrigation and livestock-raising.

Surveys of the territory around the ancient city confirm the diverse rural landscape of the Hellenistic/Republican period portrayed in the tabula.[82] The densest areas of settlement are those closest to the city and the River Tusa. These areas were probably divided into small, highly productive properties where mixed farming of olives, grapes, fruits, and cereals was practiced. Settlement is less dense (though not sparse) in areas farther from the city and concentrated around water sources and transportation routes. A mixed economy probably existed in those areas, where forestry (especially of oaks, whose tannin was used in tanning) could be practiced alongside ranching. Survey has also shown that the territory of Halaesa was integrated into the commercial networks of the central Mediterranean. Punic-type amphorae for fish products were found on many sites, along with Dressel 1 amphorae used for the export of Italian wine.

This landscape changed in the Augustan period and in the late first century AD with a steady and then dramatic decrease in the number of rural sites in occupation, though the territory continued to be densely settled. The sixty-eight settlements in occupation in the Hellenistic period were reduced to thirty-nine in the Augustan period, accompanied by the occupation of only a few new sites. From the end of the first century until the third century half of the remaining sites went out of occupation and only two new sites were settled. Settlement was more stable in the most geographically and economically favorable areas, however, such as the slopes and valley between the city center and the Tusa. The rural population appears to have concentrated in larger, stable settlement sites equipped with processing and storage spaces that served as centers of medium or large properties. They were located in a more extensive territory than in earlier centuries: for example, a villa site active for all of the imperial period far from the city center in Piano Fontane.

These results should be accepted with caution, however, because the diminution of settlement numbers in the imperial period was largely inferred from the absence of Italian sigillata then African sigillata from rural sites. It is risky to associate the absence of such finewares with the abandonment of a site. This may instead (or in addition) suggest changing patterns of production and exchange. Indeed, the survey directors suggest that the limited presence of transport amphorae on imperial-era rural sites may indicate their self-sufficiency in the production of wine and olive oil and perhaps their lack of integration into prevailing Mediterranean commercial networks, especially those centered on North Africa in the second and third centuries AD.

Nonetheless, the Tabula Halaesina and the results of field survey reveal much about the rural territory of Halaesa and its relation to the city center. First, the integrity of the city center and the organization of the countryside were closely connected. In addition to the parceling and leasing of lots, the city government was responsible for the creation and maintenance of the structures that organized and facilitated rural life, such as the roads that connected the city to its hinterland and the aqueduct that passed through the countryside on its way to the city, whose water was channeled to rural properties for use in irrigation. The tabula and field survey also show the importance of waterways—especially the Tusa—to rural organization and production. These watercourses provided valuable resources for agriculture and aided in communications and transportation between rural sites and between the urban center and its hinterland.

Finally, the evidence for rural settlement in the territory of Halaesa lends support to Cicero's emphasis on the city's role in *deportatio ad aquam*. Twelve rural sites were found near the interior route connecting Halaesa with Enna that ran along the western bank of the Tusa. All of these sites were occupied from the earliest period of the city's history until late antiquity. The location of the city along such important transportation routes, its role as a port, and its possession of a large, fertile, well-watered hinterland with a wide range of productive opportunities enabled a diverse and integrated urban and rural economy to develop. This helps to explain the continued prosperity of the urban center and the continued occupation of the countryside, in spite of the political setbacks, economic shifts, and natural disasters that affected the region and the island as a whole.

In past decades scholars have assumed that Halaesa experienced a precipitous decline after the second century, when monumental building activity appears to have ceased in the urban center.[83] Recent excavations in the agora/forum and necropolis areas, however, have shed light on the late and post-Roman history of the site and have provided evidence for almost-continuous occupation of the urban center at least until the tenth century, necessitating a nuancing of these earlier assessments. The agora/forum may have declined as a monumental civic space from the late second century AD onward, with few signs of new building or renovation, although the west stoa and paved plaza were in use at least until the era of Constantine. A fragmentary marble Latin inscription in honor of a *proconsul* and *c.v.* dated to the mid-third century or later is the latest published inscription from the area.[84] Some parts of the portico's external colonnade were filled in with spoliated architectural materials, perhaps in the fourth century.[85] The portico collapsed shortly thereafter and was not subsequently rebuilt.

Materials and structures from the third, fourth, and fifth centuries indicate that occupation continued in the urban center, but in a less organized fashion. Numismatic finds chart a continuity of occupation from the time of Severus Alexander through the successors of Constantine, until the fifth century AD. Later houses were often built with reused materials from earlier structures, however, and impinged on streets and other formerly open spaces.[86] The existence of a large necropolis and other structures on the slopes that extend north from the urban center toward the coast at modern Castel di Tusa has led excavators to suggest that the main area of settlement moved or dispersed down from the hill in the fourth and fifth centuries, closer to the port and to the Via Valeria, the coastal road connecting Messana to Panormus and Lilybaeum.[87] The transport amphorae used for child burials in the necropolis indicate that the settlement continued to receive imports, mainly from Africa but also from Spain. It also participated in regional trade in staples like wine, as shown by abundant finds of small amphorae produced along the Tyrrhenian coast. In addition, an epitaph in which a Christian husband possibly of Gallic or Pannonian origins honors his wife Eirena, perhaps of Jewish ancestry, in Greek and partly in verse, points to the continued diversity of the population of Halaesa thanks to its maritime links.[88]

Occupation of the ancient urban center persisted into the Byzantine period, though probably within a smaller area and at a suburban level. There are signs of scattered nuclei of religious, residential, and economic activities in the urban center in the sixth and seventh centuries, though the organization of these activities seems to have been ad hoc, without the oversight of civic authority. Scatters of tiles over the foundations of some of the agora's structures indicate the presence of simple houses in the Byzantine era.[89] After the collapse of the portico, its architectural elements, inscriptions, and sculpture were subject to spoliation. Some were collected for use in a lime kiln.[90]

The final use of the agora/forum area was as a cemetery in the sixth and seventh centuries.[91] Almost fifty burials have been found, clustered especially in the area once occupied by the portico and *sacella* of the west stoa. This cemetery covered and cut into the collapse layers of the stoa, down to the pavement of the plaza. The chamber tombs, probably of Christians, are all oriented to the east but otherwise show no signs of organization. They were often constructed of reused materials, such as tiles and stone slabs, with no *tituli*, and contain few grave goods. Contemporary with the cemetery are two parallel curving walls of uncertain purpose built of fragments of tile and stone atop the destruction layer of the agora's ancient buildings.

Despite the municipal status it regained in the Augustan era, Halaesa appears to have lacked close connections to Roman administrators and provincial elites. Its own local elite shows only limited social mobility, though this may be a result of the relative dearth of inscriptions from the imperial period. Its economy and the social connections of its leading families were also strongly oriented toward Italy. Halaesa does not show the same economic and political vitality throughout the imperial period as Lilybaeum, Panormus, Syracuse, Catina, and other cities with more extensive links to Africa and the Eastern Mediterranean, which points to the potential impact of the relative decline of Italy in the imperial export economy in the early and middle Principate on its prosperity. Nonetheless, the diversity of the roles that the urban center played, including in the administration of a fertile rural hinterland and in maritime commerce, and the socially and ethnically heterogeneous population that resulted were key to Halaesa's survival for most of the imperial period.

The adaptation of the existing monumental infrastructure instead of the construction of new monuments in the urban center should not be interpreted as a symptom of decline. Rather, it was a strategic deployment of communal and individual resources, geared mainly toward expressions of loyalty to (and solidarity with) the Roman imperial order created by Augustus. Even if the economic and political prominence of the city declined over the course of the high Empire, its urban core remained vital into late antiquity.

A collapse of civic authority can only be detected in the late Roman and early Byzantine periods, but Halaesa continued to be a center of population and economic activity until the end of antiquity.

ANALYSIS: REGIONAL AND MICROREGIONAL DIFFERENCES IN DEURBANIZATION

The gradual abandonment of Soluntum, Segesta, and Halaesa points to the complexity of the phenomenon of deurbanization in Roman imperial Sicily. These cities and those examined in chapter 1 reflect the variable effects that shifts in regional economies, as well as changing relationships with Rome, could have on the physical and political integrity of an urban settlement. The full-scale abandonment of Heraclea Minoa, Phintias, and Camarina on the south coast was significantly earlier than the abandonment of Segesta, Soluntum, and Halaesa (and even of Ietas). This reveals considerable regional and microregional disparities in the pace and extent of deurbanization. But the impact of geography on an individual settlement's viability cannot be reduced to simple contrasts between coastal and inland, south coast and north coast, or hilltop and valley settlements. An urban site's access to water and the productive potential and adaptability of its rural hinterland were also significant factors in its development. The end of intensive production and commerce at Morgantina by the early imperial period, in contrast to the continued economic vitality of the Caronia Marina site of Calacte and some parts of Halaesa as late as the Byzantine period, points to the importance of the availability of natural resources (especially water) in determining the economic connectivity of a settlement. Conversely, the geographical advantages of a city like Soluntum, which was near a protected harbor and a major coastal land route, may have mitigated environmental disadvantages like the lack of a convenient groundwater source.

Moreover, similar processes of adaptation to changing economic configurations were at work in different regions of Sicily, though at varying paces, throughout the imperial period. For example, settlement and economic activity along the south coast may have shifted gradually from the environmentally disadvantageous older coastal centers like Heraclea Minoa and Camarina, which required considerable financial and human resources for their maintenance, to smaller, less monumental, and hence less archaeologically visible landing points along the shore that also served land transportation routes. These small centers gained prominence in the historical and archaeological record as commerce between Sicily and North Africa increased in late antiquity. Similarly, along the Tyrrhenian coast, the most economically vital sectors of the settlements at Caronia and Halaesa in their later periods of occupation were the areas closest to harbors and to the main overland route along the northern coast.

Though they were themselves linked to the geographical and economic diversity of the island, the political histories of individual Sicilian cities and particularly their histories with Rome also had an impact on their development under the Roman Empire. Segesta and Halaesa (and perhaps Soluntum) stand out as the only cities examined so far with significant evidence of public building activity in the century encompassing the end of the Republic and the early Principate (ca. 50 BC–AD 50). In Halaesa such activity continued for at least a century thereafter. The continued economic integration of Segesta and Halaesa in the early and middle imperial period, however, is not a sufficient explanation for the maintenance of the urban fabric. The example of Ietas shows that the monumental infrastructure of a city could decay even as it continued to receive goods from across the Mediterranean.

In contrast to Ietas, the epigraphic and historical record of Segesta reveals considerable continuity within the local elite. The families of men like Marcus Onasus and Marcus Sopolis, who were among the latest known benefactors to the town, can be traced back at least to the Republican period. The identity and concerns of the civic body of Segesta were also consistent over time, though adaptable to the various political situations that the city faced in its long history. Most telling in this regard is the city's concern for the Temple of Astarte/Aphrodite/Venus at Eryx, which can be traced from the Athenian expedition of the late fifth century BC through the Julio-Claudian period. Over the centuries the ruling elite of Segesta proved adept at using its control over this sanctuary to its advantage in negotiations with imperial authorities and especially with the Romans, with whom they claimed kinship through the goddess and her son Aeneas. The decline of effective city government also meant the end of a community's relations with the center of power and hence of its appearance in Roman annals, so it is significant that the last of the cities thus far examined to be mentioned in the Roman historical record is Segesta. It appears in Tacitus's *Annales* in AD 25, when it sent a delegation to Tiberius to ask for his assistance with repairs to the Eryx sanctuary.[92]

As a result of this particular facility with dealing with imperial powers, Segesta and Halaesa were the only cities considered so far that possessed definite juridical status throughout the period of Roman hegemony. As already noted, the Segestans seem to have quickly parlayed their status as a *civitas immunis ac libera* (bestowed, Cicero claims, because of the city's loyalty and its ancestral links with Rome) into municipal status under the new Augustan regime. This status did not serve as a catalyst for urban development, however, but seems rather to have served as a temporary break in the process of deurbanization already at work. Some of the latest monumental building projects in the city, such as the construction of the upper wall circuit and the "restoration" of the *dei forenses* temple, can be interpreted as signs of civic distress or at least as stresses on the diminishing resources of the city government.

The local elite of early imperial Segesta were working against the main force shaping the urban landscape of Sicily: the concentration of political and economic power in coastal centers of Roman status (mainly the Augustan *coloniae*) or in coastal centers with significant political and economic advantages. These included the subjects of the next chapter: Lilybaeum, a major port and center of Roman administration, and Agrigentum, also a major port and a center of sulfur production. The complete abandonment of the urban center that eventually occurred at Segesta was not the inevitable result of this process of concentration, however, as the settlement history of Halaesa shows. As at Segesta, a tenacious local elite can be detected at Halaesa, a city with a similar history of cordial relations with Rome. Halaesa experienced a similar flurry of monumental activity in the late second century BC, with the construction of the stoa complex in the agora. It also continued to be a vital urban settlement in the first and second centuries AD. Its agora continued to serve as a space of self-promotion where socially mobile freedmen (such as the Augustales) could make their mark alongside members of the freeborn local elite. But the evidence for Halaesa's abandonment in late antiquity is less comprehensive than for Segesta's abandonment. Perhaps the site's access to overland and maritime communication routes enabled a smaller, less complex settlement to persist until the end of antiquity in and around the urban center.

The singularity of Segesta and Halaesa among the case studies of the last two chapters also demonstrates the different extents to which communities embraced characteristically Roman political forms, language, architecture, and material culture (in other words, their levels of "Romanization"). As has frequently been noted, it is difficult to separate "Roman" from "Italic"—and even from broader "Hellenistic"—cultural forms in the Republican period. Rather, the channels of influence in Rome, Italy, and other regions of the Mediterranean (including Sicily) were mutual and complex.[93] All the same, the Roman/Italian architectural influences visible in the urban landscapes of Ietas and Heraclea Minoa, Morgantina, and perhaps Camarina have been linked to direct (though limited) interventions by Roman authorities after the servile wars, the Second Punic War, and the First Punic War, respectively.

The indirect influence of Roman and Italian culture can also be seen in several cities. These influences probably stemmed from commercial contacts between Sicily and Italy. Cities in the interior (Segesta) as well as on the northern (Calacte) and southern coasts (Phintias, Heraclea Minoa) imported Italian wine in the Republican period or at least consumed local imitations of it, as shown by the presence of Greco-Italic and Dressel 1 amphorae. The paintings that adorned the walls of fashionable houses in Soluntum were executed in styles similar to those found in houses of Pompeii and other central and southern Italian cities, and an Italic influence may be detected in the later phases of the residential quarters of Morgantina.[94]

Segesta and Halaesa are the cities with the greatest bodies of evidence for the adoption of Roman and Italian architectural forms in the late Republic and early Principate. During this period Segesta's agora was restructured in "forum terms" by the addition of the triangular forum and *macellum* and the construction of the small Italic podium temple in the main square. It is also the only city (besides Halaesa) to produce a significant number of Latin inscriptions, a marker of the political and cultural integration of its ruling class. The development of the architecture and material culture of Segesta and to a lesser extent of Ietas and Soluntum may have been influenced by these cities' links with larger coastal centers like Thermae, Panormus, and Lilybaeum in the early imperial period that were more fully integrated into Roman economic, political, and cultural currents. But, in contrast to these cities, Segesta shows little sign of any impetus from the imperial center, Roman administrators, or the emerging class of provincial elites toward further urban development. With the exception of a few dedications to the imperial cult, the inscriptions of Segesta record changes to the urban fabric that were initiated by locals, were local in scope, and were framed in local language. They give little indication of links between the city's elite and the wider social and political world of the province and empire.

Halaesa's cultural "Romanization" under the Republic was linked to the early presence of Italian and Roman residents. The city's connection to Italy persisted into the imperial period, as is apparent from the architecture of the tombs on its periphery. As in Segesta, Greek had ceded to Latin as the main language of public inscriptions by the early Principate. In addition, the city's Hellenistic-era public spaces were adapted to the political, cultural, and religious institutions of the imperial-era *municipium*. Most notably, at least one of the rooms of the stoa was renovated to serve as a space for the veneration of the emperor.

Though they lack significant evidence of political or cultural "Romanization," most of the other Sicilian centers that continued in occupation in the early imperial period did receive high quantities of characteristically Roman material culture, such as Italian finewares and coins issued by imperial mints—indeed, this is the main body of evidence for the latest phases of life at Morgantina and the hilltop site of Calacte. The presence of such material in urban contexts is more reflective of shifting commercial currents than of changing tastes or cultural Romanization. Almost all of the cities had imported or had themselves produced black and red-glazed dining and service vessels for much of the classical and Hellenistic periods. But the large-scale production and export of finewares from Arezzo and other central Italian production centers in the early years of the Principate seems to have squeezed out the other black- and red-gloss forms produced in southern Italy and Sicily. In the workshops at Morgantina, for example, potters experimented with new forms of red-gloss wares (presigillata), but these experiments ceased with the destruction ca. 35 BC, after which Italian wares dominate the ceramic assemblage. Similarly, while an estimated 80 percent of the Hellenistic finewares found at the Marina site of Calacte were of Sicilian origin, Italian finewares dominated the assemblage between ca. 30 BC and the end of the first century AD.[95]

DEURBANIZATION AND RURAL SETTLEMENT

The urban histories of this chapter also refine the interpretation of the relationship between urban occupation and rural settlement put forward in chapter 1. In the cities where survey of the hinterland has accompanied excavation in the urban center, no one pattern of distribution or development of rural settlement is visible. In some areas both rural settlement and urban settlement appear to contract in the late Republic and early Empire. Surveys around Heraclea Minoa indicate a rise in rural settlement coinciding with the contraction of the urban center in the third century BC, but an apparent diminution followed in the first century BC and continued into the early imperial period. The early imperial period shows no signs of the development of villas or the emergence of other forms of new settlement. But a few larger sites—perhaps villas or large farming establishments—grew out of older Hellenistic settlements in the middle and late Empire. Rural settlement in the vicinity of Heraclea Minoa appears to have suffered, along with the urban center, from the shift of commerce away from the south coast by the late Republic. It did not resume until new, revived patterns of exchange implicated the area in late antiquity. Survey in the hinterland of Morgantina has similarly suggested a substantial decline in the number of rural sites, their size, and their artifact densities. This probably reflects both a decline in rural population numbers and a divestment from agricultural production after the Roman siege and takeover of the urban center from which the region never fully recovered.

While the Heraclea Minoa and Morgantina surveys show that the abandonment of an urban center could be accompanied by a diminution of rural sites in its territory, the opposite seems to have occurred in other areas. The rise in rural settlement numbers in the territory of Ietas culminates in the mid-first century AD, the same period as the disintegration of the urban center. These sites appear fully integrated into Mediterranean exchange networks: in particular, as the plentiful finds of Campanian wine amphorae hint, the exchange of Italian wine for Sicilian grain.

The territory of Segesta, like that of Heraclea Minoa, shows a high density of settlement in the Hellenistic period. This was followed by a progressive contraction in the course of the second and first centuries BC, especially of small and medium-sized sites, perhaps indicating the concentration of properties rather than an actual demographic decline. The diminution of rural sites continued in the first century AD, especially in the area around the urban center. In the high Empire settlement gradually concentrated in villages and large farms at a distance from the former city center, in well-watered valleys that were accessible to transport routes—a development also observed in the territory of Morgantina in the second century BC and into the Principate. Although the specific pattern and chronology of rural settlement around Segesta differed from settlement in the vicinity of Morgantina and Ietas, in all three territories there was a gradual shift away from the urban center as the main pole of economic activity and a weakening of links between urban and rural settlement, coupled with an emergence of new patterns of rural settlement based around new nonurban centers of processing and distribution. The urban center of Halaesa remained in occupation through most of the imperial period, but a similar shift toward larger, more widely distributed rural settlements, coupled with a reduction in the total number of sites in occupation, occurred in its hinterland.

These developments are mirrored even in regions where field surveys have not been conducted but where something is known of rural settlement patterns, such as the south coast and southeastern interior. Many areas show caesuras in settlement in the late Republic and early Principate, followed by a gradual shift to new centers of processing and distribution, both on the coast (as at the Marina site of Calacte and probably along the southern coast around Camarina) and along interior land routes (as in the area of Morgantina). In the interior these new centers took the form of villas or other agglomerations (villages, *vici*) that were connected to each other and to the cities of the eastern, northern, or western coasts via land routes and watercourses. As noted above, smaller landing points developed on the coast that also served overland routes.

CONCLUSION

The settlements examined here and in chapter 1—along with other Sicilian towns where the archaeological and historical evidence for abandonment is suggestive but not as comprehensive (e.g., Helorus, Apollonia, and Entella)—demonstrate that deurbanization was a real phenomenon in the Roman imperial period in Sicily. By the era of Augustus the social, political, and economic structures that had governed *polis* life in previous centuries had begun to weaken. As a result, many urban centers gradually went out of occupation in the first through third centuries AD. Nonetheless, deurbanization was a complex phenomenon, subject to variations in pace and extent according to variables such as a city's geography, economic basis, and political history as well as other factors (including the changing tastes, economic means, and identities of urban residents) that cannot be fully recovered from fragmentary literary and material-cultural evidence.

The next three chapters examine the concentrated urban system that emerged in Sicily to replace the old, diffuse network of autonomous *poleis*. This new system centered on existing cities that were notable for their economic dominance over their respective regions and also for their economic diversity. These cities' roles as centers of commerce, political power, and social prestige gained monumental form and were manifested in the urban landscape in numerous ways over the course of the Principate.

THREE

THE SOUTHWESTERN COAST

Economic Integration, Political Privilege, and Urban Survival

The two preceding chapters have described deurbanization as a significant and complex phenomenon in Roman imperial Sicily. The classical *polis* ceased to be a significant form of settlement in many regions but especially along the southern coast and in the more isolated sections of the mountainous interior. In other parts of Sicily, however, cities remained a vital part of the settlement landscape. This chapter and the next two chapters examine several of these cities, with a particular focus on their place in the emerging urban hierarchy of the early Principate.

In Sicily, like the rest of the Greco-Roman Mediterranean, the urban core of each *polis* or *civitas* served as a center of government and administration for itself and for an agricultural territory and also as a center for the processing and marketing of its agricultural products. Independent political entities (such as the classical Greek *poleis*) and cities that were subordinate to larger imperial systems also served as collection points for tribute and tax. This fiscal role could be facilitated by the minting of coins in the urban center, whether in the name of the *polis*/*civitas* itself or in the name of the larger imperial entity.

Ancient urban centers were the main place of residence of an elite class of rentiers whose wealth was based in agriculture (the ownership, and perhaps also leasing, of agricultural land) but who were engaged in economic, cultural, religious, and political activities in the urban center (e.g., service in magistracies and priesthoods). Considerable social prestige was attached to these public vocations. Therefore, they are highly visible to modern scholars, particularly in monumental epigraphy and other material acts of self-promotion in urban space. Besides this elite class, ancient cities had substantial populations of varying legal status (freeborn, freed, or enslaved and citizen or resident noncitizen) whose livelihoods were not directly related to agriculture and who were instead engaged in occupations related to government (e.g., public slaves), the provision of services (innkeepers, builders, fullers), and the processing and marketing of the raw goods produced in the rural hinterland (bakers, potters, weavers, merchants). This nonagricultural population, especially in "megacities" like imperial Rome and classical Athens, had to be sustained by the surplus alimentary resources of the territory or by the importation of such resources.

Under the Roman Empire, in which the central state's authority was embodied in the emperor but maintained in most regions by a skeletal staff of administrators, cities were also the main places from which information and policy originating in the imperial center were disseminated to subjects. This dissemination could occur through formal channels, such as imperial decrees; letters and embassies between local governments and imperial officials; visits of emperors and provincial administrators to individual cities (e.g., on the "assize" circuit); and the circulation of images originating in Rome, such as coins and statuary. It could also occur less formally through the social networks that developed among urban populations, spreading downward from elite to nonelite social levels, laterally from public to private contexts, and outward from urban to rural settings.

This chapter begins to explore how and to what extent Sicilian cities fulfilled these roles and whether a particularly Sicilian form of Roman urbanism can be distinguished. As discussed in the previous two chapters, while the specific economic changes of the late Republic and early Principate (including potential changes in the taxation system) are elusive, the body of archaeological evidence for urban and rural settlement indicates no island-wide economic crisis that adversely affected urban life in general. Rather, the social and political change brought by the Principate that had the greatest impact on urban life in Sicily and was linked to changing patterns of land tenure (the accrual of land previously owned and exploited by cities and their citizens into Roman senatorial and imperial hands) was the obsolescence of the system of relationships between local urban elites and Roman noble families founded on friendship and mutual obligation (*amicitia*, *hospitium*, and *clientela*). These relationships, and the patchwork of urban statuses and privileges that had been negotiated through them, can be seen most clearly in Cicero's Second Verrine Oration. Under Augustus, these ad hoc relationships were replaced with a regularized system of provincial administration that was based on the formalization of the juridical status of Sicilian communities as *coloniae*, *municipia*, or *stipendiarii*. The emperor, rather than the Roman senatorial class and its leaders, was at the top of this system and was the ultimate source of authority and prestige.

Chapter 2 has demonstrated how some previously integrated and thriving urban centers failed, for various reasons, to find an enduring place in this new and evolving imperial system. In other cities, however, the organic spread of Roman citizenship, coupled with the expansion of Mediterranean commerce in the early Principate, fostered the creation of powerful elites (and their *familiae* and *clientelae*) with origins in or strong links to Sicily as well as to other parts of the Mediterranean imperial core. Archaeological evidence, coupled with the testimony of Cicero, shows that this process of establishing connections among Sicily, Rome, and other parts of the empire (particularly Italy and North Africa) was underway even in the middle and late Republic, with the rise of wealthy "entrepreneurial" classes. They had economic, political, and social connections beyond their cities of origin and even beyond Sicily itself. However, with the Principate came the opportunity for local elites to expand their spheres of influence and to become part of the wider ruling order of the Empire as fully fledged Romans. As the Ciceronian distinction between "Roman" and "Sicilian" became less acute over the course of the Principate, the relationship of Sicilian elites to their native communities changed with their rising social and political ambitions. This change had a profound effect on the urban landscape.

The next three chapters continue to argue for the early Principate as a transformative period for Sicily. The cities discussed—Lilybaeum (modern Marsala) and Agrigentum (Agrigento) in this chapter; Tyndaris and Tauromenium (Taormina) in chapter 4; and Centuripae, Catina (Catania), and Syracuse in chapter 5—share several features, especially regarding the nature of their archaeological records. One commonality is the persistence of occupation in modern times, making full-scale excavation in the urban center impossible. In contrast to the cities in the previous two chapters, which were abandoned in antiquity and not resettled on a large scale thereafter, Lilybaeum/Marsala, Catina/Catania, Tauromenium/Taormina, Syracuse, and Agrigentum/Agrigento remain major urban centers. Modern buildings obscure their ancient levels of occupation, and ancient materials (including inscriptions) have frequently been reused in postantique structures. The complicated stratigraphy resulting from centuries of occupation, combined with the depredations of time (such as the pilfering of building materials), makes it difficult to date standing ancient structures like the theater of Catina and the amphitheater of Syracuse. Even in Tyndaris, which was abandoned after antiquity and has been the subject of extensive modern archaeological research, long traditions of antiquarian exploration have resulted in muddled archaeological and epigraphic records in which important items of material culture have been lost or lack clear provenance. An additional challenge for many cities is the lack of full publication, especially for excavations that took place in the nineteenth and early twentieth centuries.

This set of challenges is more acute in Panormus (Palermo), Messana (Messina), and Thermae Himeraeae (Termini Imerese), even though knowledge of their Roman-era topographies has improved dramatically over the past several decades. Historical sources assign these cities a primary place in the urban landscape of Roman Sicily. They possess considerable epigraphic corpora and other material indications of prosperity, but many aspects of their topographical development remain obscure. Therefore, they are not included as case studies in the next three chapters, though they are addressed as comparanda. The cities chosen for detailed analysis are distinguished not only by persistent occupation throughout the Roman period but also by a well-published record of excavations conducted throughout the ancient urban center or in substantial sections of it.

This chapter discusses two cities, Lilybaeum and Agrigentum, on the southwestern coast, the region of Sicily closest to Africa and with the strongest historical links to that continent. Neither city became a *colonia* or received any special attention from Rome in the early decades of the Principate, but both remained dynamic urban centers until the end of antiquity. The variety of economic and political roles that these cities played both within Sicily and in broader Mediterranean networks (a result in part of their favorable geographic position) contributed to their long vitality.

LILYBAEUM (MARSALA)

Located at the western tip of Sicily, Lilybaeum was settled around the second quarter of the fourth century BC by the displaced residents of the Phoenician island colony of Motya, which had been destroyed by Dionysius I of Syracuse in 397 BC (Diod. Sic. 13, 14, and 22). Its foundation was primarily strategic: to provide the Carthaginians with a naval stronghold from which to maintain their political and economic dominance over the western half of the island. The strategic significance of the site is reflected in the extensive defenses constructed in the Punic period, which consisted of a wall circuit, ditch, and a series of tunnels (see figure 3.1). The city also possessed at least three ports. In addition, the availability of spring water was probably an important consideration in the original foundation (one still-active spring is underneath the church of San Giovanni, discussed below).

Although the modern city of Marsala overlies much of the ancient urban center of Lilybaeum, Capo Boeo, the southwestern sector of the city closest to the harbor, has remained undeveloped since the Middle Ages. When it was used as a vineyard and storage complex in the eighteenth and nineteenth

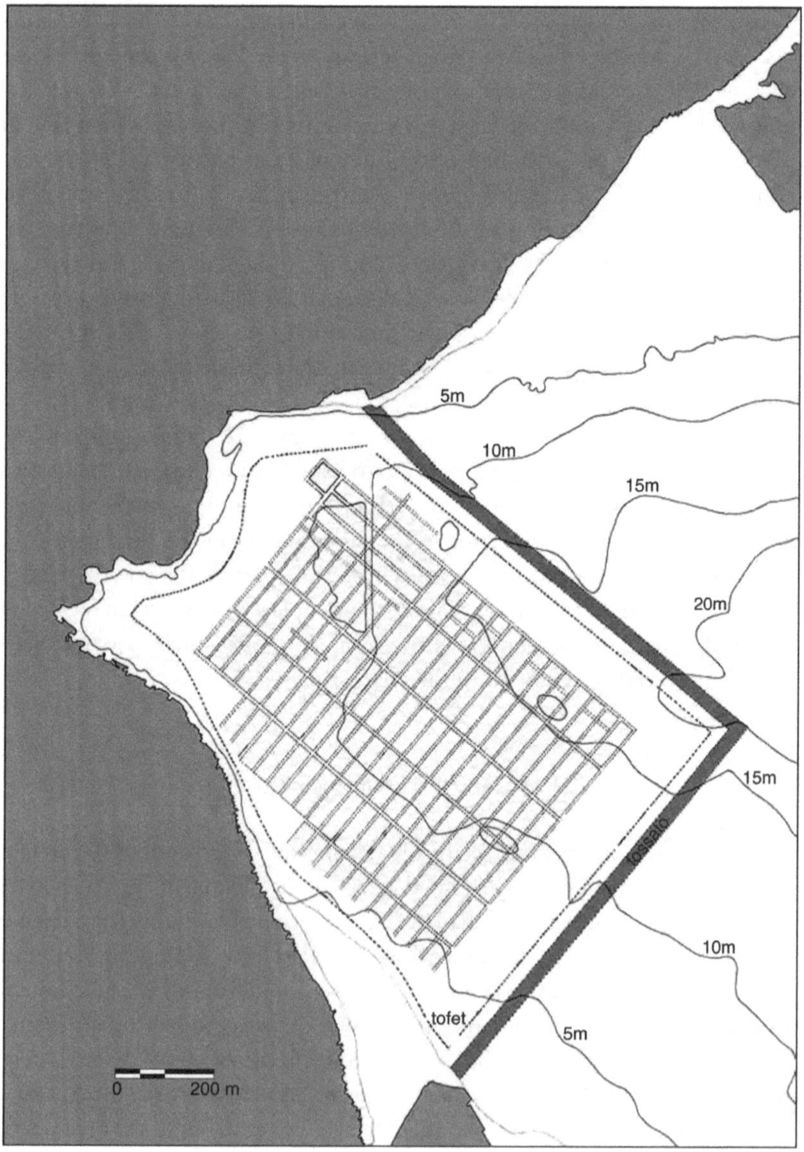

FIGURE 3.1.
Plan of Punic-era Lilybaeum (E. Caruso, with modifications by K. Rasmussen).

centuries, Capo Boeo was the site of chance finds of inscriptions and other artifacts. Systematic archaeological research began there in the early twentieth century. Scattered rescue excavations in the modern urban center north and east of Capo Boeo have also yielded traces of ancient occupation.

Little physical evidence of the original fourth-century BC settlement remains besides the fortifications and the traces of houses found underneath later residential areas.[1] Nor is much known of the city's rural territory in this period, though the foundation of Lilybaeum seems to have coincided with an upswing in commerce and settlement in the countryside in the fourth century, indicating substantial Carthaginian involvement in the rural hinterland of its Sicilian domain.[2] In the century following the First Punic War, when the city came firmly under Roman control, Lilybaeum developed a hybrid role as a Roman administrative center and military stronghold and as an autonomous *polis* with a Greek (or Hellenized) ruling elite. It was also a key node in the expanding commercial route between Italy and North Africa, with a substantial population of merchants from across the Mediterranean. The city assumed key military and administrative roles, particularly in the context of Rome's wars with Carthage and imperial expansion. In addition to serving as a base for the Roman fleet, the town was the seat of one of the quaestors of the *provincia* by the end of the third century; export taxes (*portoria*) were collected from its port (Cic., II *Verr.* 2.185). Lilybaeum's primary role in the development of the Roman province is also reflected in the creation (or continuation) of a mint in the city after the First Punic War.[3]

Amphorae found in urban excavations and in the waters surrounding the city attest to the importation of wine from southern and central Italy and the Eastern Mediterranean and of olive oil from North Africa. Large numbers of stamped Rhodian wine amphorae dating from the late third century to the mid-second century BC were excavated in the Via del Fante necropolis, along with Naxian and Coan wine amphorae and Greco-Italic and Apulian vessels.[4] Moreover, kilns in the area of Capo Boeo produced a range of Punic-style transport amphorae in the third and second centuries.[5] The most vivid illustration of the city's commercial prominence is the Greek epitaph of Poseidermos, a citizen of Massilia (Marseilles) and perhaps a merchant, who was buried in post-Punic War Lilybaeum.[6]

In addition to serving as a Roman administrative center and Mediterranean emporium, Lilybaeum was also an autonomous *polis* with an extensive and fertile rural territory. The few public inscriptions from the second and early first centuries BC commemorate members of a Greek or Hellenized local elite who performed acts of euergetism in the community. They hint at a government that largely followed the model of other Hellenistic *poleis*, with a citizen body (*demos*) divided into tribes and probably represented by a council (*boule*).[7] More private forms of epigraphy point to a mixed Greek, Italian, and Punic urban population. A distinctive carved bone *tessera hospitalis* from the first century BC commemorates the guest-friendship (*xenia*) between Imulch Inibalos Chloros, son of Imilchon, and Lyson, son of Diognetos. Lead curse tablets found in the necropolis are inscribed in Greek and contain names such as Allia Prima, Gaius Vibius, Agbor Bouki, Apithambal, Numerius, and Zopyrion, son of Mymbyr.[8] A field survey in the southeastern sector of the hinterland has revealed traces of centuriation that were perhaps connected to the consul Laevinus's reforms after the Second Punic War and the subsequent influx of new Italian and Roman landholders to the city.[9] The large Italic tetrastyle atrium featured in the second-century house excavated in Via Sibilla reflects not only the wealth of its occupants but also the city's cultural ties to Italy.[10]

The Punic and Republican-era necropolises, which occupy an extensive area east and northeast of the ancient urban center (with the greatest concentration of excavated burials between the modern Via del Fante and Piazza Borsellino), provide further information about the mixed population of Lilybaeum. The hundreds of excavated burials range in date from the mid-fourth century BC to the mid-fourth century AD. While the locations remained consistent, with Roman-era graves next to or overlying Punic burials, the forms of burial changed dramatically with the transition from Punic to Roman control.[11] After the mid-third century BC, inhumations in chambers or trenches carved deep into bedrock gave way to cremation burials with monumental superstructures.[12] The monumentality of the necropolises increased in the second century BC, when painted stone *epitymbia*, elaborate mausoleums, and in one case a *tholos* on a podium marked the locations of individual or family tombs. The *epitymbion* burials at Lilybaeum are most closely paralleled in second-century cemeteries in the territory of Carthage. The form later spread through the African provinces and elsewhere in the Roman world. Another indication that the city retained ritual links to the Punic world is the Carthaginian coin (ca. 290–260 BC) found with the remains of a horse sacrifice (ca. 180–150 BC).[13]

Although Lilybaeum gained no special juridical privileges under the Republic, the long-standing presence of Romans and Italians, especially in the spheres of government and commerce, led to the development of strong ties of patronage with powerful Romans and grants of Roman citizenship to individual citizens of the town by the first century BC. Cicero refers to a community of *negotiatores* at Lilybaeum (II *Verr.* 2.153) as well as a *conventus civium Romanorum* (5.10, 140). Among the victims of Verres's abuses are numerous citizens or residents of Lilybaeum with Roman citizenship and/or links of patronage with Roman nobles (including with Cicero himself). These include Pamphilus of Lilybaeum, a "friend and host" of Cicero, and his son-in-law, the Roman citizen Diocles Popilius; Marcus Coelius, a young *eques* at Lilybaeum; Lyso, a leading citizen of Lilybaeum who had hosted Verres; a young member of the Heius family of Messana and ward of C. Marcellus, whose property at Lilybaeum was stolen; and Diodorus of Melita, a resident of Lilybaeum who fled to *patroni* and *hospites* in Rome after being hounded by Verres (4.32–41).

Inscriptions also attest to the spread of Roman citizenship. For example, Diognetos Megas, son of Demetrios, was a *euergetes* commemorated in a Greek honorific inscription whose son, M. Valerius Megas Chorton, was in turn honored in Greek and Latin inscriptions as *patronus* of the early imperial *civitas* of Lilybaeum.[14] The spread of Roman citizenship organically among the elite of the town, by means of immigration and individual grants, is borne out epigraphically by the presence of at least eight Roman tribes by the middle Empire. By contrast, only two tribes are attested at Thermae Himeraeae, a difference attributable to the establishment of an Augustan veteran colony in Thermae with a more homogeneous group of Roman citizens.[15]

Lilybaeum's strategic importance made it a center of the conflict between the Second Triumvirate and Sextus Pompey in the last years of the Republic. A monumental Latin inscription found at Capo Boeo attests to the presence of a Pompeian force under the command of L. Plinius Rufus and commemorates efforts to repair and improve the town's defenses (*AE* 1895.23).[16] The impact of the Augustan "settlement" of 21 BC on the administrative status of Lilybaeum is unclear, though the town was not the site of a colony.[17] Like Segesta and Halaesa, Lilybaeum appears to have become a *municipium* under Augustus. The full range of municipal institutions and offices (the *ordo* of *decuriones*; quaestor, aedile, duumvir) are attested in inscriptions from the early and middle Principate. There are dedications to the *genius* of the *municipium*, and the imperial cult was present in the city by the first century AD.[18]

The public epigraphy of Lilybaeum also reflects the cultural changes that the town underwent in the transition to the Principate. Although it never completely disappeared from use, and indeed was revived in later centuries, Greek ceded to Latin as the dominant epigraphic language as the town became a Roman *municipium* and as members of its elite gained Roman citizenship. This transition occurred alongside the spread of Latin in the city outside public contexts and at lower social levels, perhaps encouraged by the long presence of Romans and Italians as administrators and merchants (as well as the more recent presence of Roman soldiers in the civil war). This new "bilingualism" is hinted at by the Latin and mixed Latin and Greek graffiti discovered in private contexts.[19]

The changes to the urban fabric of Lilybaeum in the late Republic and early Empire mainly consisted of the improvement of existing infrastructure. The main excavated residential areas continued in occupation, with some renovations. Recent excavations in Capo Boeo have revealed traces of the city's *decumanus maximus*, which was paved at the initiative of a *praetor designatus* whose name was inscribed in the white marble pavement.[20] The Punic fortifications were also abandoned, probably by the early Principate, and residences were eventually built in the space that they once occupied.[21] Epigraphic evidence also indicates imperial intervention in the first century: the restoration and improvement of an aqueduct sponsored by Domitian in AD 84 (*CIL* 10.7227). This is a rare case of imperial benefaction in Sicily, probably linked to the city's continued role in provincial administration and substantial population of Roman citizens.

Lilybaeum administered a rural territory whose considerable size is hinted at by an inscription commemorating the *concordia* with Agrigentum (140 kilometers down the coast) that was achieved during the reign of Nero (*CIL* 10.7192, discussed below). Survey in the hinterland has pointed to a diverse rural landscape where a combination of cerealiculture and arboriculture was probably practiced. Both large- and small-scale surveys have indicated a general continuity of occupation of rural sites from the Republic to the early Empire. A gradual consolidation of landholdings seems to have occurred in the first and second centuries AD, with the disappearance of some sites and the growth of others into villas or agricultural villages.[22]

The second through fourth centuries saw the most extensive urban development. This period of prosperity was undoubtedly linked to the economic rise of the African provinces and the increased commerce between Rome and North Africa, much of which would have passed through the port of Lilybaeum, to the advantage of its resident merchants and landowners. The bulk of public inscriptions from the city date to this period and reveal a fully developed urban social hierarchy. They also show the impact of individuals of diverse ranks, ranging from slaves and freedmen to imperial administrators and the emperor himself, on the topography of the city.

The public process of negotiation for status and privileges by local, provincial, and imperial authorities is visible in an inscription of ca. AD 170 recording the paving of the *platea* of the Cereres.[23] This sort of benefaction, made in cities throughout the empire, was intended both to improve local infrastructure and to enhance the reputation of the benefactor. The inscription begins with a dedication in honor of Marcus Aurelius and a prayer for the emperor's health. The dedicator, L. Annius Tertius, is a member of the Lemonia tribe, not otherwise attested outside Italy, hinting at peninsular origins for him or his ancestors. The inscription gives the municipal *cursus* of Tertius in descending order, from duumvir down to *curator muneris publici gladiatorii* (an indication, incidentally, that the city hosted gladiatorial games, perhaps in a still-undiscovered theater). According to the text, Tertius had promised 25,000 sesterces on the occasion of his appointment as aedile (*summa honoraria*), which he paid only upon his assumption of the duumvirate, for work to be overseen by the Roman quaestor stationed at Lilybaeum, Valerius Seponianus, who had died by the time of the actual dedication. This work consisted of the paving of the *platea* (probably a plaza or monumental street) of the Cereres, to which 13,000 sesterces was devoted, with the remainder going as a gift to the decurions.[24] The very existence of the dedication suggests that Tertius in turn received (or expected to receive) some honor or benefit from Marcus Aurelius.

It is also possible to trace the rise of wealthy local families into the ranks of the equestrian and senatorial elite through inscriptions. The most explicit evidence of this process is the public commemoration of local notables who held imperial offices. One inscription in honor of M. Marcius Bietis Glaucus records his adlection into the senate, probably by Commodus; his son was also a senator (*CIL* 10.7237). Two members of another local family, C. Bultius Geminius Titianus, proconsul of Sicily in the late second or third century, and his son, C. Bultius Geminius Marcellus, were honored as patrons by the town's twelve tribes (*CIL* 10.7206, 7233). Later inscriptions honor the senator L. Cassius Manilianus, who returned to serve as *curator rei publicae* of his *patria*, probably in the third century, as well as two fourth-century *consulares*, Alpinius Magnus Eumenius and Julius Claudius Peristerius Pompeianus, who were likely citizens of Lilybaeum.[25]

As members of the local elite began to participate in the Roman imperial social, political, and religious order, members of their *familiae* and *clientelae* become visible in the epigraphic record engaging in similar acts of self-commemoration. For example, a *sevir* dedicated a statue in honor of a son of Marcus Aurelius (*AE* 1906.75a). An inscription found in excavations of the *decumanus maximus* records the donation of funds for the paving of the *platea Aelia*, a street named after Hadrian (perhaps the *decumanus maximus* itself), by P. Stertinius Threptus, probably a freedman of the Stertinii, a senatorial *gens* with extensive links to Sicily, Spain, and Africa Proconsularis that had achieved the consulship under Trajan.[26]

Lilybaeum's cosmopolitan urban culture, derived from its continued role as a major central Mediterranean port, was reflected in the diversity of its religious landscape. A large sanctuary discovered in recent excavations in Capo Boeo was devoted to Isis, a cult of Egyptian origin that spread across the Mediterranean mainly through maritime commerce and is found in many ports of the Roman Empire. The sanctuary was probably established in the second century BC but rebuilt in the second century AD.[27] A long-lived cult complex centered on a spring has also been excavated under the medieval church of San Giovanni in Capo Boeo.[28] A fine marble statue of Venus and a Latin dedication to that goddess by an anonymous Roman magistrate identify the recipient of these rites.[29] The mosaics in this complex are comparable to African examples of the second and third centuries AD.[30]

Lilybaeum's economic prosperity and participation in Mediterranean-wide cultural currents are also reflected in the domestic architecture of the middle and late Empire. A revival of building activity in the residential areas began in the early third century, including the addition of thermal complexes to residences and the installation of fine mosaic floors.[31] The most conspicuous residence of this period was excavated in the 1930s in Capo Boeo. In the late second or early third century a townhouse occupying an entire *insula* was built over residences of the second or first century BC—probably two separate houses, one with a tetrastyle atrium or peristyle.[32] This new luxury residence, whose plan resembles the mid- and late imperial *domus* of Ostia and African coastal cities, included spacious rooms with elaborate polychrome mosaic floors and marble wall facings distributed around a tetrastyle atrium and a large peristyle courtyard. It was also equipped with a thermal complex and service rooms.

The most significant political development of this period was the grant of colonial status under Septimius Severus (or, less likely, under his predecessor Pertinax), which is attributable to and probably in turn contributed to the furtherance of Lilybaeum's economic prosperity and connection with North Africa, its links of patronage with Roman administrators, and the social promotion of its leading families.[33] The favor and attention shown by Severus and members of his dynasty probably had their roots in the links of patronage that arose during the emperor's time as governor of the island as well as in his more general efforts to build and reward loyalty in the economic and political core of the empire.[34] Although no standing remains of public structures from this period have been found, the grant of colonial status clearly had an impact on the urban landscape. An inscription attests to the presence of a *septizodium*: a monument taking its name from the fountain complex built by Severus in the heart of Rome and replicated in other parts of the empire, especially those favored with the dynasty's benefactions (mainly North Africa and Asia Minor).[35]

In contrast to the full Romanization of the town's government, the population of Lilybaeum began to revitalize older Punic burial traditions and places in the mid-imperial period. The transition from cremation back to inhumation was complete by the second century AD, when burials in the monumentalized sections of the Republican necropolises petered out. Thereafter, the burial chambers of the Punic period were increasingly reused as individual and family tombs, continuing into the Christian period, when the catacomb complexes expanded beyond the pagan burial areas.[36] The best-known mid-imperial tomb is an underground chamber in the heart of the Punic necropolis that was reused in the second century AD. It contained six burials as well as an altar in its center.[37] One of the deceased, Crispia Salvia, aged forty-five, was commemorated in a Latin epitaph by her husband, Julius Demetrius. The walls of the chamber were adorned with rich polychrome paintings probably executed by a local workshop. Subsequent burials and decorative phases in the chamber extend into the fourth century.

Lilybaeum remained a prosperous settlement that was fully integrated into the Roman political, economic, and social order through the mid-fourth century AD. The city still attracted the patronage of provincial elites (some of whom had family ties to the town). Building and renovation work on public infrastructure (including the street system) and in domestic contexts continued (e.g., fourth-century renovations to the bath complex of the Capo Boeo luxury residence). A recently discovered inscription from the mid-fourth century also confirms that the town became a *statio* on the *cursus publicus*, warranting the visit of an imperial official (*ducenarius*).[38] Beginning in the late fourth century, however, the urban fabric progressively weakened. The traditional interpretation of the archaeological record of late Roman Lilybaeum held that the fourth-century destruction layers visible in many residential areas were connected to the earthquake of AD 365.[39] This destruction was followed by some rebuilding, as seen in the latest phases of renovation of the bath complex of the Capo Boeo luxury residence. But the Vandal incursions of the fifth century represented the final blow to the urban fabric and were followed by abandonment and demographic contraction.[40]

Recent excavations in Capo Boeo have refined this image of late and post-Roman Lilybaeum. They indicate that the spread of burial areas within the ancient urban center and onto the remains of former public and residential structures began in the late fourth century, though some older structures (including the cult complex of Isis) remained in use in the fifth century.[41] This slow and uneven expansion of burial areas into the ruins of the Roman imperial city is most visible around the *decumanus maximus*. This road was in use, with its pavement maintained at least until the fourth century AD. But it went out of use in the fifth century, when the paving stones were covered by a series of beaten-earth surfaces. Tombs were placed above the paved road surface in the late sixth or early seventh century, in the leveled, ceramic-rich strata of destruction and burial of Roman-era structures. A possible apsidal basilica was discovered near the *decumanus maximus* and following its orientation, around which these burials may have gravitated. A further indication of the primarily Christian orientation of the Capo Boeo area is the transformation of the complex beneath the medieval church of San Giovanni into a Christian cult center, along with the installation of a new mosaic floor in one of its rooms in the late fourth or fifth century.[42]

The epigraphic and historical record indicates that Lilybaeum remained an important political and religious center in the post-Roman period. The city was in the border zone between the Gothic and Vandal successor kingdoms to the Roman Empire in Italy and Africa.[43] The Ostrogothic king Theodoric the Great gave the city to his sister Amalafrida upon her marriage to the Vandal king Thrasamund around 500, an indication of the city's importance to the Vandals for the defense of Carthage (Procopius, *History of the Wars of Justinian* 3.8.13). An inscription, now lost, from the environs of the city marked the boundary between Vandal and Gothic territory (*CIL* 10.7232). The dense, extensive cemeteries and catacombs on the city's outskirts were used by a large Christian community established by the late fourth century. A letter of Pope Leo from AD 447 mentions a bishop of Lilybaeum, Pascasinus; the diocese had been instituted in the early fifth century, in the time of Pope Zosimus.[44]

The rural hinterland of Lilybaeum also shows less disruption than might be expected. The Timpone Rasta villa in the territory of Mazara continued to be occupied until the end of the sixth century. A field survey in the surrounding area revealed a consistent occupation of rural sites from the first century AD through the mid-fifth century AD, with some sites occupied as late as the seventh century.[45] These sites produced large quantities of African sigillata and late Roman amphorae, pointing to the continuity of trade with North Africa after the Vandal conquest. The surveys and excavations conducted by the Marsala Hinterland Survey similarly found little evidence of abandonment of the countryside in the late and post-Roman period. The Roman villa site at Genna, for example, continued in use until the sixth century and possibly as late as the ninth century.[46]

AGRIGENTUM (AGRIGENTO)

Agrigentum (Greek Akragas) is one of the most renowned ancient cities of Sicily. Its most famous monuments are the archaic and classical Greek temples situated on a long ridge, the Collina dei Templi, looking south toward the sea and north to the medieval city of Agrigento (Girgenti). The main residential and public areas of the ancient city lay on an extensive (though never fully utilized) site on the south-facing slopes of the hill of medieval/modern Agrigento and in the valley extending to the Collina dei Templi. The urban area is delimited to the east by the River Akragas (the modern San Biagio) and to the west by the rocky gully of the Hypsas (Drago). It was further demarcated in antiquity by a wall circuit with several gates on each side.

Colonists from Gela settled the area in the early sixth century BC. An urban plan began to take shape within a century of foundation, as residences and sacred and public buildings were built on the terraces that had been the agricultural plots of the early colonists. In the first half of the fifth century the tyrant Theron initiated a program of public works that included the construction of the famous temples on the southern edge of the city and the creation of a regular street grid (see figure 3.2). Because of the lack of hard stone quarries in the territory the city streets had beaten-earth surfaces in all periods of antiquity.

While little is known of the Carthaginian occupation that began in the late fifth century, the decades after the city was freed from Carthaginian control in 338 saw the further development of its public and sacred areas. Most significantly, an *ekklesiasterion* and *bouleuterion* were constructed, probably in association with the restoration of the city's autonomy, in the "upper agora." This public complex was located on a hillock (now occupied by the Church of San Nicola and the Museo Archeologico Regionale) north of the Collina dei Templi that had previously been occupied by sacred buildings. A period of relative inactivity followed that coincided with the First and Second Punic Wars, during which the city changed hands several times. At the beginning of the First Punic War the city was controlled by the Carthaginians, who used it as a base against the Romans. In 262 BC the Romans besieged the city for six months, forced the Carthaginians to abandon it, then sold its inhabitants into slavery. Seven years later, the Carthaginians attacked the city again. In 213 BC, during the Second Punic War, the city was reconquered by a Carthaginian fleet and remained in Carthaginian hands even after the fall of Syracuse.[47] Hoards of coins and other valuables from this period found throughout the city indicate considerable demographic upheaval and loss of wealth. In addition, little new building activity took place in the city center,

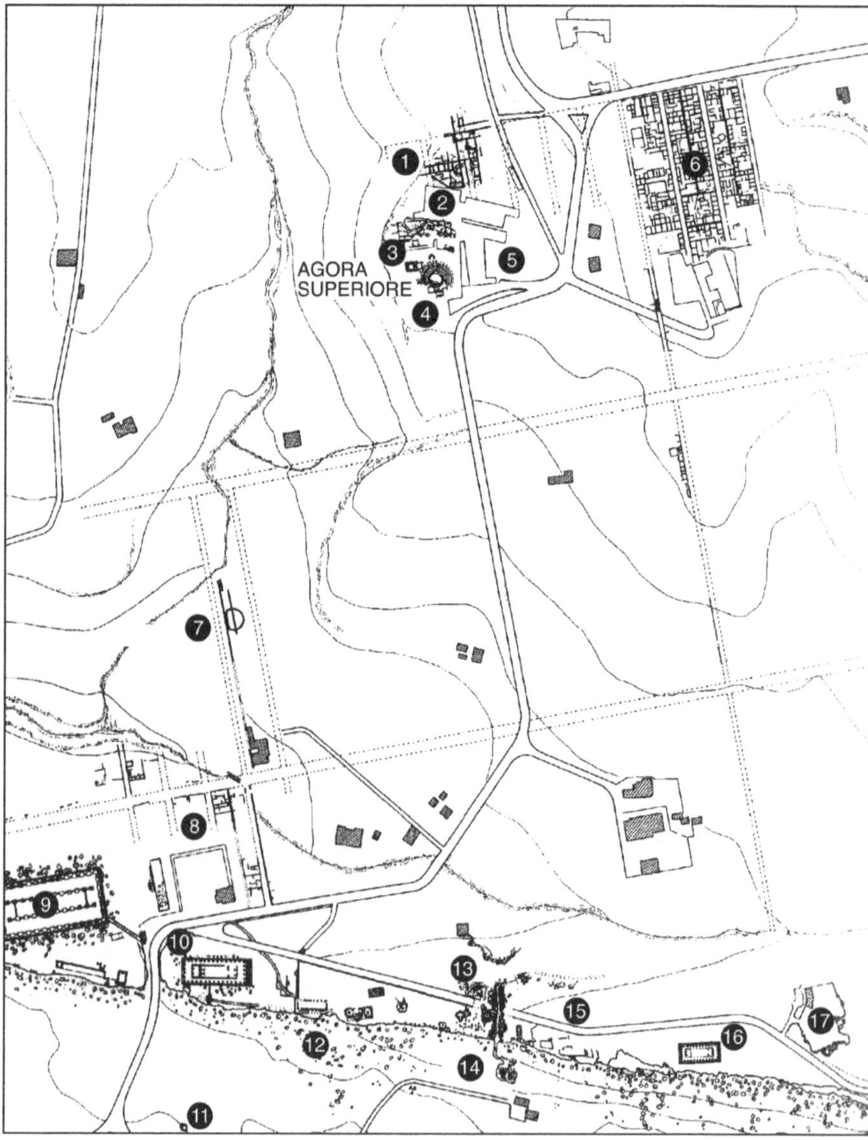

FIGURE 3.2.

Plan of Agrigentum: 1. bouleuterion*; 2. Museo Archeologico Regionale; 3. Oratory of Phalaris; 4.* ekklesiasterion*; 5. S. Nicola; 6. Hellenistic-Roman quarter; 7. gymnasium; 8. Lower Agora; 9. Temple of Zeus; 10. Temple of Heracles; 11. Tomb of Theron; 12. Gate IV; 13–15. Roman and Early Christian burial areas; 16. Temple of Concord; 17.* hypogea *(De Miro and Fiorentini 2011, reproduced with permission of Fabrizio Serra Editore, with modifications by K. Rasmussen).*

some extraurban sanctuaries went out of use, and residential areas show signs of abandonment and spoliation.[48]

After the Punic Wars the intramural urban core appears to have shifted northward, gravitating around the upper agora. For example, a former residential and industrial area below the Collina dei Templi (just north of the Temples of Heracles and Concord) was not systematically reoccupied after the late third century and was frequented only sporadically until the development of a necropolis in late antiquity.[49] Recent excavations on the southern edge of the upper agora have brought to light the remains of a theater whose first visible phase of construction appears to date to the late third or early second century BC.[50]

The city experienced a revival in the first half of the second century BC, perhaps following its reorganization at the behest of the Romans. According to Cicero, the praetor T. Manlius augmented Agrigentum's population with settlers from other Sicilian towns, while a Scipio reworked the city's laws for council membership in order to accommodate this new class of citizens (Cic., II *Verr.* 2.123).[51] Agrigentum joined the dozens of Sicilian cities with active mints around this time. It also participated in the main Mediterranean commercial circuits of the period, importing Rhodian and Italian wine.[52]

In the second half of the second century BC the city underwent a new monumental phase. The first phase of the gymnasium complex below the upper agora dates to this era. In the upper agora, the *ekklesiasterion* fell into disuse, perhaps reflecting changes to the city's government in the early decades of provincialization.[53] A new plaza centered on a small podium temple (the so-called Oratory of Phalaris) was built over the *cavea* of the *ekklesiasterion* in the second or early first century BC, creating an open agora (see figure 3.3).[54] A Latin dedication by a Roman citizen of the tribe Teretina to *matrem suam* found nearby suggests that this temple was created or enhanced at the private initiative of a resident Roman or members of the Roman community and that it may have been dedicated to Cybele/Magna Mater, a deity associated with Demeter/Ceres.[55] An altar was built in front of the temple, and a semicircular exedra and bases for honorific statues filled the open space of the new plaza.

The *bouleuterion*, north of this new plaza, was also expanded and renovated, with the addition of three seating rows to its upper *cavea*, perhaps in association with the expansion of the citizenry recorded by Cicero.[56] Around the same time, construction of a new monumental complex began on the terrace just north of the *bouleuterion*.[57] This complex consisted of an open plaza surrounded by porticoes on three sides; at the center was a simple podium temple (similar in appearance to the nearby Oratory of Phalaris) accessed via a frontal staircase. Construction of this temple and the surrounding porti-

FIGURE 3.3.
Agrigentum: Oratory of Phalaris (author photo).

coes was interrupted, however, and only taken up again a century later, as discussed below.

The Hellenistic-Roman residential quarter just east of the upper agora also saw a revival of activity in the second and first centuries BC with the creation of new lots, the construction of new houses, and the renovation of existing ones. The largest houses were concentrated in the western sector, in the vicinity of the upper agora, with lot sizes diminishing in the eastern sector.[58] Most of the townhouses follow plans typical of the late Hellenistic central Mediterranean, such as the two atrium houses and the house with a large peristyle in Insula I.[59] Based on the presence of a slotted screen wall and a bank of basins, a distinctive suite of rooms accessible both from the interior (via a peristyle) and from the street in the House of the Aphrodites appears to have been used for the secure collection of cash or other valuables from members of the public.[60] This suite, similar to rooms in Soluntum's House of Leda and to the third-century BC Public Office in the agora of Morgantina, perhaps functioned as a private bank or as the office of the local representative of a *societas publicanorum* and points to one of the potential sources of wealth for the Republican-era urban elite.

As with Lilybaeum, much of the evidence for Agrigentine government and society in the Republican period comes from the Second Verrine Oration. According to Cicero, Agrigentum was a *civitas decumana* and was treated as a *socius*. The city served loyally in the Third Punic War, perhaps as a Roman naval base, for which Scipio Africanus Minor rewarded it with a statue of Apollo by Myron that was housed in the Temple of Asclepius as a *testimonium societatis* (4.93). Cicero ranks the city among the largest in Sicily, with an important port and a role in Roman administration as a stop on the governor's assize circuit (2.185, 4.27). He also ascribes to it a considerable population of Roman citizens who lived harmoniously with the Greek population and whose business activities were probably connected to the port (2.153, 4.93).[61] The town's leading *negotiatores* and *aratores*, including a certain Nymphodorus (4.48) and L. Titius, a Roman citizen and *paterfamilias* (4.58), are among Verres's victims. The Greek ruling class of Agrigentum, like that of Lilybaeum, had social connections to Roman senatorial notables and played a leading role in denouncing Verres. Most notably, Sosippus of Agrigentum delivered a speech on behalf of the entire province to the consul Cn. Pompeius in which he detailed the distress of the *aratores* (3.204).

The few public inscriptions from Republican Agrigentum reveal a government structured along similar lines to that of other Hellenistic Greek cities, with a citizen body (*demos*) represented by a council and reliant on wealthy benefactors, especially in times of economic difficulty.[62] According to Cicero, the governing council of the city was composed of old and new citizens, with the old citizens holding a majority of seats, following the arrangements made by Scipio. This indicates that the citizenry was still divided by family origins several generations after the augmentation of the city's population.[63] In addition, Cicero, in his narration of Verres's attempted theft of the city's public statues, alludes to magistrates responsible for the management of sacred buildings and other parts of the urban infrastructure (4.93–95).

By the late Republic, the archaeological, historical, and epigraphic evidence points to a prosperous mixed Greek and Roman urban population at Agrigentum. The town's economic and cultural connections to Italy were mediated through its port, which served as an export point for tax grain and other goods produced along the southern coast and in the interior. The city also received substantial imports of early Italian terra sigillata beginning around 40 BC.[64]

The city appears not to have suffered extensive or lasting damage in the civil war; nor did it receive any special rewards (or punishments) from Octavian in the aftermath. Pliny describes it as an *oppidum*—that is, a major coastal urban settlement without special Roman juridical status. However, considerable numismatic and epigraphic evidence indicates that Agrigentum became a *municipium* under Augustus.[65]

The early decades of the Principate brought changes that speak to Agrigentum's continued prosperity and close connections to Italy. On the terrace north of the *bouleuterion* in the upper agora, the porticoed temple complex was completed in the early first century AD, probably in the reign of Tiberius.[66] The complex was entered from the street on its south side, perhaps through a monumental propylon. The porticoes on the other three sides of the temple plaza were lined with sandstone statue bases. Two togate statues—now headless, but probably originally portraying local notables or members of the imperial family—were excavated in the area of the porticoes in 2005 and have been dated to the Julio-Claudian era on stylistic grounds. Two similar togate figures in the collection of the Museo Archeologico Regionale may also have adorned the porticoes.[67]

The completion of this temple complex began the final stage in the refocusing of the religious and political landscape of the city onto the upper agora, whose public space increasingly took on the appearance and ideological associations of a Roman forum. One indication of the extralocal imperial resonances of the renovated temple complex is the marble base found nearby that was inscribed with Latin dedications to Augustus and his grandson Gaius Caesar. The dedicators, the brothers Publius and Marcus Annius, were members of a *gens* attested among the freedmen proprietors of sulfur *praedia* in the territory of Agrigentum (discussed below).[68]

The *bouleuterion* itself was enlarged and refurbished in the late first century BC, perhaps to serve as the *curia* of the new *municipium*.[69] The gymnasium below the upper agora was also renovated in the Augustan period, with the addition of a new water system, platforms, and seats for spectators. A fragmentary Greek inscription running across the back of the seats suggests that individual Roman citizens who held public office in the city (probably including the gymnasiarchy) financed these renovations.[70] The end of the first century BC saw widespread redecoration of individual houses in the Hellenistic-Roman residential quarter, such as the embellishment of atriums and the renovation of paved floors and wall paintings in reception rooms.[71]

After the major building projects of the early Principate, most of the changes to the urban fabric consisted of improvements to existing structures: for example, renovation of the podium temple in the porticoed complex in the second century and minor work on the gymnasium at the end of the first century.[72] Most changes in the Hellenistic-Roman residential quarter were aimed at further defining and demarcating elite residences, as some older houses were combined to form larger single residences and fine mosaic pavements became more common in reception rooms.[73]

The most significant political change at Agrigentum in the high imperial period was the elevation from *municipium* to *colonia* under Septimius Severus, but this grant had so little discernible impact on the urban fabric that few scholars suspected that the city achieved this status until the recent discovery at Marsala (Lilybaeum) of an inscription confirming the existence of a Colonia Septima Augusta Agrigentorum.[74] This grant of colonial status was probably made at a similar time and for similar reasons as the grant to Lilybaeum (as a reward for loyalty and as a recognition of economic importance), but it does not appear to have been commemorated with new monuments in the urban center. The only development dated roughly to this period is the destruction and abandonment of the gymnasium.[75] This lack of a clear impact on the public spaces of the city may be due to the largely symbolic nature of the grant, which, unlike the *coloniae* created under Augustus, would have brought few significant changes to the structure of civic government or to the composition of the urban population.

It is also not surprising that the evidence for the grant of colonial status to Agrigentum comes from Lilybaeum, a city with a richer epigraphic record that is partly attributable to its greater proximity to sources of hard stone, such as the white Trapani marble used to pave its streets. Most of the relatively few Roman imperial inscriptions from Agrigentum come from funerary contexts.[76] These inscriptions, in both Greek and Latin, are chronologically diffuse, ranging from the first/second century AD until the Christian period, and reflect the socioeconomic and ethnic diversity of the urban population. For example, one Latin epitaph commemorates a man, probably from a family with Roman or Italian origins, who had held the entire range of municipal offices (*qui omnibus municipalibus honoribus functus*) (*AE* 1966.168).

Although it lacked good quarries, Agrigentum is unique in Sicily in the amount of evidence for nonagricultural production in its territory: the mining, processing, and export of sulfur in the high Empire. Sulfur had a wide range of uses in the Roman world, including as a preservative for wine, an ingredient in salves, a fabric brightener, and a pesticide.[77] Therefore, regular and reliable sources of the mineral were highly valued. The evidence for the organization and operation of the sulfur industry of Agrigentum consists of mines and workshops excavated in the city's territory as well as the locally produced ceramic tiles (*tegulae* or *tabulae*) that were stamped with a series of names or monograms and affixed to the batches of processed sulfur for transportation and export.[78]

Although it is impossible to get a full understanding of the organization of sulfur mining from the mostly fragmentary *tegulae*, it appears that all social levels were involved. Families of freedmen (including the Annii) managed the mines and the workshops (*officinae*) that processed the sulfur and arranged for the warehousing and marketing of the finished products. Families of senatorial rank, such as the *gentes* Cassia, Annia, and Porcia, owned the land on which the mines and *officinae* were located. The Roman emperors themselves had acquired many of the properties (*praedia*) by the Tetrarchic period, perhaps taking them completely out of private ownership, although their management seems to have remained in local hands.[79] The many *tegulae* found in the Hellenistic-Roman residential quarter of Agrigentum—and especially in Casa F (the Casa delle Vaschette), which was divided into distinct residential and workshop spaces—suggest that activities related to sulfur production and export were not confined to the outskirts but also took place in the city center.[80]

Although little is known of Agrigentum's ancient port in the imperial era, the activity of the sulfur industry and the numerous imported goods found in the city itself suggest that it remained a vital shipping center. There is little evidence of the export of sulfur from Agrigentum specifically, but the mineral would have been highly desired in most urban centers as well as in regions where wine was produced and exported. A few shipwrecks carrying sulfur ingots ("loaves") have also been found, such as the Capo Granitola B wreck of the third or mid-second century BC, not far from Agrigentum on the southwestern coast.[81] The southwestern coast of Sicily was not directly on the main Africa–Italy *annona* route, which likely passed further to the west. But the presence of imported Italian sigillata (perhaps carried as cargo on longer *cabotage* journeys from Italy) reflects the continued integration of the port and urban market of Agrigentum into other central Mediterranean exchange networks.[82]

Agrigentum's ceramic assemblage also reflects the eventual shift of large-scale production and export of finewares from Tyrrhenian Italy to the North African coast (and especially to the area around Carthage). The city was a precocious importer of African terra sigillata beginning with the earliest Flavian-era forms, reflecting its proximity to the African coast and the trade routes emanating from it. These routes were increasingly dominated by the export of African cereals and olive oil to Rome, to which batches of finewares were probably attached as secondary cargoes and thereby made their way to Agrigentum and other coastal cities of the central Mediterranean.

With the obsolescence of Heraclea Minoa and Phintias by the early Augustan period, Agrigentum was left as the dominant urban center of the southern coast, though *stationes* like Thermae Selinuntinae (Sciacca) later emerged along the coastal land route. It can therefore be inferred that the city administered a sizable *territorium* stretching east and west and into the interior. A Latin inscription found on the Collina dei Templi lends support to this inference (*CIL* 10.7192). The inscription, dated to the mid-first century AD, commemorates the *concordia* between the Agrigentines and the *res publica Lilybitanorum* under the auspices of the proconsul M. Haterius Candidus and the quaestor L. Cornelius Marcellus. The inscription provides little further information. But a dispute between cities located almost 140 km apart, perhaps over boundaries or another administrative issue,[83] suggests that the *territorium* of Agrigentum extended a considerable distance northwest, perhaps as far as modern Sciacca (60 km) and presumably even farther southeast.

No systematic survey has yet been undertaken in the rural hinterland of Agrigentum, but the scattered settlements excavated in its territory include a *villa maritima* at Durrueli and a long-lived rural villa in Contrada Saraceno. The villa at Durrueli (or Realmonte) is located just beyond the shoreline ca. 10 km west of Agrigento. Although little excavation has taken place since its discovery in the early twentieth century, the villa complex appears to have consisted of a residence centered on a peristyle that held a garden and was surrounded by a roofed *ambulacrum*. Most of the rooms around this peristyle, including smaller *cubicula* as well as larger display rooms, had floors paved in tesserae or polychrome marble pieces, some of which were imported from Africa. The residential complex dates between the end of the first century AD and the first half of the second century AD. A bath complex, also with fine mosaic floors (many depicting nautical scenes), was added onto the western part of the residence around a half-century later. Although much of the villa and the area around it has not been explored, the apparent lack of a *pars rustica* suggests that the residence served as a luxury retreat for a member of the Agrigentine elite.[84]

Another large excavated villa is in contrada Saraceno, on the outskirts of modern Favara.[85] This farm-villa complex was conveniently situated less than 10 km from Agrigentum and close to the southern coastal road, on the slopes of Monte Saraceno, in an area of fertile soil and plentiful water. The villa was constructed around the mid-second century AD (finds of African terra sigillata were common in construction and occupation levels). It consisted of a small bath complex, residential rooms, and agricultural "service" rooms or workspaces (some with *dolia*), all oriented around a central courtyard, as well as water tanks in what was probably a garden. Agricultural activity seems to have played an important though secondary role in the villa's first phase of life. Given its proximity to Agrigentum, the complex may have served primarily as the country residence of an urban notable.

Agrigentum and its hinterland experienced continued economic prosperity in the mid-third through mid-fourth century AD. While the extent and pace of new public building was modest compared to the monumental program that the city had undertaken in the early Principate, the building that did take place considerably altered the nature of the public spaces of the city. The porticoed temple complex in the upper agora continued to be used and maintained. The nearby *bouleuterion* was renovated again in the second half of the third century or early fourth century, with the addition of new mosaic floors to its orchestra and perhaps a partial roof over the seats, thereby transforming it into an odeum. This transformation may reflect the changing nature of public life in the city. A more limited circle of participants perhaps required a monumental space for the public display of their *paideia* through philosophical discussions or declamations.[86]

In the area once occupied by the gymnasium, which had been abandoned for almost a century, a new complex arose in the Constantinian era that consisted of a large circular building with an interior colonnade flanked by two large rectangular buildings looking onto a paved rectangular plaza as well as a fourth much smaller building.[87] The function of these buildings, with foundations cut into the abandonment strata above the gymnasium and partly constructed with reused materials, is unclear. Excavators hypothesized that they formed a commercial complex or a new athletic center. In any case, the complex proved to be short-lived and was abandoned in the 360s AD.

The street grid in the Hellenistic-Roman residential quarter was maintained in the late Roman period, with structural changes largely taking place within individual houses and lots, such as the fusion of two houses in Insula I (one of which was itself created from two smaller late Hellenistic houses) to create a larger *domus*.[88] Other changes to the urban fabric of Agrigentum in the third and fourth centuries can be tied to the early development of its Christian community. Burial areas sprang up within the city walls, in previously unoccupied spaces around the Collina dei Templi and in areas that had been abandoned centuries earlier. For example, a *sub divo* (open air) necropolis developed in the second half of the third century on the northern slope of the Collina dei Templi, between the Temples of Heracles and Concord. This shift of burial activity into the intramural area of Agrigentum is not necessarily a sign of urban decay. The sheer extent of the paleochristian burial areas (which cover almost all of the Collina dei Templi from the Temple of

Heracles to the Temple of Juno), their monumentalized communitarianism (in the form of extensive networks of catacombs centered on rotundas), and their long periods of use (as long as four centuries in some sectors) suggest a large and prosperous Christian community. However, this community conceived of monumental urban space in a fundamentally different way than its pagan predecessor did.[89]

The sulfur industry continued to play an important role in the economy of Agrigentum's *territorium* in late antiquity, with *tegulae* found at several sites into the early fifth century (and at one site until the sixth century).[90] Alongside sulfur production, agriculture also retained its prominence in the rural economy, as indicated by the continuous occupation of several villas. The Saraceno villa, for example, underwent a new phase of renovation around the second quarter of the fourth century AD with the addition of a new water tank and the enlargement and paving of the courtyard.[91] The site also continued to receive considerable quantities of African sigillata, particularly forms produced in northern Tunisian workshops.[92]

The fourth and fifth centuries AD saw dramatic changes in the uses of both public and private space in the urban center, though we should be cautious about characterizing these as urban decline or linking them to specific events like the earthquakes of the 360s and the Vandal incursions of the early 440s rather than to long-term trends such as the growth of the Christian community. Recent excavations of the early imperial porticoed temple complex have focused on its latest phases.[93] The complex as a whole remained in use at least until the sixth century, although the temple and porticoes appear to have been gradually robbed of their stone building materials in the fourth century, leading to their collapse. In the fifth century the plaza was used as a refuse dump, resulting in the raising of the ground level. The finds from this dump hint at a wide range of activities taking place in the vicinity, including bone-working, pottery production, metal-working, the stabling of domestic animals, and the rendering of stone (including imperial-era statues) into lime. The dump also contains plentiful fragments of transport amphorae, especially from North Africa but also from the Eastern Mediterranean and Italy, as well as African red-slip finewares and lamps.

The transformation of the Greco-Roman urban area from a center of concentrated political and residential activity into more dispersed islands of production, habitation, religious activity, and burial is also indicated by the disaggregation and decay of the houses of the Hellenistic-Roman residential quarter in the fourth through sixth centuries.[94] Finds of tiles, mosaic pieces, and fragments of plaster and stone flooring indicate that the dump in the porticoed temple complex received the remains of demolished houses in the vicinity. In the sixth and seventh centuries groups of tombs with stone coverings were built into houses that were later at least partially abandoned.

As the imported ceramics found in the dump indicate, the late antique and Byzantine-era transformations of the urban space of Agrigentum were not necessarily accompanied by economic decline. Further evidence for the continued economic integration of the city and its territory comes from rural settlements as well as from recent excavations of the ancient port at the mouth of the River Akragas. The villa complex at Saraceno that had been renovated only a few decades earlier was destroyed, perhaps by the earthquakes of the AD 360s. The site was reoccupied a half-century later, though the nature of settlement changed considerably. Nine large *pithoi* were added to the rooms of the *pars rustica*, perhaps for grain storage, and a new ground level was created by the spreading of terracotta tiles.[95] About a century later rooms were built west of the older villa site that were mainly used for agricultural processing and storage, based on the materials found in them (including amphorae, plow parts, and a bronze cauldron). In the fifth through seventh century AD the former villa site—now better described as a farm complex perhaps entirely lacking residential quarters—continued to receive African finewares, an indication of the continued and strong connection between the southern coast of Sicily and Africa.[96] Further evidence of persistent connections with Africa comes from recent excavations of the port area (*emporion*) on the left bank of the River Akragas—most conspicuously, in the African cylindrical transport amphorae reused for burials from the late fourth until the seventh century.[97]

By the early Byzantine period the boundaries between urban and rural space in Agrigentum had become porous. In the seventh century a grape press was built in the area once occupied by the gymnasium. In addition, as the concentration of burials in the southern sector attests (including in sections of the Greek city wall), religious activity was no longer concentrated around the nodal points of the Greco-Roman city. Instead it was centered around Christian sites on its edges, including the church that was eventually created within the shell of the Temple of Concord. This transformation facilitated the ancient monument's unusual degree of preservation down through the centuries (see figure 3.4).

An extraordinary glimpse into life in early Byzantine Agrigentum is provided by the *Life of Saint Gregory*, the alleged biography of a late-sixth and early-seventh century bishop of the city.[98] Although the date, authorship, and veracity of the *Life* are all disputed (indeed, the very existence of a Bishop

FIGURE 3.4.
Agrigentum: Temple of Concord (author photo).

Gregory of Agrigento has been questioned), the author was clearly acquainted with the city and its topography. Though well beyond the end of its ancient phase of habitation, the Agrigento of the *Life* remains a regional center of religious, economic, and political life, and its port continues to link the southern coast of Sicily to the wider Mediterranean world. For example, the young Gregory escapes from Agrigento by going down to the river port (*emporion*) and gaining passage on a boat destined for Carthage, which he reaches after a three-day journey (*Life*, 7–8). When he returns to Agrigento as bishop, Gregory must contend with the plotting of rival clerics and their secular allies in a series of episodes that recall the civic disputes that Cicero had described centuries earlier in the Verrine Orations.[99]

Recent excavations in the urban center and at the river port reveal a reduction in activity after the seventh century that was perhaps connected to the fall of Carthage to the Arabs in AD 698 and the subsequent disruption of links between the southern coast of Sicily and Africa.[100] Yet the vibrancy of the port, burial areas, and churches as well as the continuous occupation of the agricultural and industrial hinterland in the centuries preceding this apparent rupture indicate that Agrigento retained a strong sense of communal identity and cohesion, even if it no longer bore much physical resemblance to its classical or Roman imperial-era incarnations.

ANALYSIS

Lilybaeum and Agrigentum became the main urban centers on the southern, Africa-facing coast of Sicily during the Principate. Their coastal locations allowed them to embrace both terrestrial and maritime hinterlands and to participate in local and trans-Mediterranean exchange networks. Both cities maintained their strategic importance throughout the Roman era. The contrast between their frequently troubled histories under the Republic and their prosperity during the Principate hints that the civic statuses and privileges bestowed in the former period on favored communities (and potentially taken away from recalcitrant ones) lost significance in the latter's new social and political order.

Lilybaeum developed from a Carthaginian military stronghold into one of the main centers of economic and political power and poles of elite activity in western Sicily. One indication of the city's regional economic dominance is the size of its territory, which apparently extended several miles down the southern coast and included smaller, dependent (though economically prosperous) urban centers like Mazara. Lilybaeum shared this preeminence in western Sicily with two cities on the Tyrrhenian coast, Panormus and Thermae Himeraeae. Although less is known of the topographical development of Panormus and Thermae, their epigraphic records highlight the extensive ties among the three cities, particularly among their leading families.[101]

The inscription commemorating the paving of the *platea* of the *vicus* of the *septizodium* at Lilybaeum provides insight into this elite network. The exact date and nature of the project commemorated is unknown because the beginning of the text is missing, but it is clear that the work was overseen and dedicated by the *quaestor pro praetore* of Sicily, Q. Fabius Caesilius Modius Titianus, who was based in Lilybaeum. This individual belonged to a prominent family with western Sicilian links of long duration, especially to Thermae and Panormus, where some of the family's branches may have been based. He was the grandson of Q. Aquilius Niger, a proconsul of Sicily who was commemorated in an inscription from Panormus (*CIL* 10.7287). Through this maternal grandfather, he was also related to C. Maesius Aquillius Fabius Titianus, who was honored as a patron of Thermae (*CIL* 10.7345, ca. mid-third century) and who is probably the C. Maesius Titianus who was *consul ordinarius* in AD 245.[102] This consul was in turn related to—and perhaps was the son of—the *clarissimus puer* Maesius Fabius Titianus who, with his sister, had made dedications in the late second century to the Severan family in Panormus and Thermae (*CIL* 10.7276, 7343). The consul of 245 married into the Fonteii Frontinii, a notable senatorial family with extensive links of patronage to African cities. He seems to have retained links with his probable hometown, however, as his son was honored in Thermae by an *eques* upon his receipt of the *toga virilis*, probably in the second half of the third century (*CIL* 10.7346).

The traces of centuriation revealed in field survey hint that some of the rural territory of Lilybaeum became *ager publicus* held and leased by the Roman state rather than by the city itself under the Republic. There is also epigraphic evidence of senatorial landholding in the region: two *cippi* from Valderice (northeast of Trapani) dedicated by two *epitropoi* to an early/mid-third century senator of consular rank, C. Asinnius Rufus Nicomachus Julianus (*IG* 14.283–4).[103] After the transitional period of the late Republic and early Empire, the continuity of occupation evidenced by imported pottery at rural sites like Timpone Rasta and Genna points to the continued fertility, diverse agricultural potential, and economic integration of the region, which made farming profitable and land in the territory of Lilybaeum desirable to both absentee and resident owners and tenants. This stability of the rural landscape would have contributed to and would also have been reinforced by the continued vitality of the urban center of Lilybaeum, as the agricultural products of the territory continued to require a marketing and embarkation center.

The development of the urban center of Lilybaeum itself shows the significance of varied and diverse urban roles and the presence of a heterogeneous population (in terms of occupation, wealth, and cultural orientation) as the basis for sustaining urban life and infrastructure. The richness of Lilybaeum's social, economic, and political connections with other parts of Sicily and with the wider Roman world was also key to its survival in the imperial period (a connectivity that it shared with Agrigentum and with the cities discussed in the next two chapters).

Agrigentum, like Lilybaeum, played a key strategic role in Rome's wars with Carthage in the third century BC. In spite of this troubled history, by the early first century AD Agrigentum was the only remaining substantial urban center on the southern coast of Sicily. The city's resilience in the second century BC, its development in the Augustan period, and its continued prosperity in the high and late Empire were all closely linked to the importance of its port and to the flexibility and diversity of its urban and rural economy. Agrigentum's proximity to shipping routes, the fertility of its agricultural hinterland, and its possession of mineral resources (chiefly sulfur) made it an attractive place to own land and enabled the growth of a considerable urban, nonagricultural population engaged in activities such as tax collection and the processing, marketing, and export of the resources of the territory. Under the Empire, this territory was probably wider than at any previous period in the city's history, with maritime links across the central Mediterranean and directly to the center of power in Rome. The city's persistent economic and cultural links with Africa even in times of political unrest in late antiquity also contributed to the early development of a Christian community that endured and gradually developed its own *loci* of religious, social, and productive activities, even after the abandonment of the classical urban center.

CONCLUSION

The development of Lilybaeum and Agrigentum reflects the fruition of the social and political processes—such as the transition from *civitas* to *municipium*—that were begun but remained unfulfilled in the cities discussed in chapter 2. The key factor that allowed Lilybaeum and Agrigentum to flourish under the Principate was the diversity of the political and economic roles that they played within their regions. The next two chapters further refine this analysis of the emerging urban landscape of the province by examining cities in northern and eastern Sicily with diverse political and economic orientations that, like Lilybaeum and Agrigentum, gained primacy in the island's urban hierarchy.

FOUR

THE NORTHEASTERN COAST

Civil War and Colonization

The cities examined here and in the next chapter share several features. Like Lilybaeum and Agrigentum, all (except possibly Tyndaris) remained in occupation until the end of antiquity and sometimes beyond. Despite vicissitudes in their postantique histories—including volcanic eruptions, earthquakes, and warfare—all (except Tyndaris) remain vital urban centers today, complicating the reading of their ancient archaeological records.

All of these cities are located on or near the eastern, Ionian coast of Sicily, in regions with long histories of Greek colonial settlement that remained outside Carthage's sphere of influence in the fifth and fourth centuries BC. In general they shared stronger economic, cultural, and political links with the Hellenic communities of the eastern Mediterranean and southern Italy—and weaker historical links with Carthaginian North Africa—than their western Sicilian counterparts. Most of them were under the political and economic influence of Syracuse for much of their pre-Roman history. Along with other communities in eastern and northeastern Sicily, all were touched by the decisive military campaign of the triumvirate against Sextus Pompey in 36 BC. In the aftermath all received Roman juridical status as a means of ensuring future political and economic stability: Tyndaris, Tauromenium, Catina, and Syracuse received colonies, while Centuripae retained its Republican-era privileges as a community of Latin status. Therefore, their subsequent development provides clearer insight into the impact of the Augustan settlement of Sicily on the island's urban landscape than any of the cities previously discussed.

This chapter examines Tyndaris and Tauromenium, cities on the portion of the northeastern coast closest to Italy (approximately 70 km west and south of the Strait of Messina, respectively). Because of this proximity, both cities exhibit close cultural ties to central and southern Italy in the Republican period and would play key strategic roles in the conflict between Sextus

Pompey (based in eastern Sicily) and Octavian (based in Italy). The aftermath of this war marked a political and cultural turning point, as Roman colonists were settled in each city, perhaps after the displacement of some of the original population.

TYNDARIS

Ancient Tyndaris was located on a high, rocky coastal promontory overlooking the Gulf of Patti to the west and the Bay of Oliveri to the east (the probable location of the ancient city's harbor).[1] The city lay in an easily defendable location, accessible only from the southwest with difficulty. However, it is in one of the most seismically active areas of Sicily; in fact, it gives its name to a system of faults that extends from the Ionian coast northeast of Etna to the central Aeolian islands.[2]

According to Diodorus (14.54), Tyndaris was founded in 396 BC by Dionysius I of Syracuse as a home for his Messenian mercenaries (and as a strategic outpost on the northern coast) in territory taken from the interior hilltop city of Abakainon. For the rest of its pre-Roman history the city lay firmly in the political orbit of Syracuse. In the First Punic War, Tyndaris fell into the hands of the Carthaginians, who used it as a naval base and deported most of its leading citizens to Lilybaeum when it tried to go over to the Romans (Diod. Sic. 23.5). After the fall of Panormus, Tyndaris was finally able to surrender to the Romans, along with Soluntum and Ietas (among other cities) in 254 BC (Diod. Sic. 23.18). The city remained loyal to Rome for the remainder of the Republican period.

Although the site was not occupied after antiquity, many aspects of the topographical development of Hellenistic and Roman Tyndaris remain obscure. Periodic excavations in the eighteenth and nineteenth century resulted in the dispersal of many of the city's ancient inscriptions and sculpture to museums across Sicily, often with little indication of their provenance. Systematic excavation began after World War II, and the most recent excavations took place in the 1990s and 2000s. The main excavated section of the urban center is located on a plain between two summits. This plain slopes gently north toward cliffs that drop sharply to the sea, the result of periodic landslides. By the Roman imperial period the city occupied more than 27 hectares and was surrounded by a three-kilometer perimeter wall. However, it is likely that the original Messenian settlement occupied a smaller area in the southeastern section of the promontory and expanded gradually north and west (see figure 4.1).[3]

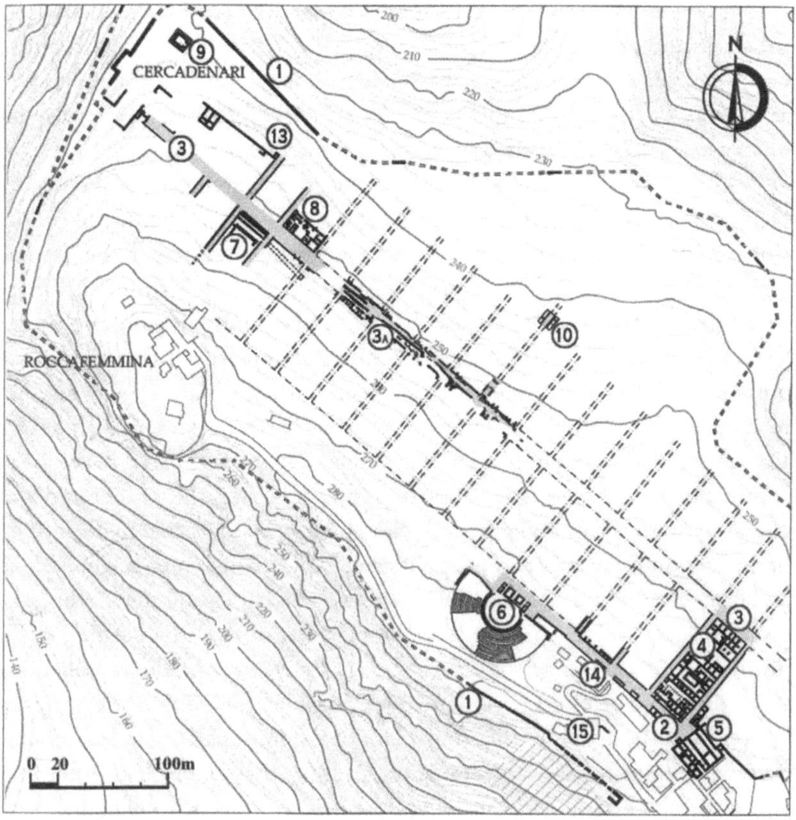

FIGURE 4.1.
Plan of Tyndaris: 1. wall circuit; 2. upper decumanus; *3 and 3a: middle* decumanus; *4. Insula 4; 5: "basilica"; 6. theater; 7. monumental building; 8. Cercadenari* domus; *9. funerary monument; 10. excavated* cardo *(2004); 13. Roman-era* latrina; *14. antiquarium; 15. entrance to the archaeological site (Spigo 2005, reproduced with permission of the Soprintendenza BB.CC.AA. di Messina).*

The development of the city from its foundation until the second century BC is not well documented, and the dating of the original urban plan remains controversial. Mid-twentieth century excavators believed that Tyndaris's orthogonal layout dates to the period of Timoleon, while recent researchers have suggested disparate dates ranging from the Dionysian foundation to the post–Punic War years.[4] The construction dates of the theater and wall circuit are also uncertain, although both structures clearly underwent several subsequent phases of renovation or reconstruction.[5]

The Second Verrine Oration supplies a great deal of information about the status and obligations of Tyndaris under the Roman Republic. According to Cicero, the city was among the *civitates decumanae*.[6] It had been treated as a *socius*, contributing ships to Roman military expeditions. After the fall of Carthage, Scipio rewarded it for its loyal service with a statue of Mercury (4.84).[7] Cicero also includes Tyndaris among the "seventeen loyal cities" of Sicily (5.124), an honor that probably came with further defense obligations (for example, furnishing troops for the Eryx garrison). Although the city had regular tax and occasional military obligations to Rome, with them perhaps came greater local autonomy as well as the opportunity to gain booty (like the statue of Mercury) in Rome's wars of expansion. The city's strategic importance is reflected in the activities of its mint, particularly during and immediately after the Second Punic War, when it issued coins that followed Roman standards—an indication that Roman troops were based in the area.[8]

Most of the visible urban fabric of Tyndaris besides the theater and wall circuit dates to the imperial period. Nonetheless, it is possible to glean signs of an economically prosperous, politically vital urban center in the second and first centuries BC. The location of the agora/forum is unknown: the most probable locations are in or near the highest part of the urban center, either just below the theater or southeast of it, in the vicinity of the so-called basilica (discussed below).[9] Cicero provides valuable insight into the city's public areas and the activities that took place in them. In particular, he recounts Verres's attempt to seize the statue of Mercury that Scipio had gifted, for which the city held an annual festival (4.84–92). After the local council and its president (*proagorus*) Sopater refused Verres's request for the statue, the governor had Sopater flung from the *porticus* where he was presiding into the open space of the forum and flogged. Verres then ordered that the unfortunate Sopater be put astride and bound to the equestrian statue of C. Marcellus that was on display in the forum along with statues of other Marcelli. When the council finally gave in and turned over the statue of Mercury, Verres (according to Cicero) ordered the erection of an equestrian statue of himself on a higher pedestal, near the statues of the Marcelli—a statue that the Tyndaritans mutilated and took down after Verres left the province (4.90 and 2.160).

From this dramatic (and probably exaggerated) account we can glean that the city's government was in the hands of a council (*senatus* or *boule*) led by a *proagorus* and that this council was not afraid to stand up to and even legislate against a Roman governor.[10] The city possessed at least one public plaza (Cicero's "forum") framed by porticoes that could be used as meeting places: this is where Sopater encountered Verres. The plaza was filled with honorific statues by the early first century BC, including those of the town's Roman patrons, the Marcelli. The statue of Mercury itself would have been displayed in or near the town's gymnasium, since Cicero notes that the *gymnasiarchus*, Demetrius, was responsible for its removal (4.92).

The magistrates and other citizens involved in the Mercury incident, as well as the wealthy townspeople who were the victims of Verres's other thefts, mostly appear to be of Greek origin.[11] However, by the time of Cicero, many members of this ruling class had forged social and political links with members of the Roman senatorial elite, as the statues of the Marcelli in the forum hint. Cicero includes among Verres's victims a certain Cn. Pompeius, "formerly known as Philo" (*Philo qui fuit*), who gave a dinner for Verres at his villa outside Tyndaris (*apud villam in Tyndaritano*) (4.48). As his name indicates, this man received Roman citizenship from Pompey the Great, perhaps not long before Verres's governorship. Verres had further social ties to Tyndaris: Cicero claims that Dexo, the father of the captain of the ship that the city contributed to Verres's pirate campaign, was a *hospes* of the governor (5.108).

What is known of the residential areas of Tyndaris in the Republican period confirms Cicero's portrait of a wealthy local elite with social connections to influential Romans and cosmopolitan tastes. The most extensively excavated residences in the city are Casa B and Casa C, neighboring *domus* that were built in the late second or early first century BC on lots that each fill roughly one-third of the *insula* between the city's central and upper *decumani*.[12] To accommodate the slope, the houses were laid out on a series of terraces in an area previously occupied by several smaller residences.

The larger house, Casa B, occupied an area of about 900 m^2 above a series of shops flanking the city's central *decumanus*. Its main residential area was articulated around a large peristyle that itself was the size of one of the previous residences in the *insula*. The peristyle was flanked by two large rooms (*oeci*) to the north and south, both adorned with wall paintings. The house was accessed from the *stenopos* west of the *insula*, originally through an atrium. The adjacent, two-storied Casa C was slightly smaller, accessible from the eastern *stenopos*. It followed a completely different (and more traditionally Hellenistic) plan, with a peristyle at its center around which all the rooms gravitated.

As La Torre has pointed out, these large *domus* are products of the *luxuria asiatica* embraced by the elites of Rome, central and southern Italy, and many Sicilian cities between the mid-second and mid-first century BC. The houses had large peristyles, colonnaded exedras, *oeci*, spacious *andrones*, and similar spaces dedicated to entertainment and to the display of fine objects and decor. These rooms had pavements in polychrome mosaics, stuccoed and painted walls in the First and Second Pompeian styles, Corinthian columns and (we can infer from the *Verrines*) precious metal adornments and fine textiles. The fully realized, high-status residences of late second/early first century BC Tyndaris contrast with the excavated houses of Phintias and Heraclea Minoa, where there are signs only of the nascent preference for residential spaces devoted to display and self-promotion. Any attempts at the transformation and renovation of domestic spaces seem to have been abandoned or curtailed by the mid-first century BC. The houses of Tyndaris provide evidence of a local aristocracy that had acquired economic surplus and required new means of displaying its status and ambition.[13]

Cicero indicates that local notables such as Cn. Pompeius owned villas in the city's territory—residences that were large and fashionable enough to receive the governor (4.21). A further indication of the presence of a wealthy rural elite is the coastal villa excavated at Castroreale Bagni (Contrada S. Biagio) about 15 km east of Tyndaris. The first phase of this villa, which was centered on a large peristyle and equipped with a bath complex, dates to the first half of the first century BC.[14] A recent surface survey in the territory of Tyndaris has pointed to an upswing in rural settlement, especially on open, accessible, and fertile sites, after the Second Punic War.[15]

Although relatively little is known about the urban economy of Tyndaris, black- and gray-glaze wares provide evidence of ceramic production in the city center or in its territory. These resemble Syracusan Campana C but are likely of local manufacture: an indication of the city's participation in the diffusion of this fineware from regional production centers. The city also hosted a significant workshop producing Megarian bowls and imported the typical range of late Republican ceramics, including eastern sigillata and presigillata.[16]

Tyndaris gained strategic importance during Sextus Pompey's war with the triumvirs as one of the main defendable ports of the northeastern coast. In addition, as indicated by Cicero, some members of the community had links of patronage to the family of Pompey by the early and mid-first century BC. Tyndaris may have issued coins during the Pompeian occupation as a *municipium* (following Julius Caesar's grant of *ius Latii*), though these coins bore the same civic symbols as earlier issues (such as the heads and attributes of the Dioscuri, the main civic cult).[17] Agrippa seized the city with difficulty in 36 BC then used it as a base for taking Messana (Cassius Dio 49.7).[18] Tyndaris became a colony under Augustus, probably in 21 BC. The main evidence for the city's colonial status are the so-called foundation issues minted in the name of Augustus, the proconsul of Sicily, and the duumvirs in the years after the deduction and, more securely, later Latin inscriptions recording the deeds of the Colonia Augusta Tyndaritanorum.[19]

Due in part to the uncertain dating of the deduction of the colony and in part to the multiple imperial-era layers of occupation, destruction, and rebuilding in many sectors of the city, the impact of the colonial settlement on the urban plan is unclear. A monumental structure on the central *decumanus* at the western end of the city appears to date to the early imperial period and may have formed part of a second forum associated with the western entrance to the city.[20] The street grid was also renovated in the early imperial period, perhaps in association with the foundation of the colony. The streets were paved in blocks of local limestone and a more extensive and complex system of underground drainage channels put into place.[21]

Similarly unclear is the impact of an earthquake in the early first century AD that, according to Pliny, resulted in the destruction of half of the city from landslides (*HN* 2.206). None of the excavated buildings or infrastructure appears to have been affected by such a destructive event. The major changes visible in the urban fabric date instead to the mid-first century AD or later. For example, Casa B was renovated in the Neronian or Flavian period, when the original floors were replaced with black and white mosaics. The main reception rooms were also redecorated with marble facings and new wall paintings. A *domus* constructed along the central *decumanus* in the late Republican or Augustan period was also refurbished around a half-century later. In this second phase the house's *triclinium* received a new mosaic pavement and polychrome wall paintings.[22]

Other early and mid-imperial changes to the urban fabric consist mainly of alterations to existing buildings and monuments. The theater was transformed into a space for gladiatorial games and *venationes* in the Flavian or Hadrianic/Antonine period. The orchestra was converted into a small, irregular arena by the removal of the first four rows of seats and the construction of a high railing to protect spectators, a wall extending to the stage building, and service rooms at the base of the *cavea*. These alterations in part utilized older architectural elements.[23] At some point in the imperial period the *domus* occupying the third and highest (southernmost) lot in Insula IV next to the two larger *domus* was transformed into a bath complex, with the peristyle becoming the *palaestra* of the baths and the service corridor that adjoined the main thermal rooms built in part onto the upper *decumanus*.

Some scholars have interpreted the second and early third centuries as a time of financial stress for the city, as it was apparently not able to construct new public buildings (such as an amphitheater) or maintain its existing infrastructure to a high standard.[24] They cite as further evidence of financial disarray the presence in the Antonine period of a *curator rei publicae*, M. Valerius Vitalis (*CIL* 10.7474–7475).[25] These developments have parallels in other cities that flourished in the high imperial period, however, including Tauromenium (Taormina), Lilybaeum, Panormus (Palermo), and Catina

(Catania). The adaptation of existing infrastructure to serve new purposes—such as the conversion of a theater into an arena—and the presence of a designated magistrate with financial oversight here and in other Sicilian towns may instead be interpreted more neutrally, as symptoms of a community's desire to participate in prevailing imperial cultural and social trends while staying within its financial means. This desire was supported by imperial and provincial authorities, who could be called upon to help the community prioritize its building projects or to resolve internal tensions over expenditures.

Most evidence for the public life of the *colonia* in the high Empire comes from monumental inscriptions and sculpture, although many of their original locations are unknown. The sculpture from the site includes two *togati* (probably honorific statues of Augustan and Julio-Claudian magistrates), a colossal head of Augustus, Claudius in the guise of Jove, three members of the Julio-Claudian imperial family (including Drusus Minor and Antonia Minor), and a cuirassed torso, probably of Trajan.[26] These images of emperors and their families, along with the portraits of magistrates and statues of deities, perhaps formed a group originally dedicated to the *gens* Augusta shortly after the foundation of the colony. This group may have been set up in the forum or in one of the nearby buildings and augmented over time, as was the case with the statuary groups around the forum of Centuripae (discussed in chapter 5).[27]

Latin inscriptions, moreover, attest to the centrality of the imperial cult to the public religious life of the *colonia* and to the active role of the government in paying homage to emperors and their families. The activities of the Augustales are visible in the epigraphic record—for example, honoring their patron, the city's quaestor (*AE* 1989.338i). The *res publica* itself was also active in promoting the imperial cult and in honoring living emperors, particularly in the reigns of Trajan through the Severans. These displays of loyalty and civic self-promotion, along with the presence of a *curator rei publicae*, were probably related to imperial sponsorship and/or oversight of building activities in the town.[28]

Tyndaris continued to participate in Mediterranean economic circuits in the high Empire. Large numbers of coins have been found on the site, leading excavators to name one area Contrada Cercadenari. The issues of imperial mints supplanted the civic mint by the Augustan period, with numerous series of sesterces and asses circulating in the city center until a drop-off in the fourth and fifth centuries.[29] The city received lamps and other ceramics from Africa in the second century and had access to goods of more limited regional circulation, such as the Proclos Agyrios lamps (almost certainly produced in Sicily, perhaps in Agyrium) and terracottas from Catina.[30]

Rural settlement around Tyndaris remained vital in the early and middle

Principate, though perhaps less dense and less widely dispersed than in the Republican period. The two residential villas in its territory that have been excavated, at Castroreale San Biagio to the southeast and at Patti to the west along the coast, point to the continued existence of a wealthy rural elite.[31] The late Republican villa at Castroreale underwent considerable renovations, including the repaving of floors in the thermal complex and main residence in black-and-white mosaics under the Julio-Claudians and the addition of a *pars rustica* in the mid-imperial period.[32] The Patti *villa maritima*, located 10 km from Tyndaris, may have been the country retreat of a wealthy citizen in its obscure first phase, dated broadly to the second and third centuries AD.[33] Recent surface survey around the Patti villa and throughout the hinterland of Tyndaris has identified dozens of potential rural settlements. These sites are marked especially by finds of transport amphorae of local provenance (the Ostia II 522 and 523 wine amphorae, produced in northeastern Sicily and exported to Italy and Africa in the first and second centuries) as well as amphorae produced in Italy, the Aegean, Tripolitania, and Baetica.[34]

The deterioration of the urban fabric of Tyndaris had begun by the early third century AD, when some of the buildings on the western edge of the city were abandoned or destroyed.[35] The necropolis also began to spread within the walls of the settlement, with monumental tombs built on the lower (northern) terraces of the town's western edge. A seismic event usually linked to the earthquake of AD 365 did extensive damage to the urban fabric and helped to usher in the post-Roman phase of settlement. Its most visible effect is the scattered upheavals in the pavement, particularly in the central *decumanus*.[36] This event probably caused the destruction of some houses, such as the large *domus* and bath building in Insula IV, and the landslides that covered already-abandoned structures, such as the monumental building along the central *decumanus*.[37]

Although many structures were abandoned after this event, smaller residences were built over the remains of the bath building in Insula IV. Rebuilding and restoration also commenced in other areas of the city, often using materials (and even inscriptions) from older structures.[38] Though its dating is controversial, the so-called basilica, a mysterious stone structure flanking the southeastern end of the central *decumanus*, may also have been constructed after this earthquake over the remains of an earlier residential *insula* (see figure 4.2).[39] This earthquake seems to have been responsible for the collapse of the villa at Patti, which may have been abandoned shortly before, though it had been reconstructed and expanded into a palatial luxury retreat only a few decades earlier.[40]

Occupation of the site continued for nearly five centuries more, though probably on a smaller, suburban scale. Tyndaris became the seat of a bishop by

FIGURE 4.2.
Tyndaris: "basilica" (author photo).

the early sixth century, but no Christian structures (or burials) have yet been found in or around the site.[41] Rather, the emphasis of the late Roman/Byzantine occupation seems to have been on defense and on the delineation and protection of property, with settlement in scattered nuclei across the former urban center—a phenomenon also seen in Segesta and Halaesa in their late phases. Parts of the wall circuit were renovated. Remains of long walls have been found above the former central *decumanus*, on a different alignment and mostly built with reused materials. These were perhaps intended to delimit and protect properties within a smaller, differently organized, more rural settlement.[42] The villa at Patti also shows signs of occupation in the Byzantine period, with materials from the ruined villa reused for structures.[43]

Apart from its colonial status, Tyndaris shares many features with the settlements discussed in chapters 1 and 2. These commonalities may help to explain its relative lack of success as an urban settlement in the imperial period compared with the other Augustan colonies. Like Heraclea Minoa and Camarina, Tyndaris was in a raised and somewhat unstable coastal location; unlike those two cities (but like Calacte), Tyndaris was also in a region prone to seismic activity. In addition, like many of the cities that were abandoned in the Principate, it lacked abundant freshwater sources in its immediate vicinity and its location on a steep coastal promontory made it difficult to access sources in its hinterland.[44]

Tyndaris held strategic importance in the pre-Roman geopolitical system of northeastern Sicily as an outpost of Syracuse along the Tyrrhenian coast. It again played a key role in the late Republican period in the war between Sextus Pompey and the triumvirs. While the establishment of a Roman colony in the city had a clear strategic purpose (to displace members of the local elite who supported the Pompeian faction and to maintain the peace along the northeastern coast), it may have outlived its geopolitical relevance with the Mediterranean Pax Romana of Augustus.

The city was also relatively distant from the Rome–Africa commercial routes that fed the growth of Lilybaeum, Agrigentum, and other western coastal centers and from the routes from the Eastern Mediterranean and Tripolitania through the Strait of Messina to the Tyrrhenian coast of Italy, on which the eastern coastal centers of Tauromenium, Catina, and Syracuse served as stopping points. The territory of Tyndaris was not especially fertile or rich in nonagricultural resources. For all of these reasons, the urban center did not attract the activity or patronage of provincial and imperial elites and Roman authorities to the same extent as the other Augustan colonies.

While indications of stress on civic resources and the weakening of the material forms of the city appear as early as the third century, Tyndaris remained in occupation as an urban center for almost all of the Roman period and at a suburban level for several centuries thereafter. This continuity of settlement, as at Halaesa, was probably due to Tyndaris's location on the major maritime and land routes of northeastern Sicily. In addition, as a colony, Tyndaris played a primary political, social, and economic role in its region and possessed an extensive territory that probably included the lands of former urban centers like Abakainon/Abacaenum. Therefore, Tyndaris occupied a middle rung in the hierarchy of urban settlement in Roman imperial Sicily. It was a substantial urban center with important regional economic and political roles and with an elite resident in the city or in its hinterland that fulfilled these roles in most periods. But it was a city of minor importance on the provincial economic, social, and political scale.

TAUROMENIUM (TAORMINA)

Tauromenium/Tauromenion was founded in 358 or 357 BC on a series of natural terraces on Monte Tauro, a promontory overlooking the Ionian Sea approximately midway between Messina and Catania (Diod. Sic. 14.59 and 16.7). The city is in a transition zone between the volcanic foothills of Etna to the south and the Peloritani mountains that extend north and west. The terraces of Monte Tauro overlook the bay and promontory of Giardini Naxos to the south. This was the site of the archaic Greek *apoikia* of Naxos (discussed in chapter 7), which had been destroyed by Dionysius I of Syracuse several decades before the foundation of Tauromenion. The site chosen for the new city shares important features with two other foundations of the late fifth and early fourth centuries, Tyndaris and Thermae Himeraeae. All three cities are on promontories that dominate maritime and land-based routes, with good harbors below.[45]

Tauromenion was under the influence of Tyndaris until the fall of that city's tyranny in 270 BC. It remained under the political sway of Syracuse for the rest of the third century BC, as Hieron II extended his city's power and influence over much of eastern Sicily.[46] Little is known of the city's early topography, but it is clear that it underwent a major phase of development in the mid- to late third century under the influence of Hieron. The first phase of the famous theater, built into a slope looking out to the bay of Naxos and Mt. Etna, probably dates to this period (see figure 4.3). The main public areas took shape on a series of terraces west of the theater (see figure 4.4). These areas, in turn, were connected by two principal roads, one running northwest-southeast between the probable agora (the modern Piazza Vittorio Emanuele II) and the other running southwest-northeast and aligned with the modern Corso Umberto I. Little is known of the agora in this period, though the peripteral temple on its western side probably dates to the Hieronian era.[47] In the second half of the third century or the second century BC a plaza fronted by a stoa—perhaps a second agora or the agora's lower square—was built just off the southwest-northeast main street, in the area later occupied by the "naumachia."

Although its status after the First Punic War is debated, Tauromenium became a *civitas foederata* by 210 BC, after the collapse of the Syracusan kingdom. Tauromenium had negotiated a special treaty with Rome that left it exempt from the grain tithe and other obligations, such as providing a ship to the Roman fleet (II *Verr.* 3.13, 5.50).[48] Most of the Greek public inscriptions from the city date to its two centuries under the Roman Republic. They shed much light on civic government and financial institutions in this period of semiautonomy. Probably the earliest of these inscriptions is a *cippus* listing the two *strategoi* who were the city's chief magistrates, with each pair listed under the heading of an eponymous magistrate (*IG* 14.421).[49] A stele that lists the city's two annually elected gymnasiarchs (*IG* 14.422) and provides a

FIGURE 4.3.
Tauromenium: theater (author photo).

brief account of the gymnasium's yearly activities and finances is of a similar Republican-era date.

Most valuable for the town's institutional and economic history is a series of inscribed financial accounts (*IG* 14.423–30).[50] These list the monthly deposits, withdrawals, and balances of the magistrates, beginning with the *hieromnamones* (officials in charge of the revenues derived from the properties of sanctuaries), followed by the *tamiai* (civic treasurers, in charge of public accounts), *sitophylakes* (in charge of accounts related to cereals and other commodities), *agertai* (answerable to the *sitophylakes* and responsible for the collection of tithes, probably in kind, from lessees of sacred public lands), and *sitonai* (responsible for the purchase and storage of cereals). Among the city's revenues, in addition to agricultural products like grain and broad beans, these accounts mention high-quality worked stone from local quarries and wood from forests in the *chora*, both probably intended for export.[51] The accounts reflect a highly monetized urban economy, in which officials were responsible for the leasing of public houses and lands, for the collection of tithes, for the acquisition of some commodities using civic funds, and for the sale of others on the market (*IG* 14.426, col. I, ll. 10–15, for such sales).

The other Greek inscriptions from Republican Tauromenion include several statue bases containing honorific decrees of the *damos* from the second half of the second century BC. Two of these—one in honor of the benefactor Nymphodoros, son of Eukleidas, the other in honor of Nymphodoros, son of Philistion—were found in excavations on the northern side of Piazza Vittorio Emanuele II, the probable site of the main agora. The bases were inserted into a paved area that appears to have been a courtyard or peristyle connected to a vestibule leading to a large room or hall: perhaps the *bouleuterion*.[52] Excavations also turned up fragments of financial accounts.[53] Two statue bases had previously been discovered in the same area: one dedicated to Olympis, son of Olympis, a victor in the Pythian games (*IG* 14.434), and the other to C. Claudius Marcellus (*IG* 14.435), probably the proconsul of 79–78 BC and certainly a member of the Roman senatorial family (the Claudii Marcelli) who were notable patrons of Sicily. Cicero indirectly provides further evidence of the community publicly honoring leading Romans, noting that the

FIGURE 4.4.
Plan of Tauromenium (L. Campagna).

people of Tauromenium tore down a statue of Verres in the forum but kept its pedestal as a reminder of his abuses (II *Verr.* 2.160).

Besides the public building (*bouleuterion*?) in the agora, only a few other structures from the Republican period are known. The most notable is the complex identified as a library-gymnasium on the slopes below the theater. This complex was built in the last quarter of the third century and renovated around the end of the second century BC.[54] The most significant finds from it are fragments of plaster inscribed in Greek with the names of authors and summaries of their work, which appear to be the remains of a library catalogue. It is unclear whether this complex was a true civic gymnasium or formed part of a private residence.[55] In addition, the Temple of Serapis and Isis on the northern edge of town probably dates to the late third or early second century BC.[56] As in Lilybaeum, the presence of this Egyptian cult reflects the city's integration into key commercial and cultural routes, particularly those connecting Tyrrhenian Italy to the Eastern Mediterranean.

The epigraphic record of Tauromenion between the Second Punic War and the defeat of Sextus Pompey reflects a prosperous, effectively autonomous community, though increasingly influenced by Roman institutions. In addition, like many other Sicilian cities (e.g., Lilybaeum, Agrigentum, and Halaesa), Tauromenium had a considerable population of resident foreigners by the end of the Republic, including Roman citizens, who were attracted by the business opportunities of the town and the fertility of its hinterland. Cicero mentions two Roman citizens, M. and P. Cottius, *ex agro Tauromenitano* (5.64), while one of the later financial accounts records the leasing of houses and lands to *xenoi*.[57]

The last years of the Republic and the early years of the Principate brought a complete political (and probably demographic) reorganization, although its chronology is controversial. Appian reports that Tauromenium, which had been a Pompeian stronghold in whose vicinity many of the key naval and land battles in Sicily had been fought (cf. *Civil Wars* 5.105 and 109), was punished by Octavian after the war by the expulsion of its citizenry and, along with the other cities of Sicily, by an indemnity of 1,600 talents (5.129). Diodorus Siculus records that Octavian expelled the inhabitants of Tauromenium and installed a colony of Roman citizens but does not indicate the date of this event (16.7.1), though none of the other historical events he mentions are known to postdate ca. 30 BC. The main scholarly debate concerns whether the founding of the Roman colony at Tauromenium and the deportation of the city's citizens date to the immediate aftermath of the civil war (36–35 BC) as a punitive measure against the partisans of Pompey or the Augustan "settlement" of Sicily in 21 BC (cf. Cassius Dio 54.7.1). Most scholars now favor the later date. Wilson, for example, argues that Octavian only expelled the city's leading citizens after the conclusion of the war, since it is implausible (lacking any archaeological indication) that the town lay deserted for fifteen years.[58]

Whatever its exact date, the foundation of the colony marked a new phase in the political life of the city and initiated a new program of construction that incorporated buildings and monuments common in *coloniae* and *municipia* across the empire. The probable agora of the Greek *polis* (covered by the modern Piazza Vittorio Emanuele II) underwent a complete restructuring and rebuilding. The archaeological remnants of the renovated agora/forum include terracing walls on the eastern and northern sides as well as a number of large paving stones and architectural décor, including granite columns and a large marble basin.[59] The eastern entrance to the forum may also have held an arch.[60] Recent excavations around the Hellenistic peripteral temple on the western side indicate that it had fallen out of use by the Augustan period and a wall was built in front of it, thereby cutting it off from the main space of the agora.[61] The public building (*bouleuterion*?) on the northern side also underwent renovations in the Augustan period, including the paving of the portico that surrounded its courtyard—a project that (perhaps intentionally) covered up the bases of the honorific statues dedicated by the free *damos*.[62]

Further indications of the impact of the establishment of the colony on public life are the fragments of a calendar and *fasti consulares* discovered in the forum area, documents rarely found outside Italian *municipia* and *coloniae*. The calendar, of which only the months of September and October are preserved, was inscribed in Latin on Luna marble. It appears to date between the foundation of the colony and 19 BC, based on the months and the festivals included in it, though it may have been inscribed later in the Augustan period or under Tiberius. The two fragments of the *fasti consulares* preserve the years 39–36 and 31–30 BC.[63] The theater may also have been renovated or redecorated under Augustus. Although few of its architectural elements date to this era, a statue group that included Niobe and Artemis probably from the stage does appear to be Augustan, as do some portraits of magistrates as well as a portrait head of Augustus himself.[64]

The public life of Tauromenium is more obscure after the Augustan period due to the sparse epigraphic record: unsurprisingly for a *colonia*, the few fragmentary nonfunerary Latin inscriptions are mostly dedications to emperors.[65] Likewise, the imperial-era changes to the city's topography are difficult to date with precision due to the absence of ancient stratigraphy around surviving monuments like the theater. Some older structures, including the gymnasium-library complex, remained in use until the mid-imperial

FIGURE 4.5.
Tauromenium: odeum (author photo).

period.[66] It appears that most alterations to the urban fabric after the Augustan period consisted of renovations, refurbishments, and adaptations of existing structures. A few new buildings of the Roman type were added, many of which were geared toward spectacle and the improvement of residents' quality of life.

In the late first or second century AD an Augustan-era bath building north of the forum was expanded, covering over the Hellenistic public building (*bouleuterion/curia*?).[67] Around the same time, on the western side of the forum, an odeum was built onto the back of the Hellenistic peripteral temple, using the Doric colonnade of the temple as a sort of *scaenae frons*, with the *cavea* partly cutting into the slope of Monte Tauro (see figure 4.5).[68] Although it follows a basic design common across the empire, the positioning of this monument directly behind the southern side of the Hellenistic temple, in perfect symmetry with the earlier structure, is more unusual. Its construction may indicate a "secularization" of a once-sacred area, with the temple building functioning only as an impressive backdrop for musical and rhetorical events held in the odeum.[69]

Major building projects of the middle Empire away from the forum also

FIGURE 4.6.
Tauromenium: "naumachia" (author photo).

emphasize urban splendor and quality of life. The city was equipped with two aqueducts that furnished public and private supplies of water. The first, constructed in the first century AD, fed into large reservoirs in the city center. The second, constructed in the second century, supplied the public baths as well as other reservoirs in the city center. These reservoirs in turn fed smaller private cisterns, some dating back to the Hellenistic period.[70]

In keeping with the emphasis on public splendor and luxury, this era also saw the transformation of the public area once occupied by a Hellenistic stoa and paved plaza into the "naumachia": a mysterious elongated rectangular building, much of which still stands, with a brick façade consisting of eighteen large semicircular apses (see figure 4.6). This structure was connected with the distribution of water, probably functioning as the monumental façade of a reservoir or as a *nymphaeum*. Like the odeum, the form of this building—an isolated monumental façade with wide apses—is uncommon. Its closest parallel is perhaps the mysterious Bagni building (public baths or a *nymphaeum*) on the outskirts of Centuripae. Its brick architecture suggests an earlier date than the other major Roman monuments of the city, perhaps between the deduction of the colony and the Flavian period. Many of the bricks bear the stamp "TAUROMENITAN" in Greek, indicating that a special commission of bricks from a large (public?) workshop was made for the construction of the monument.[71] The niches of the façade would have held statues, such as the Parian marble torso of Apollo found nearby. The complex may have been associated with the imperial cult, harnessing the ideological power of water in a manner presaging later imperial monuments such as the Severan *septizodia* found in Rome, Sicily (in Lilybaeum), and North Africa.[72]

The late Trajanic/early Hadrianic period saw the most conspicuous change to the urban fabric: a major renovation and expansion of the spectacular Hellenistic theater into the completely brick structure visible today.[73] A further transformation of the theater into an arena for *venationes* and gladiatorial combats followed, probably in the Severan period, reflecting the increased popularity of Roman-style games in the provinces. Similar modifications to theaters were made around the same time in Tyndaris and elsewhere in the empire, especially in Greece and in cities of Greek origin in southern Italy, Asia Minor, and Cyrenaica. Most of these cities had centuries-old theater buildings whose adaptation into arenas was more cost-efficient and space-efficient than the construction of purpose-built amphitheaters.[74] This transformation was accomplished in Tauromenium by the removal of the stage and the lowest rows of seats, thereby lowering the level of the orchestra. A curved, vaulted corridor was constructed around the new arena space, and rooms were added beneath the arena floor.[75]

Little else is known of the urban fabric of the imperial period. No new cult buildings have been identified, though the Hellenistic temple of Isis and Serapis on the northern edge of town remained in use at least until the middle imperial period. A small marble base with a Latin dedication to Serapis and Isis by C. Ennius Secundus (*CIL* 10.6989) was found near this temple, along with a late second-century statue of a young priestess, made of marble perhaps imported from the Aegean.[76] Little can also be said about the domestic architecture of the imperial city. The few structures that have been excavated, however, suggest that the city's elite maintained a high standard of living. For example, a vast and long-lived *domus* built on two terraces, with one level centered on a large peristyle surrounded by rooms with mosaic floors, was discovered near the Serapis and Isis sanctuary.[77]

The burial spaces and practices of the imperial period reflect strong Roman influence and suggest the presence of families of Roman or Italian origin among the colony's elite. On the northern and northwestern slopes are twelve vaulted chamber tombs ("house tombs") built using concrete, some with brickwork, mostly from the second century AD.[78] All are rectangular in plan and placed on high podiums. The architectural styles and building techniques used in these tombs are central Italian in origin; their closest parallels are in Rome, Ostia, Portus, and Campania and in other Sicilian cities with similarly strong Roman social elements. Like the columbarium of Halaesa, these tombs were probably used for the burial of leading local families and their associates. The interior of the La Guardiola tomb, for example, contains niches for ash urns (including one made of glass and another of alabaster), with fifteen sarcophagus tombs of the first and second centuries AD nearby.[79]

Some scholars see the location of the burial areas as an indication that urban habitation had contracted by the second and third centuries AD.[80] Relatively little is known about the later Roman phases of the city. The bath building near the forum underwent a second, obscure phase of use after the thermal apparatus ceased functioning.[81] A cistern was carved into the bedrock on the eastern side of the forum in the fifth century and subsequently filled with fragments of Hellenistic sculpture.[82] The ancient urban fabric appears to have maintained its integrity until the Byzantine era (seventh and eighth centuries), when the forum was abandoned and converted into a burial ground.[83]

Although no field survey or other archaeological research has been done in the territory of Tauromenium, scattered literary and epigraphic evidence indicates the strength and diversity of the city's Roman-era economy. The financial accounts of the second and first centuries BC show that the city gained revenues from the export of colored marble from quarries in its hinterland and timber from extensive forests on the slopes and foothills of Etna. But the most important component of the economy of the city and its territory was wine. Northeastern Sicily had been renowned for viticulture since the sixth century BC, when the colony of Naxos was one of the key centers of the wine-producing region stretching across the slopes and foothills of Etna, from the Bay of Naxos down to the outskirts of Catania. Like the Bay of Naples, this area was blessed with fertile volcanic soil. The cultivation of vines was possible up to 1,000 meters on the slopes of Etna.[84] Although little is known of the infrastructure of this wine production, its iconography (such as the head of Dionysus and grape clusters) appeared on the coins of classical Naxos and of its successor city, Hellenistic Tauromenion.

The wine industry continued to be a key component of the economy in the imperial period, when it penetrated the Italian and Roman market: according to Pliny, the city exported a noteworthy wine bottled in small amphorae (*lagonae*) (*HN* 14.66). *Tituli picti* from amphorae in Pompeii and Herculaneum and tablets from the Murecine archive indicate that this wine was distributed, probably through the port of Puteoli, to the urban markets of the Vesuvian region.[85] Most of the warehousing and ancillary activities associated with the export of wine and other commodities took place around the Bay of Naxos below Tauromenium, as indicated by the remains of the Roman and late antique settlement at Naxos discussed in chapter 7.

Tauromenium's integration into Mediterranean trade, especially between Tyrrhenian Italy and the Eastern Mediterranean, is further indicated by the imperial-era shipwrecks off Capo Taormina and in the bay below the city.[86] One wreck off Capo Taormina, dating approximately to the reign of Hadrian, had a cargo of thirty-seven columns and two blocks of green stone probably destined for the Roman or Italian market. Another third-century wreck in the Bay of Naxos had a cargo of twenty-four columns of Cipollino marble from Carystos in Euboea and thirteen blocks of white Aegean marble.

CONCLUSION

Like Tyndaris, Tauromenium underwent considerable political, cultural, and demographic change in the transition from Republic to Empire. The imposition of the *colonia*, whether in 36–35 BC or 21 BC, marked a clear break in the institutional and cultural history of the city. Efforts to introduce a new political culture centered on Rome are seen in the inscribed *fasti* that were probably set up in the main public area of the city. The urban fabric, and particularly the main centers of public activity, began to assume a new character with the spread of Roman and "imperial" building types (public baths, odeum, *nymphaeum*, and arena) and construction techniques (in particular, the use of concrete and brick). In this respect, Tauromenium differs from Lilybaeum, Agrigentum, and Halaesa, where the transition from Greek *polis* to Roman *civitas* (and eventually *municipium* and *colonia*) was more organic and gradual. In the latter three cities this transition began as early as the first century BC and was led by resident Romans and Italians who had business interests in those communities as well as by local elites who possessed social and economic connections to Rome and perhaps even Roman citizenship.

As in the case of Lilybaeum and Agrigentum, the diversity of Tauromenium's economy and the strength of its connections with the wider Roman Mediterranean were key to its success in the imperial period. As a key port on the eastern coast of Sicily, with access to the markets of Tyrrhenian Italy and the Eastern Mediterranean, Tauromenium was a major center for the production and export of wine produced from grapes grown on the fertile slopes of Etna. In this respect the city experienced continuity from the Hellenistic/Roman Republican period, when financial accounts attest to the revenues that the government derived from the sale and export of commodities from its territory. So it appears that in both Tyndaris and Tauromenium the foundation of a Roman colony was a significant political turning point but not a decisive blow (or boost) to the city's economic fortunes. The next chapter continues to explore the link between political changes (particularly those implemented by Augustus in the aftermath of the Roman civil war) and economic integration in three cities in eastern Sicily: Centuripae (modern Centuripe), Catina (modern Catania), and Syracuse.

FIVE

EASTERN SICILY

From Syracusan to Roman Hegemony

This chapter examines three cities in eastern Sicily: one inland (Centuripae) and two on the coast (Catina and Syracuse). All three were settled in the archaic period. They maintained close political, social, and economic connections with one another throughout their long ancient histories, especially during Syracuse's extended periods of hegemony in the region. These cities were implicated in different ways in the civil war between the triumvirs and Sextus Pompey, and their subsequent histories provide further evidence of the long-term impact of that war and its resolution on the urban landscape of Sicily.

CENTURIPAE (CENTURIPE)

Permanent urban settlement began on the site of Centuripae by the eighth century BC, as part of a process of agglomeration or synoikism of native settlements in the interior in response to the Greek colonization of the Ionian coast. The hilltop site, now occupied by modern Centuripe, is 733 meters above sea level and extends across five ridges roughly in the shape of a cockspur (see figure 5.1). Though difficult to access (and easy to defend) thanks to its steep slopes, it is in a key strategic position in the eastern interior, between the slopes of Etna to the northeast, the plain of Catania to the south, and the hills of the Enna province to the west. The town is well situated to control key overland and riverine routes, such as the Salso (Chrysas), Simeto, and Dittaino (Kyamosoros) Rivers and the road following the Simeto valley northwest from Catania to the Tyrrhenian coast at Thermae Himeraeae. The town's immediate hinterland is suitable for agriculture, with plentiful water and some mineral resources.

Centuripae/Kentoripai had a long history of contact with the Greek cities of the coast, and particularly with Katane (Catania), but it came firmly under

Syracusan influence in the time of Timoleon.[1] In 339–338 BC Timoleon oversaw the deportation of the town's native population to Syracuse and its replacement with new colonists. Kentoripai's ties to Syracuse were not always detrimental, however: for example, Hieron II granted it part of the territory of neighboring Ameselon in 269 BC (Diod. Sic. 22.13.1). Though little is known of the ancient urban center before the third century, the ceramic industry for which it would become famous was in operation on the outskirts, in areas also occupied by necropolises, by the fourth century BC.[2]

Centuripae submitted to Rome early in the First Punic War (263 BC). Like other cities that did likewise, including Halaesa and Segesta, it was awarded

FIGURE 5.1.

The modern town of Centuripe (US Army Map Service, 1943, courtesy of the Perry-Castañeda Library Map Collection, University of Texas: https://legacy.lib.utexas.edu/maps/).

the status of *civitas libera ac immunis*, which exempted it from regular formal tributary obligations to Rome (obligations that became the *decima* after the Second Punic War), and probably left it greater autonomy.[3] The town's place in the geopolitics of Sicily between the First and Second Punic War is unclear, since it lay outside the territory directly administered by Hieron II of Syracuse. Nonetheless, it remained active in the commercial circuit centered on Syracuse in which other towns of the eastern interior, like Morgantina, participated. This circuit was geared toward the production and export of grain accompanied by mass-produced, low-value items like ceramics. Excavations of the kiln complexes that ringed the city center reveal the explosive growth of the ceramic industry in the third century, with production in some workshops continuing into the early Principate.[4] These kilns produced terracottas used in cult and domestic contexts as well as fine tablewares, such as the Campana C produced in other eastern Sicilian centers. The growth of the ceramics industry was probably linked to the city's location along key transportation routes and its favorable political and economic status after the First Punic War, especially compared to previous centers of ceramic production, such as Lipari, that had been damaged in that war.

After the Second Punic War, as the entire island was incorporated into the Roman province, the elite of Centuripae gained advantageous positions in agriculture and commerce. The immunity of the city's lands from Roman taxation meant that a greater share of its surplus could go to the community itself and to its individual cultivators. The wealth generated from this surplus could in turn be spent on the monumentalization of the urban fabric (as seen also at Segesta and Halaesa in the second century BC) or reinvested in more land. After the Second Punic War, the city and its residents expanded their landholdings at the expense of less-favored communities. For example, after the destruction of Leontinoi in 214 BC, *aratores* from Centuripae acquired much of the former territory of that city, now Roman *ager publicus* (Cic., II *Verr.* 3.114). Indeed, Cicero calls Centuripae the "wealthiest of Sicilian cities" (4.50) and claims that the *aratores Centuripini* are tenants of the lands of many Sicilian cities, including much of the fertile territory of nearby Aetna (3.108). As such, they came into contact—and competition—with the entrepreneurial Romans who also leased the most fertile Sicilian land, like Q. Lollius, an *eques* and *arator* in the territory of Aetna (3.61).

The incidents that Cicero recounts as evidence of Verres's abuse of these *aratores* provide valuable insight into the activities, background, and connections of the landed elite of Centuripae in the early first century BC. For example, he cites the case of Nympho, an *arator* with a lease on a large farm, who had invested a large sum in equipment but who was forced to flee to

Rome as a result of Verres's harassment (3.53–54). He also claims that the brothers Sostratus, Numenius, and Nymphodorus were forced to flee the land they worked in partnership (3.57). According to Cicero, Verres's thugs seized the brothers' equipment, slaves, and livestock (*pecus*)—an indication that they had used the land for both agriculture and animal husbandry. Most, if not all, of the Centuripean *aratores* appear to be of Greek origin and to lack Roman citizenship, though they did possess social connections to members of the Roman elite, as the case of Nympho suggests.[5] These connections, and the mobility of the Centuripean elite, are also reflected in the fact that the city could send *legati* to Rome to present evidence against Verres (2.120, 156).

The most important evidence of Centuripae's links with Rome and Italy, and for the presence of Centuripeans in Italy, comes from a Greek inscription found in Centuripae that records an embassy of three men sent to Rome and Lanuvium, perhaps in the second or early first century BC.[6] The main result of this mission, as recorded in the inscription, was a *senatus consultum* of Lanuvium affirming the *syngeneia* or *cognatio* between the two towns. This kinship was traced back to the legendary Lanoios, a Centuripean who followed Aeneas to Latium and founded Lanuvium (making Lanuvium, in a sense, an *apoikia* of Centuripae).[7] Such *syngeneia* carried great symbolic force, linking Centuripae to the origin story of Rome through Lanuvium, an ancient city in Rome's Latian heartland. It reinforced Centuripae's long history of loyalty to Rome, while also affirming Centuripae's significance and autonomy, at least in the sphere of peaceful interurban relations. Such a connection may also have had practical benefits, giving members of the Centuripean elite a foothold in Italy for travel to Rome, where public lands in the provinces (*agri publici*) were leased, a procedure that usually favored Roman entrepreneurs.

In addition to these links with Italy, there is evidence for the participation of Centuripae's citizens in other Mediterranean networks: for example, a second- or first-century BC inscription from Oropos in Boeotia (*IG* 7.420) that lists Emmenidas of Centuripae as one of the victors in the Amphiaraia games. Coins of Republican Centuripae have been found as far afield as Albania. The movement of people and goods from across the Mediterranean into Centuripae is also attested archaeologically. Large amounts of Rhodian wine amphorae have been found in the city, though wines of Tyrrhenian Italy (in Dressel 1 amphorae) supplanted these imports as Rhodes lost its commercial dominance after 167 BC.[8]

This body of evidence paints a picture of Republican Centuripae not only as the home of an elite whose wealth was based in landholding, agriculture, and livestock but also as a city strongly connected to other regions of the Mediterranean. The city is relatively deep in the interior, so this connection would have been mediated through one of the ports of the eastern coast, such as Catania (about 40 km east) or Syracuse (about 100 km southeast). Nonetheless, the active participation of Centuripae in maritime commerce is suggested by the presence of the cult of Zeus Urios, the patron of sailors (*IG* 14.574). And, as Cicero attests, the city was able to provide a quadrireme with a crew and captain to Verres's ill-fated expedition against the pirates who plagued Sicilian waters (II *Verr.* 5).

The presence of the modern town has prevented extensive archaeological exploration of the ancient urban center. But the excavations that have been possible, especially on the outskirts, have hinted at the expansion of Centuripae in the third century BC, when areas once occupied by necropolises were covered by residences and industrial establishments, such as potteries.[9] While little also remains of the public buildings of the Republican period, the literary and epigraphic record suggests that Centuripae possessed all of the buildings that a self-respecting Sicilian city would require, including a gymnasium and an agora with spaces for elite self-promotion and for meetings of the local council and assembly.[10]

Excavations around the urban center have revealed evidence of damage and destruction to many residential and industrial areas in the late first century BC, however, resulting in their permanent abandonment and in a contraction of the settled area.[11] This destruction and contraction may have occurred during the war with Sextus Pompey. Strabo singles out the city as the object of Augustus's restoration efforts, suggesting that it had suffered in this conflict but subsequently gained the attention of the *princeps* because of its long history of loyalty to Rome.[12] Although the early Augustan period may have been transitional for the urban fabric, there was no clear change in Centuripae's juridical status: Pliny includes it among the cities of Latin status in the Sicilian interior, along with Segesta and Netum. Little further evidence is available for the town's status under the Principate, though public epigraphy attests to the typical range of institutions and magistracies found in *municipia* (e.g., *CIL* 10.7004, a second-century dedication by a father and son who had achieved the duumvirate).

The advantageous position of the wealthiest citizens of Centuripae in Sicilian agriculture and commerce continued into the Principate and enabled members of the local elite eventually to join the ruling classes of the province and empire. The roots of this social mobility lay in the town's political and social connections to Rome and Italy, which are evident by the early first century BC. The paths of some local families can be traced somewhat tentatively from the late Republic into the early Empire. For example, Pompeius Grosphus, a wealthy owner of land and herds in Sicily and an acquaintance of the poet Horace (*Epistle* 1.12; *Ode* 2.16), was probably a descendant of the Eubulidas Grospus whom Cicero mentions among the *aratores* of Centuripae. The cognomen Grosp(h)us is of Siceliot origin and has also been documented at Pompeii and in Samothrace, perhaps another indication of the participation of wealthy Centuripeans in overseas commerce.[13] A member of the family had probably been granted Roman citizenship by Pompey the Great, a leading patron of wealthy Sicilian families since his service in Sicily in the Marian wars.[14]

As they rose through the ranks of the provincial and imperial elite, establishing and exploiting links with other powerful families in Sicily and beyond, the leading families of Centuripae also left their mark on the urban fabric of their home city. The most conspicuous example of their impact is the cycle of honorific statues dedicated by Q. Pompeius Sosius Priscus in the second century AD. Several scholars have attempted to trace the career and social connections of this man, his ancestors, and his descendants. But here it suffices to note that the family of Priscus, who achieved the consulship in AD 149, had extensive social connections through adoption and marriage to the leading families of Sicily, Italy, and Africa and probably had large landholdings in those areas.[15] The family joined the ranks of the imperial elite in the Flavian period and reached its social apogee in the second century, when its most prominent members achieved the consulship and were the intimates of emperors.[16] The geographic roots of the family are obscure, though it is probable that at least some of the ascendants of Priscus were prominent citizens of early imperial Centuripae.[17] Whatever its origins, as the statues dedicated by Priscus make clear, the family retained close ties to Centuripae in the high Empire.

The statue cycle was displayed in the probable forum of Centuripae, only a small section of which, the "ex Mulino Barbagallo" complex, has been excavated.[18] Located on a northeast-facing slope just below the summit, with a panoramic view of Etna and the valley of the Simeto, the principal construction phases of this complex date roughly to the Hadrianic and Antonine periods. The excavated portion centers on a street or plaza whose pavement contains spaces for statue bases. A rectangular building overlooking this paved street or plaza was identified as a temple, though it more likely served as a meeting space, perhaps for the Augustales attested in inscriptions found nearby (discussed below). South of this building is another room opening onto the plaza, with a façade of two columns and a floor paved in brick and colored marble. On the southwestern edge of the plaza is a building with a different alignment, perhaps from a different phase of construction, with fine mosaic floors. While the precise function of these buildings is unknown, their lavish decoration suggests that they were of some public importance. In addition, the area was littered with statues of Augustus, Julio-Claudian emperors, and members of the imperial family. A colossal head of Hadrian was also found nearby, perhaps connected to the emperor's visit to Sicily (and Centuripae?) in AD 128.[19]

Although its exact composition cannot be reconstructed with certainty,[20] Priscus's statue cycle was clearly intended to celebrate his family and the community of Centuripae and their prominent place in the Roman imperial order. Over life-sized statues of the Pompeii would have been surrounded by images of emperors and members of the imperial family, in the middle of the civic space of Centuripae that the Pompeii had helped to monumentalize.[21] The statue cycle may even have celebrated the legendary links among Centuripae, Lanuvium, and Rome, with the family joined by their mythical ancestor Lanoios.[22] R. P. A. Patanè suggests that the project was inspired by Q. Pompeius Falco's proconsulship in Asia Minor (AD 123–124), where he would have seen similar statue cycles in cities like Perge.[23] There are a few roughly contemporary Sicilian parallels: as discussed in previous chapters, similar but less-complete statue groups commemorating local elites, members of the imperial family, and their connection to deities emblematic of the imperial order have been found in Halaesa and Tyndaris.

Other areas of the city were also embellished, especially in the Hadrianic period and after. Traces of at least two bath complexes were found in the city center, one only 100 m from the forum.[24] A large brick vaulted structure in Contrada Bagni, just outside the town, that served as a *nymphaeum* or bath complex dates to the late second or early third century.[25] Further evidence of urban embellishment in the high Empire includes the dedication of a *sphaeristerium*, probably an exercise area attached to a bath complex, by a father and son *pro honore IIviratus* (*CIL* 10.7004).

The monumental tombs in conspicuous locations on the outskirts of the city center are another indication of the wealth and prominence (as well as the Italian cultural connections) of the elite of Centuripae. The so-called Castello di Corradino, a rectangular brick mausoleum on a high platform, is particularly visible, located at the farthest point of the ridge extending east from the summit of the hill looking out over the surrounding countryside toward Etna and the plain of Catania (see figure 5.2). A number of fine Roman marble ash urns have been found around the city, often in the vicinity of monumental tombs.[26] These urns, some of which are inscribed, held the ashes of wealthy freedpersons, slaves, and other social dependents, perhaps clustered as "entourages" around the tombs of elite families.[27]

The commemoration of multiple social levels in the funerary realm is mir-

FIGURE 5.2.
Centuripae: Castello di Corradino (author photo).

rored in the public sphere. As in Halaesa, the social ranks below the provincial and local elite participated in shaping the urban topography, often as a means of asserting their status in the community and in the Roman imperial order. The Augustales are attested in inscriptions from the second-century forum complex, where they may have had their seat. For example, L. Calpurnius Apthonetus, a *quattuorvir Augustalis* who made a dedication to the *lares Augusti*, was a freedman of a *gens* attested at Centuripae and elsewhere in Sicily (*AE* 1955.193). Inscriptions recording embellishments to the forum also speak to the connections between local elite families and between elites and freedmen. The monuments sponsored by the Pompeii perhaps served as focal points for advertising these connections. For example, the Coelius Lupus who sponsored the mosaic pavement of a building in the forum complex was a relation of Q. Pompeius Falco, the father of Priscus. Another relative of the Pompeii was M. Roscius Cironnus, who dedicated a statue of his deceased wife Manlia in the forum.[28]

Research on settlement in Centuripae's hinterland has been limited to surface survey.[29] The plains and low hills surrounding Centuripae have yielded evidence of extensive rural settlement, especially from the Hellenistic period (late fourth century BC) until the late Empire, centered around agriculture, ranching, quarrying, and the exploitation of mineral resources, including sulfur and gypsum.[30] The Hellenistic/Republican era appears to be the period of densest rural settlement, with numerous clusters of small farms spread throughout the territory, along with a few larger hamlets, such as the former hilltop center of Monte Ficarazza. The first and second centuries AD perhaps saw a reduction in settlement numbers, but no definite major change in settlement patterns. The third century AD brought a sharper reduction in the number of farms, perhaps due to the agglomeration of landholdings, with the few remaining farms continuing in occupation into the fourth and fifth centuries. The three rural sites identified in the survey as occupied continuously from the Hellenistic period into late antiquity share desirable features such as fertile soil, easy access to transportation routes, and proximity to mineral resources.[31]

Centuripae is distinguished from the urban centers in the interior examined in chapters 1 and 2 by its advantageous combination of a strategic position along key communications routes; possession of a fertile, well-watered hinterland, in which pastoralism and exploitation of mineral resources were possible; political shrewdness, as seen especially in its relations with Rome; and an ambitious local elite whose wealth was based in landholdings beyond the territory of the town itself. Members of this elite were able to join the provincial and imperial ruling classes in the Principate by exploiting their social and economic connections beyond Sicily. They became full participants in the maintenance of the Roman order, imbued in imperial ideology through service in Rome and in the empire and through links of patronage to their hometown.

The connection between landholding—not just (and probably not primarily) within the boundaries of Centuripae—and social mobility is particularly clear, beginning in the last century of the Republic and continuing into the imperial period. In this regard Centuripae contrasts with Segesta, where no persistent landholding local elite can be detected actively shaping the urban fabric after the early years of the Principate. Segesta, unlike Centuripae, was a city largely ignored by the provincial ruling class. This ruling class was active instead in western Sicilian centers like Lilybaeum, Panormus, and Thermae. Although leading families like the Pompeii remained patrons of Centuripae, their connections extended beyond the town; such families became more "Roman" and "imperial" than "Sicilian." The urban development of Centuripae thus shows that the question of the Sicilianness of the province's urban upper class under the Principate is somewhat irrelevant: the families who shaped the urban fabric of Centuripae were deeply interconnected with each other and with other prominent families in the provinces and in Italy and held land (and ties of patronage to cities) in multiple provinces, making them members of a truly "imperial" elite.

CATINA (CATANIA)

Ancient Catina/Katane was situated just south of Mt. Etna, on two coastal terraces at the mouths of the Longane and Amemano Rivers, whose courses are now almost completely covered by the modern city. Periodic eruptions of Etna and associated earthquakes have had devastating effects on settlement. The eruption of 1669 was particularly destructive, producing a lava flow that covered much of the city (including several surviving ancient structures), moving the coastline forward 600 meters and raising the ground level. As a result, the development of the ancient city is difficult to trace. Our knowledge of Roman Catina's topography stems mostly from the standing remains of ancient buildings scattered throughout the modern city. This knowledge is slowly improving with excavation in the city center, however, especially on the upper coastal terrace (the Montevergine hill) that probably served as the ancient acropolis.

According to Thucydides (6.3), Chalcidians from Naxos founded Katane shortly after Leontinoi in 729 or 728 BC. The archaic and classical history of the Greek *apoikia* was dominated by its geographical significance. It served as the Mediterranean port for a fertile territory that extended north to the slopes of Etna, west into the valley of the Simeto, and south into the plain of Catania but was also vulnerable to Etna's eruptions, which led to demographic and political instability. The city's position by the sea gave it an economic, strategic, and political advantage over the Sicel centers of the interior (especially Aitna/Inessa) and made it a potential rival of Naxos to the north and Syracuse to the south. But the eruptions of Etna contributed to the persistent demographic disruptions and political upheavals that the city experienced in the fifth and fourth centuries, especially at the hands of Syracuse. Most significantly, an eruption appears to have prompted the tyrant Hieron I's movement of the remaining population of Katane to Leontinoi in 476 BC (as the new *polis* of Aitna), beginning a pattern of Syracusan intervention that persisted until the First Punic War.[32]

After the earliest phase of settlement in the eighth and seventh centuries BC (a few walls and other structures have been excavated), little is known of the urban plan or monuments before the Roman imperial period. Earlier building phases were obscured first by Roman-era construction, later by lava flows, and finally by the construction of the modern city. Recent excavations in the Monastero dei Benedettini have revealed traces of urban organization beginning in the mid-sixth century BC.[33] Strata of destruction dating to the first quarter of the fifth century BC may be related to the Hieronian conquest and refoundation of the city. The city was rebuilt under Dionysius I (ca. 403) on a new plan. Thereafter there was little apparent change in the urban plan until the first century AD.

After its early surrender in 263 BC Catina enjoyed stable relations with Rome and was loyal during the Second Punic War, though it received no special privileges and remained a *civitas decumana* through the Republican period. A series of volcanic eruptions in the second half of the second century caused considerable damage to the city and its territory, however, prompting the Roman Senate to grant a ten-year exemption from the grain tithe.[34] Excavations in the former Reclusorio della Purità near the Monastero dei Benedettini have identified a thick layer of volcanic sand corresponding to the last of these eruptions, covering strata of the first half of the second century BC and covered by strata from dumping and leveling activities.[35]

The city underwent an economic revival in the early first century BC when it served as one of the main ports of eastern Sicily, attracting Roman and Italian merchants, administrators, and tax collectors and sending its own citizens across the Mediterranean. Coins of the city have been found at Delos, presumably carried there by merchants or sailors. A Catanian was among the victors in the games at Oropos, and the name of a certain Apollonos Poplios Katanaios is found in an inscription from Smyrna. In Catina, as in Tauromenium, Egyptian cults had an early presence in the civic pantheon, with their iconography appearing on coins of the first century BC.[36]

Cicero affirms that the prosperous city (II *Verr.* 4.50: *oppidum locuples, honestum, copiosum*) was a main port for the export of tithe grain and other goods (2.185, 3.192), making it a target for Verres's abuses. He notes that the city's representatives joined in denouncing the former governor (2.120, 156; 3.103, 4.114). His narrative also provides rare evidence of the town's religious life and political institutions. Cicero claims that Verres ordered the theft of the ancient statue of Demeter/Ceres, usually only viewable by women and girls, from the shrine (*sacrarium*) in the city (4.99–102). When the priestesses and wealthy local women in charge of the shrine reported the crime, Verres shifted the blame to a slave, who was then tried in accordance with city law before the council of Catina and acquitted only because of the testimony of the priestesses. A third- or second-century Doric dedication to Demeter and

Kore, accompanied by a marble relief of the two goddesses (produced by a fifth-century Attic workshop), may be related to this cult, whose presence in the port city of a major grain-producing region of Sicily is not surprising.[37]

The third quarter of the first century BC brought considerable political and demographic upheaval to Catina, caused as much by the multiple eruptions of Etna (in 49, 44, 36, and 32 BC) as by the Roman civil wars. The activities of Selurus and other bandits around Etna may have been a symptom of such regional instability (Strabo, *Geog.* 6.2.6). These difficulties in turn prompted Augustus's "restoration" of the city through the foundation of a Roman colony in 21 BC (*Geog.* 6.2.4; cf. Pliny *HN* 3.89). Little is known about the composition of this colony or the relations between colonists and native inhabitants. The assignment of lots to the colonists in the territory of the city would have been challenging, because much of the land would have been unusable or in poor condition due to the eruptions of Etna.

The establishment of the colony does seem to have prompted some changes to the urban fabric. The construction of new houses in the area of the Reclusorio della Purità around the end of the first century BC and alterations to residences excavated in the Monastero dei Benedettini may reflect the need to accommodate the new colonists in a manner befitting their status.[38] Some streets excavated in the Monastero dei Benedettini were also repaved with basalt blocks in the Augustan era.[39] The forum of Catina has not been identified, but the early phases of structures such as the theater, aqueduct, and the complex of shops and *tabernae* (perhaps part of a *macellum* or *horrea*) excavated in the Cortile San Pantaleone may also date to the Augustan colony.[40]

The tenuous traces of the Augustan colony are a symptom of the larger difficulties in understanding the development of Catina under the Roman Empire. Although the city has the most conspicuous collection of surviving Roman monuments in Sicily, these monuments are difficult to date due to lack of stratigraphy and frequent spoliation. Their relative position within the modern urban center can, however, give some sense of the extent and consistency of the ancient city (see figure 5.3). Wilson has hypothesized, based in part on the positioning of the necropolises, the amphitheater, and the circus (whose sites are firmly within the modern city but would have been on the outskirts of the ancient settlement), that at its largest ancient Catina covered approximately 130 hectares. Therefore, it would have been about half the size of Syracuse (around 280 hectares) and a fraction of the area enclosed by the walls of Agrigentum (around 500 hectares, not all of which was occupied in the Roman period). But it would have been larger than the area enclosed by the wall circuit of Lilybaeum (around 77 hectares) and roughly on a par with the largest cities of North Africa.[41] Strabo claims that Catina was more populous than Messana and Tauromenium (6.2.3).

Broadly speaking, the Flavian through Severan era was a time of significant and perhaps continuous public building in the urban center.[42] The building projects of this period utilized local materials (most conspicuously, black basalt blocks quarried from the lava flows of Etna) as well as marble, gran-

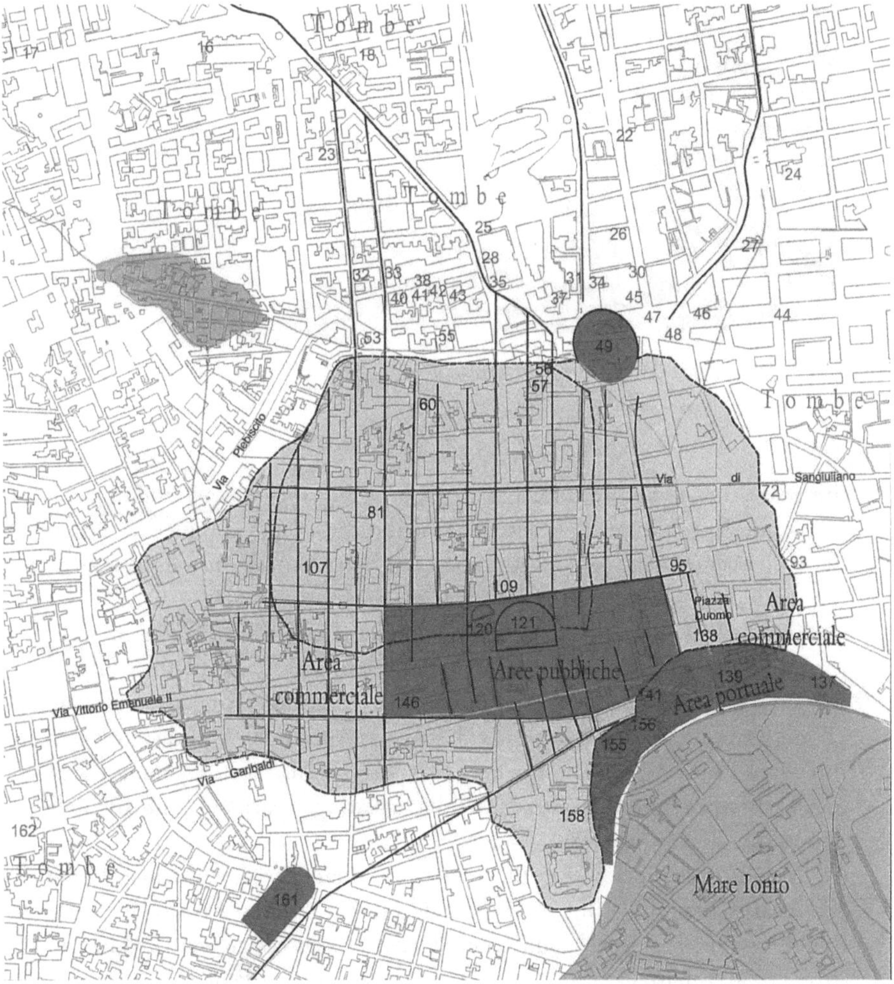

FIGURE 5.3.
Plan of Catina in the high Empire (E. Tortorici 2016).

FIGURE 5.4.
Catina: theater (author photo).

ite, and other stones from further afield. Most conspicuous are buildings for entertainment, leisure, and spectacle: the theater-odeum complex in the ancient city center and the amphitheater on the northern edge as well as numerous bath complexes scattered throughout the city.

The theater was altered or renovated numerous times in the imperial period. After smaller-scale works in the Augustan/Julio-Claudian and Flavian periods, the most dramatic renovations took place under Trajan or Hadrian. These renovations perhaps stretched into the Antonine era and were taken up again in the late Severan period.[43] In its current form, a palimpsest of these periodic renovations, the theater has a seating capacity of approximately 7,000 (see figure 5.4).

The seating area closest to the orchestra was faced with white marble and Euboean Cipollino.[44] But the richest decoration was reserved for the stage building. A range of local and imported stones was used, including white and rose-colored marbles from the area of Tauromenium; Pentelic, Proconnesian, and Luna white marble; polychrome marble from Teos; and colored stones from African and Eastern Mediterranean quarries.[45] The stage building's sculptural friezes, probably executed by itinerant craftsmen from the

Aegean in concert with local workshops, included a gigantomachy;[46] a triumph scene with victories, soldiers, trophies, and conquered barbarians; and smaller panels adorned with vegetation, animals, and Erotes. These friezes participated in a decorative program that exulted Roman victory over outsiders and beneficence to insiders, while connecting these imperial themes to local history. The stage building and the *porticus post scaenam* were also adorned with freestanding sculpture, much of which was found in situ in eighteenth-century excavations, including Hercules, Apollo, the Muses, Roma, other female personifications, and imperial portraits, such as the head of a youthful Marcus Aurelius and a cuirassed bust (probably an emperor) holding a mantle and scepter.[47]

Almost certainly after the construction of the theater, and probably under the Antonines or the Severans, an adjacent odeum was built to the northwest. This structure, though smaller than the theater, was similarly sumptuous and sophisticated in its architecture and decor. Its orchestra was paved in white marble. Its external façade consisted of a series of vaulted arches; the arches not connected to the auditorium were presumably used as shops or storage spaces.[48] A large amphitheater was built on the northeastern edge of town in the late first or early second century AD to hold *venationes* and gladiatorial games, the Roman-style spectacles gaining popularity across the empire.[49] Unlike the theater, the foundations of the amphitheater were placed on open ground, in keeping with Italic tradition. In its second phase under the Antonines or Severans the amphitheater was strengthened and stabilized—perhaps as an antiseismic measure—with the construction of an additional ambulatory.[50] Recent research has also indicated the presence of an imperial-era podium temple in the vicinity of the amphitheater, on the site of the future Church of Sant'Agata al Carcere.[51]

On the other side of the city, on its southern outskirts, was a circus/hippodrome perhaps also used for *naumachiae* that was covered by the lava flow of 1669 and is now known only from antiquarian descriptions.[52] The bath complexes that cropped up in the city center between the first and third century completed the city's leisure and entertainment facilities. The best-known complexes are the Terme Achilliane (underneath the Duomo), the Terme della Rotonda (just above the theater on Montevergine hill), the Terme dell'Idria and Terme del Reclusorio delle Verginelle (in the Montevergine residential area), and the Terme dell'Indirizzo.[53]

Recent archaeological research has shed considerable light on the domestic architecture of the imperial city. Excavation in the Monastero dei Benedettini and former Reclusorio della Purità has revealed that the middle of the Montevergine hill, above the theater-odeum complex, was a prosperous residential area with lavish *domus* from the mid-first through third century AD. These *domus* were interspersed with public buildings and facilities, including at least three bathhouses and a *nymphaeum* fed by the city aqueduct, within the paved street grid that connected the neighborhood to the amphitheater to the north.[54] Occupants had a high standard of living. In the first and second centuries houses were adorned with floors paved in mosaics, with their lots increased in size to accommodate large peristyles holding fountains, *nymphaea*, and *balnea*. For example, Domus A of the Monastero dei Benedettini complex, originally built in the first century AD over a late Hellenistic house, had an entrance room with a paved *lacus* leading to the *ambulacrum* of a vast colonnaded peristyle. The rooms surrounding this peristyle included *cubicula* and a large *triclinium*. The house was renovated in the first half of the second century AD and again in the late imperial period.[55]

In contrast to its poorly documented topographical development, Catina possesses one of the richest Roman imperial epigraphic records in Sicily. Here and in Syracuse the study of the use of Latin and Greek in public and private epigraphy has shed light on the linguistic, political, and cultural changes that accompanied the Roman colonization of the eastern coast. Knowledge of the epigraphic record of Catina essentially begins with the imposition of the Roman colony, after which the public monumental space was practically unilingual. In this respect the city was similar to the colonies of Tyndaris, Thermae Himeraeae, and Syracuse and to Lilybaeum, Agrigentum, and Halaesa, where strong public Latin epigraphic cultures had also emerged by the early imperial period (though perhaps more organically in the latter set of cities, through the presence of substantial populations of Italians and Romans).

However, as Kalle Korhonen has noted, private inscriptions in Catina (including funerary epitaphs and religious dedications) show a greater diversity of linguistic practices, as might be expected in a city whose middling social levels were bilingual or solely hellenophone. Latin predominates in pagan funerary epigraphy, perhaps reflecting a perceived prestige derived from its use in public epigraphy. Though pure bilingualism is uncommon in funerary inscriptions, the formulation of the epitaphs themselves involved considerable mixing of Greek and Latin phrases and syntax as well as the occasional use of Greek letters in Latin names.[56] Greek also persisted in private religious inscriptions under the Empire, such as a statue of Priapus with a bilingual dedication in Greek verse and Latin prose and a hexameter dedication of a statue to Apollo (*IG* 14.451).[57]

In the realm of public epigraphy Latin and bilingual inscriptions shed considerable light on the political, religious, and cultural institutions of the Roman city and on the individuals and groups involved in the development of the urban fabric. Numerous public inscriptions—including a colonial "album" from the late 260s AD listing the city magistrates for each consular year (*CIL* 10.7025)—attest to the typical magistracies found in Roman colonies, such as *duoviri* (*CIL* 10.7028–9 and 7023, in honor of a magistrate who also served as *praefectus fabrum*), aediles (*CIL* 10.7026), and quaestors. Local elite families probably descended from Augustan colonists are also present in funerary epigraphy. One Latin epitaph records that Grattia Paulla, the wife of C. Ofillius and mother of C. Ofillius Verus, both duumvirs, was honored with a public funeral and a statue in the forum (*AE* 1989.341m).

A wide range of cults and religious practices is also attested. In the realm of civic religion, the L. Rubrius Proculus honored on a statue base of the second century served as *augur* as well as *duovir quinquennalis* (*CIL* 10.7028), while *seviri* Augustales are attested in the high Empire (*CIL* 10.7027). In the fourth or early fifth century a *consularis* made a Latin dedication to the *genius* of Catina (*CIL* 10.7014, found in the area of the theater). Striking evidence of the continuity and strength of the city's cultic and cultural traditions is a reused marble base with a Latin inscription of the late fifth or early sixth century that commemorates the restoration of the statues of the *flammifugae fratres*, probably to their traditional place of honor in the theater, by the *consularis* and *v.c.* Merulus (*AE* 1956.259).[58] The *pii fratres* Amphinomos and Anapius/Anapias had been venerated as the city's protectors from the dangers of Etna at least since the Hellenistic period. Their images had appeared on coins until the Augustan era, and they continued to be celebrated in the high Empire (Strabo also mentions the brothers: 6.2.3).[59] Further indications of their continued prominence and association with the city in late antiquity are their inclusion in the poems of Claudianus (*Carm. min.* 17: *De piis fratribus et de statuis eorum quae sunt apud Catinam*) and Ausonius (*Ordo urb.* 92–3: *Catinam ... ambustorum fratrum pietate celebrem*).

Inscriptions also attest to the involvement of many social levels in the development of the urban fabric. The *curatores* of the city aqueduct, all Roman citizens, are commemorated on a basalt block found near the aqueduct's point of origin some 25 km outside the city center (*CIL* 10.6999). The local and provincial elite were also involved in the costly development of the city center: a fragmentary Latin dedication on marble from the late first or early second century AD attests to a construction project costing HS 50,000 and involving a certain [B]etilius Secund[us] (*CIL* 10.7030). In the Severan period a certain [T]ralia[nus] made a donation, probably of marble sculpture, as *summa honoraria*, while one Seius Agathos was honored with a statue for his funerary gift of HS 50,000.[60]

Inscriptions also attest to the involvement of imperial administrators in building activities, especially in the intense monumentalization of the Antonine and Severan eras. The most vivid testimony of the social, economic, and political forces shaping the built environment is a letter sent around AD 164–166 by the *curator* Julius Paternus to the emperors Marcus Aurelius and Lucius Verus, apparently regarding a dispute with the *decuriones* over the restoration of a *porticus* (or perhaps *portus*), a copy of which was inscribed on marble (*CIL* 10.7024).[61] The involvement of imperial authorities like the *curator rei publicae* T. Clodius Pupienus Pulcher (ca. 226) and the proconsul Q. Lusius Laberius (the lost *CIL* 10.7018, attesting to work on bath buildings) in the development of the city continued in the late Severan period. Numerous inscriptions attest to the beneficence of imperial notables in later centuries. For example, a Latin text commemorates improvements to the city water supply (the *nymphaeum* near the *castella aquarum in moenibus*) sponsored by the *consularis* Fl. Arsinius in the late fourth century (*CIL* 10.7017).[62] Such beneficence extended to the sponsorship of spectacles, as a late third- or fourth-century hexameter inscription honoring the agonothete Severus, son of Zosimianus, attests (*IG* 14.502). From the last years of the Roman city, in addition to the above-mentioned dedication of Merulus, a monumental Greek inscription commemorates the restoration of the Thermae Achillaeae (Terme Achilliane) by the *consularis* Fl. Felix Eumathios in 438 (*IG* 14.455).

The presence in the 220s of the *curator rei publicae* T. Clodius Pupienus Pulcher, the son of a future emperor, hints at the political interests connecting Catina with Italy and North Africa, especially as the economic prominence of the latter region grew. Pupienus's family rose to prominence under the Severans, and his own career included administrative positions in Italy, Sicily, and North Africa (including the curatorship of Leptis), culminating in the consulship. His *cursus*, including his position in Catina, is commemorated in an inscription from Tibur in Latium (*CIL* 14.3593).[63]

Furthermore, Catina's role as an export point for the agricultural products of the most fertile regions of Sicily and its location on trade routes connecting the Eastern Mediterranean, the North African coast, and Tyrrhenian Italy made it the focus of the economic interests of many leading families of the province. These included the Roscii, a wealthy *gens* that had attained senatorial rank by the time of Domitian or Trajan. Several members are attested in cities and rural communities across eastern and central Sicily, particularly within the triangle formed by Centuripae, Catina, and Syracuse.[64] For example, the *eques* L. Roscius Rufus, whose *cursus* included *praefectus cohortis equitatae*, was honored at Catina in the late first or early second century AD (*CIL* 10.7019). As noted above, the Roscii were connected by marriage and adoption to other leading landholding families of Sicily, North Africa, and

Italy, including the Pompeii of Centuripae. A highly fragmentary second-century inscription appears to commemorate at least one member of this family, probably descendant(s) of Q. Sosius Senecio (*CIL* 10.7021). The wider *familia* of freedpersons and other dependents of the Roscii can also be traced in the funerary realm. Roscius is among the most common gentilicians found in Greek and Latin pagan epitaphs, with six known individuals.[65]

Such inscriptions contain little substantive demographic information about the nonelite population of Catina, but in aggregate they present an image of a prosperous urban middling class engaged in a variety of nonagricultural activities. These included freedmen connected to the senatorial families of eastern Sicily who looked after the business and administrative interests of their patrons; *collegia* of tradespeople associated with the activities of the port; and individuals engaged in the banal aspects of civic and provincial government and in the provision of the range of services (entertainment, health, etc.) in demand in a large cosmopolitan urban center. Individuals of enslaved or freed status who were probably engaged in the business interests of the provincial elite appear in funerary epigraphy, such as the epitaph of a *fidelissimus vilicus* (*CIL* 10.7041).[66] Freedmen were also employed in the administration of the imperial patrimony: a Latin epitaph commemorates an *Augusti libertus tabularius* (*AE* 1933.28),[67] while another set of epitaphs in Latin and Greek points to the presence of the *familia* of M. Vipsanius Agrippa (e.g., *IG* 14.495).

As one of the major ports in eastern Sicily, Catina was also the home of several professional *collegia*, *sodalicia*, and *conviviae* associated with processing and export activities, including *marmorarii* (*CIL* 10.7039), *cuparii* (*CIL* 10.7040), *saccarii*, and *mensores*. The *fabri navales Catinenses* (*CIL* 14.364) shared a patron, C. Granius Maturus, with an Ostian corporation.[68] Epitaphs further attest to individuals who provided a range of services to the urban community, including actors and gladiators (e.g., *CIL* 10.7046: a female *mimas*), and a physician (*IMCCat* 171: the *iatros* Bassos). Unusually for Sicily, Catanian epitaphs also commemorate soldiers, veterans, and other Roman citizens who were perhaps colonists or their descendants.[69]

The variety of social ranks and occupations attested epigraphically in Roman Catina, which represent only a fraction of the actual population and their activities, reflects the economic diversity of the city. This diversity derived from the city's dual role as the administrative center of a large and fertile territory and as a port along important shipping routes of the central Mediterranean. However, as Strabo's account of the banditry of Selurus hints, the urban center's relationship with this territory was complicated by the eruptions of Etna, which periodically rendered some lands uninhabitable and forced the reconfiguration of boundaries. The letter of the *curator* Julius

Paternus implies, furthermore, that some parcels of civic land were no longer occupied by the mid-second century and hence could be sold by the city.[70]

The city shows no sign of centuriation, making the extent and division of its territory after the deduction of the Augustan colony unclear. Were the lands of pro-Pompeian Catanians confiscated and redistributed to colonists, did colonists resettle abandoned lands around Etna, or were colonists assigned territory of abandoned cities? Multiple methods may have been used. The territory could not have extended substantially north beyond the southern and eastern slopes of Etna, due to the presence of the Roman *colonia* at Tauromenium. It is likely that it expanded west and south instead, into the plain of Catania, the valley of the Simeto and the *ager Leontinus* (probably shared with Centuripae), and the Hyblaean plateau (shared with Syracuse).[71] As the presence of the provincial and imperial elite and their *clientelae* in Catina implies, this territory contained substantial private and imperial landholdings. Additional evidence of such landholding is a late Republican or early imperial basalt milestone that was reinscribed in the second or third century to mark the *fines* of the property of Vibius Severus (*CIL* 10.7022b).

The presence of such substantial wealth—and the need to integrate rural productive units with larger settlements and with the port of Catina—is reflected in the numerous building projects in the hinterland, beginning with the Augustan-era aqueduct that brought water into the city from the southern foothills of Etna. Bridges built over the Simeto in the first and second century improved transport and communications between Catina and its inland rival, Centuripae.[72] Substantial residential and productive centers also arose in the territory of Catina. West of the city at Misterbianco a bath complex perhaps attached to a villa was built in the late second century. Along the coast to the north at Santa Venera al Pozzo near Acireale a bath building, small temple, and kiln complex have been excavated: perhaps remnants of a small marketing center or thermal spa and cult complex.[73] Amphorae were produced around Santa Venera from the early first century through the fifth century AD, probably in multiple workshops (though with minimal variation in material and technique). They were likely used to transport wine produced in the plain of Catania to markets across the Mediterranean and northern Europe: most notably, Leptis Magna, where almost two hundred examples have been found in the Thermes du Levant.[74]

Although field survey in the immediate vicinity of the city has been limited, research along the coast and in the plain of Catania suggests a substantial rural population, particularly in the early imperial period. The range of goods received at rural sites is reflective of wider commercial trends in the Mediterranean, as imports from Italy gave way to provincial products in the second, third, and fourth centuries, including African olive oil and fish sauce and eastern Sicilian wine.[75] In turn, the diverse agricultural potential of the hinterland is reflected in the activities at the port of Catina: the *collegia* of *cuparii*, *saccarii*, and *mensores*, for example, were involved in the storage and export of wine and cereals.

The presence of *marmorarii* at Catina points to another important urban industry, the transport and working of stone. The eastern coast of Sicily lay along one of the principal shipping routes for building materials directed to Rome. These routes have left traces in the numerous wrecks of large valuable cargoes of stone in the shallow waters between Capo Passero and the Strait of Messina.[76] Although little is known of Catina's port facilities, the use of valuable stones from across the Mediterranean in public monuments as well as in public and private inscriptions suggests that the city received at least some of this trade. Furthermore, the black basalt from the lava flows of Etna was used as a building material in Catina and nearby settlements, especially for paving stones, walls, foundations, and other substructures.

Catina maintained its political and economic importance and integration with the wider Mediterranean well into the late Roman and early Byzantine periods. In the late fourth century Ausonius celebrated it along with Syracuse as one of the leading cities of the Roman Empire in his *Ordo urbium nobilium* (16–17), though the significance of this inclusion should not be overstated. Another manifestation of the city's continuing prominence is the long life of its public infrastructure, which was maintained and expanded at least through the fourth century.[77] As noted above, a court official restored the Thermae Achilleae in 438, and the nearby Terme dell'Indirizzo were also renovated. The orchestra of the theater was enlarged to accommodate aquatic shows in the fourth or fifth century, while the inscription of Merulus celebrating the restoration of the *pii fratres* implies that the theater was used and maintained even in the last decades of Roman rule.[78]

Catina's continued integration into Mediterranean economic, cultural, and religious currents is also reflected in the presence of an early and extensive Christian community. Around 150 epitaphs from the necropolises on the city's northern fringes attest to the size and prosperity of this community, which existed alongside a small Jewish community.[79] Christian burials in the urban necropolises had begun by the 330s AD, but the community was probably established somewhat earlier: the epitaph commemorating Julia Florentina, who died shortly after baptism at Hybla but was buried at Catina, dates roughly to the Diocletianic persecutions.[80] The inscription is valuable additionally as evidence of the early Christians' veneration of martyrs, since Julia Florentina was buried *pro foribus martyrorum*.[81] The abandonment and collapse of the imperial-era residences excavated in the former Reclusorio della Purità in the course of the fifth century points to the contraction of the settled area. Necropolises expanded into former residential and public areas, especially on the northern edge of town, including in the vicinity of the abandoned amphitheater.[82]

The Christian community's maintenance of a strong civic identity helped to shape the city's post-Roman phase. By the seventh century, as the infrastructure of the imperial city decayed, the northern, formerly extramural zone that included the Roman amphitheater and necropolises emerged as the center of organized religious activity. The palimpsestic nature of the urban fabric of early Byzantine Catania is encapsulated in the Terme della Rotonda, a bath complex in the heart of the ancient city, which was transformed into a church in the late sixth century at some point after falling out of use. Excavations of the complex recovered the seal of Barbatus, *rectoris sanctae ecclesiae ravennatis* during Constans II's sojourn in Sicily, indicating that the church was an important part of the city's religious landscape in the seventh century.[83] Survey along the coast and in the interior suggests that the hinterland of Catania remained inhabited in the sixth and seventh centuries and that rural sites continued to receive imports. Wine was supplied from the Eastern Mediterranean and the northeastern Sicilian coast rather than from Africa after the Vandal conquests.[84]

The Roman-era development of Catina can profitably be compared to that of the other major cities of the eastern coast: Tauromenium to the north and Syracuse to the south. All three were Augustan colonies, but they were set up for different reasons and according to different models. A colony was created at Tauromenium for punitive and strategic purposes, accompanied by the transformation of the topography of the civic center. The foundation of the Roman colony at Catina, in contrast, was intended to restore political, demographic, and economic order in a region devastated by eruptions of Etna and the civil wars. Unlike Syracuse, the administrative heart of the island, Catina developed primarily as an economic center. Although it did not possess the largest or best port in the region, it controlled an extensive and fertile hinterland. Like Lilybaeum on the western coast, Catina was positioned on shipping routes connecting the long North African littoral, with its booming export economy, to Rome and central Italy. As the adornment of the urban center with valuable marbles and imported stones shows, the city was also a port of call on the route connecting the main stone-producing regions of the Central and Eastern Mediterranean (North Africa, Egypt, and the Aegean) to Rome. For these reasons Catina attracted the economic activity and patronage of the leading families of the province and the attention of Roman administrators. Along with Centuripae and Syracuse, it formed an alternative triangle of elite activity to rival Lilybaeum, Thermae, and Panormus in the west.

Catina maintained its urban fabric as well as a strong civic identity until (and even beyond) the end of Roman hegemony. This persistence can in part be attributed to the economic and social diversity of its population. As the epigraphic record reveals, the city was home to multiple social levels, from slaves to officials of the imperial court, engaged in a variety of occupations. This economic and social heterogeneity meant that the city remained attractive both as a population center and as an object of elite patronage. In this respect Catina offers a contrast to the cities examined in chapters 1 and 2. Their economies followed the traditional *polis* model of land ownership and exploitation of agricultural resources in the hinterland—an economic basis for urban development that came under strain in the imperial period.

SYRACUSE (SIRACUSA)

Syracuse was the most prominent city in Sicily from its foundation (ca. 734 BC) until the end of antiquity. Its political, cultural, and economic influence on the island diminished only after the Arab conquest in the late ninth century. Despite (or perhaps because of) its turbulent political history, with dynasties of tyrants alternating with democratic and oligarchic governments, Syracuse was highly active on the Mediterranean political, cultural, and economic stage from the archaic period until its fall to Rome in the Second Punic War and the end of its effective autonomy. Hence more literary testimony exists for Syracuse than for any other Sicilian city, especially regarding the third century BC, when Agathocles and Hieron II reasserted Syracuse's political, military, cultural, and economic dominance in Sicily.

Thanks to the efforts of Agathocles and Hieron, Syracuse was the only truly hegemonic city in Sicily in the third century. These men crafted styles of personal rule heavily influenced by contemporary Hellenistic monarchs, incorporating ideological elements such as "spear-won land," the defense of the Greeks against barbarians (the Carthaginians), cultural patronage within the Syracusan realm, competitive euergetism beyond Sicily (mainly the supply of grain to other cities and kingdoms), and the assimilation of the ruler and his family with Olympian deities. Hieron's interactions with the Roman state anticipated those of the Attalids and other Hellenistic dynasts, as he successfully balanced expressing loyalty (or fealty) to Rome with maintaining his personal authority and the autonomy of his kingdom.

By the third century the urban center of Syracuse was organized into four districts: Ortygia, Acradina, Neapolis, and Tyche (see figure 5.5). Bridges connected the island of Ortygia, the site of the original *apoikia* that remained the political and religious heart of the city, to the mainland. Acradina (or Achradina), the mainland district closest to Ortygia, developed on a regular plan with long, wide streets radiating northwest from the city's two harbors. It eventually extended over the necropolises that ringed the archaic and classical urban center. Neapolis developed in the third century BC on the higher ground northwest of Acradina, in an area formerly occupied by necropolises, small suburban residential and industrial settlements, and the famous quarries of the classical period. The precise boundaries of Tyche, a mainland district bordering Neapolis, are unknown.

Syracuse's political, military, economic, and cultural revival, initiated in the mid-fourth century under Timoleon and continued in the third century by Agathocles and Hieron, saw the expansion of the city into areas of Acradina and Neapolis formerly occupied by extraurban necropolises.[85] Although the chronological and topographical details remain uncertain, it is generally agreed that Hieron was responsible for the monumentalization of Ortygia, Acradina, and Neapolis in the decades after the First Punic War, when his savvy dealings with Rome positioned Syracuse as the preeminent political and economic power in eastern Sicily. Hieron is said to have built his palace (Cic., II *Verr.* 4.118) and monumental granaries (*horrea publica*: Livy 24.21) on Ortygia, though no trace of them remains.[86] In the agora, presumably in Acradina though its precise location is disputed, Hieron built a new Olympeion to supplement the archaic sanctuary of Olympian Zeus south of the city center. Again, no trace of this building remains (Diod. Sic. 16.83.2; Cic., II *Verr.* 4.119, cf. 4.128). He also expanded the monumental fortifications built by Dionysius I and renovated by Agathocles at Epipolae, north of the city center.[87]

Hieron made his greatest impact in Neapolis, where he assembled a monumental complex that celebrated his personal power, legitimated his family's claim to dynastic rule, and reinforced the civic identity of Syracuse in the decades after the First Punic War, at a time when the city was celebrating the quincentennial of its foundation and enjoying renewed political, economic, and cultural prestige in Sicily and beyond. The centerpiece of this complex was the theater built into a gently sloping terraced hillside looking out to Ortygia and the harbor (see figure 5.6). Although it is unclear whether Hieron created this theater *ex novo*, he was certainly responsible for a program of nearly complete renovation and expansion that obliterated any trace of earlier structures and resulted in the basic form visible today. The theater was one of the largest in the Greek world, with a capacity of around 14,000 specta-

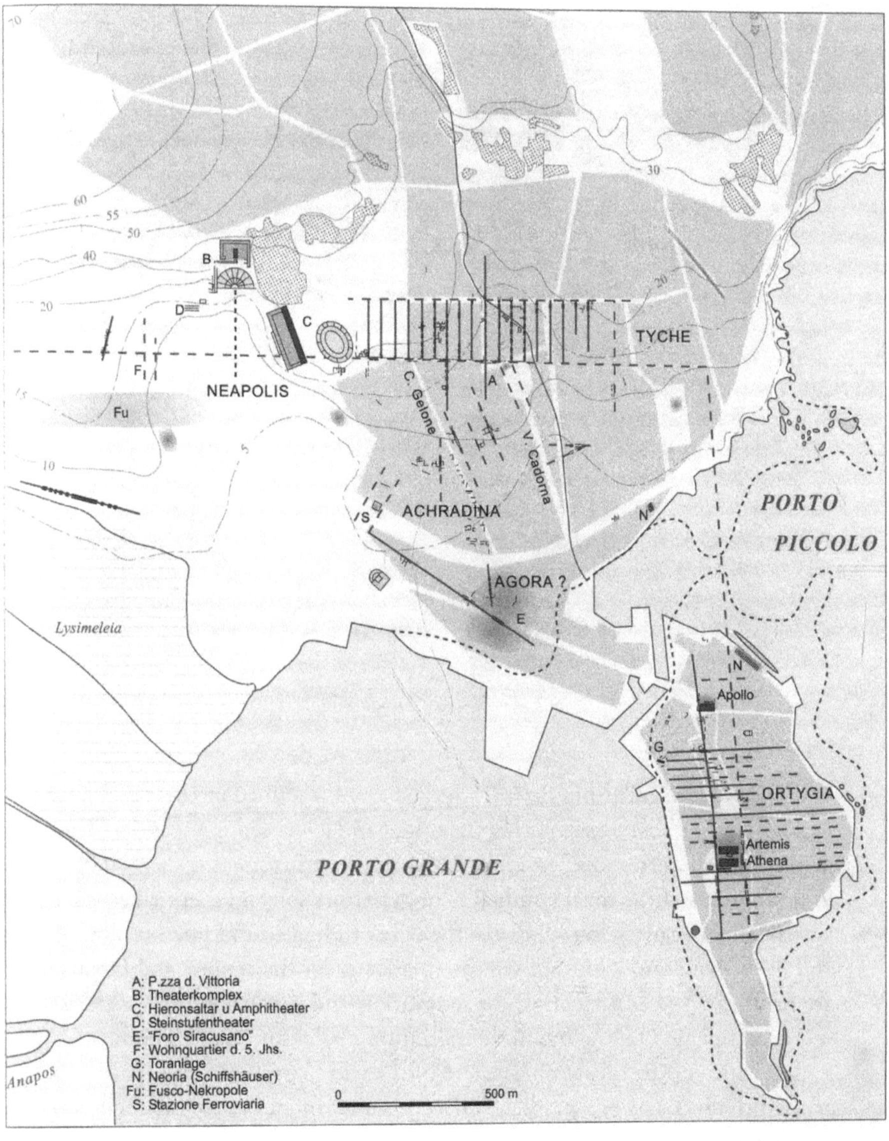

FIGURE 5.5.
Plan of Syracuse (© D. Mertens).

FIGURE 5.6.
Syracuse: theater (author photo).

tors.[88] Its link to Hieron is clear from the names inscribed in large Greek letters across the *diazoma* separating the upper and lower seating sections. These names, which correspond to each of the nine seating areas (*cunei*), include four members of the royal family (Gelon, Hieron's son and eventual co-ruler; Nereis, the wife of Gelon; Philistis, the wife of Hieron; and Hieron himself) and five Olympian deities, of whom only Zeus (in the center) and Heracles are legible.[89] The construction (or renovation and expansion) of the theater was accompanied by the monumentalization of the surrounding terraces.[90]

Just south of the theater, at the end of the wide east-west street that served as the principal axis of Acradina, Hieron built a monumental altar, cited by Diodorus as an emblem of Syracusan prosperity in the century after Timoleon (16.83.2). This altar, whose foundations are still visible, was one of the largest in the Greek world, almost 200 meters long and over 20 meters wide.[91] It was fronted to the west by a large paved plaza that underwent several alterations in later eras; its original form is uncertain. The specific divinity (or divinities) to whom the altar was dedicated is likewise unclear, though it was clearly intended for large-scale public sacrifices.

The nature of Hieron's building projects, and the motives and ideologies behind them, largely align with those of Hellenistic kings in the Eastern Mediterranean. The theater-altar complex in Neapolis—and especially the monumental inscription on the *diazoma*—was a means of legitimating and strengthening Hieron's rule by creating an association of the *basileus*, his family, and the Olympian deities. At the same time, the Neapolis complex celebrated Syracuse's power and autonomy and served as a new monumental space for public processions, performances, and sacrifices, thus bringing the populace closer to its ruler.[92]

The Olympeion in the agora further assimilated Hieron with Zeus, the chief tutelary deity of the Greeks and a divinity closely linked to Syracuse's origins and history. This temple was also the site of Hieron's dedication of Gallic and Illyrian spoils: gifts from Rome in thanks for the king's (financial and logistical rather than military) assistance in the wars of 225–221 BC (Livy 24.21). This gesture shows the success of Hieron's philo-Roman policy as a means of bolstering his stature as a military leader, despite his lack of real autonomy in foreign policy under the Romans.

The construction of monumental granaries on Ortygia—also the site of Hieron's palace—tied the political power and legitimacy of the king to the economic power of Syracuse, which was from the grain tithe that Hieron instituted across eastern Sicily. (It was subsequently adopted by Rome, as Cicero's *lex Hieronica*, as the taxation system for the entire province.) The granaries also served as a conspicuous reminder of the king's beneficence both to his people and to other communities, including Rome. The Attalids of Pergamon likewise built granaries in association with their palaces, as a means of demonstrating the economic security of the state.[93] Hieron's improvement of the city's defenses and famed patronage of the Syracuse-born and Alexandria-trained Archimedes demonstrate an interest in military technology even after the First Punic War.[94] He shared this interest with other Hellenistic kings and with Dionysius I and Agathocles, earlier Syracusan rulers who had possessed stronger military credentials.

Hieron's interest in military technology is symptomatic of the elevated intellectual and cultural climate of Syracuse under his rule—a cultural revival attributable to the kingdom's connections with Ptolemaic Egypt and the Hellenistic Eastern Mediterranean. This integration into Mediterranean artistic, architectural, and cultural trends is visible in the material culture of the city: wealthy homes were adorned with sculpture from or influenced by Alexandrian workshops, many of which are now on display in the Museo Archeologico Regionale Paolo Orsi. According to Cicero, the city's temples and public buildings were also adorned with fine paintings and sculpture from the East, such as the statue of Sappho by Silanion, a contemporary of Alexander the

Great, that stood in the *prytaneion* (II *Verr.* 4.126). The religious syncretism apparent in material culture, including objects related to the cults of Cybele, Demeter, Dionysus, and Isis, also derived from the city's close and enduring links to the Eastern Mediterranean.[95]

The impact of Hieron and his building program in cities under Syracusan control or influence, such as Morgantina, Tauromenion, Megara Hyblaea, and Akrai, is hard to assess because of the difficulty of dating many monuments. Such structures as the granaries of Morgantina, the Hellenistic temple in the probable agora of Tauromenion, and the public bath complexes at Morgantina and Megara Hyblaea cannot firmly be attributed to the personal initiative of Hieron, though they were probably constructed during his reign.[96] Additionally, the impact of the innovative architecture and scale of Syracusan monuments (particularly the theater) is visible in cities beyond Hieron's realm. For example, in the decades after his reign new stone theaters were built in western and northern Sicily, including in Segesta, Soluntum, and Ietas.

After the death of Hieron in 215 BC and the short rule of his young grandson Hieronymus, Syracuse plunged into turmoil once again (Livy 24.4–7, 21–24). The city turned against Rome in the Second Punic War, was famously besieged by the Romans in 214–213, and finally was sacked by M. Claudius Marcellus in 212 BC (Plut., *Marc.* 14–19). This last event effectively ended the city's hegemonic political and economic position in Sicily, as Syracuse and the former "kingdom" of Hieron became part of the new Roman *provincia* that now encompassed the entire island. Cicero states that Marcellus forbade the Syracusans from occupying Ortygia in order to deny them an easily defendable stronghold (II *Verr.* 5.84). The impact of the Roman siege and takeover on the urban fabric of Syracuse is otherwise difficult to discern, though excavations have provided tentative evidence of destruction and contraction of the occupied area broadly dating to the second half of the third century BC.[97] Cicero (4.120–123) and Plutarch (*Marc.* 20) portray Marcellus as a fair, unselfish, and merciful conqueror, but they indicate that much of the cultural patrimony of the city was lost after the sack: the Roman commander and his army carried many of its notable artworks to Rome as spoils.

It appears that Syracuse was quick to recover from the trauma of the siege and to establish beneficial relations with its new Roman overlords. According to Cicero, the city was subject to the grain tithe and received no special privileges but served as the center of Roman administration. Syracuse became the seat of one of the island's two quaestors (the other was based in Lilybaeum). The palace of Hieron was taken over as the *praetorium* or *regia*, the seat of the Roman governor (II *Verr.* 4.118). Hence the city was the main location of the governor's activities, such as the administration of justice (2.37, 68; 3.27, 68, 78) and the annual contracting of the grain tithe (3.149). It was also one of the harbors from which the *portorium* was collected (2.171, 176). Shortly after the sack the Syracusans honored their conqueror, M. Claudius Marcellus, in ways befitting a Hellenistic king, instituting the Marcellia festival in his honor and erecting a bronze portrait statue in the *bouleuterion* (2.50–51 and 154). Such gestures honored the Roman promagistrate as the city's new founder or *restitutor* and helped to cement the client relationship between the Syracusans and the Claudii Marcelli that endured at least until Cicero's time (cf. 2.36).[98]

Although material evidence for the city's development in the Republican period is deficient, Cicero provides considerable information about its population, government, religious life, and topography at the time of Verres's governorship and trial. Cicero describes Syracuse as the richest and fairest (*pulcherrima atque ornatissima*) city of Sicily, and the largest and loveliest of all Greek cities (*urbs maxima, pulcherrima*) (II *Verr.* 4.115,117). As the center of Roman administration and the cultural capital of the island, in Cicero's account, the city was the site (as well as the target) of many of Verres's crimes and thus receives considerable attention in his oration.

Cicero describes Syracuse as home to a large and diverse population. Many members of its wealthy Greek elite had ties of patronage to Verres—serving as his cronies, in Cicero's reckoning—while others were subject to his abuses (2.35–36). For example, the large inheritance of Heraclius, son of Hiero, was pointed out to Verres by the Syracusan citizens Cleomenes and Aeschrio. Cicero also refers to individual Romans and Italians resident in Syracuse as well as to the city's sizable and active Roman *conventus* (4.55, 4.137, 5.94, 5.155)—including many *equites* (3.136, 4.137)—engaged in business (*negotiatores*: 2.153) and provincial administration (e.g., as tax collectors and members of *societates*: 2.171).[99] Cicero describes how Verres set up an *officina* for metalworking and engraving in his *regia* on Ortygia, summoning all skilled craftsmen on the island to this establishment (4.54), and how he induced Theomnastus of Syracuse to set up a weaving establishment at home (4.59). These allegations imply that the city was (or became under Verres) home to many artisans of luxury goods.

In his descriptions of Verres's activities, Cicero reveals valuable details about the city's public institutions and spaces. Indeed, Syracuse is the only Sicilian city whose topography Cicero describes in detail, dividing the city into four districts (4.118–119): the island of Ortygia, the center of Roman administration and the traditional religious heart of the city; Acradina and Tyche, the mainland residential and public areas;[100] and Neapolis, the theater and temple district. His descriptions of Verres's abuses hint at the vivacity of the town's civic and religious life as well as the continuity of its ancient cults. Demeter/Ceres and Kore/Persephone remained an integral part of the city's religious life, with a sanctuary of the two goddesses located in Neapolis (4.119) and an annual festival still celebrated outside the city, at the site of the legendary rape of Persephone (4.106–107). The temples of Artemis/Diana and Athena/Minerva that Cicero cites among the main landmarks of Ortygia (4.118) have been identified with some certainty, while the locations of those of Dionysus/Liber and Asclepius (4.127–128) remain unknown. Though he does not mention the archaic Apollonion on Ortygia, Cicero includes Apollo among the main deities venerated in the city, with a colossal statue of the god on display in the highest part of Neapolis (Temenites: 4.119) and another (Paean: 4.127) in the temple of Asclepius. Zeus remained the main civic deity, with his hereditary priesthood being the most prestigious position in the city (2.126, 4.127). Hieron's Olympeion in Acradina, the main urban temple of Zeus, was probably the location of the statue of Zeus Urios allegedly stolen by Verres (4.119, 128). Cicero also alludes to the religious syncretism that came from Syracuse's links to the Eastern Mediterranean. He mentions a Temple of Serapis that must have had considerable prestige and visibility, since Verres set up a statue of himself near its entrance (2.160).

Cicero's description of Verres's thefts from the temples and public buildings of Syracuse (especially 4.122–132) points to their continued wealth, stature, and relevance, in spite of the plunder by Marcellus and presumably other Roman magistrates. In addition to describing the numerous honorific statues and artworks housed in the *bouleuterion* and *prytaneion*, Cicero makes clear that the city's government remained active, especially in opposing the abuses of Verres and courting the support of Cicero during his visit to Sicily, prompting Verres to attempt to dissolve the city council (4.136–149). Finally, two of Cicero's anecdotes speak to the continued prominence of Syracuse on routes connecting Rome to the Eastern Mediterranean. First, he describes Verres's harassment of Antiochus, a son of the Seleucid king Antiochus X, who stopped in Syracuse on his way home to Syria from a political mission in Rome (4.61–68).[101] Cicero also complains that tour guides (mystagogues) have nothing to show visitors because of Verres's thefts from the sacred buildings of Syracuse (4.132). He indicates at various points that his audience is familiar with sites in Syracuse, such as the engraved doors of the Temple of Athena/Minerva (4.124), so these tourists would have included wealthy Romans visiting from Italy.

Besides the account of Cicero, our knowledge of Syracuse in the late Republic largely derives from epigraphy and from other Roman literature. The appointment of prominent Romans to the quaestorship (such as P. Clodius in

61 BC) and governorship (such as Cato the Younger at the start of the Caesarian civil war) reflects both the attractiveness of Syracuse as a posting and the strategic importance of Sicily as one of the main suppliers of grain to Rome and as a bridge to Africa. Greek decrees of *proxenia* issued by the *synodos* of the *technitai* of Aphrodite Hilara to the Caesarian proconsul M. Acilius Caninus and to a certain Atilius Sarranus Sopater (early first century BC) indicate that community groups remained eager to foster patronage relations with magistrates and other prominent Romans based in Syracuse.[102]

Syracuse became a Roman colony, *Syracusae Colonia Augusta*, in 21 BC (cf. *CIL* 10.7131–7132). Strabo (*Geog.* 6.2.4) implies that the city had suffered considerable demographic and physical contraction under Sextus Pompey, prompting Augustus's restoration of the city, though there is little archaeological evidence for such a crisis in the urban fabric. Perhaps because of Syracuse's long-standing (and continuing) role in Roman provincial administration, the foundation of the Augustan colony did not bring about the dramatic linguistic shift from Greek to Latin seen in the epigraphy of other colonies. Nonetheless, with the transition to the Principate, Latin became the predominant language of monumental public inscriptions, with the use of Greek largely confined to religious and spectacular contexts. However, there is at least one instance of bilingual communication between the city and the imperial center. As part of his efforts to restore Syracuse, Augustus sponsored construction of a bridge between Acradina and Ortygia, accompanied by statuary and a Greek dedicatory inscription (*SEG* 38.967); in roughly the same period, the city honored him with a statue with a Latin dedication (*AE* 1989.342b).[103] Although epigraphic evidence for the government of the *colonia* is lacking, Roman citizens are visible in early imperial religious and cultural life—for example, as cult officials of the *dea Syria* in a lost inscription (*IG* 14.9), though it is unclear if these are colonists or enfranchised members of the Greek local elite.

Strabo describes considerable changes to the urban fabric in the transition from Republic to Principate, including a reduction of the occupied area (*Geog.* 6.2.4), but few monuments or alterations to the urban plan securely date to the Augustan period. If Ortygia remained unoccupied by the Syracusan citizenry and served exclusively as the center of Roman administration, the main residential and public areas would have remained in Neapolis and Acradina (though perhaps now in a more restricted area).[104] Indeed, it is exclusively these mainland districts that have furnished scattered evidence of settlement and monumentalization in the early imperial period. Excavations in Acradina have revealed a series of new streets carefully paved in limestone blocks that appear to date to the Augustan period.[105]

The monumental complex of Neapolis also underwent changes in the Augustan period that were perhaps linked to the desire of the new colony's government (or the wish of the *princeps* himself) to make a firm break with the city's autonomous past and foster loyalty to the new ruling regime in Rome. The theater and altar of Hieron were the most conspicuous legacies of this not-so-distant era of nominal independence. The altar underwent significant alterations in the early imperial period. The plaza on the western side of the altar was enclosed by a 200-meter portico, the longest such structure found in Sicily. The paved plaza itself, which had probably held the crowds and sacrificial animals for the rituals performed at the altar, seems to have been transformed into a garden with an ornamental basin or pool at its center and trees planted in neat rows throughout the open area.[106] The new square resembled the *palaestrae* of Pompeii and Herculaneum, which also took shape in the Augustan period (located near the amphitheater in the case of Pompeii).[107] The transformations obscured the altar as a monument in its own right, reducing its visibility, eliminating its sacrificial function, and redefining it as merely the back wall of an enclosed garden. Along with the construction of the amphitheater (which blocked access from the east), the changes to the altar redefined the Hieronian monumental complex of Neapolis as a center of Roman-style leisure and spectacle rather than as a true civic center where the religious and political rituals of *polis* life were performed.[108]

The first phase of the amphitheater just east of the altar of Hieron may also date to the Augustan period, though the chronology is controversial (see figure 5.7).[109] The amphitheater was medium-sized, accommodating around 20,000 spectators.[110] Mostly built into bedrock, it was oriented to the street grid of Acradina. A Roman street on its eastern side, surmounted by an honorific arch possibly set up in commemoration of Augustus's visit in 21 BC, led to a residential quarter.[111] The amphitheater, though built in isolation, stood at the head of the street grid of Acradina and served as the new focal point of the monumental complex of Neapolis. It drew attention away from the Hieronian structures, with the altar of Hieron (now an enclosed garden) and the theater spatially peripheral and subordinate to it.

The periodic visits of emperors, beginning with Augustus in 22–21 BC on his way to the eastern provinces (Cassius Dio 54.7),[112] reflect Syracuse's continued position at the top of the urban hierarchy of Sicily. It remained the center of Roman administration and an active port. The city's public and residential areas also continued to be used and embellished in the high and late Empire. Apart from the amphitheater, the most conspicuous (and enigmatic) imperial-era structure is the so-called Roman gymnasium in the southwestern sector of Acradina, near the ancient city walls. A four-sided portico ad-

FIGURE 5.7.
Syracuse: amphitheater (author photo).

joined by an Italic podium temple and a small theater or odeum, this structure is better characterized as a small temple-theater complex. The portico is the earliest structure, dating to the second or first century BC, and may originally have enclosed a small temple/*heroon* or funerary monument. The temple and theater were constructed over the western side of the portico, probably after the reign of Tiberius, turning it into a *porticus post scaenam*.[113] A well and perhaps an altar stood in front of the temple. The theater/odeum could seat 100–200 people and may have been roofed.[114] The complex underwent further renovations around the second century AD, when it was adorned with imported marble and granite columns and architectural elements.[115] The deity worshipped in the complex is thought to be an eastern import: Isis/Serapis, Cybele, or Atargatis/*dea Syria*.[116]

The presence of the theater/odeum made the complex an attractive space for public commemoration. White marble portrait statues of a Flavian/Trajanic-era woman and a late Hadrianic togate magistrate with a document box, both now in the Orsi Museum (inv. nos. 697–698), were among those found in nineteenth-century excavations in the area. The complex is unique in Sicily; the closest comparandum is perhaps the odeum built onto the back of a Hellenistic temple in Tauromenium (discussed in chapter 4). It has a few parallels elsewhere in the Roman world (theaters associated with temples and porticoes of roughly the same date can be found, for example, at Ostia) but stands out for its small size and for the asymmetrical spatial relationship among the portico, theater, and temple. Like the "basilica" of Tyndaris and the odeum and "naumachia" of Tauromenium, the Syracuse "Roman gymnasium" is an example of the eccentric architectural forms that arose in Sicilian cities from the modification of existing structures within the confines of an already highly developed urban landscape in order to create new, more Roman (or imperial) monuments.

The main public area of Syracuse in the imperial period appears to have been the so-called Foro Siracusano, near the Great Harbor and in the heart of Acradina, though few traces remain of its structures or layout. Two Julio-Claudian imperial portraits now in the Orsi Museum were found in this area, though the visible remains, a small stretch of white limestone pavement and a portico in the northwest corner, date roughly to the second century AD.[117] Another probable public area is the so-called triangular forum to the northwest,[118] sections of which were excavated in the 1960s. This area had public buildings (including a portico) and residences by the early first century AD, as indicated by finds of a monumental marble base with a Latin inscription, marble columns and architectural elements, traces of a *nymphaeum* or fountain complex, and a *domus* with mosaic floors.[119] Though little is known about the appearance of either supposed forum, Syracuse's public areas were clearly objects of civic pride: fine portrait sculpture and architectural elements, many crafted from valuable imported granites and marbles, have been found throughout the city.[120]

Further modifications to the urban fabric in the high and late Empire consisted mainly of improvements to infrastructure and alterations or renovations to existing monuments: updates to bring older structures into line with new architectural styles, building materials, and tastes. The Augustan street excavated in Piazza della Vittoria was repaved in the second or third century.[121] The monuments in Neapolis also continued to be used and renovated: a monumental stage building was added to the theater around the late first century, and the orchestra was adapted around the fourth century to host the water spectacles gaining popularity across the empire. A Latin inscription set up by the *consularis* Neratius Palmatus (*CIL* 10.7124) may relate to this latter transformation. The amphitheater also underwent at least one additional construction phase (including an expansion around the second half of the first century AD) and renovations (including the addition of a marble parapet) in the second or early third century.[122]

Syracuse possesses the most extensive corpus of imperial and late Roman inscriptions of any Sicilian city. We are particularly well informed about the religious and cultural life of the city as well as the ethnic composition and economic status of the nonelite, thanks to the hundreds of epitaphs found in imperial and late antique cemeteries and catacombs. To turn first to religious life, there is evidence for the continued veneration of the traditional civic pantheon. An Augustan-era altar with a Greek dedication by a certain Markianos to Zeus and Tyche (*SEG* 44.787) was found in northern Acradina. In addition, C. Marcius Zoilus made a Latin dedication to Minerva on a marble candelabrum (*CIL* 10.7120).

Even more evidence indicates the continuity of cults of Eastern Mediterranean origin. A now-lost inscription recorded the priestly hierarchy of the cult of *dea Syria*, and some scholars have linked the Roman gymnasium complex to that goddess. A small white marble statue of Attis now in the Orsi Museum (inv. no. 45921) found in a house in Acradina provides evidence of the private veneration of Cybele, whose cult had been part of the public religious life of the city since the early fourth century BC. Syracuse is the only city in Sicily where a Mithraeum has been found, though these excavations in Acradina were not published.[123] The Orsi Museum houses Mithraic cult statuary found elsewhere in the city, including a second- or third-century marble relief of Mithras slaying the bull (inv. no. 8478) and a third-century marble image of the god that once formed part of a *taurocthonia* (inv. no. 50712).

There is also plentiful evidence for the cult of Isis and Serapis. The public cult is referenced in two early imperial Latin inscriptions. One found near the San Giovanni catacombs commemorates the restoration of a sacred building by a *flamen* of Serapis, Papinius Flavianus (*AE* 1951.174). The other is an epitaph of a *scoparius* of Isis, C. Julius (*CIL* 10.7129). In addition, a fragmentary early imperial marble statue of a female holding a cornucopia and bearing a *situla* (either Isis herself or a priestess of the cult) was found in Acradina (Orsi Museum inv. no. 713). Many objects relate to the private, personal veneration of these Egyptian cults. These include a small ceramic head of Isis and a bust identified as Serapis found in a *hypogeum* in Acradina and dated to the second or third century as well as numerous third- and fourth-century lamps that depict the deities.[124]

The painted, etched, and inscribed grave markers from Roman-era burial areas shed considerable light on the economically, socially, and ethnically diverse population that lived and died in Syracuse. The locations of these burial grounds are themselves significant because they indicate the extent of the imperial and late antique city. The largest above- and below-ground cemeteries fan out around the northern edges of Acradina and Neapolis. They occupy peripheral areas that had been used for earlier burials, industrial establishments, or suburban agricultural production. Areas of exposed and malleable limestone bedrock, some of which had been quarries in earlier centuries or were excavated to serve as water tanks and conduits, were especially well suited, since tombs could be cut directly into the rock.[125] The main burial areas were in use almost continuously from the second century until the sixth century AD, expanding outward from the urban center to the east beginning in the mid-fourth century, indicating that Acradina did not contract in the middle and late imperial periods.[126]

Most of the funerary inscriptions are relatively terse, making it difficult to date them precisely. However, they can be used to draw some general conclusions about the consistency of the population of Roman Syracuse. First, both Greek and Latin were used in funerary epigraphy in all periods, though Greek is far more common. As in Catina and other Sicilian cities where Latin was used in monumental public inscriptions, it was perceived as a high-status language in Syracuse and was employed especially by individuals who wished to advertise their social position. One potential indication of nonelite Syracusans' adoption of Latin is its use in the epitaphs of individuals with "Greek" or "mixed" *nomina*: for example, by the mother Thyche for her young sons Euangelus and Thychicus (*CIL* 10.7150).

Latin funerary inscriptions also commemorate slaves and freedmen, some of whom were owned by (or were formerly in the service of) Roman officials stationed in Syracuse. For example, Eros, a young *servus cubicularius* of the proconsul Junius Julianus, was buried with the freedman Junius Alcibiades in the late second or early third century (*CIL* 10.7127). The use of Latin in their epitaphs may reflect their Roman owners/patrons or perhaps their own non-Sicilian origins. Thanks to the continued presence of Roman administrators and other "foreigners" from across the Mediterranean, the use of Latin in funerary epigraphy persisted in late antiquity, as in the *titulus* of Atinodorus, the young son of the *primicerius* Mucianus, who may have been stationed in Spain at the time of his child's death.[127]

In the much larger corpus of Greek epitaphs we can also trace the presence of Roman, Greek, and mixed names in the imperial period and late antiquity. For example, K. Kornifikios Stephanephoros (Q. Cornificius Stefaneforus), a Roman citizen (perhaps from the Caracallan grant) of Greek origins, was linked to the Cornificii, a prominent *gens* of the third century (*AE* 1975.455). Nor was the use of Greek confined to the epitaphs of low-status individuals: costly sarcophagi and tombs within monumental *hypogea* also bear Greek *tituli*.[128] The Greek epitaphs attest to a wide range of occupations and social statuses. The professionals and businesspeople buried in Syracuse include doctors (*iatroi*), a veterinarian, ship owners (*naukleroi*: *SEG* 4.21, 15.590), former soldiers, and intellectuals (including a professional philosopher and a female poet).[129] There are also artisans, such as a dyer of purple cloth and a weaver. These occupations, as in the Verrine Oration of several centuries earlier, were probably linked to the city's role as a major port and as a center of wealth and culture in eastern Sicily.[130] Additionally, Greek funerary inscriptions commemorate slaves and freedpersons (e.g., *IG* 14.19).

Mariarita Sgarlata has summarized the epigraphic evidence for the burial of "foreigners" in the three large, mostly Christian catacombs of late antique Syracuse (Vigna Cassia, Santa Lucia, and San Giovanni). Of the 680 individuals attested on *tituli* studied by Sgarlata, 23 (mostly buried in Vigna Cassia and San Giovanni) indicate non-Sicilian origins; 6 of these were Syrian, including a *naukleros Leptimagnensios* buried in Vigna Cassia in the fourth or fifth century (*SEG* 4.21).[131] The catacombs also held several individuals from Lycia (including another *naukleros*: *SEG* 15.590) and elsewhere in Asia Minor.[132] Some of those buried in the catacombs were not far from their places of origin, including Rome, Catina, and the Sicilian interior.[133] There is also evidence of individuals of African origin: most notably, the *hypogeum* that contained the second or third-century tomb of Kloutoria, daughter of M. Kloutorios, of Ptolemais in Cyrene.[134]

The Roman-era epigraphic record of Syracuse is most similar to that of Catina. Both epigraphic corpora are extensive compared to other Sicilian cities and give the impression of socially, economically, and ethnically diverse—and relatively literate—urban populations. The mixture of Latin and Greek in both cities, especially in the funerary realm, reflects the persistence of Greek as the language of everyday life (and probably as the first language of the majority of the population) and the perceived prestige of Latin derived from its dominance in public contexts.

In addition to burials, the edges of the ancient urban center hosted agricultural and industrial establishments. These zones are farthest from the medieval/baroque city center of Ortygia and the harbors of Acradina, so they did not see widespread residential development until after World War II, enabling more extensive excavation than closer-in neighborhoods. Thus we are considerably better informed about their ancient settlement history. The urban status of these areas fluctuated during antiquity, with dense residential occupation alternating (and sometimes coexisting) with industrial production, scattered suburban agriculture, and use for burials.

Many kiln complexes have been found on the fringes of ancient Acradina, in a "potter's quarter" on the bank of a watercourse rich in clay deposits.[135] Excavations of these complexes have confirmed the large-scale production of finewares and coarsewares in Syracuse from the early Hellenistic period until the late Republic/early Principate. One such complex on the northeastern edge of Acradina was established in an area of archaic tombs. Houses and ceramic workshops, including at least three kilns, wells, and cisterns, were in use from around the second century BC until the first century BC. Some small-scale production followed in the second and third centuries AD before the area was again occupied by tombs in late antiquity.[136] Another industrial complex was excavated on the site of the catacomb of Santa Lucia, on the eastern fringe of the ancient city close to the shoreline. The kiln in this complex was in operation by the late fourth century BC and was most active in the third and second centuries. It was destroyed while still in operation in the first century AD.[137]

These kilns and others excavated nearby (including near the late antique Vigna Cassia cemetery) produced a range of vessels during their long histories of production, including Gnathian ware, Campana A and B, and thin-walled wares. Most significantly, the excavation of these complexes has shown that Syracuse and its hinterland were major production centers of Campana C, a black-glaze fineware type that was produced and distributed widely in the Mediterranean basin in the Hellenistic and Roman Republican periods.[138] Mineralogical analysis of vessels from Syracuse and from the kiln complexes at Morgantina (see chapter 1) has affirmed that most were made from eastern Sicilian clays, further confirming that the region was a major producer of this ware. It remains difficult, however, to distinguish the products of the Morgantina kilns from those of Syracuse and its hinterland.[139]

Campana C vessels have been found throughout Syracuse in a variety of archaeological contexts, including occupation strata, cisterns and other fills, and as grave goods. They have also been found in urban and rural sites across eastern and southeastern Sicily, including at Camarina. Examples have also been found in northeastern Sicily, including at Tyndaris, and along the central southern coast (e.g., at Heraclea Minoa and Agrigentum). Campana C is rarer in western Sicily, with distribution extending only as far west as the coastal centers of Halaesa and Soluntum, perhaps owing to the difficulty of overland transport across the island and the different orientation of western Sicilian maritime networks.[140]

The distribution of Campana C also reflects Syracuse's position in Mediterranean trade. Though the volume and extent of Sicilian exports are unclear, it appears that Campana C from eastern Sicily reached Italy (mainly the southern Tyrrhenian coastline), coastal regions of Gaul, North Africa, and Spain, and interior centers located on navigable rivers. The Sicilian wares also spawned local imitations, especially in Spain.[141] The beginning of production of Campana C in Sicily follows the extension of the Roman *provincia* across the island after the Second Punic War and may have been partly instigated by the fall of Carthage and the entry of Italian finewares onto the island's markets.[142] The ware's origin in Syracuse is not coincidental: the city was already the artistic and cultural capital of the island, with a substantial population of artisans who were aware of cultural, artistic, and technological developments in the Eastern Mediterranean and Italy. The widespread production and capillary distribution of Campana C from centers like Syracuse and Morgantina was facilitated by the peaceful conditions of the Roman *provincia* and by the overland transportation networks and infrastructure that developed to enable collection of the grain tithe. Its distribution outside Sicily was possible because of the expansion of Rome's empire across the Mediterranean and with it Greco-Roman cultural tastes and social practices, such as wine consumption, that required the use of high-quality tablewares and service vessels. Syracuse was also advantageously positioned as a major export center for grain and other goods, including artworks and luxury items, as the Verrine Orations make clear.

This distribution across the central and western Mediterranean ended around the early Augustan period. The kilns in Syracuse ceased production of Campana C at the same time or slightly later, just as the kilns of Morgantina went out of production around 35 BC.[143] The end of production and export of Campana C can be linked to the growing dominance of Italian sigillata across the Mediterranean. Italian finewares were exported to provincial markets along with wine and other commodities from the mid-first century BC until the late first century AD, when they were themselves supplanted by African finewares. The novelty of the shiny red glaze of Italian sigillata, which was produced in massive quantities in the industrial workshops of central and northern Italy (most notably at Arezzo), along with its consistently high quality and low price, helped it gain widespread popularity in the provinces and crowd out older, less sophisticated local products like Campana C.

Even after the end of large-scale ceramic production and export, Syracuse remained an important port center, attracting goods and people (and their ideas, beliefs, and tastes) from across the Roman Mediterranean. In addition to the large quantities of imported marble and granite used in public buildings, shipwrecks with cargoes of marble found in the waters off Syracuse and along the southeastern coast are evidence of the region's integration into the maritime trade in fine stones. These include two of the ancient wrecks found in the bay northeast of Marzamemi, 60 km down the coast from Syracuse.[144] One of these wrecks (Marzamemi A), from the first half of the third century, had as its main cargo at least fifteen blocks of grayish-white Attic marble as well as Greek amphorae and smaller quantities of African amphorae, leading its excavator to hypothesize that it was journeying from the Aegean to Carthage, following a deep-water course across the central Mediterranean.[145]

Many of the other Roman-era ships discovered in the waters off Syracuse and southward to Capo Passero carried mixed cargoes of diverse origins, pointing to the multiplicity and complexity of the southeastern coast's maritime links, particularly in the second through fourth centuries. Three wrecks just south of Syracuse, Plemmirio A and B and Terrauzza, contained cargoes, respectively, of bronze tablewares, tools, and fixtures from the fourth or fifth century; African olive amphorae and iron bars from ca. AD 200; and Greek amphorae from the late second or early third century.[146] Other wrecks with mixed cargoes farther down the coast may reflect *cabotage* between the ports of the main export regions of the central and western Mediterranean.[147]

Additional evidence for Syracuse's status as a major port comes from the journey of Paul to Rome narrated in Acts 27–28:16. The apostle embarked in a Lycian ship at Caesarea Maritima, stopping at Sidon, then following the Syrian coast and turning west, skirting the coast of Cilicia, Pamphylia, and Lycia (Acts 27:2–5). He and the other passengers transshipped in Lycia to an Alexandrian vessel bound for Italy that continued west in rough waters along the southern coast of Crete, making an additional stop (27:5–8). The ship's journey toward the southern coast of Sicily was interrupted by a severe storm, pushing it south and causing it to wreck at Malta (27:13–28:10). After a three-month stay in Malta, Paul and the others set sail in another Alexandrian ship, landing at Syracuse and staying there for three days before proceeding to Rhegium then Puteoli (28:11–13). This account confirms that Syracuse was one of the first major landing points on the most difficult part of the route between the Eastern Mediterranean and Rome: the long open stretch of sea between the western coast of Crete and the eastern coast of Sicily. Along with Malta, the city was also one of the first refuges on the shorter open-sea route from Leptis Magna in Tripolitania favored by ships bound from Egypt to Italy.[148] A more local perspective on Syracuse's port role is offered by the graffiti on wall plaster excavated in Via G. Natale in Acradina. These etchings, from the third or fourth century, include names, human figures, different types of ships and boats, and, rather charmingly, curved lines to indicate waves. The figures appear to form a scene of embarkation, perhaps of the sort that the artist(s) witnessed regularly in the port of Syracuse.[149]

Less is known of settlement and production in the hinterland of Syracuse, especially in the Roman imperial period. We have evidence from a few excavated farms, villas, and rural settlements in southeastern Sicily, most of which (in the absence of another large urban center in the region) must have been in Roman Syracuse's territory.[150] One of the most extensively excavated rural settlements is in Contrada Aguglia, in a hilly area 40 kilometers southwest of Syracuse and midway between ancient Akrai (Roman Acrae, modern Palazzolo Acreide) and Netum (near modern Noto), medium-sized urban centers that were occupied at least until the high imperial period.[151] Excavations in the 1960s uncovered a farmhouse and cistern surrounded by a dense surface spread of ceramics and building materials, suggesting that the complex originally consisted of several edifices, perhaps forming a rural hamlet.[152] Finds from the complex included cylindrical ceramic vessels for measuring dry goods, two of which were stamped with the Greek *akribazontos* (of the one who measures accurately), indicating that a magistrate, perhaps in Akrai or Netum, had approved their proportions. Similar measuring cups have been found at Morgantina, a major grain storage and marketing center of the south/central interior. This led the excavators of Aguglia to hypothesize that the farm mainly cultivated grain and that the measures, along with the lead weights found in excavations, were used in the collection of the Hieronian and/or Roman grain tithe.[153]

Along with the ceramics found in the farm building itself, the approximately 170 complete or fragmentary vessels found in the fill of the nearby cistern have augmented knowledge of the forms of Campana C and other local ceramics. The excavators hypothesized that the farm, though apparently on a relatively small and isolated property and lacking extensive and lavishly decorated residential quarters, achieved a certain prosperity (as evidenced by its material cultural assemblage) and was consistently occupied between the second half of the third century and the late first century BC.[154]

We lack substantial evidence for settlement in the early and high Empire in the hinterland of Syracuse, and the evidence for late antiquity is only slightly better. A large, luxurious villa on the Tellaro River 40 km south-southwest of Syracuse and near the site of ancient Helorus has been the subject of extensive excavations that have not yet been published. This villa, whose visible form dates to the mid-fourth century AD, is notable for the high-quality polychrome mosaics in its reception and dining rooms,[155] including a depiction of the ransom of Hector. It is thought to be the center of a *latifundium* on the basis of its splendor and its felicitous (though rather isolated) location in an area of rich agricultural land, overlooking a watercourse and well positioned to receive southerly winds. It perhaps operated in association with the small late Roman/Byzantine settlement at Cittadella, closer to the coast and approximately 7 km south of Helorus, which would have functioned as a marketing center and road station for estates in the vicinity. Limited survey southwest of Syracuse around modern Canicattini Bagni has pointed to growth in the rural population in the second and third centuries, with an increase in the number of visible farm sites, villas, and other rural structures.[156]

In contrast, the late antique history and archaeology of Syracuse itself is relatively well documented. Although ancient sources claim that marauding Franks devastated the city in 278, this event left little discernible impact in the archaeological record. But there is considerable evidence for the maintenance and improvement of the city's physical fabric in the late Roman and Byzantine periods. Syracuse also remained an administrative and economic center and the home of a large and diverse population. The theater was renovated with financial assistance from Neratius Palmatus *v.c. cons.* (*CIL* 10.7124), a member of the imperial court probably stationed in Syracuse.[157] Additional evidence for the activity of high-ranking officials in the last centuries of Roman rule includes a bilingual dedication (probably of a statue) by the *populus Syracusanus* to Perpennas Romanus *v.c. cons.* (*IG* 14.14 = *CIL* 10.7125) and a dedication by another official, Fl. Valerius Busiris, that refers to the *praetorium* (*AE* 1946.207). Syracuse is included among Ausonius's major cities of the empire along with Catina and is mentioned in the *Expositio totius mundi* (65).

The late antique history of Syracuse is dominated by the spread of Christianity into the physical fabric of the city and among the population. Given the city's long history of receptivity to foreign religious influences, it is hardly surprising that Christianity was introduced at a relatively early date, almost certainly from the Eastern Mediterranean. Although it is unlikely that the Christian community had its origins in Paul's brief visit, it was firmly in place and relatively substantial by the mid-third century, when the oldest Christian burial area (Santa Maria di Gesù) was established. The city had achieved metropolitan ecclesiastical rank by the time of Constantine.[158]

The most conspicuous evidence of the early Christian community is the presence of underground communal burial areas (catacombs) used most intensively in the third through fifth centuries. These catacombs—first Santa Lucia, Santa Maria di Gesù, and Vigna Cassia, followed by San Giovanni and Villa Maria—were located in the same extraurban zone as pagan burial areas, on the fringes of Acradina and Neapolis, thus respecting the classical urban center. They have been described as second only to the catacombs of Rome in size and significance; the San Giovanni complex, the second-largest in the city, contains approximately ten thousand tombs.[159]

The size and careful layout of these catacombs, along with the *tituli* from the graves themselves, speak to the consistency, cohesion, and vitality of the Christian community and also to its ethnic and economic diversity. The community was increasingly stratified in the post-Constantinian era, however, as members of the imperial elite converted to Christianity. More prestigious burial areas in the newer catacombs of the fourth century and later were established in expansive underground chambers that contained large, elaborate graves. These prestigious areas held members of the Roman imperial elite like Adelphia, wife of the *comes* Valerius, who was entombed in a fine sarcophagus of Luni marble with scenes from the Old and New Testaments. This sarcophagus, one of the most notable examples of late Roman art in Sicily (now on display in the Orsi Museum), was originally set in a monumental *arcosolium* adorned with an architrave and columns.

The catacombs also reveal the development of the ecclesiastical hierarchy and the formation of a communal identity among the Christians of Syracuse. Clergy, some of whom originated outside Sicily,[160] and other venerable members of the community were given prestigious burial places. These include two elderly women, Photis and Philoumene, who may have belonged to a religious order. As in Catina, the veneration of martyrs took hold relatively early. The cult of Saint Lucy, a young girl martyred during the Diocletianic persecutions, had been established by the early fifth century.[161] She remains the patron saint of the modern city.

Shipwrecks in the harbor of Syracuse and in waters off the southeastern coast attest to continued integration into major commercial routes, and especially a strong maritime connection to the Byzantine Empire. Two of the ancient wrecks found in the Great Harbor (Siracusa A and B) carried cargoes of Byzantine-era amphorae (fifth-seventh centuries AD).[162] The Marzamemi B wreck further down the coast held a cargo of architectural elements carved from *verde antico* and white Proconnesian marble, which are thought to have been intended for a small Justinianic basilica, perhaps in Cyrenaica.[163]

As a result of its continued economic and political importance, the ancient urban center had a long life, with occupation at an urban level extending well into the Byzantine era. The city played a role in Belisarius's conquest of Sicily and hosted such notables as the historian Procopius (AD 533) and the emperor Constans II, who established a mint and briefly (AD 663–668) made Syracuse the de facto capital of the Byzantine Empire.[164] The city's political prominence, and perhaps even the presence of the emperor himself, may have been the reason for the continued maintenance and improvement of urban infrastructure even in the late seventh century AD, including renovations to the amphitheater and the repaving of the Roman-era street in Piazza della Vittoria.[165]

While the occupied area of the city appears to have contracted in the Byzantine era, many neighborhoods—especially those closest to Ortygia—continued to be inhabited and show signs of destruction only during the Arab invasions of the late ninth century. The monumental complex of Neapolis was partly abandoned by the mid-fifth century, when a necropolis was established on and around the upper terrace of the theater.[166] An ancient neighborhood on what would have been the southeastern edge of Acradina also shows signs of reduced occupation. Although the neighborhood's main paved Roman street was maintained until the sixth century, the seventh- and eighth-century street surfaces were unpaved. The drainage system was no longer maintained, perhaps reflecting reduced traffic and the street's obsolescence as a primary urban thoroughfare. The width of the roadway was also gradually reduced as walls of new, irregularly aligned structures were placed onto the Roman-era roadbed.[167]

The visibility of Christianity in the urban landscape also increased in the Byzantine era with the construction of churches in the city center. Burials shifted to areas close to these churches even within the intramural area, and the extraurban necropolises established by the early Christian community declined in use.[168] Many of the city's first churches, built in the late fourth century by the bishop Germanus, underwent substantial renovation and expansion in the sixth century. The most significant Christian complexes were located on or near the sites of the catacombs, such as the church of San Pietro *extra moenia*, mentioned in a letter of Gregory the Great from 598. In the sixth century the grand San Giovanni basilica was built on the site of the namesake catacombs, over the crypt dedicated to the first bishop of Syracuse, Marcianus.[169] Some of these new Christian buildings, such as the sixth-century church of San Martino, utilized fine stones spoliated from ancient structures, a practice that continued in the medieval and baroque periods.[170] The new Christian religious landscape also incorporated pagan temples in the heart of the city, such as the archaic Athenaion and Apollonion on Ortygia, which were converted into churches beginning in the sixth century.[171]

To summarize, the development of Syracuse in the Roman period can be fruitfully compared and contrasted with the development of Catina and Morgantina, which had been within Syracuse's sphere of influence for much of their pre-Roman histories. The end of Syracusan political hegemony in eastern Sicily after the Second Punic War had profound effects on the economy, government, and society of Morgantina that are visible in the urban fabric in the second century BC. Like Syracuse itself, Morgantina was transformed under the Roman *provincia* into a major regional production and marketing center, a role reflected especially in the growth of the pottery industry. Unlike in Syracuse, however, where this industry developed on the urban fringes, ceramic workshops took over structures in the heart of Morgantina, including residences and monumental stoas in the agora that had previously been used for grain storage and public administration.

The pottery industry in Morgantina declined along with activity throughout the city center after the mid-first century BC as a result of a series of destructions as well as shifts in inland commercial routes. The economy of Syracuse, by contrast, was diverse enough to survive the end of the pottery industry. The city remained a vital civic center and the home of a large, diverse population throughout the imperial period. The growth of ceramic production in second- and first-century BC Syracuse had been opportunistic, taking advantage of the opening of the Mediterranean to expanded commerce under Roman rule, the city's port, and its long-standing economic hegemony in eastern Sicily. The growth of the ceramic industry in Syracuse had a trickle-down effect, fostering the development of secondary regional production and distribution in inland cities like Morgantina. After the decline of this industry, probably as a result of increased competition from imported Italian finewares, Syracuse's port allowed it to remain integrated into prevailing Mediterranean commercial routes. Its status as a *colonia* and Roman administrative center brought the continued attention and beneficence of imperial authorities.

Syracuse shared with its northern neighbor Catina a diverse economy and population in the imperial period. The ancient urban fabric of both cities had a long life, extending beyond the end of Roman rule in Sicily. The similarities between the two cities are attributable to the persistence of a strong local (but now colonial) elite (although the activities of its members are less visible in Syracuse) as well as the continued presence of provincial elites and imperial authorities. Both cities also had vital ports that catered especially to vessels traveling between Italy and North Africa and the Eastern Mediterranean.

The urban fabric of Syracuse underwent several transformations under the Romans and beyond, from *colonia* to early Christian center to Byzantine capital. These transformations allow us to reject the notion of the city's decline beginning in the Augustan period. Though the urban culture of the city became less distinctively Syracusan under the Roman Empire, Syracuse was very much an imperial city, with a full set of monuments, including a theater, amphitheater, baths, and lavishly decorated public areas. It was also one of the most cosmopolitan urban centers on the island, remaining receptive to cultural and religious influences from across the Mediterranean.

CONCLUSION

The cities examined in this chapter and in chapter 4 received varying treatment in Augustus's settlement of Sicily. The immediate effects of such changes as the introduction of colonists and the redistribution of civic land are rarely visible in the archaeological record, however, and the long-term impact of the Augustan settlement in each city is similarly difficult to discern. As with Lilybaeum and Agrigentum, it appears instead that each city's economic diversity, and the engagement of local and regional elites in its public life, was more vital to its long-term vitality than the active intervention of the imperial center (for good or for ill). The next chapter is a broader analysis of urbanism in Sicily under the Roman Empire. It highlights common trends visible in the development of cityscapes across Sicily but also explores regional variations in the pace and extent of urban change on the island, especially in the late Republic and early Principate.

SIX

ROMAN URBANISM IN SICILY

Unlike the cities examined in chapter 1, all of the cities discussed in the preceding three chapters acquired elements of the monumental set found in urban centers across the Roman Empire. Some of these were new buildings: Catina and Syracuse each had large amphitheaters, a novel building type in Sicily, by the second century AD. These amphitheaters were located on the fringes of the urban center as was customary. Catina also had a circus on its outskirts and a new theater-odeum complex in its center. Lilybaeum, Catina, and Tauromenium were each equipped with at least one aqueduct, which took monumental form in the case of Catina and probably Lilybaeum. The water supplied from aqueducts was used in new public bath complexes, fountains, and *nymphaea* attested at Lilybaeum, Centuripae, Tyndaris, Tauromenium, Catina, and Syracuse.

Most of the known public building work in Sicilian cities in the imperial period, however, involved the modification and refunctionalization of existing monuments and public spaces. This is not surprising, because the high level of urbanization of the island and the antiquity of its cities meant that many urban centers already possessed extensive and elaborate monumental public spaces, and is not necessarily a symptom of urban decline, neglect, or poverty. Most conspicuously, the Hellenistic theaters of Tyndaris, Tauromenium, and Syracuse were renovated, often multiple times, to bring them up to date with architectural and cultural tastes. For example, elaborate stage buildings were added, and the orchestras were modified to accommodate gladiatorial games, *venationes*, and water displays. Such adaptation of existing structures (in place of the construction of separate amphitheaters) is paralleled in Greece, where older theaters were modified over the course of the Empire—for example, by adding removable gratings (in Argos) or removing lower rows of seats (in Corinth)—to facilitate gladiatorial combats.[1]

In Sicily there is also a trend beginning in the Augustan period and continuing into the second century toward the "Romanization" or "forumization" of older public spaces, though it is often difficult to identify forums and agoras with certainty, on the basis of the existing evidence. This trend is broadly paralleled in Greece, where the agoras of cities both large and small were expanded and embellished in the imperial period. New cult buildings were erected, such as the temples of Augustus and Caesar in the agora of Sparta, and new commercial spaces were created, such as the Roman Agora of Athens.[2]

As discussed in chapter 2, this process of forumization is visible in Sicily in the early Principate in the renovation of the second-century BC stoa at Halaesa to include space for the veneration of the emperor and in the construction of a triangular forum in Segesta, adjoining the old agora and using some of its structures. The early imperial phases of the likely forum of Centuripae are obscure, but it is clear that in the high Empire it became a monumental complex devoted in part to the veneration of the emperor. A cult building and other structures opened onto a paved space containing monumental Latin public inscriptions and statues of emperors and civic benefactors.

Much of the so-called upper agora of Agrigentum is obscured by post-antique structures, so our understanding of the impact of the imperial-era changes traced in recent excavations (the completion of a new temple precinct) on the city's existing public areas and structures remains incomplete. The agora/forum of Tauromenium also cannot be identified with certainty, but it is clear that several older public buildings underwent dramatic modifications in the early and middle imperial periods. The Hellenistic public building (*bouleuterion*?) in the area traditionally identified as the ancient agora was obliterated by a Roman bath building after a brief possible use as a *curia*. An odeum was built onto a long-disused Hellenistic temple nearby. In another public area a Hellenistic stoa was transformed into the monumental façade of a reservoir (the "naumachia").

It is difficult to attribute any of these developments to a deliberate monumental program, let alone to assign them to the initiative of any one individual. But we can detect a clear process of urban embellishment and beautification beginning in the Augustan period and continuing over several centuries. In Syracuse, Tauromenium, probably Lilybaeum, and less certainly Tyndaris this program was clearly announced by the construction of monumental arches: markers of civic pride and distinction but also unambiguous monuments of the ruling order of Rome. In Greek cities like Athens, Argos, Mantineia, Maroneia, and Kos the construction of monumental gates at the entrances to agoras and other public spaces similarly completed the architectural reframing of those spaces.[3] The paving of streets in durable, aesthetically pleasing, expensive hard stone—as seen at Lilybaeum, Catina, Tyndaris, and

Syracuse—was in keeping with the Augustan ideology of urban restoration and beautification. It was also a way to make a conspicuous impact on (and mark the prestige of) residential and public areas within older urban plans. Perhaps in Catina, Tyndaris, and Syracuse the paving of streets marked the new political and social regime of the Augustan colony.

The monuments constructed over the course of the imperial period hint at the nature of Sicilian urban life under Rome and at the priorities of the individuals and groups guiding urban development. One trend is the construction of monuments that utilized large quantities of water in conspicuous and elaborate ways, such as aqueducts, fountains, public gardens, *nymphaea*, and bath complexes—monument types also favored by the older cities of Italy, Greece, and especially Asia Minor as a way of "modernizing" their infrastructure.[4] In addition, many Sicilian cities saw the construction of new buildings for spectacle and performance (amphitheaters, odeums, circuses) or the modification of their older Greek theaters for these purposes. In Greece, too, odeums were popular additions to the urban landscape. All three known examples from the Peloponnese—in Argos, Patrae, and Corinth—were constructed close to theaters (as in Catina) and were built or remodeled at some point in the second century AD, likely in connection with the cultural revival of the Second Sophistic.[5]

These trends in Sicily can be interpreted in several ways. They may be symptoms of a de-emphasis on buildings related to public life and civic administration by sponsors (whether civic authorities or individual benefactors)—particularly structures that facilitated the participation of nonelites, such as *ekklesiai*—accompanied by a new taste for buildings devoted specifically to leisure and spectacle. Given that many urban centers already possessed buildings suitable for the public functions of government and administration, such as *bouleuteria* and stoas, the creation of new structures devoted to leisure and spectacle may have been seen as a more conspicuous and effective way of enhancing urban infrastructure. They also may have fulfilled the perceived need to keep up with cultural tastes and with an ever-expanding range of new building types and to proclaim the city's (and its elite's) political and social prestige. Greek cities also managed to maintain and renovate their older infrastructure while enhancing the urban landscape with new building types, such as public baths. Even the small city of Thera saw renovations in the second century AD that included the transformation of an older stoa into a multifunctional building and the construction of a small bath.[6]

The types of structures absent from the monumental landscape of Sicilian cities (at least on the basis of current knowledge) may also be significant. For example, no *macella* like the ones built in second-century BC Morgantina and late Republican/early imperial Segesta have yet been found in the cities examined in chapters 3 and 4. This stands in contrast to the Greek East, Italy, and North Africa, where the construction of market buildings continued into the imperial period.[7] In Greece, in addition to the Roman Agora of Athens and the first-century AD market of Corinth, *makelloi* are attested in Mantineia, Sparta, Andros, and Tegea.[8] In Asia Minor, where purpose-built market complexes had a long history (as seen, for example, in the fourth-century BC North Market of Miletus), market buildings also continued to be constructed in the imperial period.[9] In the towns of Italy, as in Sicily, *macella* first appeared in the second century BC (e.g., at Pompeii and Alba Fucens) but were most popular in the first and second centuries AD.[10] Although *macellum* construction in North Africa peaked under the Severans, the earliest examples (at Leptis Magna and Thugga) date to the Augustan and Julio-Claudian eras.

If the absence of *macella* in the cities of Roman imperial Sicily is not simply the result of our limited knowledge,[11] it may reflect a change in architectural tastes and in the perception of the role of monumental urban space. Most of the cities examined in chapters 3 and 4 possessed extensive fertile agricultural territories. They served as major import and export centers, maintained extensive maritime connections with other regions of the Mediterranean, and housed a substantial nonagricultural population. Therefore, they probably hosted significant markets, even if they did not possess purpose-built market buildings. At least in some of these cities, the activities associated with *macella* (the sale to urban residents of foodstuffs, and especially higher-price, perishable items like meat, fish, fruits, and vegetables) may have occurred in other places, such as *tabernae* located in residential insulae or in the rooms behind porticoes. Indeed, Emanuel Mayer argued that the development of such "*taberna* economies" was one of the major features of the spread of Roman urbanism beginning in the first century BC.[12] In addition, Sicilian urban centers may no longer have served as the primary markets for residents of their rural hinterlands. The sustenance needs of this population were instead met in markets in smaller settlements, such as the *stationes* arising along Roman roads discussed in the next chapter.

No construction of new gymnasia in Sicily in the imperial period has been archaeologically attested. Under the Republic these institutions had played an integral social and political role in many cities, including Centuripae, Tauromenium, Tyndaris, Agrigentum, and Syracuse. Epigraphic and historical attestations of gymnasia in Sicily also cease after the Augustan period, in contrast to cities in the Eastern Mediterranean. There these civic institutions continued to be used and expanded, sometimes taking on new functions (e.g., as law courts and imperial cult spaces).[13] The magistracies associated with gymnasia also persisted in some cities of Magna Graecia. At Velia the gymnasiarchy is attested alongside Roman municipal offices in the first century AD, and at Naples it persisted along with other Greek magistracies until the third century.[14]

Though the gymnasium in Agrigentum continued to be used in the second century, the Augustan-era renovations significantly altered its character, emphasizing the spectacle aspect of the athletic activities that it hosted. The apparent obsolescence of Sicilian gymnasia as centers for the military, athletic, and intellectual training of the citizen body—and especially of the local elite—may reflect the reduced political power and autonomy of urban communities and their traditional ruling classes in the post–civil war period. As gymnasia became obsolete, other types of buildings (such as bathhouses) that did not have the same potentially dangerous association with civic autonomy and military readiness took up their roles as exercise spaces and leisure centers and became objects of elite benefaction. This is seen at Centuripae, where a father and son sponsored a *sphaeristerium* (exercise area) in honor of their appointment as *duoviri*.

In addition, few new cult buildings are known to have been constructed in the imperial period in the cities examined in the previous three chapters. The small number of new religious structures that have been identified tend to be associated with cults outside the traditional Greco-Roman pantheon, such as the long-known but poorly attested Mithraeum in Syracuse and the recently discovered Iseum in Lilybaeum. Most cities show evidence of the imperial cult, though the buildings associated with this cult have not been identified with the possible exception of Centuripae (and Halaesa). On the basis of the limited evidence, it appears that emperor worship in Sicilian cities was grafted onto existing religious structures and spaces and provoked little new construction.[15]

Finally, the more private realms of city life also reflect the changing tastes and priorities of urban residents but also show greater continuities. For example, funerary spaces and structures were largely unaltered from Hellenistic and Republican times: burial spaces remained communal, relatively inconspicuous, and located on the fringes of the urban center, as seen most clearly at Syracuse and Lilybaeum. In Tauromenium, Tyndaris, and Centuripae (and at Halaesa), however, new types of funerary monuments emerged in the imperial period. Employing the Roman technologies of brick and mortar construction, these monumental "house tombs" and mausolea, probably used by single wealthy families and their dependents, were located on the urban periphery but in conspicuous locations (e.g., near the city gate, in the case of the Halaesa columbarium). They proclaimed their owners' awareness of and adherence to burial practices in vogue in Italy and may have belonged to families of Roman or Italian origin.

All of these commonalities in urban development show that all of the cities analyzed in chapters 3 and 4 remained centers of residence for local elites in the early and middle imperial periods, in contrast to the cities examined in chapter 1. This continuous elite presence is most clearly evidenced by the periodic building and renovation of urban residential areas. Changes to existing residential areas in Catina, such as the construction of new houses or the renovation and remodeling of existing ones, may be linked to the imposition of the *colonia*. In Lilybaeum and Agrigentum, in contrast, similar changes at a later date may simply reflect the growing prosperity of the local elite over the course of the Principate. None of the cities show a clear link between the decline of prestigious urban residential areas and the growth of suburban or rural residential villas before late antiquity.

All of the cities examined in chapters 3 and 4—as well as those omitted for lack of substantial or coherent archaeological evidence, including Panormus, Thermae Himeraeae, and Messana—manifested a distinct Romano-Sicilian urbanism. It was characterized by the adoption of a limited range of new monument types (especially specialized leisure and entertainment buildings). With the possible exception of Tauromenium, older buildings and public spaces were rarely destroyed or obliterated to make way for new ones, as occurred most dramatically, for example, in the creation of the early imperial *coloniae* of Corinth and Carthage. Instead, new construction projects were accommodated within the existing urban plan and conformed to existing spaces and structures. Older structures, such as theaters and stoas, were frequently modified to serve new purposes. The early stages of this urbanism are visible in the cities examined in chapter 2 in the decades before their abandonment, most conspicuously in the forumization of their public spaces.

Sicilian urbanism in the Principate was the product of the desire of civic authorities to showcase their cities' prestige and cultural currency by creating new monuments, while at the same time maintaining the existing urban fabric. This distinctive form of urbanism was forged from the tension between the perceived need to adhere to imperial norms and the desire to maintain a more local identity. As a result, it is characterized as much by idiosyncrasy as by standardization and conformity. Such singular structures as the Tyndaris "basilica," the Syracuse "Roman gymnasium," and the Tauromenium "naumachia" are equally as characteristic of this Sicilian Roman urbanism as amphitheaters, bath buildings, and paved streets—if not more so. They are a testament to the creativity and ambition of the individuals and groups shaping the urban fabric, not evidence of the backwardness of Sicilian architecture and craftsmanship in the imperial period.

THE COMPARATIVE DEVELOPMENT OF SICILIAN CITIES UNDER THE ROMAN EMPIRE

What were the reasons for the emergence of this Sicilian Roman urbanism and its local variations? The preceding chapters have shown that a combination of interrelated geographic, political, and economic factors influenced the development (or lack thereof) of individual cities by facilitating (or hindering) their essential role as the center of an economically and socially diverse population headed by a resident local elite. Among the cities of chapter 4, Centuripae stands out as a winner in the political order established under the Roman Republic, despite its apparent geographic disadvantage: its hilltop location. Unlike the similarly privileged Segesta and Halaesa, however, Centuripae prospered for most of the imperial period. It was positioned along major overland transportation routes and in the heart of an agriculturally fertile region that also possessed mineral resources. Under the Republic, the city's leaders fostered political and social links with other cities (including Rome) and gained advantageous economic positions, acquiring land in the territories of other Sicilian cities. A Romanized, socially mobile local elite whose wealth was based in commerce and landholding had emerged by the first century BC. This elite endured and ascended the imperial social ranks during the Principate, to the continued advantage of Centuripae itself.

Halaesa also had early links with Rome and Italy—including a substantial population of individuals of Italian origin—thanks to its position on the Tyrrhenian coast. Like Centuripae and the other cities examined in chapters 3 and 4, it possessed an extensive hinterland and had gained regional economic hegemony by the late Republic. Yet, despite its prosperity under the Republic and early Principate, it persisted as a politically vital urban center only until the third century AD, around the same time as the final abandonment of Soluntum and Segesta. Like those two cities, it may have been disadvantaged by its hilltop location as well as by competition from the colonial centers of the northern coast: Panormus, Thermae Himeraeae, and Tyndaris.

As discussed in chapter 3, the advantageous strategic and economic positions of Lilybaeum and Agrigentum drove their continued prosperity and development, especially in the high and late Empire, despite their earlier troubled relations with Rome. Tyndaris, Tauromenium, Catina, and Syracuse also followed diverse courses of development under the Principate, although all were Augustan colonies. The imposition of a colony was most clearly punitive in the case of Tauromenium, where it seems to have resulted in the obliteration of institutions and structures associated with the old *polis*. The city continued to thrive under the new colonial ruling order, however, apparently on the same economic basis as before: as a major port on the northeastern coast and as the center of a famous wine-exporting region.

The Augustan colony seems to have stimulated only limited development at Tyndaris, whose imperial-era history was dominated by severe periodic seismic movements that caused extensive damage to the urban fabric. The creation of colonies at Catina and Syracuse had a visible impact on the built environment, introducing new Roman-style monuments and bringing about the extensive modification of existing public areas. However, both of these cities thrived under the Empire not only (or even primarily) as a result of their colonial status but also because of their continued (and perhaps expanded) roles as Mediterranean ports and regional economic centers.

The comparative development of the cities discussed in chapters 1 through 4 suggests a gradual recentering of economic, political, and social activity away from the urban centers of the northern coast and toward the cities of the western and eastern coasts that reached its climax in the late second century AD. These western and eastern coastal cities remained economically and politically vital well into the fourth (and in some cases fifth) century. The northern coastal centers of Soluntum, Halaesa, Calacte, and even Tyndaris, along with Segesta and Ietas (interior centers closely linked to that coast), exhibit signs of decreased political and economic activity, though at different paces and to different extents, between the early first century and late second century AD. Two triads of cities emerge as centers of economic activity and elite patronage in the same period: Panormus, Thermae Himeraeae, and Lilybaeum in the West and Syracuse, Catina, and Centuripae in the East. One explanation for this shift is the decline of Italy as an exporter of commodities (mainly wine) to the provinces over the course of the first century AD, supplanted first by Spain then by North Africa. The eastern and western coasts were particularly well positioned to take advantage of the increasing volume of commerce directed at Italy from North Africa, making them more attractive bases for the economic activities of elites.

ELITE PATRONAGE AND URBAN SURVIVAL

The family backgrounds, social and political aspirations, and personal relationships of some of the local and provincial elites most active in shaping the urban fabric of Sicily can be traced in the imperial-era epigraphic record. Chapters 1 and 2 have pointed to the absence of such elites as a major cause of the disintegration of cities that were abandoned in the early and middle Principate. However, the short- and long-term patronage relationships that communities fostered with wealthy, politically influential families and individuals, whether Roman or Sicilian, could be a significant factor in their continued cohesion and vitality under the Roman Empire.

As is clear from Cicero's Second Verrine Oration, individual notables as well as entire Sicilian communities had already begun to form patronage relations with members of the Roman senatorial elite under the Republic. In addition, expatriate Romans and Italians had become socially prominent and politically influential residents of many Sicilian cities. These early links continued to have an impact, especially in the cities of northern and western Sicily, into the imperial period. One result was that Roman citizenship had spread to many prominent families in these cities even before the Augustan era—a factor that may have contributed to the apparent stability of the ruling order of cities like Halaesa, Lilybaeum, and Centuripae in the transition from Republic to Principate. An early Roman/Italian presence and strong economic and social links to Italy also affected the language of governance: Latin was adopted in public epigraphy in Halaesa, Segesta, Lilybaeum, and Agrigentum earlier than in cities like Catina and Tauromenium, where the earliest Latin inscriptions date to the Augustan era.

The Augustan era was an important point of transition for the urban elites of Sicily and for their relations with their home communities and with Rome. The imposition of colonies, the confiscation and redistribution of land (especially from partisans of Sextus Pompey), and the formation of imperial estates undoubtedly affected the economic and political power of these elites, but the specific impact of these measures is difficult to trace in the epigraphic and archaeological record. Change is most visible at Tauromenium, where the historical record shows that the population was deported to make way for the Augustan colony as a punitive measure for the community's support of Sextus Pompey. The formerly vital institutions of the *polis* government then fall silent in the epigraphic record, and the structures and monuments associated with it are obliterated in the archaeological record.

We can infer from the changes to the built environment and epigraphic records of Syracuse and Catina (as well as Thermae Himeraeae), such as the construction of amphitheaters and other Roman buildings, that the new colonists took leading roles in city government and in shaping the urban fabric, perhaps in collaboration with imperial authorities. But the pace of change in the composition of local elites (and in their building priorities) in the Sicilian colonies should not be overestimated; the construction of amphitheaters in Sicily may serve a rough proxy. In contrast to Italy, where veterans' affinity for gladiatorial games meant that an amphitheater was one of the first buildings that a new colony acquired (and that neighboring communities then emulated),[16] amphitheater construction was not immediate in all Sicilian colonies (e.g., Catina). Tyndaris and Tauromenium may never have acquired such a structure. As in the provinces of mainland Greece, where amphitheaters are found only in the Roman colonies of Corinth and Dyrrhachium (not in Patrae),[17] the building type appears to have had little or no impact beyond the Augustan colonies of Sicily. The noncolonies of Centuripae and Lilybaeum, moreover, seem to show little disruption to the local elite in the post–civil war period. We can even trace the continued activity of certain individuals and families into the early imperial period. Perhaps in these cities the ruling class was gradually augmented, rather than displaced, by individuals and families from abroad with economic interests in Sicily.

Also difficult to untangle, but undoubtedly key to the continued cohesion of urban communities, is the relationship of landholding, political status, and social mobility in the imperial period. Most, if not all, of the cities examined in chapters 3 and 4 administered extensive territories by the early Principate. They were responsible for the assessment and collection of tax and for the maintenance of infrastructure (such as roads), though they had limited authority to collect revenues from this land by leasing or selling it. These limitations can best be seen by contrasting the Tabula Halaesina with the letter of Julius Paternus concerning the public finances of second-century AD Catina. While the former document shows a *polis* exercising close control over its hinterland and overseeing the leasing of land in accordance with its own institutions, the latter reveals the limited means that a city government possessed for raising revenues and the potential for Roman authorities to intervene in this process.

The limited financial resources of urban communities during the Principate was one result of the divorce of landholding in the territory of a city from membership in the urban community. This process had already begun in the Republic with the leasing of Roman *ager publicus* formerly administered by Sicilian *poleis* to Sicilian, Roman, and Italian *aratores*. Under the Empire, in addition to the growth of the imperial patrimony, it became common for wealthy individuals and families of equestrian or senatorial rank to own extensive properties in many parts of Sicily as well as outside the island. These individuals and families become visible in the epigraphic record as participants in provincial administration and as patrons of Sicilian cities over the course of the Empire. The classic case is the Maesii Titiani of Thermae and the Fabii Titiani, probably of Panormus. The members of these related senatorial families held multiple administrative posts in Sicily and elsewhere in the empire, especially in the third and fourth centuries, but remained active in their home cities and in Lilybaeum.

For families like the Maesii of western Sicily and the Pompeii of Centuripae, the political and social distinction between provincials and Romans grew less acute over the course of the Principate, as the ranks of the imperial elite opened to provincial notables. Social mobility was achieved through the acquisition of property, by the forging of links to other notable Italian and provincial families through marriage and adoption, and by participation in the administration of the empire, rather than through participation in *polis* government, as had been the case for previous generations of Sicilian elites.

Keeping this in mind, the lack of Sicilians in the senatorial ranks of the high Empire compared to the large numbers of senators of Spanish and African origin becomes more explicable. Domenico Vera attributed this absence partly to the lack of ambition of Sicilian notables and to their ambiguous relationship with the Roman ruling order.[18] As a result of Sicily's long-standing links to Italy, and as a consequence of the emphasis of the Augustan settlement on the redistribution of landed wealth and political prestige from old urban elites to colonists and individual landowners, the imperial period saw the increased activity of individuals and families of equestrian and senatorial rank on the island rather than the emergence of a provincial elite class rooted in the old Hellenistic *polis* order. Many of these individuals and families also had links to Italy and Africa. Their wealth and social mobility were closely tied to their economic interests in Sicily: one reason for their patronage of the most politically and economically vital Sicilian communities. The upward mobility of families with roots in or long-standing links to Sicilian cities, such as the Pompeii of Centuripae, was the result of their social and economic links with other wealthy families in Italy and Africa as much as of their activities in Sicily.

Although Sicilian cities were not the main *loci* for elite social mobility, considerable social changes did take place among other sectors of the urban population under the Roman Empire. One development visible in the epigraphic record (and especially in funerary *tituli*) of cities like Catina and Syracuse is the emergence of freedmen—and even some slaves—in the middling urban social ranks. Their presence was related to senatorial and imperial landholding on the island: some would have been stationed in Sicilian cities (especially ports) in order to manage their patrons' economic interests (e.g., as *tabularii*), while others would have been involved in the administration of rural properties (as *vilici*). However, as the example of the Annii of Agrigentum shows, some freedmen also had opportunities to enrich themselves by participating in production and commerce based in urban centers. One way in which they used this wealth to enhance their social prestige was through participation in the imperial cult, especially as *seviri* Augustales.

THE ROMAN EMPEROR IN SICILY

The figure of the emperor played an essential role in the religious and political life of urban communities in the Roman Empire.[19] In Sicily, as in the cities of the Greek East, the imperial cult and other expressions of loyalty to the emperor had antecedents in the elaborate honors that communities paid to Hellenistic kings and later to Roman Republican magistrates. Such practices were particularly well established in Syracuse, where Hieron II modeled his personal rule after the dynasties of the Hellenistic East. Even with no official "ruler cult," the king made a concerted effort to accrue divine qualities to himself and to his family, especially through his building program. In the decades after the creation of the Roman *provincia*, the Syracusans transferred the honors previously paid to Hieron to leading Roman magistrates (especially the Marcelli), dedicating statues and instituting festivals in their honor.

The epigraphic evidence for the imperial cult and other commemorations of the emperor is lacunose, with some cities (e.g., Lilybaeum) probably overrepresented and others (Syracuse) underrepresented. But it does appear that the emperor was a visible presence in Sicilian cities from an early date. The Syracusans dedicated a statue to Octavian early in his reign (*AE* 1989.342b), while the *municipium* of Halaesa made a dedication to Augustus a few decades later (*CIL* 10.7458). Few dedications to the Julio-Claudians or Flavians survive, and most evidence for honors paid to emperors comes from the reign of Trajan through the Severans.

The epigraphic evidence for the imperial cult and other displays of loyalty to the emperor can be divided into two broad categories: dedications by individuals and products of community initiatives. Displays of loyalty to the emperor sponsored by civic bodies (*res publicae*, *municipia*, and *coloniae*) are rare and mostly come from the Augustan colonies (particularly Tyndaris) and from Lilybaeum, especially after it gained municipal and colonial status. The epigraphic record of the cities examined so far contains only one reference to a civic priesthood of the imperial cult: an inscription honoring a *flamen divorum Augustorum*, probably of Lilybaeum, found at Mazara (*CIL* 10.7212).[20] In addition, no cult buildings associated with the community-wide or province-wide veneration of the emperor of the type found in other provinces (e.g., the Maison Carrée in Nimes, the Temple of Roma and Augustus in Leptis Magna, and the imperial cult complex at Tarraco) have been identified in Sicily. In contrast to the Aegean Greek world, there is no epigraphic evidence of such institutions.[21]

Dedications made by individuals are more common. Especially in Lilybaeum, members of the local and provincial elite made numerous dedications that refer to the emperor and sometimes also to his divine quality (*numen*), often in the context of public works or other benefactions, such as a local magistrate's donation of funds for the paving of a *platea* in honor of Marcus Aurelius.[22] An example of a more personal form of veneration also comes from Lilybaeum: a dedication to Mercurius Augustus made by two Roman citizens (*CIL* 10.7224).

Most of the individual dedications that refer to the emperor and the imperial cult were set up by *seviri* Augustales, freedmen who were chosen by the *municipium* or *colonia* to maintain the structures and oversee the rituals associated with the local imperial cult. All of the cities discussed in the last three chapters except Tauromenium and Agrigentum have produced secure epigraphic evidence for the Augustales. In Centuripae (and in Halaesa), the location of their office or cult building has been identified with some certainty. The relative prominence of the Augustales in the epigraphic record is a reflection of the success of this institution in fostering community cohesion and loyalty to the ruling order of Rome. It facilitated the participation of *liberti* in the public life of their cities and offered them opportunities for self-promotion in the service of the Roman emperor. All of the known dedications of the *seviri* are in Latin, and many were displayed in prestigious public spaces (such as the agora/forum of Halaesa).

The veneration of the emperor in Sicily conformed to imperial norms in its rituals and institutions, though it was apparently embraced with limited enthusiasm by the urban ruling classes, except at certain historical moments when displays of loyalty were politically necessary or expedient, such as the receipt of a benefaction or political privilege (e.g., the bestowal of colonial status on Lilybaeum). The lack of internal initiative—the apparent lack of interest of local elites in the imperial cult and in other displays of loyalty to the ruling order of Rome—is in keeping with this chapter's suggestion that urban centers were not the main *loci* of elite social advancement in the imperial period. However, the apparently enthusiastic embrace of the imperial cult by wealthy freedmen accords with the role of Sicilian cities as centers of economic and social activity for freedmen and other nonelites.

POINTS OF TRANSITION IN THE URBAN LANDSCAPE

The analysis so far has emphasized broad changes in the urban landscape of Sicily, such as the shift in activity away from the south coast and interior in the first century BC and then away from the north coast and toward the western and eastern coasts in the high Empire. However, these broad trends mask the different extents to which the human and natural events that befell Sicily in the imperial period affected individual cities. In fact, numerous significant points of transition are visible in the urban communities discussed in chapters 3 and 4. The political events of the late Republic and the Augustan period left the most visible impact on the urban fabric of Tauromenium and Syracuse. In Centuripae, in contrast, the middle imperial period, and especially the reigns of Hadrian and the Antonines, seems to have been an era of particular prosperity and urban development. Lilybaeum reached the peak of its political and economic fortunes under the Severans, as reflected in the embellishment of its public and residential areas. Agrigentum also achieved renewed political prominence in the Severan period with the bestowal of colonial status. Overall, however, the development of the built environment in all of these cities can be characterized as slow and piecemeal, rather than quick and dramatic. The case of Catina is typical: no single moment of extensive urban development took place after the creation of the Augustan colony, but instead a gradual reshaping of the urban plan in the first, second, and third centuries to include bathhouses, an amphitheater, and a theater-odeum complex, reflecting the emergence of a prosperous urban residential class with a taste for Roman leisure pursuits.

Likewise, it is difficult to discern processes of quick, dramatic urban decline in any of the cities. While the seismic events of the 360s AD did great damage to Tyndaris, the urban fabric shows signs of deterioration even earlier. Occupation continued on the site at a suburban level for several centuries after. As Christian communities emerged in late antiquity, their impact on the urban fabric consisted of reprioritization or reclassification, rather than neglect. The fourth and fifth centuries saw the emergence of new centers of activity and novel practices in the ancient urban cores of Lilybaeum, Agrigentum, Catina, and Syracuse that reflect the different social and religious priorities of Christian communities. New communal burial areas were established (sometimes within city walls), and pagan temples began to be converted into churches, though these transformations were not fully realized until the Byzantine period.

CONCLUSION

We can see especially in the epigraphic record the disappearance of Greek local elites as the public face of many Sicilian cities by the Julio-Claudian period. These elites were replaced with—or perhaps merged into—new, interrelated social groups that drove urban life and development in the imperial period: colonists, freedmen, and wealthy, politically prominent families with extensive landholdings on the island. For these groups and for what remained of the Greek local elite, Roman citizenship and social status were as important as (if not more significant than) local identity based in *polis* citizenship. The accumulation of wealth, effective social networking, and participation in Roman religious and political institutions, many of which were based in cities, were as key to social mobility in Sicily as they were in other provinces. Urban public space was the most effective venue for individual and communal displays of adherence to the Roman imperial order.

The addition of Roman monuments to the built environment of Sicilian cities, or the modification of existing buildings to accommodate Roman institutions, can therefore be seen as part of local and extralocal "conversations" involving the sponsor(s), the community as a whole, the Roman state as embodied in the emperor, and more immediately the provincial magistrates who represented him. The local context of the monument made its message more effective. The statue cycle of Q. Pompeius Sosius Priscus in Centuripae was located amid other monuments celebrating the imperial order, such as the "seat of the Augustales," some of which were also sponsored by the Pompeii. The paved *platea* in Lilybaeum funded by a local magistrate in honor of Marcus Aurelius was associated with the Cereres (Ceres and Proserpina), a cult with a long history in Sicily and associations with the island's agricultural fertility.

The effectiveness of the message of monuments also depended on the financial means of their sponsor(s), the skill with which they were executed, and the size and composition of their potential audience. Therefore, the economic, social, and political integration of a city was closely linked to its monumental development. However, no simple geographic determinism lay behind the Augustan reordering of the Sicilian urban hierarchy or the subsequent development of cities under the Roman Empire. Rather, a combination of geographic and environmental factors and historical circumstances fostered (or hindered) the ambitions, means, and connections of urban residents from provincial and local elites down to freedmen and slaves and their ability to participate in and enhance the economic, political, and social life of cities.

In closing, it is important again to emphasize that the urban centers examined in the previous chapters lie at one extreme of the settlement spectrum of Sicily and that they are distinguishable from other forms of settlement mainly in the intensity of their economic, political, and social roles and the corresponding heterogeneity of their populations. The next chapter moves away from the political and social world of cities to explore the new forms of settlement that emerged in Sicily under the Principate. These new settlements arose organically and apparently without direct encouragement from the Roman state, sometimes on the sites of long-abandoned *poleis*. Their development sheds further light on the density and complexity of the Sicilian settlement landscape under the Principate as well as on the economic, social, and political relations between urban settlements and their hinterlands, both territorial and maritime.

SEVEN

NEW FORMS OF SETTLEMENT IN ROMAN IMPERIAL SICILY

The preceding chapters have examined the impact of the economic, political, and social changes brought by the Principate on the urban fabric of Sicilian towns (the former Greek *apoikiai* as well as Hellenized Phoenician and indigenous *poleis*). In some towns certain urban functions, and especially the role of the town as an administrator of a defined territory and a *locus* of elite residence and activity, became obsolete in the new political and economic order of the early Principate. This obsolescence was accompanied by the contraction and deterioration of the urban fabric. But other towns adapted—sometimes (but not usually) with the encouragement or direct assistance of imperial authorities—to the political and economic exigencies of the evolving Roman imperial system and became provincial centers of administration, commerce, and elite activity. These developments point to a stratification of the Sicilian urban system as a smaller number of towns came to assume a wider range of political, social, religious, cultural, and economic roles; to administer a larger amount of territory; and perhaps to acquire larger populations. Yet in Ietas, Segesta, and Halaesa the economic integration of the urban center continued amid, or after, the decline and disappearance of its political authority. In Calacte and Halaesa changing patterns of Mediterranean connectivity were at least partly responsible for the shift of settlement to better-integrated locations. Moreover, new settlement at Segesta emerged on the old urban site to take advantage of new production regimes and commercial patterns, even after a period of abandonment.

One aspect of the urban landscape of Sicily remains to be examined further: the extent and nature of the new settlements that arose in the Roman imperial period (whether they can be considered urban) and their social, political, and economic relations with existing urban and nonurban settlements. The emergence of *stationes/mansiones* and "agro-towns" (often along major Roman routes, sometimes also near the coast, and usually in areas of high agricultural potential) has long been cited as an aspect of the ruralization of Roman Sicily in the imperial period.[1] It was accompanied by the obsolescence of former *poleis*—particularly those located in the interior—that were distant from such routes. Like the assumption of the decline of the urban centers of Sicily in the imperial period, this picture of the ruralization of the Sicilian settlement network must be nuanced and refined, particularly in light of recent archaeological work.

SOFIANA: A NEW ROMAN TOWN IN SICILY?

The settlement in Contrada Sofiana, in the territory of Mazzarino in the hilly south-central interior, is the archaeologically best-attested new settlement that emerged in Roman imperial Sicily (figure 7.1). The site, on a low ridge overlooking the Nocera River in terrain now devoted to cereal production, viticulture, and forestry, was first identified and excavated in 1954 and 1961. These early excavations uncovered a late Roman bath complex and a Christian basilica surrounded by a cemetery on the southwestern edge of the site, though little about the stratigraphy or finds has been published.[2] Excavations in the 1980s and 1990s focused on the area north of the late Roman baths,

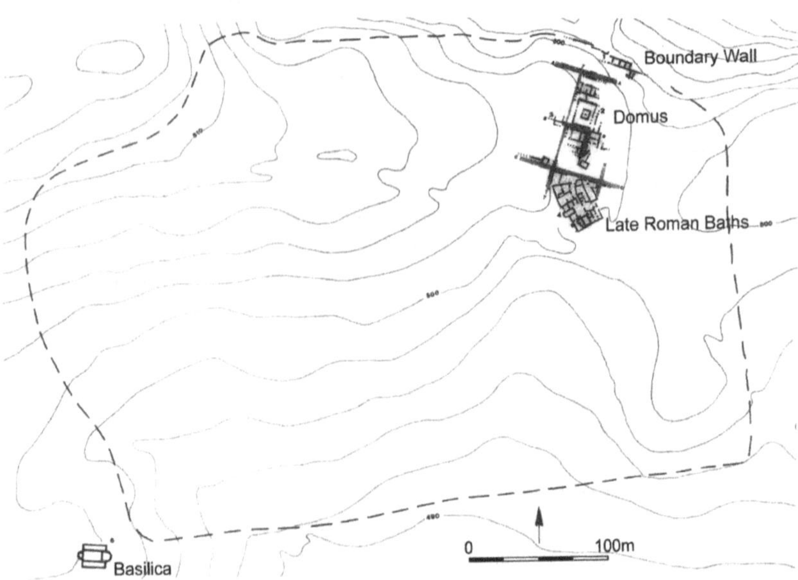

FIGURE 7.1.
Plan of Sofiana (K. Bowes/G. F. La Torre).

uncovering several buildings and a system of paved streets, and on the necropolises surrounding the settlement.[3] A project of excavation, magnetometry, and field survey begun in 2009 focused on determining the extent of the settlement and the uses of space within it as well as on understanding the evolution of the site and its relationship with the surrounding area, from antiquity through the medieval period.[4]

Dinu Adamesteanu identified the Contrada Sofiana settlement as the *mansio* of Philosophiana of the *It. Ant.* (94.5, also listed as *Gela sive Filosofiana* at 88.2) that lay along the inland route between Catina and Agrigentum, based on the similarity of the modern toponym and stamped tiles ("FIL SOF") found in the site's late Roman structures.[5] The Sofiana settlement is nearly unique in the Sicilian archaeological record in the *ex novo* nature of its development in the imperial era, with little evidence of frequentation before the Augustan period. Few such settlements have been identified in Sicily, and even fewer have been excavated.

The approximately eight hectares of the settlement at Sofiana excavated since the 1950s have revealed a complex and lengthy, though still lacunose, history of occupation. Though Adamesteanu hypothesized the existence of a farm on the site in the fourth century BC, a recent intrasite survey found no materials earlier than the first century BC.[6] Excavations in the 1980s and 1990s in the area north of the baths uncovered numerous structures—most notably, a peristyle *domus*—lining a series of paved orthogonal streets as well as a section of a northern perimeter wall. These structures were attributed to the first phase of occupation and dated to the Augustan period. Further construction, including the first phase of the bath complex on the same orientation as the peristyle *domus*, took place in the Julio-Claudian period and in the second century AD. In addition, from an early stage the settlement was equipped with a water collection and distribution system: an aqueduct following the orientation of the streets probably brought water from nearby springs to the bath complex.[7] Excavations and intrasite survey have shown that the settlement received large quantities of imports in its first phase, including Italian and African finewares, coarsewares, and transport amphorae.[8]

Although a gap in occupation may have occurred in the second century AD, more securely attested are the destruction of several structures in the late third century (including the *domus* and other buildings along the early imperial streets), the decline in the quantities of ceramics found in intrasite survey, and the end of use of the necropolises. A new phase of building and occupation had begun by the early fourth century, whose most prominent feature was a new bath complex on a different orientation than the early imperial building. The use of these new baths lasted perhaps only a few decades; by the late fourth century the building seems to have been occupied by industrial workshops and residences. The first phase of construction of the Christian basilica in the southwestern sector of the site dates to around the same time.

Recent magnetometry and survey have shed light particularly on this late antique phase of occupation (fourth–sixth century AD), when the settlement reached its greatest physical extent, covering an area of ca. 21 hectares excluding the cemeteries. Geophysical prospection has indicated the existence of buildings apparently arranged on a street grid, pointing to a replanning of the settlement in the fourth century AD, as well as the presence of at least two kilns, one of which produced tiles. Extrasite survey has revealed the proliferation of sites—apparently small farmsteads or houses—in the immediate vicinity of the settlement in the fourth and fifth centuries.[9] Although little is known of the settlement after this period, it appears from the high number and wide dispersion of ceramics that life continued on the site in the eighth and ninth centuries.[10]

The recent research at Sofiana supports the hypothesis that the settlement was a planned entity during its late antique phase and probably even as early as the first century AD. Recent excavators have therefore described Sofiana as "urban-like" or "urban-style." It most closely resembles the type of ancient settlement usually described as a *vicus*, or agro-town: a very large rural settlement or agglomeration that lacks an urban designation but shows signs of urbanism.[11]

Sofiana in both its early imperial and late antique phases can be described as an urban settlement in some respects. It possessed a relatively dense, cohesive, and permanent population, which can be deduced archaeologically from the presence of multiple differentiated dwellings arranged within a network of streets or around other forms of open communal space (not necessarily planned). At least in its late antique phase, it also performed higher-level economic roles that both tied it to and differentiated it from other settlements in the area: the manufacture of goods from raw materials, as evidenced by the kilns in its vicinity and the evidence for glassmaking and other industrial activities in the remains of the bath complex. The evidence for commerce and production in both phases of settlement as well as the peristyle *domus* of the early imperial settlement also point to the presence of a heterogeneous and economically and socially differentiated population not engaged solely in agricultural production, headed by a defined, embedded elite. Further confirmation of the (perhaps periodic) presence of an elite stratum in the late antique settlement comes from a monumental tomb in the eastern necropolis whose grave goods included a pair of gold earrings.[12]

In both stages of settlement at Sofiana, however, it is difficult to identify the authority (or authorities) overseeing the development of its infrastructure and buildings. Sofiana displays urban characteristics such as a relatively high concentration of population and evidence of nonagricultural economic activity as well as structures and institutions that indicate a civic identity, such as a perimeter wall, an aqueduct and public baths, and a street grid. But the settlement shows no physical indications of the existence of civic authority: no public administration or government buildings.

Whether this lack of clear evidence of civic authority points to Sofiana's political and economic dependence on another settlement in the area is an open question. The original excavators of Sofiana (Dinu Adamesteanu) and of the Villa del Casale near Piazza Armerina (Andrea Carandini) believed that the former settlement was a dependency of the latter: Sofiana developed in late antiquity as a *vicus* or peasant village that housed the agriculturalists who worked the land owned by the wealthy notable who resided at the villa, approximately 6 km away.[13] This hypothesis was based largely on the proximity of the two sites, the extreme wealth and luxury of the Villa del Casale, and the likelihood that the toponym "Philosophiana" derives from the name of the *praedia* within which the settlement was situated.

The extensive and complex remains of the early/mid-imperial and late antique settlements found in more recent fieldwork at Sofiana, however, necessitate a revision of this theory. At the time of the early/mid-imperial phase of settlement at Sofiana, the Villa del Casale would have been considerably smaller and less elaborate—perhaps merely a *villa rustica* or *vicus*—and presumably in control of a smaller territory.[14] As for the dependence of the late antique settlement on the Villa del Casale, the recent excavators of Sofiana have argued that the estate-derived toponym indicates only the proximity of a *praedia* Philosophiana, not a proprietary relationship; *mansiones* in Italy located on or near imperial and senatorial estates may have been named in a similar fashion.[15] In addition, Wilson has argued against characterizing the Villa del Casale as an "estate-center,"[16] given the lack of evidence that it served as anything other than the luxurious personal retreat of a wealthy individual.

Moreover, the recent geophysical and survey work at Sofiana has suggested that the site remained a planned entity in late antiquity and became the center of an extensive network of smaller settlements, casting further doubt on the hypothesis that it was a simple peasant village dependent on the Villa del Casale. Extrasite survey has revealed dozens of small concentrations of building materials, pottery, and *dolia* within a kilometer of Sofiana, mostly dating to the fourth and fifth centuries. These have been interpreted as the remains of small farmsteads or peasant houses.[17] Surface survey within the site has pointed to a significant increase in ceramic quantities beginning in the early fourth century and continuing into the first half of the fifth century, roughly corresponding to the phase of greatest expansion of the Villa del Casale. This intrasite survey has shown, however, that Sofiana remained a center of economic activity in the eighth and ninth centuries, long after the abandonment of the villa.[18]

Much remains to be learned about the shape and extent of the settlement at Sofiana and its relationship to the Roman road network and to other settlements in the area.[19] But research conducted in and around the site has hinted at the complexity of settlement patterns in the Sicilian countryside under the Principate. The development of the rural landscape was not simply a process of the ruralization of older *poleis* and of the emergence of *latifundia* and dependent settlements to take their place. Rather, new settlements could emerge that did not fulfill the political roles of the *poleis* but possessed considerable wealth and served as centers of population and economic activity. Sofiana is unusual in the current state of research on Roman Sicily in the extent of its *ex novo* development, in a locality with no substantial earlier occupation. As the next section shows, in other regions of Sicily with longer and more substantial histories of settlement, emerging Roman-era settlements sometimes adapted older, long-abandoned urban sites, especially to create infrastructure for the processing, transportation, and export of agricultural produce.

NAXOS AND MEGARA HYBLAEA: THE RURALIZATION OF THE *POLIS*?

Chapters 1 and 2 have discussed the settlements that reemerged at or shifted to a site near the former *poleis* of Segesta, Halaesa, and Calacte in the imperial period or late antiquity. This section examines two settlements, Megara Hyblaea and Naxos, that arose on or near the sites of long-abandoned Greek *apoikiai* on the eastern coast in the imperial period. It considers whether the emergence of these and similar settlements is a separate phenomenon or a symptom of the same economic, political, and social processes that led to the emergence of the settlement at Sofiana.

Settlements like the imperial and late antique reoccupations of the former *poleis* of Naxos and Megara Hyblaea appear more frequently in Sicily than *ex novo* settlements like Sofiana, but this may be the result of bias in the archaeological record. The former two settlements lie on or near the extensive monumental remains of archaic Greek *poleis* and thus have been easier to detect and have attracted more attention than "isolated" sites in the interior like Sofiana. Nonetheless, much less is known about the later stages of occupation at Naxos and Megara Hyblaea than about their earlier, classical-era phases of settlement, especially because later occupation strata lie closer to the surface and have been more vulnerable to plow damage.

The founders of Naxos and Megara chose sites along the coast with good visibility, on sheltered bays that offered natural harborage (figure 7.2). According to Thucydides (6.3), Naxos was the first Greek colony in Sicily, founded by Chalcidians from Euboea a year before Syracuse (735–734 BC). Megara was founded a few decades later and went on to establish its own colony at Selinus in the following century (6.4). Both sites were on or close to the coastal land route that developed to connect the urban centers of the eastern coast from Syracuse north to Zancle/Messana (the Via Pompeia of Roman times).[20] Naxos was situated on Punta Schisò, a flat, low-lying peninsula between the mouth of the Santa Venera torrent and the Bay of Giardini Naxos, next to a sandy beach that provided a safe, accessible landing point. The city was redeveloped on a new urban plan in the fifth century, probably following its conquest by Hieron I of Syracuse in 476 BC.[21] This settlement was destroyed in 403 BC by Dionysius I of Syracuse. Most of its population was transferred in subsequent decades to Tauromenion, a more easily defendable settlement on a hill above the Bay of Giardini that assumed most of the urban roles of Naxos.

Excavations within the Greek colony and around the modern city of Giardini Naxos to its north, however, have shown that the site was not completely abandoned after the Dionysian destruction. But the Hellenistic phase of settlement (ca. fourth or third to first century BC) appears to have been restricted to a small area of the classical city. In the imperial period settlement shifted away from the site of the Greek colony on the Schisò peninsula toward the southwestern corner of the Bay of Giardini, where an agglomeration formed close to the ancient port and along the coastal road to Messana.[22] This settlement has been identified as the Naxus or Naxos listed in the *It. Ant.* as a stopping point and exit for travelers to Tauromenium on the Ionian coastal leg of the long route between the Strait of Messina and Lilybaeum (86.2–89.2, at 87.2). Structures excavated within the settlement indicate that it functioned as a node for maritime and land traffic. A bath building dated to the second century AD was supplied, perhaps along with the rest of the settlement, through a system of water distribution evidenced by the numerous ceramic tubes found in the area. A warehouse complex was located between the baths and the ancient port (where traces of colonial-era slipways remain). Its first phase dates to the first century BC or first century AD, when it consisted of a long portico extending along the Messana road, parallel to

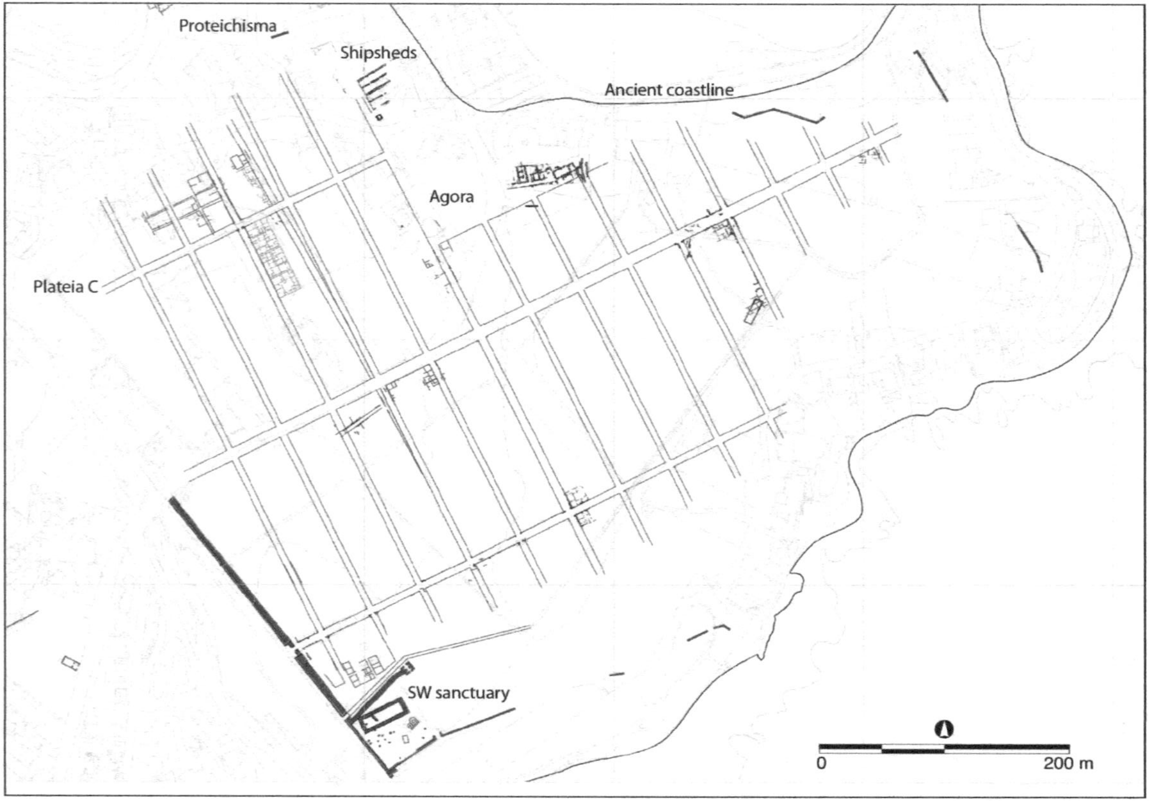

FIGURE 7.2.

Plan of Naxos (J. Pakkanen, with modifications by K. Rasmussen).

the coastline. Seven *dolia defossa* that probably stored wine were found in the two rooms at its southern end. A row of pilasters was added to the eastern side in the second century AD and the building was subdivided into a series of small rooms, apparently transforming it into a *horreum* accessible only from the port.

Settlement also continued outside this harbor/roadside agglomeration. A few burials of the second and third centuries AD have been found in the archaic necropolis, and a possible mid-imperial *villa maritima* has been uncovered near the Giardini Naxos train station. In addition, remains of a mid-imperial settlement were found west of the Santa Venera torrent, close to the modern coastal road. The structures of this settlement align with the extramural course of the classical-era Plateia C, indicating that the settlement developed near or along the coastal road running south toward Catina.

Occupation of the area continued and perhaps increased in the late Roman and Byzantine periods. The entire arc of the Bay of Giardini appears to have been settled in this period, including the area of the road station and, from the fourth/fifth century, parts of the Schisò peninsula once occupied by the Greek colony.[23] Excavations in the area of the colony, and particularly on the site of the classical shipsheds, have revealed numerous structures from the late third century AD and after.[24] The structures from this phase, mostly identified as houses, partly followed the plan of the archaic Greek settlement. At least one, located near the classical shipsheds, contained a storeroom with two *dolia*. Other evidence of this latest ancient phase of settlement includes a small *tepidarium* built above the colonial fortification wall; the fourth- or fifth-century kiln complex excavated in the 1980s in Contrada Mastrociccio, in the area of the road station (discussed below); numerous tombs; and two coin hoards, one dating to the mid-fifth century and the other to the end of the eighth century.[25]

The most significant body of evidence for Hellenistic, Roman, and late antique occupation of Naxos relates to ceramic production, particularly to the production of wine amphorae. The several kilns in and around the settlement—and the numerous transport amphorae found on land and in the surrounding waters—point to uninterrupted production and export activity from the third century BC until the fourth and fifth centuries AD.[26] Indeed, the production and export of wine is an element of continuity between the archaic/classical and Hellenistic/Roman settlements. The Greek colony had multiple extramural ceramic production areas, and bunches of grapes appear on many of its coin issues. Numerous fragments of MGS III-type wine amphorae have been found in the area of the classical slipways, which had probably been converted to pottery production after the destruction of the *polis* (ca. fourth-third century BC).[27] Fragments with the stamp "Naxios" have been found in the area of the suburban sanctuary, on several other sites in Sicily, and in Athens and northern Italy.[28]

Potters could take advantage of numerous clay deposits around the colony, including on the eastern slopes of the Larunchi hill and at the mouth of the San Giovanni torrent at the center of the Bay of Giardini. The earliest excavated complexes include a group of three kilns west of the Santa Venera that were active in the third century BC and two kilns on the Larunchi hill that were active in the third/second and first centuries BC, neither of which appears to have produced amphorae. A mid-imperial (second/third century) ceramic workshop was found in the city of Giardini, north of the colonial site and close to the modern coastline. This complex consisted of a large room with two *dolia defossa* adjoining two kilns that produced flat-bottomed MR1 amphorae and a separate kiln. In addition, a straight, long basin for the decantation of clay was found in the area of the archaic necropolis, built over and partly destroying tombs. This basin was filled with small flat-bottomed imitations of Dressel 2–4 amphorae as well as early examples of the MR1 type.[29] Most substantial is the kiln complex found in Contrada Mastrociccio, near the clay deposits at the mouth of the San Giovanni. This complex included areas for the working and storage of clay as well as five kilns active in the late fourth and fifth centuries, some producing striated tiles and others producing Keay 52 amphorae.[30]

In addition to these kiln complexes, deposits of amphorae, wasters, and other ceramics in and around Naxos provide evidence for the chronology and extent of ceramic production in the area. Most notably, a first or early second century AD deposit of flat-bottomed amphorae was found on top of one of the slipways of the classical-era naval yard. These amphorae appear to be vessels of local production that were discarded before use, perhaps because of poor firing, as their interiors lack traces of the resin lining that would have been applied before they were filled with liquid.[31]

Recent research on these kiln complexes and ceramic deposits, and comparison with vessels found on other sites in and beyond Sicily, has shed considerable light on the history of wine production and export in the region. As the MGS III vessels attest, local production of transport amphorae had begun by the early Hellenistic period. This production increased in the late second/early first century BC, as indicated by deposits of wasters of Dressel 1-type amphorae.[32] By the first century AD the Naxos kilns appear to have specialized in the production of small, flat-bottomed amphorae of a basic form that was widely diffused in the Western Mediterranean. This production expanded and evolved in the second century with the appearance of new variations on this form and continued into the fourth and fifth centuries, when the Mastrocicio kilns produced Keay 52 vessels.

These amphorae were probably used to transport the wines for which northeastern Sicily was famous in the imperial period. Literary sources attest that fine wines from Tauromenium and Messana reached the Roman market by the third quarter of the first century AD. Certain similar types of amphorae found in Italian assemblages, including vessels from the eastern slope of the Palatine in Rome and larger amphorae from Pompeii with *tituli picti* alluding to Tauromenium, were probably used to transport and distribute these wines beginning in the first century AD and continuing in Rome into the fifth and early sixth centuries.[33] Moreover, the forty-five amphorae found in the deposit in the area of the classical shipsheds, probably discarded from a nearby (as yet unidentified) production site, match the eight complete amphorae found in a shipwreck near Capo Sant'Alessio, 15 km north of Naxos. This Sant'Alessio type has been dated to the Julio-Claudian period based on comparison with similar vessels found in Ostia, Naples, Leptis Magna, and shipwrecks off the western coast of Sicily.[34]

The formal evolution of the amphorae produced at Naxos, their distribution beyond Sicily, and their relationship to typologies produced and distributed in other regions of the Central and Western Mediterranean provide hints about the nature of production at Naxos and the site's external economic links. The early products of Naxos that were found in the decantation basin in the area of the port (ca. first century BC to first century AD) derived from forms originating in Italy (namely, Dressel 1 and Dressel 2–4). The handle of one of these locally produced Dressel 2–4 amphorae, which bears the stamp "DA[MOSION]," points to some form of public control over production (from Tauromenion?): perhaps a public workshop whose products were destined for sanctuaries or for public supplies of daily commodities.[35] However, the lack of uniformity of amphorae even of the same typology—such as the vessels of the Sant'Alessio type found in the shipwreck and in the deposit in Naxos—indicates the nonindustrial, manual nature of production. The stamps found on the handles of some of these vessels (e.g., "CAPITO" and "VAL") also suggest the involvement of an ethnically Latin population in their production, unsurprising given the proximity of the Roman colony of Tauromenium.[36]

The evolution of the forms produced at Naxos over the course of the empire reflects the site's connections to other regions of the central Mediterranean, especially southern Italy and North Africa. Production between the first and fifth centuries can be divided into three principal forms: the Sant'Alessio type; the intermediate Spinella type, a variant of the MR1 form similar to Peña's Palatine East I, found in a deposit in insula C3 of the classical *polis*; and Keay 52. The beginning of production of Keay 52 vessels in the Mastrociccio kilns can be linked to northeastern Sicily's proximity to South Bruttii and the growth of wine production there for the Roman market in the fourth and fifth centuries—a market that Sicilian wines also supplied.[37] Reynolds and Peña hypothesize that the export from northeastern Sicily to Ostia, Rome, and Tripolitania of variations on the MR1 amphora, and later of Keay 52 vessels, took advantage of prevailing routes from the Eastern Mediterranean, Tripolitania, and central Tunisia to Rome via the Strait of Messina.[38] The settlement at Naxos would have been well positioned to participate in the production, packaging, and export of wine, if not directly overseas then via intermediate ports like Catina or Messana. Its kilns had access to plentiful supplies of clay and the settlement itself was easily accessible both by sea and by road, including the secondary interior routes connecting the coast to vineyards in the foothills of Etna and the Peloritani.

Little is known of rural settlement away from the coast, so there is almost no evidence for wine production in the region beyond the statements of Pliny and other historical sources. One of the few rural sites in the area to have been identified and excavated is at Scifì in the Agrò valley, approximately 8 km northwest of Capo Sant'Alessio. This site, which was inhabited by the second century BC, was occupied in the fourth century AD by a villa or *villula* that probably served as a stopping-point along a secondary route connecting the Ionian and Tyrrhenian coasts through the Peloritani.[39] The site was involved in production, storage, and exchange with the coast: fragments of African terra sigillata and transport amphorae are relatively abundant, as are flat-bottomed amphorae of Naxian and/or northeastern Sicilian production. Large storage *dolia* have also been found on the site as well as evidence for tile production on site or nearby.

The colony of Megara Hyblaea lay in the middle of a sheltered bay approximately 20 km north of Syracuse, across from the modern city of Augusta and in a narrow coastal plain now dominated by oil refineries and other heavy industry. The archaic city was destroyed in 483 BC by Gelon of Syracuse but rebuilt and resettled under Timoleon in 340 BC. This settlement was in turn destroyed by the Romans in their campaign against Syracuse in the Second Punic War.[40] The site of the archaic *polis* was excavated sporadically in the nineteenth and early twentieth centuries and has been the object of regular excavation since the late 1940s.[41]

As these excavations have shown, like Naxos after the Dionysian destruction, the site of Megara was not fully abandoned after the Roman destruction: settlement resumed on a smaller scale by the second century BC. The earliest signs of reoccupation are in the area of the fortifications, where houses and farms were built onto the remains of the city wall in the second and first centuries BC. The remains of these habitations include a press with a cement cistern used to collect liquid (oil or wine?). A row of shops built partly over the ruins of a Hellenistic portico in the city center may also date to this period.[42]

After a possible interruption connected to the war with Sextus Pompey,[43] occupation continued on the site until the fourth century AD, with settlement concentrated in the westernmost part of the ancient *polis* in the area closest to overland transportation routes (primarily, the north–south Via Pompeia). The structures excavated in this area, including a lime kiln built into the western fortification wall that was broadly dated to the Roman period, have not been fully published and are therefore difficult to date precisely.[44] The most significant is a rectangular building east of the lime kiln. This building has a central colonnade with seven surviving column bases and thirteen *dolia* in its pavement. Its precise date and function are uncertain: the current excavators hypothesize that it was built in the Hellenistic period and reused as part of a large Roman-era *villa rustica*. Giuseppe Cacciaguerra, however, describes it as a warehouse belonging to the roadside *mansio* that developed on the site in the imperial period and dates its destruction and abandonment to the late third century AD.[45]

At least a dozen Roman-era and late antique tombs have been found in the area of the archaic necropolis immediately west of the city wall.[46] In addition, excavators have uncovered late antique structures in the area of the Hellenistic fortifications, with some built over the remains of the city wall (whereas structures from earlier Roman-era occupation had been built into it). One room of a third- or fourth-century house near the wall had a floor in *opus signinum* with the Greek inscription "Gnaiou Modiou." Attached to this house was a small thermal complex with three entrances (two from the outside, one from the house itself), which was apparently intended to service the other late Roman houses in the area.[47] In the southern gate of the Hellenistic wall excavators found the remains of a late Roman agricultural installation on two levels, with a vat for the collection of grape or olive juice from a press. They also found a late Roman and Byzantine-era structure of an uncertain nature in the area of the classical agora.[48]

BEYOND SOFIANA, NAXOS, AND MEGARA: NEW SETTLEMENT (AND RESETTLEMENT) IN ROMAN SICILY

These three sites are examples of the new forms of settlement that replaced or supplanted the *polis* in the landscape of Roman imperial Sicily. Naxos and Megara Hyblaea in particular share several characteristics. Both were close to major overland routes (different sections of the Via Pompeia) and to maritime outlets, and both were in the immediate hinterland of major Roman urban centers (Tauromenium and Syracuse, respectively). Both settlements were also spread out over a wide area, with many nuclei of activity and little evidence of internal organization. Much of the activity on both sites was related to the processing, storage, and distribution of agricultural products. Both sites also bear evidence of long, if not uninterrupted, frequentation in the imperial period. Each settlement is therefore better characterized not as a defined urban center (as it had been in the archaic and classical periods in its *polis* phase) but as part of a regional system of suburban settlement that included smaller, less archaeologically visible, perhaps economically dependent sites (farmsteads, villas, hamlets, etc.). Surveys have traced such systems of rural settlement in the imperial period in the area of Segesta, centered on Aquae Segestanae and later perhaps on the village that arose in the ruins of the urban center of Segesta (see chapter 2), and in other parts of Sicily.

It is not yet possible to assess Naxos in its regional context because of the urbanization of the surrounding coastline and the lack of survey in the interior. The coastal plain around Megara, however, has been subject to extensive research, in spite of the difficulties of tracing ancient occupation in such a heavily industrialized area. This research has centered on the industrial town of Priolo Gargallo, situated less than 7 km southwest of Megara in the center of a small, fertile coastal plain.[49] A Roman-era and late-antique settlement system developed there that had Syracuse at its head and was integrated into the island's broader economy via overland and maritime transportation routes.

Surveys have revealed traces of the paved Roman Via Pompeia, which probably followed the course of a much older coastal route, and a series of Roman-era monuments and settlements oriented around this road and the numerous maritime landings along the bay. Evidence of Roman-era occupation includes the remains of a monumental tomb (Guglia di Marcello) located a few meters away from a paved section of the Via Pompeia. At least three large rural settlements of long duration, occupied in most cases from the classical period through late antiquity, have also been identified. In one of these settlements, in Contrada Fico-Pezzagrande, an honorific Roman marble statue was found along with kiln wasters, indicating the presence of an imperial-era kiln producing roof tiles. The Fico-Pezzagrande settlement has been interpreted as the *pars rustica* of a villa complex or a residential/production area that developed in connection with the Via Pompeia. The settlements have similar ceramic assemblages, dominated by local and imported Italian products in the late Republican and early imperial periods (including Campana C, eastern sigillata A and B, Italian sigillata, thin-walled wares, and Greco-Italic and Dressel 2–4 amphorae) and by local and imported African products in the middle and late empire (including MR1 amphorae and African sigillata).[50]

Several new settlements of varying size (ranging from 1.5 to over 10 hectares) emerged in the late imperial period, beginning in the third century and climaxing in the fourth and fifth centuries. These are distinguishable mostly from their dense ceramic scatters, their burial areas, and, in the case of the San Foca settlement, by a church constructed in the second half of the fifth century.[51] Their development can perhaps be linked to the intensification of agricultural production for export in the region following the Diocletianic administrative reforms of the late third century and the establishment of Constantinople—and the reemergence of Sicily as a major commodity supplier to Rome—in the early fourth century. These settlements, like the older settlements in the area, were located near the Via Pompeia, with traces of secondary routes connecting them to this road. Their ceramic assemblages indicate that they also received imports, especially transport amphorae and finewares from North Africa. In addition, the variation in the monumentality of the tombs in their burial areas and in the amount and quality of goods found within tombs indicates substantial social differentiation within the population.[52]

The recent research conducted around Priolo and in other parts of the southeast shows that the coastline between Catania and Syracuse, and probably also the stretch of coast extending from Syracuse down to Capo Passero, was characterized by shifting clusters of rural settlements of various sizes and degrees of organization rather than by substantial urban settlement. Some of these settlements may have lain within larger senatorial estates, as indicated by the tiles with the stamp "HORTES" found in some sites around Megara and by the presence of the toponym "Hortesiana" in two inscriptions from Syracuse and Modica.[53] Settlement was relatively stable throughout the Roman period, and its organization was governed by the production, storage, marketing, and transportation of agricultural goods. These economic processes were mediated through a road system that connected smaller settlements to larger agglomerations (such as the station at Megara), to major urban centers, and to coastal outlets.

Other areas of Sicily had similar networks of smaller suburban settlements that emerged by the imperial period, whose activities intensified in late antiquity. The development of new settlements on the southern coast is particularly notable and may be a response to the abandonment of the region's older Greek *poleis* and the disintegration of their former territories by the first century AD. The expansion of these settlements in late antiquity may in turn be linked to the revival of the region's economic connections to the wider Mediterranean, particularly to North Africa.

Excavations in the area of modern Sciacca, probably the site of the thermal spa/road station of Aquae Larodes/Thermae Selinuntinae on the southern coastal road (*It. Ant.* 89.4 and 88.7), have revealed that settlement flourished along this section of the southwestern coast. East of Sciacca, in Contrada Locogrande, a large rural settlement arose in the late first century AD on the site of a Hellenistic farm and remained occupied through late antiquity.[54] On the coast around Sciacca archaeologists have identified three additional settlements. Excavations near the mouth of the River Carboj revealed a multiphased settlement complex around one hectare in size that was in occupation from the end of the third century BC until the seventh century AD, with a phase of intensification in the late first century/early second century AD.[55] A similar settlement (also ca. one hectare) arose in the late fourth century AD at the mouth of the River Carabollace and remained in occupation until the late sixth century.[56] The range of imported ceramics found in its buildings attests to its close connection with Africa.[57] A settlement at the mouth of the River Verdura a short distance down the coast had a similar size and period of occupation and a ceramic assemblage similarly dominated by vessels from North Africa.[58] The toponyms of Carboj and Carabollace, derived from the late Latin *carabus* (riverboat), hint at the economic orientation of these settlements. They would have served as coastal *emporia* for the processing and export of products from the interior, perhaps via the larger ports at Mazara, Lilybaeum, or Agrigentum, and for the capillary distribution of imported goods (particularly from Africa) to smaller settlements in the region.[59]

Other parts of the southern coast experienced a notable expansion of settlement in late antiquity. As discussed in chapter 1, new settlement emerged in the hinterland of the abandoned *polis* of Heraclea Minoa in the late Roman period, most likely in connection with the southern coastal road to Agrigentum. Two large late antique settlements in the interior northeast of Agrigentum have recently been excavated: Cignana in the territory of Naro and Vito Soldano in the territory of Canicattì. Cignana, approximately 8 km from the coast but close to the Roman route connecting Catina, Syracuse, and Lilybaeum via Agrigentum, was the site of an imperial-era villa (ca. first–third century AD).[60] This villa appears to have been connected in at least one of its phases to the Flavian senator M. Otacilius Catulus (cos. suf., AD 88), as several roof tiles are stamped with his name or initials.[61] The site of the villa was reoccupied around the second half of the fourth century until the sixth/seventh century by a large village (*vicus*) of ca. 15 hectares, with at least seven buildings and a necropolis. The ceramic assemblage from this village points to strong economic links with North Africa and eastern Sicily that were made possible by the settlement's proximity to the southern coast and to overland transportation routes.

The site of Vito Soldano, between the modern towns of Canicattì and Castrofilippo, shows signs of occupation of indeterminate nature in the early imperial period.[62] In the late third or early fourth century a bath building was constructed on the site, in an *insula* delimited by perpendicular streets that formed part of a larger, still-unexplored regular plan. The site was ringed by a large unexcavated Christian necropolis. The proximity of the site to the presumed course of the interior Roman road between Agrigentum and Catina has led some scholars to hypothesize that it was the *mansio* of Cosconiana in the *It. Ant.* (94.7), 33 Roman miles from Philosophiana, and that its monumentalization was associated with the reform of the *cursus publicus* in Sicily under Constantine.[63] The bath building and the dwellings around it appear to have been abandoned in the fifth century, but the streets remained in use, with some evidence of repaving, until the mid-sixth century, when kilns were constructed over the strata of abandonment.[64]

These settlements provide additional evidence that the dichotomy of urban and nonurban is not adequate for describing and understanding the development of the settlement landscape of the southern coast of Sicily in the imperial period. With the exception of Agrigentum, the Greek *poleis* in the region, along with the political structures associated with them and the territories that they had administered, had disappeared by the first century AD. Agricultural production continued, however, so new forms of settlement arose to house the population engaged in this activity, to manage production processes, and to facilitate the transport by land and sea of agricultural products. For example, the itinerary in the *It. Ant.* from Agrigentum to Syracuse "per maritima loca [*sic*]" includes seven stops at sites labeled as *plagae* or *refugia*, few of which have been securely identified. This itinerary seems to be based on a *cabotage* journey, pointing to the close integration of overland and maritime transportation in this region in the middle and late Empire as well as the ephemerality of many of the centers of such small-scale, regional exchange networks. Moreover, the growing economic significance of coastal settlements was not unique to Sicily: in Roman Cyprus, for example, small and medium-sized coastal sites played an important economic role, particularly in facilitating the exchange of local products for imported goods.[65]

The late Roman and early Byzantine period saw the growth of many of the settlements on the southern coast of Sicily in size and complexity, again in response to shifts in the region's geopolitical position as direct exchange between Sicily and North Africa increased, partly in connection with military campaigns in North Africa. The most highly developed settlement of this late period is at Punta Secca, a short distance down the coast from the site of Camarina and identified by most scholars as the anchorage of Caucana. This level of development in the late Roman/Byzantine period is perhaps unique to the southern coast, which retained direct economic contact with North Africa. But the growing body of research on rural landscapes across Sicily has pointed to intense activity (including the building of churches and other monumental structures as well as the production of ceramics) in other regions.[66]

Of the settlements discussed in this chapter, Sofiana is unique in its monumentality (with its perimeter wall, large and comfortable residences, and large bath complex), its level of internal organization, and the wide range of structures found within it. The resettlement of Megara and Naxos was part of the same process of concentration of economic activity into secondary centers, but neither site reached a similar level of monumentality or organization as far as can be discerned. The settlement at Sofiana was perhaps more autonomous and performed a greater range of services because it was located at a considerable distance (at least two days' travel) from a major urban center.[67] Megara and Naxos were closer and clearly subsidiary to important cities, situated easily within a day's journey of Syracuse and Tauromenium, respectively. Therefore, they are better seen as economic extensions of these cities; indeed, the settlement at Naxos may have served primarily as Tauromenium's port.

Although much less is known of its development, the late Roman settlement at Vito Soldano may offer the closest parallel to Sofiana of the sites examined in this chapter. Both settlements saw the extensive redevelopment of their monumental infrastructure in the late third–early fourth century, in the form of the construction of bath buildings oriented to street grids. In both settlements, this development may be linked to the reorganization of the *cursus publicus* under Constantine. The main evidence for this effort is an inscription found at Sciacca that commemorates the creation of a *sta-*

tio (probably Aquae Larodes/Thermae Selinuntinae) by imperial authorities (*CIL* 10.7200) as well as the itinerary in the *It. Ant.*, which lists *mansiones nunc institutae* (including Philosophiana) between Catina and Agrigentum (94.2–95.1).[68] Additionally, the abandonment of these monumental structures in both settlements and the transition to industrial production (in the form of ceramic kilns and possibly glassworking) may be linked to the weakening of external control over their organization and activities and/or their disintegration from extraregional networks of production and exchange and participation instead in more locally oriented networks. These hypotheses are tentative, however, and rely on still-tenuous and incomplete bodies of archaeological evidence.

CONCLUSION

Despite the sharp contraction in urban settlement in the late Republic and the slower decline that followed under the Principate, the landscape of Roman imperial Sicily was not simply decaying urban centers and emerging luxury villas. Many of the new settlements, like Naxos and Philosophiana, that arose during the Principate can be described as urban only in a loose or minimal sense, as organized centers of population and of economic (but not political) activity. These settlements are difficult to categorize: in spite of their apparently strong connection with the road system and with agricultural activity, the terms "road station" and/or "estate center" are not sufficient. Nor can we assess their development simply in terms of the ruralization of the *polis*, as part of the much-longer process of the decolonization of the Hellenic world.[69] The parallel development of Naxos and nearby Tauromenium, for example, shows the potentially symbiotic relationship between an economic center and a political/social center. Although the settlement at Naxos possessed some monumentality and organization, this was loose and limited. The settlement seems to have had no independent political existence, with the *colonia* at Tauromenium serving as the political and administrative center of the region. The Hellenistic and Roman houses, storerooms, and kilns surrounding and overlying the shipsheds of the classical *polis* of Naxos are a dramatic illustration not only of the decolonization of Sicily but also of the deprivation of most of the autonomy of its *poleis* under Rome and the concentration of symbolic power in the handful of *coloniae* that were securely loyal to the imperial center.

As the centers of symbolic power in the province, these *coloniae* saw considerable monumental building activity in the imperial period. At the same time, many of the older *poleis* that lacked such status and/or were poorly positioned to take advantage of emerging social, political, and economic networks were gradually abandoned, though settlements like Segesta, Morgantina, and Ietas remained centers of economic activity for decades and perhaps even centuries after they had lost their roles as political and social centers. Others, including Calacte, Halaesa, and perhaps Soluntum, saw shifts in activity toward more economically connected sites in their vicinity, such as coastal landings. The monumental urban center of the *polis* could, however, retain (or later regain) its attraction as a center for smaller-scale settlement activity, primarily due to the easy availability of building material and other resources. Lime kilns, for example, were prominent features of the later settlement at Halaesa and at the roadside settlement at Megara Hyblaea.

Many scholars have noted expanded settlement and an increased material presence in the Sicilian countryside in late antiquity. Some have described this expansion as a process of ruralization or as a rural revival that was linked to Sicily's renewed importance as a supplier of cereals and other commodities to the market of Rome, especially after the establishment of Constantinople and the Vandal takeover of the African provinces a century later.[70] The large and elaborately decorated villas that emerged in the third and fourth centuries on the coast and in the interior of Sicily, most notably at Piazza Armerina, Tellaro, and Patti, are the most famous manifestation of this dominance of the countryside. Nonelite rural settlement also becomes more visible in late antiquity, especially in the southeast and along the southern coast, particularly in the realm of cult, as evidence of the presence of Christian communities (such as rural churches and burial areas) increases.

But these new settlements were limited in their physical extent and in their social and political significance in contrast to regions such as North Africa and Italy, which saw the emergence of substantial rural settlements with marketing, and sometimes administrative, functions in late antiquity. In Sicily, perhaps owing to its continued political stability and economic integration with the wider Mediterranean, high-level economic, religious, and political activities—and the monumentalization of them—remained concentrated in cities. One illustration of the limited pull of the countryside even at the apparent height of its late antique prosperity is the tombstone of Julia Florentina, a young Christian who died at Hybla in the southeastern interior but was buried at Catina (*CIL* 10.7112).

Much more archaeological work needs to be done, however, in order to gain a full understanding of this rural settlement landscape and better assess the relationship between urban and rural settlement in Roman and late antique Sicily. If the case of Sofiana is any indication, the extent and complexity of this settlement landscape has been vastly underestimated. As our knowledge of the rural landscapes of Roman Sicily continues to grow, comparison with the Roman-era settlements of regions with similar histories of urbanism, such as southern Italy or Achaea, can help to shed light on their broader significance. The conclusion explores some of the areas of comparative research that may prove fruitful for better understanding the settlement landscape of Roman Sicily and its relationship with the wider empire.

CONCLUSION

The preceding chapter has shown that the new settlements that emerged in Sicily in the imperial period were mainly oriented toward the production, processing, and distribution of agricultural goods via maritime and/or overland transportation routes. However, the archaeological evidence for the connections between these new settlements, and for their relationships with the main urban centers of Sicily, is limited. It is therefore necessary to return to the most substantial surviving document of settlement connectivity in the Roman period: the Sicilian section of the *It. Ant.*[1] This text, despite its shortcomings (discussed in the introduction), sheds light on the relationship of new settlements like Sofiana and Naxos to the urban centers of Sicily. Furthermore, it shows the most likely paths by which people and goods moved into, out of, and through Sicily in the high and late Empire (see map 2).

MOVING THROUGH ROMAN SICILY

Besides a few milestones, bridge foundations, and sections of pavement, little remains of the Roman road network in Sicily upon which the routes in the *It. Ant.* were based. It is therefore nearly impossible to determine the exact courses of these roads and the locations of many of the stops listed along them. It is probable, however, that the Roman roads of Sicily largely adopted the courses and infrastructure of existing long-distance routes. Over time, Roman authorities enhanced this infrastructure in piecemeal fashion in order to meet strategic needs.[2] This enhancement of the road network occurred especially during the First and Second Punic Wars and continued under the Republic and Empire, most substantially under Constantine.

The high- and late-imperial routes preserved in the *It. Ant.* are centered on seven coastal urban centers: Lilybaeum, Messana, Tyndaris, Thermae, Catina,

Agrigentum, and Syracuse. These cities served as ports for movement in and out of Sicily (especially between Africa and Italy, as indicated by their position in the maritime itineraries). They also served as nodes in overland travel and transport and as landing-points in smaller-scale, shorter maritime movements (e.g., *cabotage*). Although they are included as stops, Panormus and Tauromenium are the only Roman *coloniae* that do not serve as the beginning or end points of individual routes or as connecting points between interior and coastal routes. Panormus, surrounded by the hills of the Conca d'Oro, may not have had direct access to major overland routes. Instead, the settlement of Hyccara, near modern Carini, serves as the northwestern node of the road system.

The Roman road system as reflected in the *It. Ant.* is clearly geared toward travel along the coasts: nine of the routes within the itineraries are coastal, while only five traverse the interior. The coastal itineraries also show the close integration between overland and maritime transportation routes, perhaps reflecting the necessity of having numerous safe havens and alternative means of transportation available in seasons when sailing around Sicily was difficult. For example, Naxos/Tauromenium is listed as a maritime landing point midway between the larger ports of Messana and Catina (491.3–4), but in the overland itineraries it is also two or three days' journey to the Straits of Messina and two days' journey to Catina (87.2 and 90.3).

Most of the interior settlements listed in the *It. Ant.* are also within two or three days' journey of the coast, with stopping-points available along the way. For example, following the various routes of the *It. Ant.*, the interior stop of Philosophiana would have been two days' journey from Catina, including a stop at the *mansio* Capitoniana (87.4–88.2 and 94.4–94.5). To get to Italy from there, a traveler could follow the overland route north to the Straits of Messina (a journey of six days or less) or travel by sea, with numerous islands and ports on the coast of Sicily and western Italy to put in at along the way. Alternatively, for a traveler headed to Africa, Agrigentum was a two- or three-day journey from Philosophiana, with stops at the *mansiones* of Galloniana and possibly Cosconiana (88.3–4 and 94.6–95.1). Lilybaeum could be reached by sea or land from Agrigentum in a four- to six-day journey. From Lilybaeum a ship could cross to Africa via the island of Marettimo (to Carthage) or via Pantelleria or Malta (to the ports of Libya).

The *It. Ant.*, when combined with our knowledge of the settlement system of Roman imperial Sicily from other sources, allows us to reconstruct the experience of a hypothetical traveler moving through the island in, say, the third century AD. Whether arriving from Italy (at Messana), from the Eastern Mediterranean (at Catina or Syracuse), or from Africa (at Lilybaeum or Agrigentum), the traveler's initial impression of Sicily would not have been unfamiliar. In each case, the traveler would have entered a recognizably Roman city, with the facilities that a cosmopolitan voyager would expect from any self-respecting urban center: theaters, amphitheaters, baths, temples, public buildings, fine houses, workshops, port facilities, and warehouses.

Travelers who took a route that followed the northern coast would pass by numerous hilltop settlements (Tyndaris, Calacte, Halaesa, Soluntum), some decaying or already abandoned and some with auxiliary settlements closer to the coastline and road. If they followed the southern coast, they would have encountered a landscape almost completely devoid of urban settlement and instead might have passed numerous small coastal and roadside settlements, each perhaps consisting of a few houses and storage buildings. Travelers who traversed the interior would have encountered a variety of settlements, including a few *poleis* reinvented as prosperous Roman *civitates* (such as Centuripae) and numerous new utilitarian settlements that had arisen on or near the road, though some, like Philosophiana, were of considerable size and architectural pretension. However, most rural settlements, where the majority of Sicilians probably lived, would have been away from the main routes and beyond the gaze of the travelers, as obscure as they are to modern scholars. But travelers who ventured off the road in many regions would have seen few indications of impoverishment and isolation. In northern and western Sicily, where field survey has been most extensive, rural settlement continued in the imperial period and late antiquity, though often in new configurations. For example, smaller, dispersed settlements agglomerated into fewer, larger settlements in some areas. The Sicilian countryside remained productive, and many of its settlements continued to receive goods from overseas.

ROMAN SICILY IN ITS MEDITERRANEAN CONTEXT

The late Roman itineraries and the diverse toponyms that they contain, from long-lived Greek urban centers to newer *mansiones* and *plagae*, hint at a Sicilian settlement landscape that was far from static. They also point to Sicilian settlements' connections to the broader Mediterranean, especially within the maritime corridor connecting North Africa to Italy. A later text that is vastly different in character, the *Life of Saint Gregory, Bishop of Agrigento* (discussed in chapter 3), similarly situates Sicily within the context of Mediterranean movement and exchange. It almost takes for granted the ease with which its subject could move from the southern coast of Sicily to Carthage, farther afield to Tripoli, Jerusalem, and Rome, and eventually back to his home city via the port of Palermo. These texts, though not primarily concerned with cities, provide further support to my contention that changes in the settlement landscape of Sicily—and particularly in the extent and nature of urban settlement—are related to broader trends in central Mediterranean politics and commerce.

The main conclusion to emerge from the case studies of the previous chapters is that three significant settlement shifts took place in the centuries between the Roman conquest of western Sicily in the First Punic War (264–241 BC) and the effective end of Roman political hegemony in the fifth century AD. First, intense urban settlement shifted away from the southern and northern coasts under the late Republic and in the early- and mid-imperial periods, respectively, to be concentrated instead on the eastern and western coasts by the third century AD. Second, from the late Republic into the imperial period, significant changes in urban forms and in the nature of urban life occurred in both "failing" and "thriving" Sicilian cities. These changes included the adaptation of existing urban structures and spaces to serve new and sometimes multiple functions as well as the dispersion (or dissociation) of centers of commercial and political activity within cities. One result of these processes of urban transformation is that few Sicilian cities conform to the norms of Roman imperial monumentality seen in provincial "showpiece cities," such as Carthage and Leptis Magna, and in Rome itself. Rather, the Sicilian cities that thrived demographically, politically, and economically in the high imperial period, such as Lilybaeum, Syracuse, Centuripae, and Catina, selectively adopted elements of the Roman monumental set that met the needs and desires of their populations and that conformed to the existing urban fabric, a process that sometimes led to singular hybrid monuments.

A third major shift in the Sicilian urban landscape occurred in the position of high-order urban centers within the broader settlement spectrum. The major eastern, northeastern, and western coastal centers consolidated their positions at the top of the provincial urban hierarchy during, and in the decades surrounding, the Principate of Augustus. Older second-order urban centers (including many former *poleis*: both Greek *apoikiai* and Hellenized indigenous settlements), first in the interior and on the southern coast and later on the northern coast, ceded to new forms of economically oriented semiurban or suburban settlement.

The key variable in all three of these shifts was the level of integration of Sicilian regions and localities into the interlinked political, social, and economic networks of the Roman Mediterranean. The eastern and western coasts of Sicily retained a high and consistent level of integration throughout the Roman period, especially with central Italy and Rome, the North African littoral, and (in the case of eastern Sicily) the Eastern Mediterranean. Such integration enabled the persistence of high-order urban centers like Syracuse, Catina, Tauromenium, Agrigentum, Panormus, and Lilybaeum. This small set of cities served as the province's poles of political and economic activity and cultural prestige. The southern and northern coasts and the interior, in contrast, were subject to more variable and irregular integration into these networks. As a result, new forms of suburban or semiurban settlement (e.g., Philosophiana) developed to take better advantage of these changing patterns of integration and especially to adapt to shifts in the dominant maritime and overland transportation routes traversing the island.

Although the geography of Sicily—most obviously, its unique position as an island at the center of Rome's Mediterranean empire—was a dominant factor in the development of its urban landscape under the Principate (as it had been in earlier periods of antiquity), these major shifts were not solely geographically determined. Nor were the urban populations of Sicily passive participants in the political, economic, social, religious, and cultural changes that their cities experienced or in the physical alterations to urban spaces through which these evolving roles were manifested. When the human actors in these processes can be observed, unsurprisingly, elites played significant roles, both in their presence and by their absence. The divestment of the political, economic, and social resources of elites from cities like Segesta and Ietas, and the concomitant contraction and decay of urban infrastructure, can be contrasted with the case of Centuripae. This inland hilltop center possessed the unique combination of an extensive and fertile hinterland, an advantageous position along interior trade and communications routes, and a local elite that was politically active and savvy from the early years of Roman hegemony in Sicily through the imperial period. A small set of interrelated, wealthy, and politically and socially prominent families of Roman citizens oversaw the development of the city, especially in the second century AD, using its public spaces as arenas for the celebration and promotion of themselves and of their *patria*.

Such elites, though they were the most visible actors in shaping the political and economic fortunes and the monumental public and private spaces of Sicilian cities, did not exist in a vacuum. Their livelihoods and activities were enabled in large part by the labors of the subelites that formed the majority of the urban population. Individuals and groups within these urban middling classes can be traced in the archaeological and epigraphic records of Catina, Syracuse, Agrigentum, Lilybaeum, and Halaesa, not only as inhabitants of urban spaces (such as residential and commercial *insulae*, markets, port facilities, offices, and—in the end—graves) but also as participants in urban political, social, and religious life, most visibly as Augustales. Evidence of similar activities can be found in inscriptions from other Sicilian cities that remained vital in the imperial period, such as Panormus and Thermae, whose topographical development is more difficult to assess.[3]

This analysis of Sicilian settlement can be enriched through comparison with other Mediterranean regions with similar histories of urban development and relations with the Roman state. Like Sicily, the Roman province of Achaea was densely settled with urban centers (*poleis*) of various sizes, many of which had existed for several centuries, had been monumentalized long before the arrival of Rome, and possessed sophisticated political institutions and highly developed economies. These cities, like those of Sicily, suffered from periodic warfare and political instability in the third and second centuries BC, both before and during their incorporation into the nascent Roman overseas empire. Nor were they immune from the unrest of the Roman civil wars of the first century BC. Strabo, for example, gives an account of the decline of urban settlement in Arcadia that echoes his description of the Sicilian interior (esp. *Geog.* 6.2.6), emphasizing the disappearance of "formerly notable" cities due to "continuous wars," and the "abundance of pasture" resulting from the desertion (ἡ ἐρημία) of the territory (8.8.1).

Over two decades ago Susan E. Alcock's groundbreaking monograph on Roman Achaea emphasized the material record of a province that, like Sicily, had been largely ignored by modern scholars because of assumptions (based on sources like Strabo) that it had been in terminal decline under the Principate. Alcock used data from field surveys and urban excavations to trace changes in the political, economic, cultural, and religious roles of urban centers and in the location, form, and intensity of nonurban settlement in the Roman period. Rather than being an absolute decline in population, Alcock hypothesized that the drop in site numbers indicated in field surveys reflected the rise of estate-based agriculture and a demographic shift from dispersed rural settlements to towns, such as the *coloniae* established by Augustus after Actium.[4] The results that Alcock relied on can now be supplemented with data from more recent projects. These findings largely confirm her broad analysis of the Achaean settlement landscape but add nuance, for example, by emphasizing the differences between regions.[5]

Given the patchy geographic and temporal coverage of field survey in Sicily (as well as the difficulty of comparing the results of multiple projects undertaken on varying scales and using different methodologies), it is more difficult to compare the evidence for nonurban settlement in Roman Sicily and Greece. Nonetheless, the available historical and archaeological evidence suggests that broadly similar processes were at work from the Hellenistic period into the Roman Principate.[6] As in Sicily, Roman Republican-era military intervention led to changes in patterns of landholding in Greece: first and most famously, the confiscation of the land of Corinth in 146 BC, most of which was handed over to Sicyon. As with Sicily, the first major alienation of Achaean land came in the civil wars and accompanied the Caesarian and Augustan programs of colonization. In Greece as in Sicily, however, it is important to recognize the gradual and differential nature of change. Transformations in rural structures, land divisions, and land ownership are more visible in the territories of colonies like Patrae and Nicopolis than in other large cities, where more traditional forms of rural settlement and exploitation could persist into the imperial period.

Italy is another geographically and ethnically diverse, relatively highly urbanized region with a long history of interactions with the Roman state as well as strong and enduring economic and political links to the city of Rome. We may expect the closest parallels to developments in Sicily to be found in Magna Graecia, the area of archaic Greek colonial settlement in southern Italy largely corresponding to coastal Puglia, Basilicata, and Calabria.[7] The Roman conquest of Magna Graecia occurred largely in the late fourth and early third centuries BC, a few decades before the earliest Roman military interventions in Sicily. The southern Italian cities' subsequent interactions with Roman power did not always prove beneficial. As with the Greek *apoikiai* of Sicily, Strabo emphasizes the devastating impact of Roman-era warfare on the cities of Magna Graecia. He claims, for example, that Taras/Tarentum and Brentesion/Brundisium are the only significant cities left in Messapia (6.3.4). Strabo says of Apulia: "Formerly the whole land was prosperous, but it was laid waste [ἠρήμωσαν] by Hannibal and later wars" (6.3.11). One important distinction is that southern Italy, unlike Sicily, was not a *provincia*. Instead, Roman control of the region before the Social War was based on a series of alliances with city-states and the implantation of colonial settlements. From 89 BC the region, along with the rest of Italy, was incorporated into Roman citizenship, with urban settlements classed as *municipia* or *coloniae*.

As in Sicily, recent research has suggested a more variegated picture of the cities of Magna Graecia under Roman rule than Strabo's description. Such variety is hardly surprising, given the region's large size. Signs of deurbanization begin in the third century BC and continue into the early imperial period. Several urban settlements, including the coastal *apoikiai* of Heraclea and Metapontum in Basilicata, either underwent severe contraction or were abandoned entirely.[8] One difference between southern Italy and Sicily is that the Italian cities, especially those in key strategic positions on harbors and/or along Roman roads, tended to attract more consistent attention from the Roman state. For example, after the Hannibalic war and continuing into the early Principate, Tarentum underwent several phases of colonization and saw its civic landscape gradually transformed, with the rebuilding of its Greek theater and the construction of an amphitheater, baths, and aqueducts.[9] As in Sicily in the post–civil war period, however, the direct Roman impact on the urban fabric of the Greek cities of southern Italy is difficult to measure. For example, scholars have recently argued against interpreting the creation of a Roman forum in the civic center of Paestum, a colony since 273 BC, as a traumatic change to the Greek-era urban fabric. Instead, the reshaping of the city along Roman lines was a more gradual process of adaptation of existing Greek (and Lucanian) public spaces.[10]

As in Sicily, the obsolescence of some older urban sites in southern Italy may be linked to their disintegration from prevailing trade routes or to mounting environmental challenges, such as the lack of a regular water supply or the silting of a river or sea port. For example, by Strabo's time, the area around Paestum had become marshy, apparently as a result of the inability of freshwater from springs in its vicinity to flow directly into the sea. Although located some 70 km away from Pompeii, the city may also have suffered damage from the eruption of Vesuvius in AD 79.[11] As with many Sicilian cities, however, it is debatable exactly when decline set in at Paestum. Although the city was struggling to maintain the passage of freshwater to the sea in the first century AD, the urban center remained occupied (though on a smaller scale) in the fourth century, with inscriptions attesting to the persistence of civic government. The site may not have been completely abandoned until the seventh century.[12]

The new forms of suburban and semiurban settlement that emerged in Sicily, sometimes on or near the sites of former urban settlements, in the imperial period and late antiquity (as discussed in chapter 7) are comparable to the "agricultural agglomerations" or *vici* that emerged in southern Italy on or near old urban sites, usually close to ports or to the Roman road network, in the fourth and fifth centuries AD.[13] In the grainlands of Puglia and Basilicata some sites of ancient cities found new life in late antiquity as centers for the processing and shipment of grain, perhaps under direct state control.[14] In a development similar to the emergence of suburban settlements along the coasts of Sicily, the old urban site of Metapontum and its port saw renewed development in the fourth and fifth centuries that was apparently aimed to facilitate the storage and export of grain produced in the hinterland.[15]

The cities of southern Italy that did survive through the Roman period have in general left a more extensive epigraphic record than those in Sicily. Inscriptions show that in Velia (Greek Elea), Naples, and Rhegium, where Latin had become the official language by the first century BC, Greek magistracies like the gymnasiarchy survived, embedded in largely Roman frameworks of government, at least until the early Principate.[16] Although many southern Italian cities remained occupied throughout the Roman era (and many persist today), they could experience widely divergent fortunes. Tarentum and Rhegium saw their power and prosperity decline under Roman rule, with Tarentum gradually ceding its regional commercial dominance to Brundisium, a rival port founded as a colony that was better integrated into the Roman road system.[17] Naples, Cumae, and Velia, however, benefited at least for a time from the political, economic, and social opportunities created by Roman imperial expansion in the middle and late Republic.[18]

I hope that this brief overview shows that a comparative approach has significant potential for increasing our understanding of the impact of Roman imperialism on the *polis* systems of Sicily, southern Italy, and Greece. The Roman-era histories and archaeologies of these regions continue to attract less attention than those of their perceived archaic and classical-era heydays. Nonetheless, the process of deurbanization that took place in Sicily appears to have no close parallels elsewhere in the Roman Empire, particularly in its extent and in its chronological course. The root causes of deurbanization in other regions in other periods were not at work in the Sicilian urban landscape of the late first century BC and early first century AD. An example is the "institutional loss" that contributed to the end of Roman urbanism in the western empire in late antiquity as Roman political and economic hegemony waned.[19] Rather, the driving forces behind the transformations observed in Sicily, including the obsolescence and disappearance of cities in some regions, were institutional changes at the island-wide, regional, and local levels that were linked to the altered political and economic place of the province within the Roman imperial system. Italy, the provinces of mainland Greece, and other regions experienced similar changes, such as the establishment of veteran colonies and the redistribution of civic land, at around the same time as Sicily, in the midst of the upheavals of Roman civil wars. Yet these regions' diverse geopolitical roles in the Roman Empire meant that these changes manifested in different ways in each of them. For example, in Achaea the newly founded Nicopolis and the rebuilt colony of Corinth served as regional centers of population, administration, and commerce. In Sicily, although populations were displaced and lands alienated after the civil war, no new cities were founded to house these displaced Sicilians or the Roman colonists newly settled on the island.

This study has highlighted the large-scale and small-scale changes that the urban landscape of Sicily underwent under Roman hegemony. It has also explored the significance of these changes for our understanding not only of the place of Sicily in the Roman imperial system but also of the multiple and complex ways in which the formal and informal—and direct and indirect—mechanisms of Roman state power could manifest over time and across the diverse political, economic, and physical geography of the empire. I hope, therefore, that it will serve as a stimulus to further research on Roman Sicily.

We still need to accumulate and analyze reliable archaeological evidence for settlement across the island and to synthesize the results of projects recently completed or currently underway. Survey and excavation continues at Morgantina, in areas of the city not previously explored; this work should provide insight into the development of public and private spaces away from the agora.[20] Excavation has recently resumed at Halaesa, also in areas of the city not previously explored.[21] At Agrigentum, new excavations in the city's main Hellenistic and Roman-era public area have brought to light evidence of a previously unknown theater.[22]

In addition, publication of long-running projects such as the Gela Survey continues.[23] New surveys have been undertaken in less well-studied rural landscapes in the past decade, like the area around the villa at Cignana (discussed in chapter 7).[24] The reexamination of structures and materials from sites uncovered in previous centuries also has the potential to enrich our understanding of rural agricultural regimes and patterns of settlement. For example, archaeological research has recently resumed at the late antique village, basilica, and necropolis at San Miceli (the *statio* of *ad Olivam*?) that Antonio Salinas first explored in the late nineteenth century.[25] Another promising avenue is geophysical survey of known or hypothesized settlement sites, an unobtrusive method that has been effective in revealing "hidden" structures in its limited application in Sicily, for example, at Sofiana and Akrai.[26] This method holds enormous promise, particularly for areas like the interior of Sicily, where the full extent of settlements (and relationships between settlements) can be difficult to detect using traditional methods like field survey and targeted excavation.

The recording, analysis, and publication of the vast existing bodies of Roman-era evidence from Sicily must also continue. For example, the I.Sicily project is a comprehensive online digital corpus of ancient Sicilian lapidary inscriptions that includes photographs and new editions of both published and unpublished texts.[27] Research on the production and distribution of ceramics in Sicily must also continue. Fabric-based analysis has enabled researchers to identify classes of vessels that were produced on a large scale in Sicily (for example, the small flat-bottomed amphorae used to transport wine) and to specify the regions (and in some cases the sites) in which they were produced.[28] Further excavation of kiln complexes and other pottery production sites is still needed in order to link individual fabrics more securely to specific localities or sites. The integration of Sicilian ceramic evidence (such as amphora and fineware assemblages) into online databases with more extensive geographical coverage is also desirable. This would enable more sophisticated analysis of the production and circulation of ceramic vessels (and in the case of amphorae the commodities they carried) within and outside the island.

The archaeologists and historians who analyze these ever-expanding bodies of evidence are faced with an increasingly complex picture of life in Roman Sicily. I hope that this study has shown that the links between Sicily and other regions, from the individual to the communal and provincial levels, offer fruitful avenues for further exploration. Although the nature and composition of many of its communities changed, Sicily remained a vital province at the heart of the Roman Empire.

NOTES

INTRODUCTION

1. Hansen 2006:44–47.

2. But see De Vincenzo 2013.

3. Thucydides (6.6–8) describes Segesta's role in prompting the Athenian expedition to Sicily in 415 BC.

4. The bronze rams (*rostra*) inscribed in Latin with the names of Roman magistrates recently excavated from the site of the decisive battle of the Aegates Islands (241 BC) vividly illustrate the nexus between Rome's conquest of Sicily and the development of its institutions of governance (Prag 2014a).

5. See Belvedere 1997b; Pinzone 1999a; Vera 1996; and Wilson 1990:33–45.

6. Cassius Dio claims that Augustus established colonies at Syracuse and "certain other cities" during his visit to Sicily in 21 BC (54.6–7). Pliny the Elder lists five colonies in Sicily: Tauromenium, Catina, Syracuse, Thermae, and Tyndaris (*HN* 3.87–89, discussed below). He calls Panormus an *oppidum*, but Strabo claims that it has a "settlement of Romans" (Ῥωμαίων ἔχει κατοικίαν) (*Geography* 6.2.5). Therefore, many scholars have concluded that Panormus was among the Augustan colonies; Wilson (1990:37) hypothesizes that it was established in 14 BC.

7. Horace's *Epistle* 1.12 is addressed to Iccius, the manager of Agrippa's Sicilian holdings.

8. The privilege was later granted to Gallia Narbonensis under Claudius (Tac., *Ann.* 12.23).

9. Laurence et al. 2011:12–63.

10. See Fournier 2010 for the development of Roman jurisprudence in the Hellenophone provinces.

11. My approach to defining urban settlement in Sicily is largely drawn from the general discussions of ancient Mediterranean urbanism and urbanization in Osborne 2005 and Purcell 2005.

12. Horden and Purcell 2000:224–230.

13. De Angelis 2009.

14. One exception is De Angelis 2003 for the archaic and classical periods.

15. The works of Bejor (1983 and others) and Wilson (1985, 1990, etc.) are exceptions,

although they predate the publication of several field surveys conducted since the 1980s. See Campagna 2003:22–25 for the impact of Bejor and Wilson's work.

16. E.g., Belvedere 1997a; Fitzjohn 2007; Perkins 2007; Spanò Giammellaro et al. 2008.

17. Dueck 2000:146–151.

18. Clarke 1999:341.

19. The tax obligations of the *stipendiarii* are obscure. Many scholars have argued that in the mid- or late first century BC the grain tithe (*decima*) was replaced by a fixed *stipendium* perhaps collected in cash but more likely still in kind. The exact nature of this change and the person responsible for it (whether Pompey, Julius Caesar, or Octavian) remain open questions. Pinzone (1999a) provides an overview of the debate and a possible solution.

20. Vera 1996; Wilson 1990:38.

21. Selinus and Himera had been destroyed in earlier wars without substantial resettlement (Wilson 1990:15, 166). Megara Hyblaea had been sacked by Marcellus (Plut., *Marc.* 18.2), but smaller-scale settlement resumed thereafter (discussed in chapter 7).

22. Keppie (1983:5) ascribes this section to Artemidorus or Varro, Nicolet (1991:173–174) tentatively to Varro. Wilson (1990:37–38) blames the inclusion of these abandoned cities on Pliny's failure to check and update his source.

23. Ando 2010:36–38; Mitchell 1999.

24. Wilson (1990:36) assigns secure locations to twenty names and tentative locations to eight and classifies the remaining seventeen as unknown.

25. Murphy 2004:129–131; Nicolet 1991:173–177.

26. Salway 2001:40n52.

27. Salway 2001:33–34.

28. Cf. the *Itinerarium Maritimum*, a collection of sea routes tacked onto the end of the *It. Ant.* that lists routes between Italy and Sicily and between Sicily and Africa (515.3–518.2).

29. The most thorough attempt to map the settlements of Roman Sicily is by Wilson (1990:10; fig. 8). This map relies heavily on the itineraries, so much of the interior of the island is empty space; Wilson only distinguishes between "major" and "other" settlements.

30. These definitions of Roman urban space structure Wilson's 1990 monograph as well as the contributions to the Sicilian volume of *ANRW* (1988) by Wilson and Belvedere.

31. Cities in Lombard Italy remained market centers and focuses of elite identity, political activity, and territorial organization despite the demonumentalization of their classical centers, the disintegration of their infrastructure, and the material impoverishment of their residents (Wickham 2005:211–213, 649–655). Although distant from the Roman Mediterranean in time and space, the ancient African "clustered cities" that McIntosh (2015:369) describes similarly defy normative models of cities as monumental expressions of concentrated political power.

32. Hopkins 1978.

33. Horden and Purcell 2000:89–122; Purcell 2005.

34. As Osborne (2005:13) emphasizes, "What is important about towns is not that they necessarily do or involve anything in particular, but that they make possible a whole range of economic, social, and political activities which cannot be managed, or managed as effectively, in other forms of settlement."

35. Horden and Purcell 2000:93 (quotation); Purcell 2005:252.

36. For the Roman state's impact on urban development in Italy and other provinces, see, inter alia, Alcock 1993; Lomas 1993; Patterson 2006; and Woolf 1998:106–168.

37. Hopkins 1980. Fentress 2013 and Keay 2013 propose alternatives to "Romanization" and its antecedents "Hellenization" and "Punicization." Mattingly (2010:22–42, 203–245) offers a notable critique of "Romanization" and other restrictive terms for describing cultural change in ancient communities and puts forward the alternative concept of "discrepancy."

38. E.g., Wallace-Hadrill 2008 and Woolf 1998:238–241.

39. E.g., by Coarelli (1980:380): "Nonostante la deduzione di numerose colonie augustee, i primi secoli dell'Impero rappresenteranno il periodo forse meno brillante per la civiltà urbana della Sicilia."

40. Tomka and Stevenson 1993:191.

41. Wickham 2005:672.

42. Faulkner 1996.

43. Ward-Perkins 1996:7–10.

44. Peña 2007a.

45. Wickham 2005:636–671.

46. Horne 1993.

47. Kulikowski 2006:129.

48. Renfrew and Poston 1979.

49. Cf. Bintliff 1997:80–86.

50. Horne 1993:48–52.

51. Mackil 2004:508–513.

52. Tomka and Stevenson 1993:192.

CHAPTER 1

1. Cassius Dio 54.6–7 (using the verb καθίστημι).

2. Thomas and Witschel 1992.

3. Most influentially Wilson 1990:143–159.

4. Wilson (1990:143–159) briefly discusses the evidence for the abandonment of Morgantina, Ietas, Helorus, Soluntum (at a later date), Mytistraton, Monte Riparato, Halaesa (later), Menae, Montagna di Marzo, Entella, and Segesta (later). I catalogue thirteen settlements that were abandoned or reduced in size in this century in the appendix to my PhD dissertation (2013) and discuss three (Helorus, Apollonia, and Entella) in greater detail in the main text.

5. This section largely follows De Miro's report (2014) on excavations from the 1950s through 2004.

6. Wilson and Leonard 1980; Wilson 1981.

7. Fiorentini 1993–1994:729–733. This road would have largely followed the southern coastal route between Agrigentum and Lilybaeum recorded in the *It. Ant.*

8. La Torre and Mollo 2013.

9. The naval battle in 249 BC described by Diodorus as taking place near Phintias (24.1) probably corresponds with the battle that Polybius placed near an anonymous *polismation* (1.53) (La Torre and Mollo 2013:465). Marcellus's final battle with the Carthaginians took place near the river in the late summer of 211 BC (Livy 25.40–41).

10. For preliminary results of the most recent excavations, see Toscano Raffa et al. 2015.

11. Campagna 2013.

12. La Torre and Mollo 2013:467. The city also issued two series of bronze coins with the legend "GELOION" in the late third century BC.

13. Toscano Raffa 2015, 2017:232–250.

14. La Torre and Mollo 2013:474–478.

15. La Torre and Mollo 2013:439–440.

16. Bell 1981; Buttrey et al. 1989; Cuomo di Caprio 1992; Stone 2014.

17. For epigraphic evidence of Morgantina's inclusion in Hieron's kingdom (along with Akrai and Camarina), see Walthall 2011.

18. The first chapter of Stone 2014 summarizes the development of the city's public spaces.

19. This hypothesized increase in rural settlement is based on the results of the Morgantina Archaeological Survey, as outlined by Thompson (1999:392–431).

20. E.g., Stillwell (1963:169–70) describes the "thorough and wanton destruction" of the "Priest's House."

21. Bell and Holloway 1988:326. The city's two public bath complexes west of the agora also went out of use by the early second century BC and were never reoccupied (Stone 2015).

22. Sharp 2015.

23. Bell and Holloway 1988:331–340; Bell 1986–1987.

24. Cuomo di Caprio 1992; Stone 2014.

25. Tsakirgis 1984:46–84, 120–227; Stone 2014 for domestic pottery deposits.

26. Thompson 1999:435–454.

27. E.g., Sjöqvist 1958:161 (the Pappalardo House), 1960:130 (the Public Granary), 1962:138 (the theater); Stillwell 1963:168 (the House of the Arched Cistern).

28. Stone 1983, reiterated in 2014.

29. Buttrey et al. 1989, catalogue nos. 48, 49, 73–76 (pp. 181–183 and 191–199); Stone 2014:24–26; Tsakirgis 1984:17–18.

30. Bell 1986–1987:120–123; Stone 2014:61–63.

31. Stone 2014:68–70.

32. E.g., in the residential quarters (Mancini 2006).

33. Stone (2014:23–24) cites 237 coins issued between 45 and 36 BC (including 217 issues of Sextus Pompey), compared to 52 from ca. 35 to 8 BC. Interestingly, a small hoard of well-worn Roman *denarii* mostly from the 80s–40s BC that was probably deposited around the time of Octavian's takeover of Sicily contains no issues of Sextus Pompey (Walthall 2013).

34. Stillwell (1961:278) notes the collapse of the walls of the shops of the West Stoa of the agora while they were still under construction, perhaps in the late third century BC, due to the shifting of the scarp of the West Hill. See Crouch 1984 for the environmental challenges of the site.

35. Tsakirgis 1984:148.

36. Crouch 1984.

37. The excavation of this fountain was reported in Bell 1986–1987; its phases of use have recently been reexamined by Bruno et al. 2015.

38. Buttrey et al. 1989:36–39. Although the chronology of their production is patchy, most coins of the HISPANORUM series are found in mid- to late second-century BC contexts. They remained in circulation well into the first century BC and are found with Roman *denarii* as late as 46 BC.

39. Cuomo di Caprio 1992. The ten late Hellenistic kilns excavated in the city belong to six workshops (five located in the agora and one in the House of the Official). The potteries in the East Granary and the House of the Official each contained three kilns, while those in the Central Sanctuary, North Stoa, and East Stoa each had one kiln, as did the Great Kiln in the city wall.

40. The production of Campana C vessels at Morgantina is most clearly linked to the House of the Official and East Granary kilns. The potters in these establishments also experimented with the production of thin-walled wares and red-gloss wares ("presigillata") (Stone 2014:139–205).

41. Bruno et al. 2015:15; Sharp 2015:175.

42. The Great Kiln, which produced mainly brick and tiles, was in use until the early first century BC. The other kilns went out of use later in that century, mostly ca. 35 BC (Cuomo di Caprio 1992:182; Stone 2014:139–141).

43. Tsakirgis 1984:149, 341. It is similarly difficult to discern if the altar built in the ruins of the theater *temenos* around the late first century BC was the result of individual or communal initiative (Stillwell 1963:166).

44. Sjöqvist 1962:136.

45. Sjöqvist 1962:138; Stone 2014:25, 61–70; Tsakirgis 1984:143.

46. Stone 2014:25; Tsakirgis 1984:316–317, 443.

47. Bruno et al. 2015:18.

48. The patterns observed in the second century and early first century BC—principally, the reorientation of settlement (both large and small sites, probably engaged primarily in grain production) toward major river valleys—appear to have continued in the later first century BC and into the Principate. These sites received considerable quantities of Italian terra sigillata, followed by a limited range of African wares (Thompson 1999:455–458).

49. Stone 1981:16; Tsakirgis 1984:18.

50. Orsi 1990; Pace 1927; Pelagatti et al. 1976; Pelagatti 1984–1985.

51. G. Di Stefano 2006.

52. G. Di Stefano 2001–2002:693–694.

53. Uggeri 2015:186.

54. Mattioli 1995:268.

55. Lucchelli 2004:54–57.

56. See *BCH* 45 (1921), 1, col. IV, ll. 90–118 for the Sicilian section of the Delphic *theorodokoi* list; *Syll.*³ 488 in honor of Aristarchos.

57. *SEG* 39.996–1002; Mattioli 1995:253–256.

58. Lucchelli 2004:60–61.

59. G. Di Stefano 2010:546.

60. Lucchelli 2004:43, 60–62.

61. G. Di Stefano 2010:545.

62. The stamped ceramic grain measure found in excavations in the agora is strong evidence for the inclusion of Camarina in Hieron's kingdom. Similar vessels bearing the same magistrate's name (Artemidoros) have been found in Morgantina and Akrai. All three appear to be the products of a single workshop, suggesting that they were manufactured and distributed across eastern Sicily for the collection of the Hieronian grain tithe (Walthall 2011).

63. G. Di Stefano 2006; Lucchelli 2004:56–60; and Mattioli 1995:260–269. See also Bell 2006 for similarities in the fifth-century urban plans of Morgantina and Camarina.

64. Collin Bouffier 2006.

65. Parker 1992, cat. nos. 163, 164, and 166 (Camarina A, B, and D), 398 (Femmina Morta), and 975 (Randello); cf. G. Di Stefano 2002. A first-century AD ship carrying numerous fine bronze vessels, lamps, and statuettes probably made in Campania—likely to be personal effects, rather than commercial cargo—was discovered in the bay in 1999 (G. Di Stefano 2003).

66. Di Stefano and Leone 1985.

67. G. Di Stefano 1994.

68. G. Di Stefano 1993–1994:1402–1406, 2005; Di Stefano and Ventura 2011.

69. Ietas (and especially its theater) is frequently mentioned in the debate over "high" vs. "low" chronologies for the development of Sicilian urban centers in the Hellenistic/Republican period; Isler (2011a) continues to defend a "high" dating of the main phase of monumental development.

70. Isler 2000:22–24.

71. Bloesch and Isler 1976:22–23 (obsolescence of the wall circuit); Isler 1980–1981:1004 (disuse of the *bouleuterion*).

72. Isler 1975:541–543, 545–546.

73. The portico in front of the late second-century BC *bouleuterion* collapsed in the late first century or early second century AD, long after the structure had fallen out of use (Isler 1982:11). The destruction of the temple on a podium in the agora dates around the mid-second century AD, based on fragments of African sigillata found under the collapse of its southern wall (Isler 1987:16). The collapse of the east portico of the agora dates to the second half of the second century AD or later on similar grounds (Isler 1992:25–27, 2006:5, 2011b:35–37).

74. Activity in and around the disused structures of the theater, including the con-

struction of hearths, is detectable from the early imperial period until at least the mid-fifth century AD (Isler 1978:10, 1979:47, 1980–1981:1008).

75. Bloesch and Isler 1971:16–17; cf. Isler 2000:23, 85. "Peristyle house 2" was abandoned around the mid-first century AD (Russenberger 2013). The peristyle houses in the eastern quarter also appear to have been destroyed around the mid-first century AD (Isler 2003a:74, 2003b:832–833, 2004:23).

76. Isler 1979:48–49, 2000:24, 42–43. There are also traces of late antique structures in the *bouleuterion*, the peristyle behind the north portico, and the east portico (Isler 1982: 11, 1992:18–20, 1993:10, 2006:5).

77. Frey-Kupper 2013:719–720. Later imperial issues (including four third-century issues of Gallic emperors) have been found in use, abandonment, and destruction layers (Frey-Kupper 2013:720–721). A coin of the Gallic chieftain Dumnorix (60–50 BC) has been found as well as an issue of a governor of Judea (AD 6–11), although in a medieval context (Isler 2009:665, 2011b:47).

78. Hedinger 1999.

79. Isler 2000:43.

80. Isler 1978:11, 1979:47–49, 1980–1981:1004, 1984:11–12, 1992:10–18. Frey-Kupper (2013:716–719) attributes the city's minting of "Romano-Sicilian" coins, followed by its own bronze issues, in the second century to this flourishing of civic culture and autonomy.

81. Isler 1989:12, 1992:10.

82. A fragmentary Latin inscription, tentatively dated to the late Republican period, was found among the refuse in the public cistern (Isler 2011b:49). Another fragmentary Latin inscription, probably late antique, was found in the agora in a medieval context (Isler 1994:30).

83. A possible exception may be the partial repaving of the agora at some point in the imperial period (Bloesch and Isler 1974:19; Isler 1992:23–24).

84. Shops and storage spaces, including a possible *thermopolium*, have been excavated in the southern zone of the agora. These structures appear to have been used from the Hellenistic through the early imperial period and were destroyed by the mid-first century AD (Isler 2001:9–11, 2002:10, 2005:6–7).

85. The stamping of roof tiles used in public buildings with the names of magistrates, which began by the third century, appears to have ended in the first century BC (Isler 1976–1977:692).

86. The occupation history of peristyle house 1 is indicative of this process of local elite migration from and disinvestment in the urban community (Hedinger 1999; Isler 2000: 66–85). At the time of its early or mid-first century AD destruction, the house was occupied by around six persons of some affluence, as indicated by the imported fine tablewares and objects of bronze and worked bone in its assemblage. Among the latest renovations is the construction of a *lararium* in Room 15 around the first century BC. Shortly after its destruction (by earthquake?), the northern part of the house was reoccupied, apparently by more than one household. Two rooms were rebuilt using in part architectural elements from the collapsed peristyle, and another was transformed into a kitchen/bath with a

hearth and a portable terracotta tub. This reuse was brief, and the house was finally destroyed by fire around AD 50.

87. Perkins 2007:38–51.

88. Bonanno 1993–1994:953–972; Lentini et al. 2002:87–89. Collura 2016 is a synthesis of recent research on the town and its territory.

89. Arena 2016; Battistoni 2010; Manganaro 2009b.

90. Scibona 1971.

91. Cascella and Collura 2016.

92. Bonanno 2009; Bonanno and Sudano 2006; Lentini et al. 2002:89–94.

93. A landslide on the hill of Caronia in early 2010 brought to light numerous ancient materials and structures (Collura 2011).

94. Bonanno 2009:33–40; Franco and Capelli 2014; Lindhagen 2006:103–106.

95. Lindhagen 2006:105–129.

96. Bonanno 2009:13, 31.

97. One of the imperial-era farm sites identified after the 2010 landslide was equipped with a kiln, probably for the production of brick or tile (Collura 2011).

98. Lindhagen (2006:137–156) discusses the role of "free market trade" versus "state-directed trade and taxation" in the economy of Calacte.

99. Mattioli 1995:231.

100. Campagna 2011a; Osanna and Torelli 2006.

101. Mancini 2006.

102. Tax collection was largely in the hands of Sicilians who contracted with Roman authorities (Prag 2003). The operation of civic mints between the Second Punic War and the reign of Augustus is one indication of the important local and regional political and economic roles of Sicilian *poleis* under the Roman Republic.

103. Cicero includes different cities in these categories at various points in the *Verrines*. At 3.13 he adds Panormus to the list of *civitates immunes*, while at 5.56 he mentions Netum as a *civitas foederata*. See 5.50 and 56 on these treaties, whose origins and specific provisions are obscure: Pinzone 1999c.

104. The confusion created by Julius Caesar's block grant of *ius Latii* to Sicily is illustrative of the fluidity and ad hoc nature of the Republican system. See Prag 2010 and Wilson 1990:35 for this grant and the probable alterations to it by Antony and Octavian.

105. The case of Sthenius of Thermae is instructive (Cic., II *Verr.* 2.82–94–36); see Pfuntner 2015.

106. Wilson 1990:44.

107. Isler 1982:11.

CHAPTER 2

1. Cutroni Tusa et al. 1994:13–15. Sposito 2014 is a recent overview of the site's topography and history of excavations.

2. Portale 2006.

3. Wolf 2014:40–42. Sposito (2014:320–321) posits a later date for the agora cistern.

4. Wolf 2014:45.

5. Cutroni Tusa et al. 1994:15; C. Greco 2005:40; Wolf 2014:42.

6. Wolf 2014:41.

7. Including the House of Leda and the house formerly called the Gymnasium (Sposito 2014:138, 167). See also Cutroni Tusa et al. 1994:63–98; De Vos 1975; C. Greco 1997, 2005:31–38, 2011; Wolf 2003.

8. Famà 1980; Tusa 1966:149–151. De Vincenzo (2013:188–196) doubts the identification of this complex as a sacred area.

9. Adriani et al. 1971:91, 109; Greco 2011:300; Tusa 1968:10.

10. E.g., in the so-called sanctuary with three altars (Famà 1980:35–36).

11. Lo Cascio 1990.

12. Greco 2005:44, 2011:300.

13. Wolf 2012:226.

14. Wolf 2014:41. Loops for tethering animals were added to some architectural features of the stoa.

15. The dating of the pavements and wall paintings in Soluntum houses is largely (and controversially) based on stylistic comparison with Pompeian examples. The last renovations to the wall paintings of the Casa di Leda have been dated to the Julio-Claudian period (De Vos 1975:201–202), the late first century AD (Cutroni Tusa et al. 1994:63), and the late first century BC (Greco 1997:51). The latest decorative scheme in the Casa delle Ghirlande appears to date to the Augustan period, while that of the Casa del Cerchio in Mosaico has been dated to the early first century AD (Cutroni Tusa et al. 1994:81, 97–98; Greco 2005:38). The mosaics in the Casa di Via Bagnera also appear to be Augustan (Greco 1997:52). In the residence originally called the Gymnasium the last phase of decoration appears to fall in the late first century BC, though a few subsequent structural changes can be attributed to a phase of occupation shortly before the end of the settlement in the third century AD (Wolf 2003:52).

16. Sposito 2014:23–25.

17. Pinzone 1999b, 99–106. This status probably implied tithe exemption for individual citizens of Segesta rather than for the community (and its lands) as a whole. So, for example, *incolae* owning or renting land within the city's territory were not necessarily exempt.

18. Camerata Scovazzo 1997.

19. De Cesare and Parra 2001; De Vido 2003; Nenci 1997, 2000.

20. Bechtold 1997; Camerata Scovazzo 1997:217.

21. Camerata Scovazzo 2008:65–67; Favaro 1997:691.

22. Denaro 1997; Garozzo 2001b:504–506.

23. Denaro 1997:539.

24. Bernardini et al. 2000.

25. Camerata Scovazzo 2008:20–21, 68.

26. Parra 2006:114–120.

27. Ampolo and Parra 2004:406.

28. Olivito 2014.

29. Ampolo and Parra 2003:400, 2004:407, 2012:275–276; Michelini 1999:441–443, 2001:441–444.

30. The settlement continued to import Italian wine in Dressel 2–4 amphorae and fruit products in Dressel 21–22s, perhaps supplemented by Sicilian fruits carried in the same vessels (Denaro 1997:541). Italian sigillata and Dressel 21–22 amphora sherds are among the ceramics used to date the construction of the *macellum* complex (Facella and Olivito 2003:413). For eastern sigillata A from the agora, see Michelini 2001:439. For African wares in use and abandonment contexts in the agora, see Gagliardi and Parra 2006.

31. Bonacasa Carra 1997.

32. Camerata Scovazzo 2008:20–22, 65–72; Favaro 1997.

33. E.g., the Casa del Navarca (Bechtold 1997:104; Camerata Scovazzo 1997:217).

34. Abate and Giaccone 2010; Gagliardi and Parra 2006; Infarinato 2010:30–31. See Facella and Olivito 2010:15–16 for the abandonment of the triangular plaza in the early third century AD.

35. The site lacks third-century African sigillata forms, and no coins have been found from AD 238–346 (Facella 2009:591–592; Gagliardi and Parra 2006:1626).

36. E.g., above the collapsed roof of the agora's north stoa (Olivito and Serra 2014:21).

37. Bernardini et al. 2000:104–114; Cambi 2005.

38. Malfitana 2008:152.

39. Facella 2009; Gagliardi 2009.

40. Nenci 1991.

41. Facella 2013:305.

42. *Liber Coloniarum* 2.11: *Territorium Panormitanorum imp. Vespasianus adsignavit militibus veteranis et familiae suae . . . Item Segestanorum ut supra* (Campbell 2000).

43. Ampolo and Parra 2012:278–280; De Vido 2003.

44. Nenci 2000:811–812.

45. Tribulato 2012:314–316.

46. Nenci 1997:1192–1196.

47. For published fragments of this inscription, see Ampolo and Parra 2004:407–408; Facella and Olivito 2004:417, 2010:12; and Serra 2010:22. A monumental Latin inscription from the late Republican period or later, as yet unpublished, was found in the same area (Facella and Olivito 2010:10).

48. De Vido 2003:378. See Ampolo and Parra 2012:274–275 for the kilns of the Onasii near Parthenicum (and within the extensive territory of Segesta). Roof tiles from these kilns were used on some of the buildings in the agora, including the western wing of the north stoa. Ampolo and Parra suggest that Onasus and Sopolis were father and son and that Sopolis completed the work begun by his father, Cicero's "Onasus Segestanus."

49. Michelini 1999:441. Ampolo and Parra (2012:276) suggest that the inscription is several decades older than the temple.

50. See Nenci 2000:813, for the possibility that an earthquake destroyed the temple.

51. Michelini 2001:441–444.

52. Michelini 1999:445.

53. *CIL* 10.7263, a dedication to *deivi filio deivo* (Augustus) by L. Sem(pronius?).

54. Carbè 2008:58–59; Scibona 2008.

55. Tigano 2008:73.

56. Tigano 2008.

57. Scibona and Tigano 2009:32.

58. Scibona and Tigano 2009:13–43.

59. Many of these inscriptions were published by Scibona (1971), so the following discussion uses his numbering. However, several inscriptions from the site remain unpublished. For a summary of inscriptions found in or near the agora, see Prestianni Giallombardo 2012.

60. *IG* 14.353–354: Scibona 1971, no. 2.

61. See Scibona 2009 for this text, found in the Casa dei Dolii, and its implications for the religious life and topography of Halaesa in the second/first century BC.

62. Scibona 1971, no. 3.

63. Facella 2006:209.

64. Scibona 1971, no. 1.

65. See Facella 2006:246–251 for the northern Sicilian "Pompeian connection," including links between Halaesa and Pompeian partisans like C. Vergilius Balbus (*IG* 14.356).

66. See Covino 2013 for this and other Roman interventions in Sicilian constitutions. Prag (2014b) hypothesizes that this dispute was between the civic body and the large and powerful *koinon* of the priests of Apollo mentioned in *SEG* 59.1100.

67. Prag 2007a.

68. Facella 2006:278.

69. Namely, four coin series issued by the *flamen aug* and *duovir* M. Paccius Maximus (Facella 2006:273–274).

70. Facella 2006:285. The city also received imports of Africana A in this period.

71. Scibona 1971, no. 8.

72. Facella 2006:210–212.

73. Carbè 2008.

74. Facella 2006:281.

75. Scibona and Tigano 2009:33–34. Torelli (2014) argues that *sacella* III–V were dedicated to the imperial cult, while *tabernae* VI and VII were devoted to traditional civic deities. In his view, the Halaesa stoa functioned as a *chalcidicum* from the time of its construction.

76. Scibona and Tigano 2009:38–39.

77. Portale 2009.

78. At least two other inscriptions found in the vicinity of the *sacella* commemorate wealthy freedman Augustales, who held that group's highest office, the sevirate (Scibona 1971, nos. 6, 7, and 9).

79. Tigano 2009b.

80. Facella 2006:187–191.

81. Burgio 2008:1–52; Manganaro 2009a; Prag 2014b.

82. Burgio 2008.

83. E.g., Wilson 1990:150.

84. Scibona 1971, no. 10. Four additional early to mid-third-century Latin honorific inscriptions probably from the agora as well as one found during the excavation of *taberna* VII remain unpublished at the time of writing. See the iSicily database (sicily.classics.ox.ac.uk) nos. 3584–3588 for preliminary information on these texts.

85. Scibona and Tigano 2009:37.

86. Facella 2006:298–299.

87. Tigano 2009a.

88. Manganaro 2006.

89. Facella 2006:302.

90. Scibona and Tigano 2009:19.

91. Scibona and Tigano 2009:15–18, 44–60.

92. *Ann.* 4.43. Suetonius records that Claudius also sponsored the restoration of the temple at Eryx, though he does not mention Segesta (*Div. Claud.* 25.5).

93. See, inter alia, Fentress 2013.

94. Mancini 2006.

95. Lindhagen 2006:117–118.

CHAPTER 3

1. E.g., houses excavated in Via delle Ninfe and Via Sibilla (*Lilibeo* 1984:104–106) and in Via del Quarto (Giglio 2003).

2. Blake and Schon 2010:56–58.

3. *Lilibeo* 1984:131.

4. *Lilibeo* 1984:126–130.

5. Bechtold and Schmidt 2015.

6. Manni Piraino 1963.

7. Manni Piraino 1963 for the dedication of the *demos* to the *euergetes* Diognetos Megas; Sartori 1957 for the twelve tribes.

8. Brugnone and Bechtold 1997; *Lilibeo* 1984:124, 159–164; Tribulato 2012:305–308. In addition, graffiti in Greek, Punic, and Latin by at least two hands, probably from different periods, has been found in a burial chamber (Giglio 2010:83–84).

9. Fentress et al. 1990:83.

10. The *insulae* in Via Sibilla and Via delle Ninfe: *Lilibeo* 1984:104–107.

11. Bechtold et al. 1999; *Lilibeo* 1984:38–77, 151–190.

12. Valente and Bechtold 1992.

13. Frey-Kupper (2014:99) notes: "Everything—the stratigraphic context, the iconography, and the early date of the coin—points to an intentional deposit in a Punic environment of Roman times."

14. Manni Piraino 1963 for the inscription in honor of Diognetos; *IG* 14.273 and 277 and *CIL* 10.7240 for M. Valerius Megas.

15. Calderone 1959. The epigraphic evidence for Roman tribes (*tribus*) in Sicily is collected in Prag 2010.

16. This is also the first datable Latin inscription from the town. Another recently discovered Latin inscription perhaps from the early first century BC remains unpublished (Giglio 2010:72).

17. Calderone 1959; *Lilibeo* 1984:145.

18. Calderone 1959; *Lilibeo* 1984:144–147. *CIL* 10.7212 refers to a *flamen* of *divus* Augustus; *CIL* 10.7224 is a dedication to Mercurius Augustus.

19. *Lilibeo* 1984:140–142 for Latin or bilingual graffiti on walls.

20. Giglio 2010:72; a monumental arch may have been constructed at the end of the *decumanus*, facing the sea. Silvestrini (2014) links the presence of this *praetor designatus* to Sextus Pompey's occupation of Sicily.

21. Giglio 2010:77.

22. Blake and Schon 2010:59–61; Fentress et al. 1990:84–85.

23. First published in Barbieri 1961:16–32.

24. The monumental colonnaded avenues (*plateae*) constructed in Eastern Mediterranean cities in the high Empire served a prime commercial function, hosting dozens of *tabernae* (Mayer 2012:79–81). Although nothing is known of the location or appearance of the Lilybaeum Cereres complex, the cult's association with grain may hint at a commercial purpose for the associated *platea*.

25. L. Cassius Manilianus: Bivona 1987; Alpinius Magnus Eumenius: Barbieri 1963; Julius Claudius Peristerius Pompeianus: *AE* 1906.75b.

26. Silvestrini 2011. Silvestrini (2014:220–223) hypothesizes that the Stertinii had their origins in Lilybaeum rather than in Spain or Africa Proconsularis.

27. Giglio 2010:77–79.

28. Giglio 2009:565–567, 2010:75–76.

29. Silvestrini (2014:212–214) tentatively identifies this *legatus pro praetore* and *praetor designatus* as L. Plinius Rufus.

30. Giglio 1997:124.

31. Giglio 1997:127–128.

32. C. A. Di Stefano 2006:547–549; *Lilibeo* 1984:134–135, 139–143.

33. Epigraphic evidence for the grant of colonial status is collected in Calderone 1959 and discussed in *Lilibeo* 1984.

34. Silvestrini 2011.

35. See Pfuntner 2016 for the Lilybaeum structure and North African comparanda.

36. Bechtold et al. 1999.

37. Giglio 2008:1535–1545.

38. Giglio 2010:74.

39. Although the mid- to late fourth century saw severe episodes of seismic activity across the Mediterranean, Kelly (2004:143–144) criticizes the tendency among archaeologists to ascribe destructions to this specific event, whose effects in the East are famously described by Ammianus (26.10.15–19).

40. Giglio 2009:561–562, 2010:74; *Lilibeo* 1984:134.

41. Giglio 2010:79.

42. Giglio 2009:561–567.

43. Gelarda 2011.

44. *Lilibeo* 1984:191.

45. Fentress et al. 1990:79.

46. Blake and Schon 2010:62.

47. See Polybius's books 1 and 2 and Livy's books 24–26 for Agrigentum's role in these wars.

48. De Miro 2009:406.

49. Bonacasa Carra et al. 1995:38.

50. See Caliò et al. 2017 for preliminary results of excavations of this structure, begun in July 2016.

51. These men are usually identified as L. Manlius Vulso, praetor 197 BC (whom Cicero erroneously calls T. Manlius), and either P. Cornelius Scipio (Africanus), consul 205 BC, or L. Cornelius Scipio (Asiaticus), praetor 193 BC. See Prag 2007b for possible identifications.

52. De Miro and Fiorentini 2011:25.

53. De Miro 2000:95. Alternatively, public meetings may have shifted to the theater (Soraci 2017:18).

54. De Miro 2012. The date of construction of the podium temple is based on the presence of Campana C in the fill of the abandoned *ekklesiasterion* (p. 105).

55. De Miro 2000:95–96; Marconi 1926:111.

56. De Miro 2006:70–78.

57. The earliest phase of this monumental complex was detected only in excavations begun in 2012 (Caminneci et al. 2015:21–38; Livadiotti and Fino 2017).

58. De Miro 2006:80, 2009:407–416.

59. De Miro 2006:79–80; Gabrici 1925:425–437.

60. Bell 2005.

61. From roughly the same period is *CIL* 6.40903, a dedication to Cn. Pompeius Magnus by Italians resident in Agrigentum (*Italicei qui Agrigenti nego[tiantur]*).

62. See Calderone 1985–1986 for a fragmentary honorific decree of the *demos* in honor of an anonymous benefactor, found near the *bouleuterion* and dated to the second or first century BC.

63. Asheri 1969.

64. Polito 2009:29.

65. Wilson (1990:42) dates the grant of municipal status between 14–12 BC and AD 14.

66. Livadiotti and Fino (2017:101–102) characterize the building in its second phase as a *templum rostratum*, an architectural type that originated in Augustan Rome and spread to other cities in the empire in the first century AD.

67. Belli Pasqua 2017.

68. Manganaro 2013:249–252.

69. De Miro and Fiorentini 2011:39.

70. Manganaro 2013. The individuals named in the inscription include S. Egnatius,

the *flamen* L. Egnatius, Augustus, Heracles, and Hermes; the last three were perhaps the honorary "owners" of individual seats.

71. De Miro 2006:80, 2009:407.

72. De Miro and Fiorentini 2011:54, 83.

73. De Miro 2006:80, 2009:407.

74. Silvestrini 2011.

75. De Miro and Fiorentini 2011:83–85.

76. An exception is the fragmentary inscription on white marble found in excavations of the porticoed temple complex in 2015 that commemorates a *curator rei publicae Liparitanorum* of the late second or third century AD (Vallarino 2017).

77. Hünemörder 2013.

78. Zambito 2014 is a recent study of the production of sulfur in Agrigentum and its territory.

79. De Miro 1982–1983; Griffo 1963; Zambito 2014:148.

80. Griffo 1963:169–170; cf. Gabrici 1925:434–435. Zambito (2014:150) links the large number of *tegulae* found in the city to its role as an export center where *portorium* would have been collected: the *tegulae* were no longer needed once the sulfur batches were counted and loaded onto ships and could be discarded or recycled.

81. Parker 1992, cat. no. 230; cf. cat. nos. 780 and 906.

82. Polito 2009.

83. Wilson 1990:178.

84. Wilson 1990:198–199.

85. Castellana and McConnell 1990.

86. De Miro and Fiorentini 2011:40–43.

87. De Miro and Fiorentini 2011:85–93.

88. De Miro 2006:80.

89. A recent overview of the early Christian burial areas is found in Ardizzone Lo Bue 2012.

90. Zambito 2014:152.

91. Castellana and McConnell 1990:32.

92. Castellana 1992:47–48.

93. Parello 2017; Scalici 2017.

94. De Miro 1982–1983:320, 2009:407.

95. Castellana and McConnell 1990:33–43.

96. Castellana 1992:45, 47.

97. Caminneci 2015.

98. Translation: Martyn 2004.

99. Martyn 2004:127–128. In Gregory's first test as bishop, his rivals Sabinus and Crescentius plot with thirty clerics and twenty-five laymen to discredit him by planting a prostitute in his room. A papal legate fails to resolve the resulting dispute in Agrigento, so Gregory is taken to stand trial in Rome, where he prevails (*Life*, 51–85; Martyn 2004: 183–231).

100. Ardizzone Lo Bue 2012:33.

101. These links are explored in Pfuntner 2016.

102. Bivona 1994:120–121; and Tav. VI.

103. The Asinii Nicomachi originated in Sardis and also had landholdings around Rome (Chausson 2016:294).

CHAPTER 4

1. Bottari et al. 2009:47–48.

2. The Tindari Fault: Bottari et al. 2009:42.

3. Spigo 2005:30.

4. Spigo 2005:33.

5. La Torre 2004:130–133.

6. Although Cicero never states this explicitly, he does not include the city among the privileged *civitates immunes ac liberae.*

7. The city also contributed a ship to Verres's ill-fated fleet (5.86).

8. Crisà 2008:240–244.

9. La Torre 2004:121; Spigo 2005:34. It is also possible that the city had two agoras/forums (Gulletta 2012).

10. Cicero notes that the council, in response to Verres's original request for the statue of Mercury, had declared it "a capital offense to touch the statue without orders" from the council (4.85).

11. Besides Sopater and Demetrius, locals involved in the Mercury incident whom Cicero calls as witnesses are Poleas, Zosippus, and Ismenias. The Tyndaritan victims of Verres's thefts include Cratippus (4.29), Aeschylus, and Thraso (4.48).

12. La Torre 2004:135–140, 2006:91–92; Spigo 2005:42–45.

13. La Torre 2006:91–92.

14. The excavation results of G. V. Gentili are noted in *FA* 6 (1951), no. 4589: 348–349; *FA* 7 (1952), no. 3693: 284–285; and *FA* 11 (1958), no. 4667: 290.

15. The ceramic markers of such settlement include the Campana C-type finewares distributed across Sicily beginning in the second century BC (Fasolo 2014:212–213).

16. Pavia and Zavettieri 2005.

17. For these coins and their attribution to the civic mint of Tyndaris, see Crisà 2008: 244–253.

18. Lentini and Blackman (2013) suggest that fragments of a stone ship's ram and prow found in Tyndaris may belong to one or more monuments commemorating Agrippa's capture of the city.

19. See Crisà 2008:253–259 for these foundation issues, whose attribution to Tyndaris is not universally accepted. *CIL* 10.7474–7476, 7478, and 7480 refer to the *colonia.*

20. Spigo 2008:107. Leone (2008:58–59) suggests that the structure was the seat of a *societas* or a cult building (perhaps related to the imperial cult), rather than a building of a more public nature, such as a *curia* or gymnasium.

21. Spigo 2006:101–103. The central *decumanus* also had raised sidewalks.

22. Leone 2008:59–62.

23. Fuduli 2011:29; La Torre 2004:130; Spigo 2005:64.

24. Spigo (2008:110) speculates, for example, that the less-frequent maintenance of the drainage system may be connected to fluctuations in the economic fortunes of the city.

25. Zambito 2007:108.

26. Spigo 2005:21–22, 74.

27. Spigo 2005:81–3.

28. For example, the *colonia* made dedications to Marcus Aurelius and Lucius Verus during the tenure of Vitalis that mention the latter's role (*CIL* 10.7474–7475).

29. Spigo 2005:25–27.

30. Pavia and Zavettieri 2005:86–87.

31. Another villa evidently occupied between the first century BC and the second century AD was uncovered in 1970 at the coastal location of Oliveri, almost 3 km south of Capo Tindari, during work on the *autostrada*. Sadly, most of the material from this structure was destroyed before it could be examined by archaeologists (Fasolo 2014:156–161).

32. Gentili in *FA* 1951, 1952, and 1958 (see note 14 above).

33. Voza 1980–1981:693.

34. Fasolo 2014:216.

35. Leone 2008:57, 62.

36. Spigo 2005:30, 68, 2006:101–103.

37. Leone 2008:57.

38. Spigo and Pratolongo 2008:74; Spigo 2005:50, 67, 73.

39. Wilson 2012:259–260. La Torre (2005), however, hypothesizes that it was built shortly after the foundation of the colony and rebuilt or restored after the mid-fourth century earthquake, and his dating has found general acceptance in Italian scholarship (Fuduli 2011:30–32).

40. Voza 1980–1981:690–693.

41. Aiello 2016.

42. Spigo 2005:40–41, 66, 2006:101–103.

43. Voza 1980–1981:690.

44. Aiello 2016:201.

45. Fasolo 2014:210.

46. Bell 1999; Campagna 2004:153–156.

47. Campagna (2016:259) dates it approximately to the third quarter of the third century BC.

48. Manganaro 1963a:21–25. Pinzone (1999c) suggests that Tauromenium's first treaty with Rome was negotiated in 241 BC, when it was still within Hieron's realm. The treaty between Tauromenium and Rome was then renewed (potentially, with some emendations) during the Second Punic War.

49. See Del Monaco 2003:34–35 for the debate over the beginning date of this list, with Manganaro favoring 241 BC, Del Monaco and Sartori favoring 270 BC, and other scholars proposing mid-third century dates.

50. Del Monaco 2003; Manganaro 1963a and 1964.

51. Manganaro 1964:51.

52. Bacci 1980–1981:739–741. Wilson (2012:248) questions this identification.

53. Manganaro 1964.

54. Pelagatti 1997.

55. Campagna 2009:210.

56. Lentini 2005:327.

57. Manganaro (1963a:20) identifies these *xenoi* as eastern Greek or Italian supporters of Sextus Pompey who had followed him to Sicily.

58. Del Monaco 2003:39; Lentini 2005:314; Wilson 1990:33–34. Campagna (2016: 270), however, leaves open the possibility that the colony in Tauromenium predated the other Sicilian colonies.

59. Bacci 1980–1981:738.

60. Campagna and La Torre 2008:135.

61. Campagna 2016:269–271.

62. Bacci 1980–1981:741–742.

63. Manganaro 1963a and 1964.

64. Lentini 2005:321. Venuti (2015:53) dates the first significant alterations to the *cavea* to the Augustan era.

65. *CIL* 10.6991–6993 and *AE* 1989.339b; *CIL* 10.6994–6995, two fragments of an inscription, perhaps from a statue base, found in the theater that commemorate the *pontifex* and *duovir* C. Mevius.

66. Lentini 2005:324.

67. Lentini 2005:322–323; Pelagatti 1964.

68. Campagna 2016; Scafidi 2007–2008.

69. Campagna 2016:271–272.

70. Lentini 2005:315–316.

71. Campagna and La Torre 2008:140–143.

72. Campagna and La Torre 2008:143; Lentini 2005:316.

73. Lentini 2005:318–319; Sear 1996.

74. Sear 1996:73–77.

75. Lentini 2005:321; Sear 1996:48, 52–53.

76. Lentini 2005:327–328.

77. Bacci 1980–1981:744; Lentini 2005:317. The University of Messina resumed excavation of this *domus* (the Villa San Pancrazio) in 2016.

78. Lentini 2005:328–329; Wilson 2003.

79. Bacci 1980–1981:745–746.

80. Lentini 2005:314.

81. Pelagatti 1964:34.

82. Bacci 1980–1981:738.

83. Campagna 2011b:17; Lentini 2005:321.

84. See Vandermersch 1994:25–50 for wine production in the archaic and classical periods.

85. Peña 2007b.

86. Parker 1992, cat. nos. 256 (Capo Taormina) and 443 (Giardini).

CHAPTER 5

1. Patanè 2006a.

2. Frasca 2006:195.

3. Pinzone 1999b:99–106.

4. Patanè 2002:153–154, 2006b; Rizza 2002:29–36.

5. Other named citizens include Heraclius (2.66); Artemo(n) and Andro(n), the town's representatives to Verres and to the Roman Senate (2.156, 3.108); Eubulidas Grospus (3.56), Diocles (3.129), Phylarchus (4.29, 50), and Phalacrus, captain of the city's ship (book 5).

6. Or, less likely, at the end of the first century BC. Manganaro published several articles on this inscription, beginning with 1963b.

7. Modern Centuripe and Lanuvio reestablished their *gemellaggio* after the discovery of the inscription in 1963 (http://www.comune.lanuvio.rm.it/pagina/lanuvio-centuripe-gemellaggio).

8. Patanè 2002:140–141.

9. Frasca 2006; Patanè 2002:142–155, 2006a.

10. A gymnasiarch is mentioned in a Greek inscription from the third or second century BC (Patanè 2002:130). Cicero relates that the city attempted to take down statues of Verres and his son, implying an open public space for the display of such statues (II *Verr.* 2.161–164). The Lanuvium inscription also contains a provision for its display in a public building in Centuripae.

11. Patanè 2002:147–152, 2006a:209–210.

12. Strabo claims that Centuripae "contributed much to the overthrow of Pompeius" but does not elaborate (*Geog.* 6.2.4).

13. Patanè 2002:133.

14. Badian 1958:270–284.

15. Eck 1996a and 1996b; Patanè 2011; see Murer 2017, cat. nos. 23 and 24 for the female portraits. The grandmother of Priscus, Clodia Falconilla, was a member of a wealthy family based in Africa. His daughter, Pompeia Sosia Falconilla, also possessed land in Africa, probably around Cirta. The family had links of adoption and marriage to the Roscii, another prominent *gens* in Sicily with roots in Italy (including in Lanuvium). Fronto mentions the family's estates in the Alban hills in a letter to Marcus Aurelius from the 140s AD (2.6).

16. Q. Pompeius Falco, suffect consul in AD 108 and father of Priscus, was a *novus homo* in Rome who began his senatorial career under Domitian as a military tribune with the Rhine legions. He was a correspondent of Pliny the Younger and seems to have married into an Italian family of consular rank. The son of Priscus, Q. Pompeius Senecio Sosius Priscus, was consul in 169.

17. The ties of Priscus to Centuripae likely came through his grandfather, Sextus Pompeius Priscus, husband of Clodia Falconilla, who was probably Sicilian and whose family presumably gained Roman citizenship from Pompey the Great. The inclusion of these grandparents in the statue cycle may indicate that Priscus traced the family's upward social mobility to this marriage.

18. Patanè 2011:33–47.

19. Patanè 2011:28. While there is no evidence that the emperor came to Centuripae, he certainly was in its vicinity when he visited Mt. Etna.

20. The reconstruction by Patanè (2011:49–91) is based partly on tenuous identifications and on sculpture of uncertain provenance.

21. A fragmentary inscription on sandstone containing the letters "MPEI" (Pompeius?) was found in the area of the portico, suggesting that Priscus or a member of his family had a role in the monumentalization of the forum complex (Patanè 2011:47).

22. The inclusion of Lanoios is based on Patanè's (2011:59–60) reidentification of a portrait head previously thought to depict Nero, on the basis of its "heroic" appearance.

23. Patanè 2011:84.

24. Patanè 2011:97–99.

25. Biondi 2008; Patanè 2011:99–100.

26. For example, the marble urn bearing the ashes of Laetus, a young slave, dedicated by his parents around the mid-second century AD was found near the monumental Castellaccio tomb (*CIL* 10.7005; Patanè 2011:107–108).

27. Patanè 2011:110.

28. Patanè 2011:73–74.

29. Biondi 2002 and 2010.

30. Like sulfur, gypsum had a variety of uses in antiquity, including as a preservative for food and wine and as an ingredient in plaster and other building materials (Hünemörder 2013).

31. Biondi 2002:79.

32. Manganaro 1996.

33. Tortorici 2016:267–281.

34. See Bottari et al. 2014:2, for a volcanological analysis of the most significant of these, the Plinian eruption of 122 BC.

35. Branciforti 2005a:52–54; Molè 2008:42.

36. Manganaro 1996:50, for evidence of the city's Mediterranean links in the first century BC.

37. Molè 2008:41. The temple of Demeter may be associated with a votive deposit dating back to the archaic period that was found in 1959 in Piazza San Francesco, on the southeastern edge of Montevergine hill (Privitera 2009:39).

38. Branciforti 2005a:58–59; Tortorici 2016:290.

39. Molè 2008:47.

40. Tortorici 2016:291; Wilson 1996:155, 159–160.

41. Wilson 1996:152–154. Cf. Tortorici 2016, Tavv. 7–10.

42. Tortorici 2016:292–296.

43. Molè 2008:48; Pensabene 2005:204; Wilson 1996:157–162.

44. Pensabene 2005:191; Soraci 1996:259.

45. Pensabene 2005:187; Wilson 1996:159.

46. Perhaps a reference to the giant Enceladus, son of Tartarus and Ge, who fought against Athena; the goddess, according to different sources, threw the island of Sicily or Mt. Etna on top of him (*RE*, s.v. Enceladus).

47. Molè 2008:48; Pensabene 2005:191–198; Wilson 1996:158–162.

48. Tortorici 2016:148–149; Wilson 1996:163–165.

49. Tortorici 2016:57–65.

50. Bottari et al. 2014:4.

51. Arcifa et al. 2016.

52. Tortorici 2016:199–200.

53. Tortorici 2016; Wilson 1996:168–169.

54. Branciforti 2005a; Tomasello 2007.

55. Tomasello 2007:151.

56. Korhonen 2004:243–249. Much of the following analysis is based on Korhonen's catalogue of Catanian inscriptions (abbreviated as *IMCCat*).

57. Korhonen 2011:11.

58. This dedication is usually attributed to the aftermath of one of the invasions (Vandal, Ostrogothic, or Byzantine) of the late or post-Roman period. However, Sami (2010: 41–43) proposes that the *pii fratres* statues had been desecrated by Christian mobs.

59. Manganaro 1996:51.

60. Pensabene 2005:204.

61. Manganaro 1959.

62. An earlier Greek text on the other side of the stone records the construction of the nymphaeum (*IG* 14.453).

63. Molè 2008:52–54; Molè Ventura 1996:202–220; Tomasello 2007:155–156. Further imperial ties to Catina and its territory are indicated by the epitaph of Abdalas, *magister ovium* of Domitia Longina (daughter of Domitius Corbulo and wife of the emperor Domitian), found at Ramacca (*AE* 1985.483); see Privitera 2009:52 for other evidence of Domitius Corbulo's connections to eastern Sicily and Syria.

64. Eck 1996a and 1996b.

65. Korhonen 2004:245.

66. Cf. *AE* 1989.341f for a possible *vilicus stationis*, the proprietor of a *statio* of the *cursus publicus*.

67. An anonymous *procurator Augusti* and military tribune is attested in a fragmentary Latin inscription (*AE* 1989.341q).

68. Soraci 1996:259–261.

69. E.g., M. Julius Sedatius of the tribe Papiria, a soldier in the seventh legion for fourteen years (*AE* 1897.132); and P. Junius Servienus of the tribe Quirina (*AE* 1989.341n).

70. Manganaro 1996:55.

71. An early Christian epitaph commemorates a child who died at Hybla but was buried in Catina, implying that the city's religious, if not administrative, territory extended substantially southwest by late antiquity at least (*CIL* 10.7112, discussed below).

72. Molè 2008:45.

73. Amari 2007; Branciforti 2005b.

74. Franco and Capelli 2014:346–347, 351–352.

75. Tortorici 2015.

76. Including, from north to south, the Capo Taormina and Giardini wrecks (Parker 1992, cat. nos. 256 and 443); Marzamemi A–C (cat. nos. 670–672); and Isola delle Correnti (cat. no. 522).

77. Tortorici 2016:297–301.

78. Wilson 1996:162–169. The *Expositio totius mundi et gentium*, which notes the *spectaculum circensium* of Syracuse and Catina (589–91), also points to the continuation of public spectacles.

79. Korhonen 2004:243.

80. Molè 2008:57.

81. Cf. *IMCCat* 189: veneration of Hilarion in the late fourth/fifth century.

82. Branciforti 2003:113–114, 2005a:59.

83. Buda et al. 2015.

84. Tortorici 2015:29–30.

85. Gentili 1956.

86. Lehmler (2005:120) hypothesizes that the palace was located in modern Piazza Archimede.

87. Lehmler 2005:151.

88. Lehmler 2005:125.

89. Bell 1999:271; Campagna 2004:174–181; Lehmler 2005:128.

90. Campagna 2004:173; Lehmler 2005:132–134.

91. Lehmler 2005:135.

92. As Campagna (2004:183) notes, Hieron's theater anticipates the function of representing personal power that Roman theaters would fulfill in the late Republic.

93. Lehmler 2005:122.

94. Lehmler 2005:151.

95. Ciurcina 2006:25–26.

96. For third-century bath complexes in Sicilian cities (including Syracuse), see Lucore 2013.

97. Basile 2001–2002:772, 782 on the destruction of a large (sacred?) building on Ortygia; Messina 2001–2002:815–819 on the abandonment of an *insula* in northern Neapolis.

98. Cadario 2005:169. Others holding magistracies in Sicily include M. Claudius Marcellus in 198 BC, C. Claudius Marcellus in 79 BC, and P. Cornelius Lentulus Marcellinus in 70 BC.

99. See Tribulato 2012:310–311 for epigraphic evidence of *negotiatores* (possibly involved in the fish trade) and *aratores* in the first century BC.

100. According to Cicero, Acradina was the site of the forum and the main public buildings, including *pulcherrimae porticus* (stoas), an *ornatissimum prytanium*, *amplissima curia* (the *bouleuterion*), and Hieron's *templum egregium* of Olympian Zeus, none of which has been identified. Tyche is the site of a *gymnasium amplissimum* and *complures aedes sacrae*.

101. Another indication of the presence of foreign notables in Syracuse is a fragmentary dedication by a certain Masteabar, son of a Numidian king, from the first century BC (*AE* 1959.230; Korhonen 2011:9).

102. This group's tutelary deity is perhaps to be identified with Venus Felix, whose cult was introduced to Rome by Sulla ca. 82 BC (Dimartino 2010). Other guilds of performing artists (a *koinon* of *technitai* of Dionysus and a *koinon* of the Muses) also issued decrees honoring benefactors (*IG* 14.12–13 and *SEG* 34.974; cf. Korhonen 2011:9).

103. Korhonen 2011:9.

104. This suggestion by Strabo finds some support in the archaeological record: e.g., the construction of a suburban villa in the late Republic or early imperial period at the northern edge of Acradina (Guzzardi 1993–1994:1308–1310).

105. See Basile 2001–2002:745–760, for the excavation of part of a wide street extending from the Foro Siracusano to the modern railway station: perhaps the main street of Acradina and Cicero's *via lata perpetua* (II *Verr.* 4.119). Basile notes that excavations in Piazza della Vittoria in northern Acradina have revealed a street leading to the amphitheater that was first paved in the second half of the first century BC, in a different technique from that used in the street near the railway station (761–765); cf. Solè 2006:25.

106. Evans 2009:140; Solè 2006:28.

107. Wilson 2012:257.

108. Bell 1999:272.

109. Valerius Maximus refers to games held under Tiberius, while Tacitus (*Ann.* 13.49) says that the city's government requested permission from the Roman Senate to hold additional games under Nero (AD 58). These early spectacles, whose sponsors and primary audience were probably Roman colonists, could also have been held in the theater. Gentili (1973) argued that the amphitheater was built in the late second century AD or early third century AD to replace the theater as the site of *venationes* and gladiatorial games. Wilson (1980) proposed an Augustan date, which has found general acceptance. Other evidence for gladiatorial games includes the terracotta statuettes of different types of gladiators found in the area of the amphitheater and housed in the Orsi Museum (e.g., inv. nos. 19736, 43002 and 36771).

110. Evans 2009:141.

111. Evans 2009:142; Solè 2006:29.

112. Other emperors to visit the city include Caligula, Hadrian, and Septimius Severus (Evans 2009:143).

113. Trojani 2005.

114. Evans 2009:142; Solè 2006:25.

115. Lazzarini 2007:110.

116. Evans 2009:142; R. Greco 1999:29; Lazzarini 2007:110; Solè 2006:25.

117. Wilson 2012:257.

118. Campagna (2004:158) hypothesizes that this was the main Hellenistic agora of Syracuse.

119. Evans 2009:142; Gentili 1961:23.

120. The sculpture found in Acradina and Ortygia and now in the Orsi Museum includes portrait busts of the emperor Nerva, Vibia Sabina, mother of Hadrian, and Faustina Minor (inv. nos. 37100, 72699, and 743). Lazzarini (2007) catalogues the imported marble and granite columns and architectural elements in the Roman imperial monuments of Syracuse as well as those reused in later buildings.

121. Basile 2001–2002:761.

122. Wilson 1980.

123. R. Greco 1999:27–30.

124. R. Greco 1999:40–41; Sgarlata 2006:1197.

125. Fallico 1971; Gentili 1956:151–164; Messina 2001–2002.

126. Agnello 2001:34–35.

127. Agnello 1960, no. 29. Other Latin inscriptions from the Christian catacombs include *CIL* 10.7167 (AD 356), 7168 (AD 431), and 7172.

128. E.g., *IG* 14.54, on a large marble sarcophagus of the late third century AD, names Phretensia Statia Skreibonia.

129. See Gentili 1961:20–21 for the *iatros* K. Kaikilios Ariston; Sgarlata 1991:132–135 for the professions commemorated in Christian epitaphs.

130. Sgarlata 1991:135.

131. Sgarlata 2006:1187–1192. Cf. *IG* 14.117 (Zodoros from Makre Kome, probably in Tyre, buried in San Giovanni); *SEG* 4.6 (an individual from Tripolis, buried in Vigna Cassia); and *SEG* 4.9 (Julia Antiochiana, buried in Vigna Cassia).

132. Another Lycian who died in Syracuse around the fourth century was Eustochios, whose sarcophagus has a lengthy metric inscription (*SEG* 44.794).

133. Cf. *SEG* 27.662, the *titulus* of Eutychia *apo Hortesianon*, probably referring to a senatorial estate in Sicily, from after AD 394.

134. Agnello 1960, no. 33, for this tomb, where a statuette of Isis and a bust of Serapis were also found (see above).

135. Pelagatti 1969–1970:79.

136. Fallico 1971.

137. Lagona 1972–1973.

138. N. Lamboglia and J.-P. Morel did the fundamental work of identification and classification of Campana C forms; see, more recently, González López 2005.

139. Morel and Picon 1994.

140. González López 2005:67; Pelagatti 1970:471–472.

141. González López 2005:67–68; Malfitana 2006:155.

142. González López 2005:69; Pelagatti 1969–1970:77.

143. The Hellenistic "ceramic quarter" of Messana also appears to have ceased production in the Augustan era. For an overview of excavated kiln sites, see Olcese 2012:449–454.

144. These wrecks were surveyed and partially excavated by G. Kapitän (Parker 1992, cat. nos. 670–679). J. Leidwanger currently leads a new program of research.

145. Parker 1992, cat. no. 670; Agnello 1987–1988:128. The other wreck, Marzamemi C (cat. no. 672), contained a column of red Nubian granite and can be dated broadly to the Roman imperial period. In addition, a third/fourth-century wreck off Isola delle Correnti, near the southern tip of Sicily, carried a large cargo of marble from Proconnesus or elsewhere in Asia Minor (cat. no. 522).

146. Parker 1992, cat. nos. 833, 834, and 1143.

147. For example, Ognina A carried amphorae from Africa, Spain, and Greece, and probably passengers, and dated to AD 215–230 on the basis of coin finds (Parker 1992, cat. no. 755). Other wrecks further down the coast include Eloro A, with cylindrical amphorae from the fourth or early fifth century (cat. no. 381); and Marzamemi D and F (cat. nos. 673 and 675), carrying, respectively, African amphorae from the second quarter of the fourth century and a mixed consignment mostly of Spanish and African amphorae of the late third century.

148. Agnello 1987–1988:128.

149. Gentili 1956:135–138.

150. Roughly, the territory of the *colonia* would have extended north to the border with Catina, as far south as Capo Passero, and west or southwest into the Hyblaean mountains.

151. Pelagatti (1970:440) hypothesized that the farm complex originally lay on or close to the ancient road connecting these two centers.

152. Pelagatti 1970:453.

153. Pelagatti 1970:490–493, 498–499; see also Walthall 2011.

154. Pelagatti 1970:497–498. The cistern was closed by the mid-first century BC, as evidenced by the lack of presigillata and Arretine ware in its fill. The farm itself apparently went out of occupation at a later date, since some Arretine ware was found in excavation.

155. Wilson 2016.

156. Cugno 2009.

157. Alternatively (or additionally), Neratius Palmatus may have owned property in the region and thus acted as a private benefactor.

158. Agnello 2001:29; R. Greco 1999:55–57.

159. Voza 1999:119.

160. For example, the clergy attested in rare Latin epitaphs from the San Giovanni catacombs: the *episcopus* Auxentius Ispanus and Superianus, *clerecus de Aquileia* (Sgarlata 2006:1199).

161. As evidenced by the epitaph of Euskia from the San Giovanni catacombs (Ciurcina 2006:33).

162. Parker 1992, cat. nos. 1092–1093. The Vendicari wreck farther down the coast also had a cargo of amphorae and dates to AD 375–625 (cat. no. 1211). The Byzantine-era Capo Passero wreck carried a mixed cargo of roof tiles, amphorae, and iron items (cat. no. 245).

163. Parker 1992, cat. no. 671. Two other Byzantine-era wrecks holding indeterminate cargoes have been found in this area (Marzamemi J and K: cat. nos. 678–679).

164. Agnello 2001:36; Evans 2009:144; Lazzarini 2007:108.

165. Agnello 2001:35–37.

166. Agnello 2001:37.

167. Basile 2001–2002.

168. Agnello 2001:37; Guzzardi 1993–1994.

169. Agnello 2001:37–45.

170. Lazzarini 2007:123.

171. Agnello (2001:51) dates these conversions to the era of Justinian.

CHAPTER 6

1. Di Napoli 2010:259–260; Gros 2011:298–301.

2. Evangelidis 2014:342.

3. Evangelidis 2014:344.

4. Evangelidis 2014:345–346; Gros 2011:418–424.

5. Di Napoli 2010:257. Gros (2011:308–316) notes the difficulty of distinguishing architecturally between odeums reserved for musical and rhetorical performances and *bouleuteria* that held city council meetings. Indeed, some buildings may have been used for both functions.

6. Evangelidis 2014:345–346.

7. Gros 2011:453–463.

8. Evangelidis 2014:341–342.

9. As at Perge, Sagalassos, and Aizanoi (Gros 2011:463).

10. Gros 2011:451–459; Patterson 2006:160–169.

11. For example, a circular building constructed on the west side of the Hellenistic agora (the modern Piazza Duomo) in Thermae Himeraeae (modern Termini Imerese) in the first century AD was tentatively identified as a *tholus macelli* or a small temple, but the presence of later buildings prevented full excavation of the area (Belvedere 2012).

12. Mayer 2012:16–19.

13. Burkhalter 1992; Maiuro 2007. Although in cities like Messene, Sicyon, and Pellene the continued prominence of the gymnasium is attested at least through the second century AD, inscriptions indicate that the gymnasiarchy and its suboffices could be expensive, burdensome liturgies (Kennell 2010; Themelis 2010).

14. Lomas 1995.

15. The cities of the Peloponnese show similar developments (Camia and Kantiréa 2010).

16. Most famously at Pompeii (Gros 2011:320–323; Patterson 2006:132–138).

17. Di Napoli 2010:258–259. Gros (2011:342) notes the Corinth amphitheater's limited architectural ambition and peripherality to the urban center. The Dyrrhachium amphitheater was not constructed until the early second century AD.

18. Vera 1996:51–58.

19. See, e.g., Price 1984 for the role of the emperor in the religious life of the communities of Asia Minor.

20. There is also numismatic evidence from Halaesa for the existence of a *flamen* of the imperial cult in Augustus's lifetime (see chapter 2).

21. E.g., the Achaean *koinon*'s veneration of the emperor at Olympia (Zoumbaki 2010: 123).

22. Barbieri 1961, no. 1.

CHAPTER 7

1. See Wilson 1990 for the concept of agro-towns.

2. Adamesteanu 1963; Bonomi 1964.

3. Bonacasa Carra 2002; La Torre 1993–1994 and 1994.

4. Bowes et al. 2011; Vaccaro 2013.

5. Adamesteanu 1963:262; La Torre 1993–1994:765.

6. Vaccaro 2013:115, 124.

7. La Torre 1994:125.

8. Bowes et al. 2011:430; La Torre 1994:136; Vaccaro 2013:124–125.

9. Bowes et al. (2011:430–438) warn against equating a high number of ceramics with a high density of occupation, because it could instead be evidence of increased dumping of waste within the site.

10. Vaccaro 2013:118–122.

11. Bowes et al. 2011:438–442; Vaccaro 2013:115.

12. Vaccaro 2013:118–119.

13. Bowes et al. 2011:425–427. Cf. Bonomi 1964:175.

14. La Torre 1994:128–129. Cf. Pensabene et al. 2009.

15. Bowes et al. 2011:445; Corsi 2000.

16. Wilson 2011:59–61.

17. Bowes et al. 2011:438.

18. Bowes et al. 2011:446, 448; Vaccaro 2013:125–127.

19. Cf. Alfano et al. 2014.

20. This name is found only in Cicero and implies that the road was the work of Cn. Pompeius Strabo (89 BC) or Pompeius Magnus (82–80 BC) (Malfitana et al. 2012:52).

21. See *BTCGI*, vol. 12 (1993), s.v. Naxos for the early history of the city.

22. Lentini 2001b:23–31.

23. Lentini 2001b:32–36.

24. See Lentini and Blackman 2009 for the excavation of these shipsheds and the Late Roman/Byzantine structures overlying them.

25. Late Roman/Byzantine tombs: Savelli 2001; coin hoards: Puglisi 2001.

26. Olcese (2012:456–465) identifies eight sites associated with ceramic production (kilns, discard dumps, etc.) in and around Naxos.

27. Lentini et al. 2009:103; MGS III amphorae: Vandermersch 1994:43–64.

28. Garozzo 2001a:41; Lentini 2001b:17.

29. Lentini 2001b.

30. Lentini 2001b:33–34; Muscolino 2009:123–125; Ollà 2001:49, 56–59.

31. Muscolino 2009.

32. Ollà 2001:47.

33. Peña 1999:11–13, 74–8, 154–155, 2007b.

34. Muscolino 2009; Ollà 1997.

35. Garozzo 2001a:43; Ollà 2001:48.

36. Muscolino 2009:116–119. Some of these Italian connections may predate the establishment of the colony (Lentini and Muscolino 2013:278–279).

37. Muscolino 2009:123–125; Peña 1999:155.

38. Peña 1999:18; Reynolds 1995:131.

39. Lentini 2001a.

40. See Vallet et al. 1983 for the early history of Megara.

41. Recent research has focused on recovering the site's Hellenistic history; preliminary reports are published in the *Chronique des activités archéologiques de l'École française de Rome*.

42. Vallet et al. 1983:7–9, 29, 174–175.

43. Hoards of silver vessels and bronze coins from this period were recovered in the ruins of a first-century house (Vallet et al. 1983:174).

44. Cacciaguerra 2007:270.

45. Cacciaguerra 2007:271; Gras et al. 2004:349–353.

46. Cacciaguerra 2007:271.

47. Vallet et al. 1983:15–20 (House 13, 22).

48. Cacciaguerra 2007:272; Vallet et al. 1983:93.

49. Malfitana and Cacciaguerra 2011.

50. Malfitana and Cacciaguerra 2011:163–168, 172.

51. Malfitana and Cacciaguerra 2011:173–186, 193–206.

52. Malfitana and Cacciaguerra 2011:279–280, 289–292.

53. Malfitana and Cacciaguerra 2011:111–142, 292.

54. Some scholars have identified this settlement as the station of Aquae Larodes/Thermae Selinuntinae: Caminneci 2010; Tirnetta 1978.

55. Polito 2000.

56. Caminneci 2010.

57. Caminneci et al. 2010.

58. Parello et al. 2010.

59. Caminneci 2010. In the coastal itinerary in the *It. Ant.* between Agrigentum and Lilybaeum (88.4–89.2), at least one of the five stops (*Ad fluvium Lanaricum*) refers to a river crossing; cf. *Mesopotamium* at 96.1, on the coastal route between Agrigentum and Syracuse. Recent research has also highlighted the production and distribution of small flat-bottomed amphorae, perhaps used to transport wine or olive oil, at many sites along the southwestern coast and in the interior (Rizzo et al. 2014).

60. Belvedere and Burgio 2009; Rizzo and Zambito 2007, 2010, and 2012.

61. Rizzo and Zambito 2007:276–277.

62. La Lomía 1961; Rizzo and Zambito 2012:291–294.

63. La Lomía 1961:163–165; Rizzo and Zambito 2012:292. Wilson (1990:224–225) doubts this identification.

64. Rizzo and Zambito 2012:292.

65. Leonard and Demesticha 2004.

66. There has been an encouraging upswing in research on settlement in late antique Sicily in the past decade, including new programs of survey and excavation at Alcamo and San Miceli in western Sicily and at the Gerace villa in the center of the island.

67. Sofiana is over 40 km south of Enna, which probably remained a significant urban center in the imperial period, though no known Roman roads connected the two settlements. In the *It. Ant.* the *mansio* of Philosophiana is 46 Roman miles (over 90 km on modern roads) from Agrigento, a journey of at least three days. It is 45 Roman miles and two days' journey (but almost 100 km on modern roads) from Catina and 21 Roman miles from the closest stop (Galloniana) in the itineraries included in the *It. Ant.*

68. A fragmentary inscription recently found in Marsala also relates to the Constantinian improvement of the *cursus publicus* (Silvestrini 2014).

69. Asheri 1996:92–94.

70. See especially the work of L. Cracco Ruggini (e.g., 1982–1983 and 1997–1998).

CONCLUSION

1. Cuntz 1929. Distances between stops are based on the estimates of Löhberg (2006: 109–117).

2. Uggeri 2004.

3. See especially Bivona 1970 and 1994 for inscriptions from Panormus and Thermae.

4. Alcock 1993 (esp. 93–128).

5. Stewart 2010.

6. Summarized in Rizakis 2013.

7. Indeed, the Greek settlements of Sicily are sometimes included as part of Magna Graecia. Lomas 1993 remains the fundamental English-language account of this region's history under Rome (with updates in Lomas 2016).

8. Giardino 2012 provides an overview of the settlement history of Basilicata from the third century BC onward. Crawford 2003 examines the deurbanization of the region, taking Metapontum as a case study.

9. Lomas 2016; Osanna 2012.

10. Crawford 2006; Gualtieri 2013.

11. See Pedley 1990:113–126, 163–164 for the Roman phases of Paestum.

12. Pedley (1990), Osanna (2012), and Lomas (2016) give varying assessments of the decline of Paestum. The Achaean *apoikia* of Croton on the Ionian coast faced similar en-

vironmental challenges ultimately caused by the deforestation of its territory (Raimondo and Ruga 2010:220).

13. This development is discussed briefly by Christie (2012:20).

14. Arthur 2004:105–107.

15. Giardino 2012.

16. Lomas 2016.

17. Lomas 1993:91–92.

18. Leiwo (1985) attributes Velia's apparent prosperity in the second century BC, despite its relatively small size and political insignificance, to the involvement of several of its citizens in Delos-based trade after the Roman takeover of the island in 166 BC.

19. Laurence et al. (2011:299–303) provide a summary and brief analysis of patterns of "urban recession" in the western Roman provinces, especially in the third and fourth centuries AD.

20. Walthall et al. 2014 and 2016.

21. These excavations are led by Lorenzo Campagna and Jonathan Prag.

22. Caliò et al. 2017.

23. Bergemann 2010.

24. Burgio 2012.

25. *Sicilia Archeologica* 108 (2016) is dedicated to the first results of this project.

26. Akrai: Chowaniec and Misiewicz 2011. See also Caliò et al. 2017 for the recent application of noninvasive research methods in Agrigento.

27. The database can be accessed at http://sicily.classics.ox.ac.uk/.

28. Franco and Capelli 2014.

BIBLIOGRAPHY

Abate, A., and N. Giaccone. 2010. "Segesta: angolo NordOvest della *stoa* Nord (2007–08)." *ASNP* 5.2.2 suppl.:34–40.

Adamesteanu, D. 1963. "Nuovi documenti paleocristiani nella Sicilia centro-meridionale." *BdA* 48:259–274.

Adriani, A., P. E. Arias, and E. Manni. 1971. *Odeon ed altri monumenti archeologici*. Palermo, Sicily: Banco di Sicilia.

Agnello, S. L. 1960. "Iscrizioni cemeteriali inedite di Siracusa." *RACr* 36:19–42.

———. 1987–1988. "Navigazione e porti nel Mediterraneo." *CronA* 26–27:127–132.

———. 2001. *Una metropoli ed una città siciliane fra Roma e Bisanzio*. Syracuse, Sicily: Fondazione Agnello.

Aiello, C. 2016. "Tyndaris nobilissima civitas: continuità e trasformazioni in età tardoantica." In *Paesaggi urbani tardoantichi: casi a confronto*, ed. M. C. Parello and M. S. Rizzo, 201–206. Bari, Italy: Edipuglia.

Alcock, S. E. 1993. *Graecia Capta: The Landscapes of Roman Greece*. Cambridge: Cambridge University Press.

Alfano, A., S. Arrabito, and S. Muratore. 2014. "La Villa del Casale e l'insediamento di Sofiana: un SIT per la viabilità tra il tardoantico ed il medioevo." In *La villa restaurata e i nuovi studi sull'edilizia residenziale tardoantica*, ed. C. Sfameni and P. Pensabene, 609–621. Bari, Italy: Edipuglia.

Amari, S. 2007. "A Late Roman Pottery and Brick Factory in Sicily (Santa Venera al Pozzo)." In *Archaeometric and Archaeological Approaches to Ceramics*, ed. S. Y. Waksman, 121–128. Oxford: Archaeopress.

Ampolo, C., and M. C. Parra. 2003. "Segesta: Scavi nell'area dell'*agora* (2002–2005, campagna primaverile): risultati e prospettive di ricerca." *ASNP* 4.8.1–2:391–402.

———. 2004. "Segesta: Scavi nell'area dell'*agora* (2005–2006): risultati e prospettive di ricerca." *ASNP* 4.8.2:405–413.

———. 2012. "L'agora di Segesta: uno sguardo d'assieme tra iscrizioni e monumenti." In *Agora greca e agorai di Sicilia*, ed. C. Ampolo, 271–285. Pisa: SNS.

Ando, C. 2010. "Imperial Identities." In *Local Knowledge and Microidentities in the Imperial Greek World*, ed. T. Whitmarsh, 17–45. Cambridge: Cambridge University Press.

Arcifa, L., G. Lanza, G. Mussumeci, and F. Trapani. 2016. "Il Sacro Carcere di S. Agata a Catania: analisi architettonica e trasformazioni urbanistiche." In *Architetture del Mediterraneo: scritti in onore di Francesco Tomasello*, ed. N. Bonacasa, F. Buscemi, and V. La Rosa, 35–64. Rome: Quasar.

Ardizzone Lo Bue, F. 2012. "Agrigento paleocristiana: un aggiornamento." In *Ceramica, marmi e pietre: note di archeologia tra Sicilia e Creta*, ed. F. Ardizzone Lo Bue, 19–42. Palermo, Sicily: Torre del vento.

Arena, E. 2016. "Il decreto onorifico tardo-ellenistico da Caronia (*SEG* LIX, 1102): per una nuova edizione." In *Studia Calactina I: ricerche su una città greco-romana di Sicilia*, ed. F. Collura, 351–367. Oxford: BAR.

Arthur, P. 2004. "From *Vicus* to Village: Italian Landscapes, AD 400–1000." In *Landscapes of Change: Rural Evolutions in Late Antiquity and the Early Middle Ages*, ed. N. Christie, 103–134. Aldershot, UK: Ashgate.

Asheri, D. 1969. "Nota sul senato di Agrigento." *RFil* 97:268–272.

———. 1996. "Colonizzazione e decolonizzazione." In *I Greci: storia cultura arte società I: noi e i Greci*, ed. S. Settis, 73–115. Turin, Italy: Einaudi.

Bacci, G. M. 1980–1981. "Ricerche a Taormina negli anni 1977–1980." *Kokalos* 26–27: 737–748.

Badian, E. 1958. *Foreign Clientelae (264–70 BC)*. Oxford: Clarendon.

Barbieri, G. 1961. "Nuove iscrizioni di Marsala." *Kokalos* 7:15–52.

———. 1963. "Due cippi di Marsala del IV sec. d.C." *Kokalos* 9:225–252.

Basile, B. 2001–2002. "Siracusa: indagini archeologiche nel biennio 2000–2001." *Kokalos* 47–48:729–782.

Battistoni, F. 2010. "Note al nuovo decreto dall'area di Caronia (ZPE 170)." *ZPE* 174: 113–117.

Bechtold, B. 1997. "Una villa ellenistico-romana sull'acropoli sud di Segesta." In *Seconde Giornate Internazionali di Studi sull'Area Elima*, 85–110. Pisa: SNS.

Bechtold, B., S. Frey-Kupper, M. Madella, et al. 1999. *La necropoli di Lilybaeum*. Rome: Bretschneider.

Bechtold, B., and K. Schmidt. 2015. "Amphorae and Coarse Ware Fabrics of Lilybaion: Evidences for Local Production and Export." In *FACEM: Provenance Studies on Pottery in the Central Mediterranean*. http://facem.at/project/papers.php.

Bejor, G. 1983. "Aspetti della romanizzazione della Sicilia." In *Forme di contatto e processi di trasformazione nella società antiche*, 345–378. Pisa/Rome: SNS/EFR.

Bell, M. 1981. *Morgantina Studies I: The Terracottas*. Princeton, NJ: Princeton University Press.

———. 1986–1987. "La fontana ellenistica di Morgantina." *QuadA* 2:111–124.

———. 1999. "Centro e periferia nel regno siracusano di Ierone II." In *La colonisation grecque en Méditerranée occidentale*, 257–277. Rome: EFR.

———. 2005. "Bankers' Houses in Soluntum and Agrigentum." In *Omni pede stare: saggi architettonici e circumvesuviani in memoriam Jos de Waele*, ed. S. T. A. M. Mols and E. M. Moorman, 92–99. Naples: Electa.

———. 2006. "Rapporti urbanistici fra Camarina e Morgantina." In *Camarina: 2600 anni dopo la fondazione*, ed. P. Pelagatti, G. Di Stefano, and L. de Lachenal, 253–258. Ragusa, Sicily: Centro Studi Feliciano Rossitto.

Bell, M., and R. R. Holloway. 1988. "Excavations at Morgantina, 1980–1985: Preliminary Report XII." *AJA* 92.3:313–342.

Belli Pasqua, R. 2017. "Statue di togati dall'area del Tempio Romano: ipotesi di restituzione dell'arredo statuario." In *Agrigento: nuove ricerche sull'area pubblica centrale*, ed. L. M. Caliò et al., 119–122. Rome: Quasar.

Belvedere, O. 1988. "Opere pubbliche ed edifici per lo spettacolo nella Sicilia di età imperiale." *ANRW* II.11.1:346–413.

———. 1997a. "Organizzazione fondiaria e insediamenti nella Sicilia di età imperiale." *Corso di Cultura sull'Arte Ravennate e Bizantina* 43:33–59.

———. 1997b. "Politica urbanistica e ideologia nella Sicilia della prima età imperiale." In *Architettura e pianificazione urbana nell'Italia antica*, ed. L. Quilici and S. Quilici Gigli, 17–24. Rome: Bretschneider.

———. 2012. "Thermae Himeraeae: dall'*agora* ellenistica al foro romano. Riflessioni sulla romanizzazione della Sicilia." In *Agora greca e agorai di Sicilia*, ed. C. Ampolo, 211–221. Pisa: SNS.

Belvedere, O., and A. Burgio. 2009. "Sulla viabilià nel territorio di Palma di Montechiaro: brevi note in margine al 'Progetto Cignana.'" In *Παλαια φιλια: Studi di topografia antica in onore di Giovanni Uggeri*, ed. C. Marangio and G. Laudizi, 515–530. Galatina: Congedo.

Bergemann, J., ed. 2010. *Gela-Survey: 3000 Jahre Siedlungsgeschichte in Sizilien*. 3 vols. Munich: Biering und Brinkmann.

Bernardini, S., F. Cambi, A. Molinari, et al. 2000. "Il territorio di Segesta fra l'età arcaica e il medioevo: nuovi dati dalla carta archeologica di Calatafimi." In *Terze Giornate Internazionali di Studi sull'Area Elima*, 91–133. Pisa: SNS.

Bintliff, J. 1997. "Catastrophe, Chaos and Complexity: The Death, Decay and Rebirth of Towns from Antiquity to Today." *JEA* 5:67–90.

Biondi, G. 2002. "Per una carta archeologica del territorio di Centuripe." In *Scavi e ricerche a Centuripe*, ed. G. Rizza, 41–81. Catania: CNR.

———. 2008. "Centuripe (EN): nuovi dati sull'edificio romano di contrada Vagni." In *SOMA 2005: Proceedings of the IX Symposium on Mediterranean Archaeology*, 487–493. Oxford: Archaeopress.

———. 2010. "Centuripe (EN): indagini su un territorio della Sicilia centro-orientale." In *Il dialogo dei saperi: metodologie integrate per i Beni culturali*, ed. F. D'Andria, 79–94. Naples: Edizioni scientifiche italiane.

Bivona, L. 1970. *Iscrizioni latine lapidarie del museo di Palermo*. Palermo: Flaccovio.

———. 1987. "Un nuovo quaestor p(rovinciae) S(iciliae) e curator r.p. di Lilibeo: L. Cassius Manilianus." *Kokalos* 33:11–23.

———. 1994. *Iscrizioni latine lapidarie del Museo Civico di Termini Imerese*. Rome: Bretschneider.

Blake, E., and Schon, R. 2010. "The Marsala Hinterland Survey: Preliminary Report." *EtrSt* 13:49–66.

Bloesch, H. and H. P. Isler. 1971. "Ricerche archeologiche sul monte Iato." *SicA* 4.15:9–18.

———. 1974. "Monte Iato: la quarta campagna di scavo." *SicA* 7.26:9–22.

———. 1976. "Monte Iato: la sesta campagna di scavo." *SicA* 9.32:9–24.

Bonacasa Carra, R. M. 1997. "Segesta: SAS 5: aspetti della ceramica da fuoco e della ceramica da cucina." In *Seconde Giornate Internazionali di Studi sull'Area Elima*, 173–181. Pisa: SNS.

———. 2002. "Sofiana." In *La Sicilia centro-meridionale tra il II ed il VI sec. d.C.*, ed. R. M. Bonacasa Carra and R. Panvini, 103–113. Caltanissetta: Sciascia.

Bonacasa Carra, R. M., V. Caminneci, and F. Ardizzone. 1995. *Agrigento: la necropoli paleocristiana sub divo*. Rome: Bretschneider.

Bonanno, C. 1993–1994. "Scavi e ricerche a Caronia e a S. Marco d'Alunzio." *Kokalos* 39–40:953–985.

———, ed. 2009. *Kalè Akté: scavi in contrada Pantano di Caronia Marina—Messina 2003–2005*. Rome: Bretschneider.

Bonanno, C., and F. Sudano. 2006. "Kale Akte: l'insediamento in contrada Pantano a Caronia Marina." In *Old Pottery in a New Century: Innovating Perspectives on Roman Pottery Studies*, ed. D. Malfitana, J. Poblome, and J. Lund, 435–448. Rome: Bretschneider.

Bonomi, L. 1964. "Cimiteri paleocristiani di Sofiana (retroterra di Gela)." *RACr* 40: 169–220.

Bottari, C., M. Coltelli, and C. Monaco. 2014. "Evidence of Late Roman Collapse at Catania (Sicily, Southern Italy): An Earthquake in the 4th Century AD?" *Quaternary International* 30:1–8.

Bottari, C., M. D'Amico, M. Maugeri, et al. 2009. "Location of the Ancient Tindari Harbour from Geoarchaeological Investigations (NE Sicily)." *Environmental Archaeology* 14:37–49.

Bowes, K., M. Ghisleni, G. F. La Torre, and E. Vaccaro. 2011. "Preliminary Report on Sofiana/mansio Philosophiana in the Hinterland of Piazza Armerina." *JRA* 24:423–449.

Branciforti, M. G. 2003. "Quartieri di età ellenistica e romana a Catania." In *Archeologia del Mediterraneo: studi in onore di Ernesto De Miro*, ed. G. Fiorentini, A. Calderone, and M. Caccamo Caltabiano, 95–120. Rome: Bretschneider.

———. 2005a. "Gli scavi archeologici nell'ex reclusorio della Purità di Catania." In *Μεγαλαι νησοι: studi dedicati a Giovanni Rizza per il suo ottantesimo compleanno*, ed. R. Gigli, vol. 2, 47–77. 2 vols. Catania, Sicily: CNR.

———. 2005b. "L'area archeologica di Santa Venera al Pozzo (Acicatena)." In *Dall'Alcantara agli Iblei: la ricera archeologica in provincia di Catania*, ed. F. Privitera and U. Spigo, 205–207. Palermo, Sicily: Regione Siciliana.

Brugnone, A., and B. Bechtold. 1997. "Novità epigrafiche da Lilibeo: la tomba 186 della via Berta." In *Seconde Giornate Internazionali di Studi sull'Area Elima*, 111–140. Pisa: SNS.

Bruno, G., L. Bobbo, and A. F. Bruno. 2015. "Evidenze di cambiamento climatico desunte da dati idrogeologici e dagli schemi di funzionamento della fontana monumentale di Morgantina (Sicilia)." *Geologia dell'Ambiente* suppl. 2:7–18.

Buda, G., F. Nicoletti, and V. Spinella. 2015. "Catania: scavi e restauri a nord della Rotonda." In *Catania antica: nuove prospettive di ricerca*, ed. F. Nicoletti, 507–572. Palermo, Sicily: Regione Siciliana.

Burgio, A. 2008. *Il paesaggio agrario nella Sicilia ellenistico-romana: Alesa e il suo territorio.* Rome: Bretschneider.

———. 2012. "Il progetto 'Cignana' (Naro-Palma di Montechiaro, Sicilia centromeridionale): prospezione archeologica intorno alla villa romana di Cignana: primi dati sulle dinamiche del popolamento antico." In *Göttinger Studien zur Mediterranean Archäologie 3*, ed. J. Bergemann, 127–139. Rahden, Germany: Leidorf.

Burkhalter, F. 1992. "Le Gymnase d'Alexandrie: Centre administratif de la province romaine d'Égypte." *BCH* 116.1:345–373.

Buttrey, T. V., et al. 1989. *Morgantina Studies II: The Coins.* Princeton, NJ: Princeton University Press.

Cacciaguerra, G. 2007. "Megara Hyblaea (Augusta, SR) tra l'età tardo imperiale ed il Bassomedioevo." *Archeologia Medievale* 34:269–281.

Cadario, M. 2005. "I Claudi Marcelli: strategie di propaganda in monumenti onorari e dediche votive tra III e I sec. a.C." *Ostraka* 14:147–177.

Calderone, S. 1959. "Lilybaeum." In *Dizionario epigrafico di antichità romane di Ettore de Ruggiero*, vol. 4.67, ed. G. Cardinali, 1069–1073. 5 vols. Rome: Signorelli.

———. 1985–1986. "Frammento di decreto onorifico agrigentino." *QuadA* 1:13–18.

Caliò, L. M., et al., eds. 2017. *Agrigento: nuove ricerche sull'area pubblica centrale.* Rome: Quasar.

Cambi, F. 2005. "Segesta: i villaggi di età imperiale." In *Paesaggi e insediamenti rurali in Italia meridionale fra tardoantico e altomedioevo*, ed. G. Volpe and M. Turchiano, 623–640. Bari, Italy: Edipuglia.

Camerata Scovazzo, R. 1997. "Note di topografia segestana." In *Seconde Giornate Internazionali di Studi sull'Area Elima*, 205–226. Pisa: SNS.

———, ed. 2008. *Segesta III: il sistema difensivo di Porta di Valle (scavi 1990–1993).* Mantua, Italy: SAP.

Camia, F., and M. Kantiréa. 2010. "The Imperial Cult in the Peloponnese." In *Roman Peloponnese III: Society, Economy and Culture under the Roman Empire*, ed. A. D. Rizakis and Cl. E. Lepenioti, 375–406. Athens: NHRF.

Caminneci, V. 2010. "Tra il mare ed il fiume. Dinamiche insediative nella Sicilia occidentale in età tardoantica: il villaggio in contrada Carabollace (Sciacca, Agrigento, Sicilia, Italia)." *Journal of Fasti Online* 213. http://www.fastionline.org/docs/FOLDER-it-2010-213.pdf.

———. 2015. "Sulle sponde del Mediterraneo: il porto di Agrigentum in età tardo antica e bizantina." In *Isole e terraferma nel primo cristianesimo: identità locale ed interscambi culturali, religiosi e produttivi*, ed. R. Martorelli, A. Piras, and P. G. Spanu, 481–490. Cagliari, Sardinia: PFTS University Press.

Caminneci, V., C. Franco, and G. Galioto. 2010. "L'insediamento tardoantico di Contrada Carabollace (Sciacca): primi dati sui rinvenimenti ceramici." In *LRCW 3: Late Roman Coarse Wares, Cooking Wares and Amphorae in the Mediterranean*, ed. S. Menchelli, 273–282. Oxford: Archaeopress.

Caminneci, V., M. C. Parello, and M. S. Rizzo. 2015. *Agrigentum: spazi di vita pubblica della città romana*. Agrigento: Parco della Valle dei Templi.

Campagna, L. 2003. "La Sicilia di età repubblicana nella storiografia degli ultimi cinquant'anni." *Ostraka* 12:7–31.

———. 2004. "Architettura e ideologia della basileia a Siracusa nell'età di Ierone II." In *Nuove prospettive della ricerca sulla Sicilia del III a.C.: archeologia, numismatica, storia*, ed. M. Caccamo Caltabiano, L. Campagna, and A. Pinzone, 151–189. Messina, Sicily: D. Sc. A. M.

———. 2009. "Urbanistica dei centri siciliani d'altura in età ellenistica: il caso di Tauromenion." In *Εις ακρα: insediamenti d'altura in Sicilia dalla preistoria al III sec. a.C.*, ed. M. Congiu, 205–226. Caltanissetta, Sicily: Sciascia.

———. 2011a. "Exploring Social and Cultural Changes in *Provincia Sicilia*: Reflections on the Study of Urban Landscapes." In *Local Cultures of South Italy and Sicily in the Late Republican Period: Between Hellenism and Rome*, ed. F. Colivicchi, 161–183. *JRA* suppl. 83.

———. 2011b. "Tauromenion: nuove ricerche sull'urbanistica e sull'architettura della città ellenistica." *FormaUrbis* 16.6:15–21.

———. 2013. "Iscrizioni: un'epigrafe ellenistica sulla curatela di lavori edili." In *Finziade I: scavi sul Monte Sant'Angelo di Licata (2003–2005)*, ed. G. F. La Torre and F. Mollo, 391–401. Rome: Bretschneider.

———. 2016. "Tauromenion (Taormina, Sicily): The Hellenistic Sacred Area near the Church of Santa Caterina and Its Transformations during the Roman Imperial Age." In *Hellenistic Sanctuaries between Greece and Rome*, ed. M. Melfi and O. Bobou, 254–272. Oxford: Oxford University Press.

Campagna, L., and G. F. La Torre. 2008. "Ricerche sui monumenti e sulla topografia di Tauromenion: una stoà ellenistica nell'area della Naumachia." *SicAnt* 5:115–146.

Campbell, B. 2000. *The Writings of the Roman Land Surveyors: Introduction, Text, Translation and Commentary*. London: SPRS.

Carbè, A. 2008. "The Coinage." In *Alesa Archonidea: Guide to the Antiquarium*, ed. G. Scibona and G. Tigano, 58–61. Palermo, Sicily: Regione Siciliana.

Cascella, S. and F. Collura. 2016. "Sigillata italica dalla collina di Caronia." In *Studia Calactina I: ricerche su una città greco-romana di Sicilia*, ed. F. Collura, 393–412. Oxford: BAR.

Castellana, G. 1992. "La sigillata africana dell'insediamento di età imperiale romana e bizantina del Saraceno di Favara presso Agrigento." *SicA* 25.78–79:45–70.

Castellana, G., and B. E. McConnell. 1990. "A Rural Settlement of Imperial Roman and Byzantine Date in Contrada Saraceno near Agrigento, Sicily." *AJA* 94:25–44.

Chausson, F. 2016. "Pour une histoire des patrimoines des sénateurs orientaux en Occident (Rome, Italie, Sicile)." In *Propriétaires et citoyens dans l'Orient romain*, ed. F. Lerouxel and A.-V. Pont, 289–311. Bordeaux: Ausonius.

Chowaniec, R., and K. Misiewicz. 2011. "Non-invasive Researches in Palazzolo Acreide (Ancient Akrai), Sicily." *Archeologia* 59:173–186.

Christie, N. 2012. "Vrbes Extinctae: Archaeologies of and Approaches to Abandoned

Classical Cities." In *Vrbes Extinctae: Archaeologies of Abandoned Classical Towns*, ed. N. Christie and A. Augenti, 1–44. Farnham, UK: Ashgate.

Ciurcina, C. 2006. *Siracusa in età ellenistica e romana: Museo Archeologico Regionale Paolo Orsi, Siracusa.* Syracuse, Sicily: Erre.

Clarke, K. 1999. *Between Geography and History: Hellenistic Constructions of the Roman World.* Oxford: Clarendon.

Coarelli, F. 1980. "La cultura figurativa in Sicilia: dalla conquista romana a Bisanzio." In *Sicilia antica, vol. 2:2: la Sicilia romana*, ed. E. Gabba and G. Vallet, 371–392. 5 vols. Naples: Storia di Napoli e della Sicilia.

Collin Bouffier, S. 2006. "La gestion des ressources hydriques de la cité antique de Camarina." In *Camarina: 2600 anni dopo la fondazione*, ed. P. Pelagatti, G. Di Stefano, and L. de Lachenal, 183–196. Ragusa, Sicily: Centro Studi Feliciano Rossitto.

Collura, F. 2011. "Dal disastro alle scoperte archeologiche: nuovi dati sull'occupazione del territorio calactino dalla frana del 2010 in c.da Lineri (Caronia, Sicilia)." Unpublished MS.

———, ed. 2016. *Studia Calactina I: ricerche su una città greco-romana di Sicilia.* Oxford: BAR.

Corsi, C. 2000. *Le strutture di servizio del cursus publicus in Italia: ricerche topografiche ed evidenze archeologiche.* Oxford: Hedges.

Covino, R. 2013. "Stasis in Roman Sicily." *Electryone* 1:18–28.

Cracco Ruggini, L. 1982–1983. "Sicilia, III/IV secolo: il volto della non-città." *Kokalos* 28–29:477–515.

———. 1997–1998. "La Sicilia tardoantica e l'Oriente mediterraneo." *Kokalos* 43–44: 243–269.

Crawford, M. 2003. "Brave New World: Metapontum after Metapontum." In *Les élites et leurs facettes: les élites locales dans le monde hellénistique et romain*, ed. M. Cébeillac-Gervasoni and L. Lamoine, 15–30. Rome: EFR.

———. 2006. "From Poseidonia to Paestum via the Lucanians." In *Greek and Roman Colonization: Origins, Ideologies and Interactions*, ed. G. Bradley and J.-P. Wilson, 59–72. Swansea: Classical Press of Wales.

Crisà, A. 2008. "La monetazione di Tindari romana con segni di valore e legende in lingua latina." *RItNum* 109:235–268.

Crouch, D. P. 1984. "The Hellenistic Water System of Morgantina, Sicily: Contributions to the History of Urbanization." *AJA* 88.3:353–365.

Cugno, S. A. 2009. "Il paesaggio rurale siracusano nella tarda età romana: il territorio di Canicattini Bagni." *FormaUrbis* 14.10:46–58.

Cuntz, O., ed. 1929. *Itineraria Romana 1: Itineraria Antonini Augusti et Burdigalense.* Leipzig: Teubner.

Cuomo di Caprio, N. 1992. *Morgantina Studies III: fornaci e officine da vasaio tardo-ellenistiche.* Princeton, NJ: Princeton University Press.

Cutroni Tusa, A., A. Italia, and D. Lima. 1994. *Solunto.* Rome: Libreria dello Stato.

De Angelis, F. 2003. *Megara Hyblaia and Selinous: The Development of Two Greek City-States in Archaic Sicily.* Oxford: Oxford University School of Archaeology.

———. 2009. "Ancient Sicily: The Development of a Microregional Tessera in the Mediterranean Mosaic." In *Société et climats dans l'empire romain*, ed. E. Hermon, 235–250. Naples: Editoriale Scientifica.

De Cesare, M., and M. C. Parra. 2001. "Segesta: area del *bouleuterion* (SAS 3; 1995, 1997)." *ASNP* 4.6.2:417–429.

Del Monaco, L. 2003. "Le istituzioni di Tauromenio ellenistico-romana." In *L'Italia centro meridionale tra repubblica e primo impero: alcuni aspetti culturali e istituzionali*, ed. M. L. Lazzarini and P. Lombardi, 33–48. Rome: Quasar.

De Miro, E. 1982–1983. "Città e contado nella Sicilia centro-meridionale nel III e IV sec. d.C." *Kokalos* 28–29:319–329.

———. 2000. *Agrigento I: i santuari urbani. L'area sacra tra il tempio di Zeus e Porta V.* Rome: Bretschneider.

———. 2006. "Agrigento in età ellenistica: aspetti di architettura." In *Sicilia ellenistica, consuetudo italica: alle origini dell'architettura ellenistica d'Occidente*, ed. M. Osanna and M. Torelli, 69–81. Pisa: Ateneo.

———. 2009. *Agrigento 4: l'abitato antico. Il quartiere ellenistico-romano.* Rome: Gangemi.

———. 2012. "Agorai e forum in Agrigento." In *Agora greca e agorai di Sicilia*, ed. C. Ampolo, 101–110. Pisa: SNS.

———. 2014. *Heraclea Minoa: mezzo secolo di ricerche.* Pisa: Serra.

De Miro, E., and G. Fiorentini. 2011. *Agrigento romana: gli edifici pubblici civili.* Pisa: Serra.

Denaro, M. 1997. "Segesta: SAS 5: tipologia delle anfore." In *Seconde Giornate Internazionali di Studi sull'Area Elima*, 537–548. Pisa: SNS.

De Vido, S. 2003. "Genealogie Segestane." In *Quarte Giornate di Studi sull'Area Elima*, 367–402. Pisa: SNS.

De Vincenzo, S. 2013. *Tra Cartagine e Roma: i centri urbani dell'eparchia punica di Sicilia tra VI e I sec. a.C.* Berlin: De Gruyter.

De Vos, M. 1975. "Pitture e mosaico a Solunto." *BABesch* 50:195–224.

Dimartino, A. 2010. "*Venus Felix* a Siracusa? Per una rilettura dei decreti della *synodos* di *technitai* di Afrodite *Hilara*." *Epigraphica* 72:21–49.

Di Napoli, V. 2010. "Entertainment Building of the Roman Peloponnese: Theatres, *Odea*, and Amphitheatres and Their Topographical Distribution." In *Roman Peloponnese III: Society, Economy and Culture under the Roman Empire*, ed. A. D. Rizakis and Cl. E. Lepenioti, 253–266. Athens: NHRF.

Di Stefano, C. A. 2006. "Lilibeo: contributo alla rilettura dell'insula I." In *Guerra e pace in Sicilia e nel Mediterraneo antico (VIII–III sec. a.C.)*, 545–553. Pisa: SNS.

Di Stefano, G. 1993–1994. "Scavi e ricerche a Camarina e nella Ragusano." *Kokalos* 39–40: 1367–1421.

———. 1994. "Distribuzione e tipologia degli insediamenti di età repubblicana ed imperiale sull'altopiano Ibleo." In *Le ravitaillement en blé de Rome et des centres urbains des débuts de la république jusqu'au haut empire*, 237–242. Rome: EFR.

———. 2001–2002. "L'attività di ricerca della Soprintendenza a Camarina e nella provincia di Ragusa fra il 1996 e il 2000." *Kokalos* 47–48:687–728.

———. 2002. "Marmi africani e garum spagnolo nel Mediterraneo centrale: tracce di alcune rotte commerciali di età romana." In *L'Africa romana: lo spazio marittimo del Mediterraneo occidentale, geografia storica ed economia*, ed. M. Khanoussi, P. Ruggeri, and C. Vismara, 627–641. Rome: Carocci.

———. 2003. "Materiali del sito e dal mare di Camarina." *SicA* 101:127–142.

———. 2005. "Nuovi mosaici dalla villa romana di Giarratana in Sicilia: notizie preliminari." In *Atti del X colloquio dell'Associazione Italiana per lo Studio e la Conservazione del Mosaico*, ed. C. Angelelli, 281–285. Tivoli/Rome: Scripta manent.

———. 2006. "Aspetti urbanistici e topografici per la storia di Camarina." In *Camarina: 2600 anni dopo la fondazione*, ed. P. Pelagatti, G. Di Stefano, and L. de Lachenal, 157–182. Ragusa, Sicily: Centro Studi Feliciano Rossitto.

———. 2010. "Camarina: pavimenti in cementizio a base fittile di età repubblicana *in situ*." In *Atti del XV Colloquio dell'Associazione Italiana per lo Studio e la Conservazione del Mosaico*, ed. C. Angelelli and C. Salvetti, 543–550. Tivoli, Italy: Mancini.

Di Stefano, G., and G. Leone. 1985. *La regione camarinese in età romana: appunti per la carta archeologica*. Modica, Sicily: Leopardi.

Di Stefano, G., and G. Ventura. 2011. "Nuovi mosaici e altri pavimenti dalle ville rurali di Giarratana (scavi 2009), Margi e Piombo (scavi 2008), nell'antico territorio di Camarina e dal *Fortilitium* di Ispica (Ragusa, Sicilia)." In *Atti del XVI Colloquio dell'Associazione Italiana per lo Studio e la Conservazione del Mosaico*, ed. C. Angelelli, 207–214. Tivoli/Rome: Scripta Manent.

Dueck, D. 2000. *Strabo of Amasia: A Greek Man of Letters in Augustan Rome*. London: Routledge.

Eck, W. 1996a. "Senatoren und senatorischer grundbesitz auf Sizilien." In *Catania antica*, ed. B. Gentili, 232–256. Pisa: IEPI.

———. 1996b. "Senatorische Familien der Kaiserzeit in der Provinz Sizilien." *ZPE* 113: 109–128.

Evangelidis, V. 2014. "Agoras and Fora: Developments in the Central Public Space of the Cities of Greece during the Roman Period." *ABSA* 109.1:335–356.

Evans, R. J. 2009. *Syracuse in Antiquity: History and Topography*. Pretoria, South Africa: Unisa Press.

Facella, A. 2006. *Alesa Archonidea: ricerche su un'antica città della Sicilia tirrenica*. Pisa: SNS.

———. 2009. "Segesta tardoantica: topografia, cronologia e tipologia dell'insediamento." In *Immagine e immagini della Sicilia e di altre isole del Mediterraneo antico: Atti delle Seste Giornate Internazionali di Studi sull'Area Elima*, ed. C. Ampolo, 2:589–607. 2 vols. Pisa: SNS.

———. 2013. "Nuove acquisizioni su Segesta tardoantica." *ASNP* 5.5.1:285–315.

Facella, A., and R. Olivito. 2003. "Segesta: aree del *bouleuterion* e della *stoa* meridionale dell'*agora* (SAS 3; 2002–2005)." *ASNP* 4.8.1–2:403–416.

———. 2004. "Segesta: area della *stoa* sud dell'*agora* (SAS 3; 2005–2006)." *ASNP* 4.8.2:414–428.

———. 2010. "Segesta: area della strada e della piazza triangolare (SAS 3; 2007–2008)." *ASNP* 5.2.2 suppl.:6–19.

Fallico, A. M. 1971. "Siracusa: saggi di scavo nell'area della Villa Maria." *NSc* 25:581–639.

Famà, M. L. 1980. "L'area sacra con altare 'a tre betili' di Solunto." *SicA* 13.42:7–42.

Fasolo, M. 2014. *Tyndaris e il suo territorio, 2: carta archeologica del territorio di Tindari e materiali.* Rome: mediaGEO.

Faulkner, N. 1996. "Verulamium: Interpreting Decline." *AJ* 153:79–103.

Favaro, A. 1997. "La sequenza stratigrafica della Porta Nord di Segesta (campagne di scavo 1990–91–92–93)." In *Seconde Giornate Internazionali di Studi sull'Area Elima*, 685–692. Pisa: SNS.

Fentress, E. 2013. "Strangers in the City: Élite Communication in the Hellenistic Central Mediterranean." In *The Hellenistic West: Rethinking the Ancient Mediterranean*, ed. J. R. W. Prag and J. Quinn, 157–178. Cambridge: Cambridge University Press.

Fentress, E., D. Kennet, and I. Valenti. 1990. "A Sicilian Villa and Its Landscape (Contrada Mirabile, Mazara del Vallo, 1988)." *Opus* 5:75–96.

Fiorentini, G. 1993–1994. "Attività di indagini archeologiche della Soprintendenza Beni Culturali e Ambientali di Agrigento." *Kokalos* 39–40:717–733.

Fitzjohn, M. ed. 2007. *Uplands of Ancient Sicily and Calabria.* London: Accordia.

Fournier, J. 2010. *Entre tutelle romaine et autonomie civique: l'administration judiciaire dans les provinces hellénophones de l'Empire romain (129 av. J.-C.–235 apr. J.-C.).* Athens: EFA.

Franco, C., and C. Capelli. 2014. "Sicilian Flat-Bottomed Amphorae (1st–5th Century AD): New Data on Typo-Chronology and Distribution and from an Integrated Petrographic and Archaeological Study." In *Archeologia classica in Sicilia e nel Mediterraneo*, ed. D. Malfitana and G. Cacciaguerra, 341–362. Catania, Sicily: CNR.

Frasca, M. 2006. "Centuripe ellenistica: il quadro generale." In *Sicilia ellenistica, consuetudo italica: alle origini dell'architettura ellenistica d'Occidente*, ed. M. Osanna and M. Torelli, 193–199. Pisa: Ateneo.

Frey-Kupper, S. 2013. *Die antiken Fundmünzen vom Monte Iato 1971–1990: Ein Beitrag zur Geldgeschichte Westsiziliens. Studia Ietina 10.* Lausanne, Switzerland: Zèbre.

———. 2014. "Coins and Their Use in the Punic Mediterranean: Case Studies from Carthage to Italy from the Fourth to the First Century BCE." In *The Punic Mediterranean: Identities and Identification from Phoenician Settlement to Roman Rule*, ed. J. C. Quinn and N. Vella, 76–107. Cambridge: Cambridge University Press.

Fuduli, L. 2011. "Nobilissima civitas Tyndaris e la ricerca archeologica." *FormaUrbis* 16.6:27–33.

Gabrici, E. 1925. "Girgenti: scavi e scoperte archeologiche dal 1916 al 1924." *NSc* 6.1:420–461.

Gagliardi, V. 2009. "Segesta tardoantica: ceramiche di importazione e circolazione di merci." In *Immagine e immagini della Sicilia e di altre isole del Mediterraneo antico: Atti delle Seste Giornate Internazionali di Studi sull'Area Elima*, 609–621. Pisa: SNS.

Gagliardi, V., and M. C. Parra. 2006. "Ceramiche africane dal foro di Segesta: dati preliminari." In *L'africa romana: mobilità delle persone e dei popoli, dinamiche migratorie, emigrazioni ed immigrazioni nelle province occidentali dell'Impero romano*, ed. A. Akerraz, 1615–1628. Rome: Carocci.

Garozzo, B. 2001a. "Alcuni bolli ellenistici da Naxos di Sicilia." In *Naxos di Sicilia in età romana e bizantina ed evidenze dai Peloritani*, ed. M. C. Lentini, 41–46. Bari, Italy: Edipuglia.

———. 2001b. "Segesta: bolli su anfore e laterizi rinvenuti nelle campagne 1995–1997 (con aggiornamento per gli anni 1990–1993)." *ASNP* 4.6.2:502–510.

Gelarda, I. 2011. "Lilibeo e i Vandali." *JbÖByz* 61:135–146.

Gentili, G. V. 1956. "Siracusa: contributo alla topografia dell'antica città." *NSc* 10:94–164.

———. 1961. "Nuovi elementi di epigrafia siracusana." *ArchStorSir* 7:5–25.

———. 1973. "Studi e ricerche su l'anfiteatro di Siracusa." *Palladio* 23:3–80.

Giardino, L. 2012. "The Farmhouse at San Biagio and the Agricultural Landscape of Basilicata in the Roman Period." In *The Chora of Metaponto 4: The Late Roman Farmhouse at San Biagio*, ed. E. Lapadula and J. Coleman Carter, 1–17. Austin: University of Texas Press.

Giglio, R. 1997. "Rassegna dei mosaici di Lilibeo e rinvenimenti recenti." In *Atti del IV Colloquio dell'Associazione Italiana per lo Studio e la Conservazione del Mosaico*, ed. R. M. Bonacasa Carra and F. Guidobaldi, 123–136. Ravenna, Italy: Girasole.

———. 2003. "Lilibeo (Marsala): recenti rinvenimenti archeologici in via Quarto." In *Quarte Giornate Internazionali di Studi sull'Area Elima*, 727–736. Pisa: SNS.

———. 2008. "Nuovi dati da Lilibeo (Marsala): mosaici e decorazioni pittoriche tra Africa e Roma." In *L'Africa romana: mobilità delle persone e dei popoli, dinamiche migratorie, emigrazioni ed immigrazioni nelle province occidentali dell'Impero romano*, ed. A. Akerraz, 1527–1548. Rome: Carocci.

———. 2009. "Lilibeo 2004–2005: la ricerca archeologica nell'area di capo Boeo." In *Immagine e immagini della Sicilia e di altre isole del Mediterraneo antico: Atti delle Seste Giornate Internazionali di Studi sull'Area Elima*, 561–571. Pisa: SNS.

———. 2010. "Capo Boeo: traffici, naviganti e divinità alla luce delle ultime ricerche nel Parco Archeologico di Marsala." In *La devozione dei naviganti: il culto di Afrodite ericina nel Mediterraneo*, ed. E. Acquaro, A. Filippi, and S. Medas, 71–87. Lugano, Italy: Lumières.

González López, M. A. 2005. "La vajilla de barniz negro: Campaniense C." In *Introducción al estudio de la ceramica romana: una breve guía de referencia*, ed. M. R. Roumens and M. I. Fernández García, 63–80. Málaga, Spain: CVDAS.

Gras, M., H. Tréziny, and H. Broise. 2004. *Megara Hyblaea 5: la ville archaïque*. Rome: EFR.

Greco, C. 1997. "Pavimenti in opus signinum e tessellati geometrici da Solunto: una messa a punto." In *Atti del IV Colloquio dell'Associazione Italiana per lo Studio e la Conservazione del Mosaico*, ed. R. M. Bonacasa Carra and F. Guidobaldi, 39–63. Ravenna, Italy: Girasole.

———. 2005. *Solunto: guida breve*. Palermo: BCA.

———. 2011. "I sistemi decorativi di Solunto: appunti e riflessioni." In *Pittura ellenistica in Italia e in Sicilia: linguaggi e tradizioni*, ed. G. F. La Torre and M. Torelli, 279–316. Rome: Bretschneider.

Greco, R. 1999. *Pagani e cristiani a Siracusa tra il III e il IV secolo d.C.* Rome: Bretschneider.

Griffo, P. 1963. "Contributi epigrafici agrigentini." *Kokalos* 9:163–184.

Gros, P. 2011. *L'architecture romaine du début du IIIe siècle av. J.-C. à la fin du Haut-Empire 1: les monuments publics*. 3rd ed. Paris: Picard.

Gualtieri, M. 2013. "Greeks, Lucanians and Romans at Poseidonia-Paestum (South Italy)." In *A Companion to the Archaeology of the Roman Republic*, ed. J. DeRose Evans, 369–386. Malden, MA: Wiley.

Gulletta, M. I. P. 2012. "Tyndaris: per uno status quaestionis sulle ipotesi di ubicazione dell'agora-foro." In *Sicilia occidentale: studi, rassegne, ricerche*, ed. C. Ampolo, 297–303. Pisa: SNS.

Guzzardi, L. 1993–1994. "Ricerche archeologiche nel Siracusano." *Kokalos* 39–40:1299–1314.

Hansen, M. H. 2006. *Polis: An Introduction to the Ancient Greek City-State*. Oxford: Oxford University Press.

Hedinger, B. 1999. *Studia Ietina VIII: Die frühe Terra sigillata vom Monte Iato, Sizilien (Ausgrabungen 1971–1988) und frühkaiserzeitliche Fundkomplexe aus dem Peristylhaus 1*. Lausanne, Switzerland: Payot.

Hopkins, K. 1978. "Economic Growth and Towns in Classical Antiquity." In *Towns in Societies: Essays in Economic History and Historical Sociology*, ed. P. Abrams and E. A. Wrigley, 35–77. Cambridge: Cambridge University Press.

———. 1980. "Taxes and Trade in the Roman Empire (200 B.C.–A.D. 400)." *JRS* 70: 101–125.

Horden, P., and N. Purcell. 2000. *The Corrupting Sea: A Study of Mediterranean History*. Oxford: Blackwell.

Horne, L. 1993. "Occupational and Locational Instability in Arid Land Settlement." In *Abandonment of Settlements and Regions: Ethnoarchaeological and Archaeological Approaches*, ed. C. M. Cameron and S. A. Tomka, 43–53. Cambridge: Cambridge University Press.

Hünemörder, C. 2013. "Gypsum" and "Sulphur." *Brill's New Pauly*. Brill Online: http://referenceworks.brillonline.com/browse/brill-s-new-pauly.

Infarinato, A. C. 2010. "Segesta: ala Ovest della stoa Nord (2007–08)." *ASNP* 5.2.2 suppl.:29–33.

Isler, H. P. 1975. "Monte Iato (Palermo)—scavi 1972–1974." *NSc* 29:531–556.

———. 1976–1977. "Iaitas: scavi della Missione Archeologica Monte Iato dell'Università di Zurigo 1973–1976." *Kokalos* 22–23:689–694.

———. 1978. "Monte Iato: l'ottava campagna di scavo." *SicA* 11.38:7–29.

———. 1979. "Monte Iato: la nona campagna di scavo." *SicA* 12.41:41–70.

———. 1980–1981. "Iaitas: scavi della Missione Archeologica Monte Iato dell'Università di Zurigo (1977–1980)." *Kokalos* 26–27:997–1008.

———. 1982. "Monte Iato: dodicesima campagna di scavo." *SicA* 15.49–50:7–26.

———. 1984. "Monte Iato: quattordicesima campagna di scavo." *SicA* 17.56:5–23.

———. 1987. "Monte Iato: diciassettesima campagna di scavo." *SicA* 20.65:11–24.

———. 1989. "Monte Iato: la diciannnovesima campagna di scavo." *SicA* 22.69–70:7–24.

———. 1992. "Monte Iato: la ventunesima campagna di scavo." *SicA* 25.78–9:7–43.

———. 1993. "Monte Iato: la ventiduesima campagna di scavo." *SicA* 26.81:7–30.

———. 1994. "Monte Iato: la ventiquattresima campagna di scavo." *SicA* 27.85–6:27–47.

———. 2000. *Monte Iato: guida archeologica*. 2nd ed. Palermo, Sicily: Sellerio.

———. 2001. "Monte Iato: la trentesima campagna di scavo." *SicA* 34.99:5–29.

———. 2002. "Monte Iato: la trentunesima campagna di scavo." *SicA* 35.100:5–29.

———. 2003a. "Monte Iato: la trentaduesima campagna di scavo." *SicA* 36.101:53–78.

———. 2003b. "Monte Iato: scavi 1998–2000." In *Quarte Giornate di Studi sull'Area Elima*, 827–838. Pisa: SNS.

———. 2004. "Monte Iato: la trentatreesima campagna di scavo." *SicA* 37.102:5–33.

———. 2005. "Monte Iato: la trentaquattresima campagna di scavo." *SicA* 38.103:5–38.

———. 2006. "Monte Iato: la trentacinquesima campagna di scavo." *SicA* 39.104:5–32.

———. 2009. "Monte Iato: scavi 2004–2006." In *Immagine e immagini della Sicilia e di altre isole del Mediterraneo antico: Atti delle Seste Giornate Internazionali di Studi sull'Area Elima*, 661–669. Pisa: SNS.

———. 2011a. "L'insediamento a Monte Iato nel IV e III secolo a.C." In *Krise und Wandel: Süditalien im 4. und 3. Jahrhundert v. Chr.*, ed. R. Neudecker, 147–173. Wiesbaden: Reichert.

———. 2011b. "Monte Iato: scavi 2007–2008." *SicA* 40.105:34–56.

Keay, S. 2013. "Were the Iberians Hellenised?" In *The Hellenistic West: Rethinking the Ancient Mediterranean*, ed. J. R. W. Prag and J. Quinn, 300–319. Cambridge: Cambridge University Press.

Kelly, G. 2004. "Ammianus and the Great Tsunami." *JRS* 94:141–167.

Kennell, N. M. 2010. "Citizen Training Systems in the Roman Peloponnese." In *Roman Peloponnese III: Society, Economy and Culture under the Roman Empire*, ed. A. D. Rizakis and Cl. E. Lepenioti, 205–216. Athens: NHRF.

Keppie, L. 1983. *Colonisation and Veteran Settlement in Italy, 47–14* B.C. London: BSR.

Korhonen, K. 2004. *Le iscrizioni del Museo Civico di Catania: storia delle collezioni, cultura epigrafica, edizione.* Helsinki: Societas Scientiarum Fennica.

———. 2011. "Language and Identity in the Roman Colonies of Sicily." In *Roman Colonies in the First Century of their Foundation*, ed. R. J. Sweetman, 7–31. Oxford: Oxbow.

Kulikowski, M. 2006. "The Late Roman City in Spain." In *Die Stadt in der Spätantike—Niedergang oder Wandel?*, ed. J.-U. Krause and C. Witschel, 129–149. Stuttgart: Steiner.

Lagona, S. 1972–1973. "Vasai a Siracusa in età ellenistico-romana." *ArchStorSir* 2:91–8.

La Lomía, M. R. 1961. "Ricerche archeologiche nel territorio di Canicattì: Vito Soldano." *Kokalos* 7:157–165.

La Torre, G. F. 1993–1994. "Mazzarino (CL), contrada Sofiana: scavi 1988–1990." *Kokalos* 39–40:765–770.

———. 1994. "Gela sive Philosophianis (*It. Antonini* 88, 2): contributo per la storia di un centro interno della Sicilia romana." *QuadA* 9:99–139.

———. 2004. "Il processo di romanizzazione della Sicilia: il caso di Tindari." *SicAnt* 1:111–146.

———. 2005. "La 'Basilica.'" In *Tindari: l'area archeologica e l'antiquarium*, ed. U. Spigo, 55–58. Milazzo: Rebus.

———. 2006. "Urbanistica e architettura ellenistica a Tindari, Eraclea Minoa e Finziade: nuovi dati e prospettive di ricerca." In *Sicilia ellenistica, consuetudo italica: alle origini dell'architettura ellenistica d'Occidente*, ed. M. Osanna and M. Torelli, 83–95. Rome: Ateneo.

La Torre, G. F., and F. Mollo, ed. 2013. *Finziade I: scavi sul Monte Sant'Angelo di Licata (2003–2005)*. Rome: Bretschneider.

Laurence, R., S. Esmonde Cleary, and G. Sears. 2011. *The City in the Roman West, c. 250 BC–c. AD 250*. Cambridge: Cambridge University Press.

Lazzarini, L. 2007. "I marmi e le pietre romane d'importazione e il loro riuso a Siracusa." *Marmora* 3:107–131.

Lehmler, C. 2005. *Syrakus unter Agathokles und Hieron II: Die Verbindung von Kultur und Macht in einer hellenistischen Metropole*. Frankfurt am Main: Verlag Antike.

Leiwo, M. 1985. "Why Velia Survived through the 2nd Century BC? Remarks on Her Economic Connections with Delos." *Athenaeum* 63:494–499.

Lentini, M. C. 2001a. "Esplorazioni a Scifì (Comune di Forza d'Agrò)." In *Naxos di Sicilia in età romana e bizantina ed evidenze dai Peloritani*, ed. M. C. Lentini, 124–125. Bari, Italy: Edipuglia.

———. 2001b. "Naxos di Sicilia dall'età ellenistica all'età bizantina." In *Naxos di Sicilia in età romana e bizantina ed evidenze dai Peloritani*, ed. M. C. Lentini, 13–39. Bari, Italy: Edipuglia.

———. 2005. "Tauromenion." In *Lo stretto di Messina nell'antichità*, ed. F. Ghedini, 313–331. Rome: Quasar.

Lentini, M. C., and D. J. Blackman, eds. 2009. *Naxos di Sicilia: l'abitato coloniale e l'arsenale navale: scavi 2003–2006*. Messina, Sicily: Regione Siciliana.

———. 2013. "Naval Monuments from North-East Sicily." *Skyllis* 13.2:149–154.

Lentini, M. C., K. Göransson, A. Lindhagen, et al. 2002. "Excavations at Sicilian Caronia, Ancient Kale Akte, 1999–2001." *OpRom* 27:79–108.

Lentini, M. C., and F. Muscolino. 2013. "Fornaci e produzioni di anfore e laterizi tra Naxos e Taormina (III–I secolo a.C.) e rapporti con le aree tirreniche." In *Immensa Aequora Workshop*, ed. G. Olcese, 275–285. Rome: Quasar.

Lentini, M. C., S. Savelli, and D. J. Blackman. 2009. "Amphorae from the Slipways of the Ancient Dockyard of Naxos in Sicily." In *Naxos di Sicilia: l'abitato coloniale e l'arsenale navale: scavi 2003–2006*, ed. M. C. Lentini and D. J. Blackman, 98–109. Messina, Sicily: Regione Siciliana.

Leonard, J. R., and S. Demesticha. 2004. "Fundamental Links in the Economic Chain: Local Ports and International Trade in Roman and Early Christian Cyprus." In *Transport Amphorae and Trade in the Eastern Mediterranean*, ed. J. Eiring and J. Lund, 189–202. Aarhus: Danish Institute at Athens.

Leone, R. 2008. "Indagini in contrada Cercadenari: considerazioni conclusivi." In *Tyndaris, 1: ricerche nel settore occidentale: campagne di scavo 1993–2004*, ed. R. Leone, M. Viara, and U. Spigo, 57–62. Palermo, Sicily: Regione Siciliana.

Lilibeo: testimonianze archeologiche dal IV sec. a.C. al V sec. d.C. Marsala, dal 3 dicembre 1984. 1984. Palermo, Sicily: Pegaso.

Lindhagen, A. 2006. "Caleacte: Production and Exchange in a North Sicilian Town, c. 500 BC–AD 500." Doctoral thesis, Lund University, Sweden.

Livadiotti, M., and A. Fino. 2017. "Il complesso porticato a Nord dell'agorà." In *Agrigento: nuove ricerche sull'area pubblica centrale*, ed. L. M. Caliò et al., 97–110. Rome: Quasar.

Lo Cascio, P. 1990. "Solanto: nuove scoperte archeologiche." *SicA* 23.73:33–39.

Löhberg, B. 2006. *Das "Itinerarium provinciarum Antonini Augusti": Ein kaiserzeitlcihes Strassenverzeichnis des Römischen Reiches.* Vol. 1: *Überlieferung, Strecken, Kommentare.* Berlin: Frank und Timme.

Lomas, K. 1993. *Rome and the Western Greeks, 350 BC–AD 200: Conquest and Acculturation in Southern Italy.* London: Routledge.

———. 1995. "Urban Elites and Cultural Definition: Romanization in Southern Italy." In *Urban Society in Roman Italy*, ed. T. J. Cornell and K. Lomas, 113–126. London: UCL Press.

———. 2016. "Magna Graecia, 270 BC–AD 200." In *A Companion to Roman Italy*, ed. A. E. Cooley, 253–268. Oxford: Wiley-Blackwell.

Lucchelli, T. 2004. "Monete dall'agorà di Camarina: analisi e contesto." In *Monete dall'agorà di Camarina: campagne di scavo 1983–1995*, ed. T. Lucchelli and G. Di Stefano, 38–62. Milan: CUEM.

Lucore, S. K. 2013. "Bathing in Hieronian Sicily." In *Greek Bath and Bathing Culture: New Discoveries and Approaches*, ed. S. K. Lucore and M. Trümper, 151–179. Leuven, Belgium: Peeters.

Mackil, E. 2004. "Wandering Cities: Alternatives to Catastrophe in the Greek Polis." *AJA* 108.4:493–516.

Maiuro, M. 2007. "Oltre il Pasquino: Achille, il culto imperiale e l'istituzione ginnasiale tra oriente e occidente nell'impero romano." *ArchCl* 58:165–246.

Malfitana, D. 2006. "Economia, territorio ed officine ceramiche nella Sicilia tardo ellenistica." In *Territorio e produzioni ceramiche: paesaggi, economia e società in età romana*, ed. S. Menchelli and M. Pasquinucci, 153–164. Pisa: PLUS.

———. 2008. "Roman Sicily Project ('RSP'): Ceramics and Trade." *Facta* 2:127–192.

Malfitana, D., and G. Cacciaguerra, eds. 2011. *Priolo romana, tardo romana e medievale: documenti, paesaggi, cultura materiale.* Catania, Sicily: CNR.

———. 2014. "La Guglia d'Agosta: indagini archeo-geofisiche per una nuova conoscenza e percezione culturale del monumento." In *Archeologia classica in Sicilia e nel Mediterraneo*, ed. D. Malfitana and G. Cacciaguerra, 161–179. Catania, Sicily: CNR.

Malfitana, D., G. Cacciaguerra, and A. Di Mauro, eds. 2012. *Il patrimonio culturale di Priolo Gargallo: paesaggi, monumenti, itinerari.* Priolo, Sicily: Alma Editore.

Mancini, A. 2006. "Architettura domestica a Morgantina." In *Sicilia ellenistica, consuetudo italica: alle origini dell'architettura ellenistica d'Occidente*, ed. M. Osanna and M. Torelli, 167–176. Rome: Ateneo.

Manganaro, G. 1959. "Epigrafi frammentarie di Catania." *Kokalos* 5:145–158.

———. 1963a. "Tauromenitana." *ArchCl* 15:13–31.

———. 1963b. "Un senatus consultum in greco dei Lanuvini e il rinnovo della cognatio con i Centuripini." *RendNap* 38:23–44.

———. 1964. "Iscrizioni latine e greche dal nuovo edificio termale di Taormina." *CronA* 3:38–68.

———. 1996. "Per una storia della *chora Katanaia*." In *Catania antica*, ed. B. Gentili, 19–59. Pisa: IEPI.

———. 2006. "Epigrafe in greco di VI sec. d.C. di Alesa (Sicilia) in versi e prosa, per la morte di Eirena Philandros, 'carissima a Botis boio-celtico.'" *ZPE* 158:89–92.

———. 2009a. "La Tabula." In *Alaisa-Halaesa: scavi e ricerche (1970–2007)*, ed. G. Scibona and G. Tigano, 202–208. Messina, Sicily: Sicania.

———. 2009b. "Un frammento inscritto erratico dall'area di Caronia (Kaleakté)." *ZPE* 170:87–98.

———. 2013. "Tre iscrizioni di Agrigento, il culto dei Caesares Nipoti di Augusto e la diffusione della gens Annia." *SicAnt* 10:247–252.

Manni Piraino, M. T. 1963. "Due iscrizioni inedite di Marsala." *Kokalos* 9:157–162.

Marconi, P. 1926. "Girgenti: ricerche ed esplorazioni." *NSc* 6.2:93–148.

Martyn, J. R. C. 2004. *A Translation of Abbot Leontios' Life of Saint Gregory, Bishop of Agrigento.* Lewiston, NY: Edwin Mellen.

Mattingly, D. J. 2010. *Imperialism, Power, and Identity: Experiencing the Roman Empire.* Princeton, NJ: Princeton University Press.

Mattioli, M. 1995. "Camarina in età ellenistico-romana." *Kokalos* 41:229–270.

Mayer, E. 2012. *The Ancient Middle Classes: Urban Life and Aesthetics in the Roman Empire, 100 BCE–250 CE.* Cambridge, MA: Harvard University Press.

McIntosh, R. J. 2015. "Different Cities: Jenne-jeno and African Urbanism." In *The Cambridge World History*, vol. 3: *Early Cities in Comparative Perspective, 4000 BCE–1200 CE*, ed. N. Yoffee, 364–380. Cambridge: Cambridge University Press.

Messina, E. 2001–2002. "Lo scavo in via Zappalà (Siracusa)." *Kokalos* 47–48:807–819.

Michelini, C. 1999. "Reimpiego di iscrizioni a Segesta." In *Sicilia epigraphica: atti del convegno internazionale*, ed. M. I. Gulletta, 439–448. Pisa: SNS.

———. 2001. "Segesta: settori occidentale e settentrionale dell'*agora* (SAS 4: 1995, 1997)." *ASNP* 4.6.2:430–446.

Mitchell, S. 1999. "The Administration of Roman Asia from 133 BC to AD 250." In *Lokale Autonomie und römische Ordnungsmacht in den kaiserzeitlichen Provinzen vom 1. bis 3. Jahrhundert*, ed. W. Eck, 17–46. Munich: Oldenbourg.

Molè, C. 2008. "L'età antica." In *Catania: storia, cultura, economia*, ed. F. Mazza, 23–75. Soveria Mannelli, Italy: Rubbettino.

Molè Ventura, C. 1996. "Catania in età imperiale." In *Catania antica*, ed. B. Gentili, 175–222. Pisa: IEPI.

Morel, J. P., and M. Picon. 1994. "Les céramiques étrusco-campaniennes: recherches en laboratoire." In *Ceramica romana e archeometria: lo stato degli studi*, ed. G. Olcese, 23–46. Florence: Giglio.

Murer, C. 2017. *Stadtraum und Bürgerin: Aufstellungsorte kaiserzeitlicher Ehrenstatuen in Italien und Nordafrika.* Berlin: De Gruyter.

Murphy, T. M. 2004. *Pliny the Elder's Natural History: The Empire in the Encyclopedia.* Oxford: Oxford University Press.

Muscolino, F. 2009. "Anfore proto-imperiali dall'area portuale di Naxos: l'inizio della produzione di anfore nassie a fondo piano." In *Naxos di Sicilia: l'abitato coloniale e l'arsenale navale: scavi 2003–2006*, ed. M. C. Lentini and D. J. Blackman, 110–133. Messina, Sicily: Regione Siciliana.

Nenci, G. 1991. "Un'iscrizione latina cristiana da Segesta." *NumAntCl* 20:253–255.

———. 1997. "Novità epigrafiche dall'area elima." In *Seconde Giornate Internazionali di Studi sull'Area Elima*, 1187–1202. Pisa: SNS.

———. 2000. "*Varia Elyma*: novità epigrafiche, numismatiche, tonomomastiche e cultuali dall'area elima." In *Terze Giornate Internazionali di Studi sull'Area Elima*, 809–821. Pisa: SNS.

Nicolet, C. 1991. *Space, Geography, and Politics in the Early Roman Empire*. Ann Arbor: University of Michigan Press.

Olcese, G. 2012. *Atlante dei siti di produzione ceramica (Toscana, Lazio, Campania e Sicilia) con le tabelle dei principali relitti del Mediterraneo occidentale*. Rome: Edizioni Quasar.

Olivito, R. 2014. "Dynamics of 'Romanization' at Segesta: The Case of the Macellum." In *XVIII CIAC: Centro y periferia en el mundo clásico*, 31–35. Mérida, Spain: Museo Nacional de Arte Romano.

Olivito, R., and A. Serra. 2014. "Agora: Stoa Nord: Settore centrale (SAS 4; 2013)." *ASNP* 5.6.2 suppl.:18–22.

Ollà, A. 1997. "Dal mare di Sant'Alessio (ME): un recupero di anfore da trasporto." *StAnt* 10:225–230.

———. 2001. "La produzione di anfore vinarie a Naxos (III a.C.—V d.C.)." In *Naxos di Sicilia in età romana e bizantina ed evidenze dai Peloritani*, ed. M. C. Lentini, 47–60. Bari, Italy: Edipuglia.

Orsi, P. 1990. *La necropoli di Passo Marinaro a Camarina: campagne di scavo 1904–1909*. Ed. M. T. Lanza. Rome: Lincei.

Osanna, M. 2012. "Magna Grecia e Sicilia." In *Storia dell'architettura italiana 1: architettura romana. Le città d'Italia*, ed. H. von Hesberg and P. Zanker, 268–295. Milan: Electa.

Osanna, M., and M. Torelli, eds. 2006. *Sicilia ellenistica, consuetudo italica: alle origini dell'architettura ellenistica d'Occidente*. Rome: Ateneo.

Osborne, R. 2005. "Urban Sprawl: What Is Urbanization and Why Does It Matter?" In *Mediterranean Urbanization 800–600 BC*, ed. R. Osborne and B. Cunliffe, 1–16. Oxford: Oxford University Press.

Pace, B. 1927. *Camarina: topografia, storia, archeologia*. Catania, Sicily: Guaitolini.

Parello, M. C. 2017. "L'area del Foro e le sue trasformazioni in età tardoantica." In *Agrigento: nuove ricerche sull'area pubblica centrale*, ed. L. M. Caliò et al., 147–156. Rome: Quasar.

Parello, M. C., A. Amico, and F. D'Angelo. 2010. "L'insediamento alla foce del Verdura in territorio di Sciacca (Agrigento-Sicilia-Italia): i materiali ceramici." In *LRCW 3: Late Roman Coarse Wares, Cooking Wares and Amphorae in the Mediterranean*, ed. S. Menchelli, 283–291. Oxford: Archaeopress.

Parker, A. J. 1992. *Ancient Shipwrecks of the Mediterranean and the Roman Provinces*. Oxford: Tempus Reparatum.

Parra, M. C. 2006. "Note di architettura ellenistica a Segesta, intorno all'agorà." In *Sicilia ellenistica, consuetudo italica: alle origini dell'architettura ellenistica d'Occidente*, ed. M. Osanna and M. Torelli, 107–122. Rome: Ateneo.

Patanè, R. P. A. 2002. "Centuripe in età ellenistica: i rapporti con Roma." In *Scavi e ricerche a Centuripe*, ed. G. Rizza, 127–167. Catania: CNR.

———. 2006a. "Centuripe ellenistica: nuovi dati dalla città." In *Sicilia ellenistica, consuetudo italica: alle origini dell'architettura ellenistica d'Occidente*, ed. M. Osanna and M. Torelli, 201–210. Rome: Ateneo.

———. 2006b. "Ceramiche e reti commerciali nella Sicilia repubblicana: il caso di Centuripe." In *Old Pottery in a New Century: Innovating Perspectives on Roman Pottery Studies*, ed. D. Malfitana, J. Poblome, and J. Lund, 477–486. Catania, Sicily: CNR.

———. 2011. *Impero di Roma e passato troiano nella società del II secolo: il punto di vista di una famiglia di Centuripe.* Rome: Aracne.

Patterson, J. R. 2006. *Landscape and Cities: Rural Settlement and Civic Transformation in Early Imperial Italy.* Oxford: Oxford University Press.

Pavia, G., and G. Zavettieri. 2005. "La ceramica ed altre attestazioni dell'artigianato e della vita quotidiana a *Tyndaris*." In *Tindari: l'area archeologica e l'antiquarium*, ed. U. Spigo, 84–88. Milazzo: Rebus.

Pedley, J. G. 1990. *Paestum: Greeks and Romans in Southern Italy.* London: Thames and Hudson.

Pelagatti, P. 1964. "Scoperta di un edificio termale a Taormina." *CronA* 3:25–37.

———. 1969–1970. "Stato e prospettive degli studi di ceramica romana in Sicilia." *RCRFActa* 11–12:76–89.

———. 1970. "Akrai: ricerche nel territorio." *NSc* 24:436–499.

———. 1984–1985. "Ricerche nel quartiere orientale di Naxos e nell'agorà di Camarina." *Kokalos* 30–31:679–694.

———. 1997. "Il ginnasio di Tauromenion: ripresa delle ricerche." *PP* 52:256–261.

Pelagatti, P., et al. 1976. "Sul parco archeologico di Camarina." *BdA* 61:122–141.

Peña, J. T. 1999. *The Urban Economy during the Early Dominate: Pottery Evidence from the Palatine Hill.* Oxford: Archaeopress.

———. 2007a. *Roman Pottery in the Archaeological Record.* Cambridge: Cambridge University Press.

———. 2007b. "Two Groups of *Tituli Picti* from Pompeii and Environs: Sicilian Wine, Not Flour and Hand-Picked Olives." *JRA* 20.1:233–254.

Pensabene, P. 2005. "La decorazione architettonica del teatro di Catania." In *Μεγαλαι νησοι: studi dedicati a Giovanni Rizza per il suo ottantesimo compleanno*, ed. R. Gigli, vol. 2, 187–212. 2 vols. Catania, Sicily: CNR.

Pensabene, P., E. Gallocchio, E. Gasparini, et al. 2009. "Villa del Casale di Piazza Armerina: nuovi scavi." *Journal of Fasti Online* no. 158. http://www.fastionline.org/docs/FOLDER-it-2009-158.pdf.

Perkins, P. 2007. "*Aliud in Sicilia*? Cultural Development in Rome's First Province." In *Articulating Local Cultures: Power and Identity under the Expanding Roman Republic*, ed. P. van Dommelen and N. Terrenato, 33–53. *JRA* suppl. 63.

Pfuntner, L. 2013. "The Changing Urban Landscape of Roman Sicily." PhD diss., University of California, Berkeley.

———. 2015. "Cooperation and Conflict between Governor and *Poleis* in the *Verrines*." *Phoenix* 69:355–375.

———. 2016. "Celebrating the Severans: Commemorative Politics and the Urban Landscape in High Imperial Sicily." *Latomus* 75.2:434–456.

Pinzone, A. 1999a. "La *cura annonae* di Pompeo e l'introduzione dello *stipendium* in Sicilia." Reprinted in *Provincia Sicilia: ricerche di storia della Sicilia romana da Gaio Flaminio a Gregorio Magno*, 173–206. Catania, Sicily: Prisma.

———. 1999b. "La 'romanizzazione' della Sicilia occidentale in età repubblicana." In *Provincia Sicilia: ricerche di storia della Sicilia romana da Gaio Flaminio a Gregorio Magno*, 91–120. Catania, Sicily: Prisma.

———. 1999c. "Sulle *civitates foederatae* di Sicilia: Problemi di storia e di cronologia." Reprinted in *Provincia Sicilia: ricerche di storia della Sicilia romana da Gaio Flaminio a Gregorio Magno*, 59–89. Catania, Sicily: Prisma.

Polito, A. 2000. "Resti di un insediamento rurale in contrada Carboj, nel territorio di Sciacca." *QuadA* 1.2:103–123.

———. 2009. *La terra sigillata italica liscia dal quartiere ellenistico-romano di Agrigento.* Rome: Gangemi.

Portale, E. C. 2006. "Problemi dell'archeologia della Sicilia ellenistico-romana: il caso di Solunto." *ArchCl* 57:49–114.

———. 2009. "Le sculture da Alesa." In *Alaisa-Halaesa: scavi e ricerche (1970–2007)*, ed. G. Scibona and G. Tigano, 67–92. Messina, Sicily: Sicania.

Prag, J. R. W. 2003. "Nouveau regard sur les élites locales de la Sicile républicaine." *Histoire et Sociétés Rurales* 19:121–131.

———. 2007a. "*Auxilia* and *Gymnasia*: A Sicilian Model of Roman Imperialism." *JRS* 97:68–100.

———. 2007b. "Roman Magistrates in Sicily, 227–49 BC." In *La Sicile de Cicéron: lectures des Verrines*, ed. J. Dubouloz and S. Pittia, 287–310. Besançon: Presses Universitaires de Franche-Comté.

———. 2010. "Sicilia romana tributim discripta." In *Le tribù romane*, ed. M. Silvestrini, 305–311. Bari: Edipuglia.

———. 2014a. "Bronze *Rostra* from the Egadi Islands off NW Sicily: The Latin Inscriptions." *JRA* 27:33–59.

———. 2014b. "Territorial Organisation in Late Hellenistic Halaesa, Sicily." In *Öffentlichkeit—Monument—Text: XIV Congressus Internationalis Epigraphiae Graecae et Latinae*, ed. W. Eck and P. Funke, 590–592. Berlin: De Gruyter.

Prestianni Giallombardo, A. M. 2012. "Spazio pubblico e memoria civica: le epigrafi dall'agora di Alesa." In *Agora greca e agorai in Sicilia*, ed. C. Ampolo, 171–200. Pisa: SNS.

Price, S. R. F. 1984. *Rituals and Power: The Roman Imperial Cult in Asia Minor.* Cambridge: Cambridge University Press.

Privitera, S. 2009. "Lo sviluppo urbano di Catania dalla fondazione dell'*apoikia* alla fine del V secolo d.C." In *Catania: l'identità urbana dall'antichità al settecento*, ed. L. Scalisi, 36–71. Catania, Sicily: Sanfilippo.

Puglisi, M. 2001. "Un tesoretto monetale tardo-antico." In *Naxos di Sicilia in età romana e bizantina ed evidenze dai Peloritani*, ed. M. C. Lentini, 63–78. Bari, Italy: Edipuglia.

Purcell, N. 2005. "Statics and Dynamics: Ancient Mediterranean Urbanism." In *Mediterranean Urbanization, 800–600 BC*, ed. R. Osborne and B. Cunliffe, 249–272. Oxford: Oxford University Press.

Raimondo, C., and A. Ruga. 2010. "Note su Crotone tra IV e VII secolo." In *Paesaggi e insediamenti urbani in Italia meridionale fra tardoantico e altomedioevo*, ed. G. Volpe and R. Giuliani, 219–232. Bari, Italy: Edipuglia.

Renfrew, C., and T. Poston. 1979. "Discontinuities in the Endogenous Change of Settlement Pattern." In *Transformations: Mathematical Approaches to Culture Change*, ed. C. Renfrew and K. L. Cooke, 437–461. New York: Academic Press.

Reynolds, P. 1995. *Trade in the Western Mediterranean, AD 400–700: The Ceramic Evidence.* Oxford: Tempus Reparatum.

Rizakis, A. D. 2013. "Rural Structures and Agrarian Strategies in Greece under the Roman Empire." In *Villae Rusticae: Family and Market-Oriented Farms in Greece under Roman Rule*, ed. A. D. Rizakis and I. P. Touratsoglou, 20–51. Athens: NHRF.

Rizza, G. 2002. "Scavi e scoperte a Centuripe nell'ultimo cinquantennio." In *Scavi e ricerche a Centuripe*, ed. G. Rizza, 9–40. Catania, Sicily: CNR.

Rizzo, M. S., and L. Zambito. 2007. "Novità epigrafiche siciliane: i bolli di contrada Cignana (Naro, AG)." *ZPE* 162:271–277.

———. 2010. "Ceramiche comuni ed anfore dal villaggio tardoantico di Cignana (Naro, Agrigento, Sicilia, Italia)." In *LRCW 3: Late Roman Coarse Wares, Cooking Wares and Amphorae in the Mediterranean*, 293–300. Oxford: Archaeopress.

———. 2012. "Ceramiche da fuoco di età tardo-antica e della prima età bizantina dal territorio agrigentino: nuovi dati da Cignana e Vito Soldano." *ReiCretActa* 42:289–297.

Rizzo, M. S., L. Zambito, et al. 2014. "Anfore di tipo siciliano dal territorio di Agrigento." In *LRCW 4: The Mediterranean: A Market without Frontiers*, ed. N. Poulou-Papadimitriou, E. Nodarou, and V. Kilikoglou, vol. 1, 213–223. 2 vols. Oxford: Archaeopress.

Russenberger, C. 2013. "A New Bathtub with Hypocaust in Peristyle House 2 at Monte Iato." In *Greek Baths and Bathing Culture: New Discoveries and Approaches*, ed. S. K. Lucore and M. Trümper, 189–199. Leuven, Belgium: Peeters.

Salway, B. 2001. "Travel, *Itineraria* and *Tabellaria*." In *Travel and Geography in the Roman Empire*, ed. C. Adams and R. Laurence, 22–66. London: Routledge.

Sami, D. 2010. "From Theodosius to Constans II: Church, Settlement and Economy in Late Roman and Byzantine Sicily (AD 378–668)." D.Phil. thesis, University of Leicester.

Sartori, F. 1957. "Le dodici tribù di Lilibeo." *Kokalos* 3:38–60.

Savelli, S. 2001. "Un nucleo di tombe tardo-antiche." In *Naxos di Sicilia in età romana e bizantina ed evidenze dai Peloritani*, ed. M. C. Lentini, 85–87. Bari, Italy: Edipuglia.

Scafidi, L. 2007–2008. "L'odeon di Taormina: un caso particolare nella classe degli odea." *Agoge* 4–5:295–304.

Scalici, M. 2017. "I reperti rinvenuti nella discarica." In *Agrigento: nuove ricerche sull'area pubblica centrale*, ed. L. M. Caliò et al., 113–118. Rome: Quasar.

Scibona, G. 1971. "Epigraphica Halesiana, 1: schede 1970." *Kokalos* 17:3–20.

———. 2008. "Story of the City: The Sources." In *Alesa Archonidea: Guide to the Antiquarium*, ed. G. Scibona and G. Tigano, 13–16. Palermo, Sicily: Regione Siciliana.

———. 2009. "Decreto sacerdotale per il conferimento della euerghesia a Nemenios in Halaesa." In *Alaisa-Halaesa: scavi e ricerche (1970–2007)*, ed. G. Scibona and G. Tigano, 97–112. Messina, Sicily: Sicania.

Scibona, G., and G. Tigano, eds. 2009. *Alaisa-Halaesa: scavi e ricerche (1970–2007)*. Messina, Sicily: Sicania.

Sear, F. 1996. "The Theatre at Taormina: A New Chronology." *BSR* 64:41–79.

Serra, A. 2010. "Segesta: area del criptoportico e sepolture tardoantiche (SAS 3 e 4; 2007–08)." *ASNP* 5.2.2 suppl.:20–24.

Sgarlata, M. 1991. *Ricerche di demografia storica: le iscrizioni tardo-imperiali di Siracusa*. Vatican City: PIAC.

———. 2006. "Morti lontano dalla patria: la documentazione epigrafica delle catacombe siracusane." In *L'Africa romana: mobilità delle persone e dei popoli, dinamiche migratorie, emigrazioni ed immigrazioni nelle province occidentali dell'Impero romano*, ed. A. Akerraz, 1185–1201. Rome: Carocci.

Sharp, H. K. 2015. "Nuove ricerche sul *macellum* di Morgantina: funzioni pratiche e metaforiche." In *Morgantina Duemilaequindici: la ricerca archeologica a sessant'anni dall'avvio degli scavi*, ed. L. Maniscalco, 172–178. Aidone, Sicily: Museo Regionale.

Silvestrini, M. 2011. "Colonia septimia Augusta Agrigentinorum." In *Scritti di storia per Mario Pani*, ed. S. Cagnazzi, 455–468. Bari, Italy: Edipuglia.

———. 2014. "Nuove epigrafi da Lilibeo." In *L'epigrafia dei porti*, ed. C. Zaccaria, 207–226. Trieste, Italy: Editreg.

Sjöqvist, E. 1958. "Excavations at Serra Orlando (Morgantina) Preliminary Report II." *AJA* 62.2:155–164.

———. 1960. "Excavations at Serra Orlando (Morgantina) 1959: Preliminary Report IV." *AJA* 64.2:125–135.

———. 1962. "Excavations at Morgantina (Serra Orlando) 1961: Preliminary Report VI." *AJA* 66.2:135–143.

Solè, L. 2006. "La città della Magna Grecia all'Impero romano: Siracusa." *FormaUrbis* 11.2:19–31.

Soraci, C. 2017. "Il contesto storico." In *Agrigento: nuove ricerche sull'area pubblica centrale*, ed. L. M. Caliò et al., 15–22. Rome: Quasar.

Soraci, R. 1996. "Catania in età tardoantica." In *Catania antica*, ed. B. Gentili, 257–278. Pisa: IEPI.

Spanò Giammellaro, A., F. Spatafora, and P. van Dommelen. 2008. "Sicily and Malta: Between Sea and Countryside." In *Rural Landscapes of the Punic World*, ed. P. van Dommelen and C. Gómez Bellard, 129–158. London: Equinox.

Spigo, U., ed. 2005. *Tindari: l'area archeologica e l'antiquarium*. Milazzo, Sicily: Rebus.

———. 2006. "Tindari: considerazioni sull'impianto urbano e notizie preliminari sulle recenti campagne di scavo nel settore occidentale." In *Sicilia ellenistica, consuetudo italica: alle origini dell'architettura ellenistica d'Occidente*, ed. M. Osanna and M. Torelli, 97–105. Rome: Ateneo.

———. 2008. "Le campagne di scavo 1993–2004: contributi conoscitivi al quadro storico e culturale di *Tyndaris* e della *Colonia Augusta Tyndaritanorum*." In *Tyndaris, 1: ricerche nel settore occidentale: campagne di scavo 1993–2004*, ed. R. Leone, M. Viara, and U. Spigo, 101–111. Palermo, Sicily: Regione Siciliana.

Spigo, U., and V. Pratolongo. 2008. "Il saggio lungo la prosecuzione Nord del *cardo* N." In *Tyndaris, 1: ricerche nel settore occidentale: campagne di scavo 1993–2004*, ed. R. Leone, M. Viara, and U. Spigo, 69–85. Palermo, Sicily: Regione Siciliana.

Sposito, A. 2014. *Solunto: paesaggio, città, architettura*. Rome: Bretschneider.

Stewart, D. 2010. "The Rural Roman Peloponnese: Continuity and Change." In *Roman Peloponnese III: Society, Economy and Culture under the Roman Empire*, ed. A. D. Rizakis and Cl. E. Lepenioti, 217–233. Athens: NHRF.

Stillwell, R. 1961. "Excavations at Serra Orlando (Morgantina) 1960: Preliminary Report V." *AJA* 65.3:277–281.

———. 1963. "Excavations at Morgantina (Serra Orlando) 1962: Preliminary Report VII." *AJA* 67.2:163–171.

Stone, S. C. 1981. "Roman Pottery from Morgantina in Sicily." PhD diss., Princeton University.

———. 1983. "Sextus Pompeius, Octavianus and Sicily." *AJA* 87.1:11–22.

———. 2014. *Morgantina Studies VI: The Hellenistic and Roman Fine Pottery*. Princeton, NJ: Princeton University Press.

———. 2015. "The Pottery Found in the Excavations of the South Baths in Area VI (Contrada Agnese), Morgantina." In *Morgantina Duemilaequindici: la ricerca archeologica a sessant'anni dall'avvio degli scavi*, ed. L. Maniscalco, 115–122. Aidone, Sicily: Museo Regionale.

Themelis, P. 2010. "The Economy and Society of Messenia under Roman Rule." In *Roman Peloponnese III: Society, Economy and Culture under the Roman Empire*, ed. A. D. Rizakis and Cl. E. Lepenioti, 89–110. Athens: NHRF.

Thomas, E., and C. Witschel. 1992. "Constructing Reconstruction: Claim and Reality of Roman Rebuilding Inscriptions from the Latin West." *PBSR* 60:135–177.

Thompson, S. M. 1999. "A Central Sicilian Landscape: Settlement and Society in the Territory of Ancient Morgantina (5000 BC–AD 50)." PhD diss., University of Virginia.

Tigano, G. 2008. "The Archaeological Site." In *Alesa Archonidea: Guide to the Antiquarium*, ed. G. Scibona and G. Tigano, 70–90. Palermo, Sicily: Regione Siciliana.

———. 2009a. "La necropoli settentrionale: scavi in proprietà Purpura (1990–1993; 2007)." In *Alaisa-Halaesa: scavi e ricerche (1970–2007)*, ed. G. Scibona and G. Tigano, 153–184. Messina, Sicily: Sicania.

———. 2009b. "La necropoli urbana meridionale: dati archeologici e prime considerazioni." In *Alaisa-Halaesa: scavi e ricerche (1970–2007)*, ed. G. Scibona and G. Tigano, 114–132. Messina, Sicily: Sicania.

Tirnetta, P. 1978. "Sciacca: insediamenti rurali di età greca e romana nel territorio." *Kokalos* 24:156–174.

Tomasello, F. 2007. "Per un'immagine di Catania in età romano-imperiale." *RTopAnt* 17: 127–158.

Tomka, S. A., and M. Stevenson. 1993. "Understanding Abandonment Processes: Summary and Remaining Concerns." In *Abandonment of Settlements and Regions: Ethnoarchaeological and Archaeological Approaches*, ed. C. M. Cameron and S. A. Tomka, 191–195. Cambridge: Cambridge University Press.

Torelli, M. 2014. "Chalcidicum Halaesinum." *SicAnt* 11:469–476.

Tortorici, E. 2015. "Catania antica: territorio costiero ed entroterra produttivo." *Orizzonti* 16:23–30.

———. 2016. *Catania antica: la carta archeologica.* Rome: Bretschneider.

Toscano Raffa, A. 2015. "Nuove acquisizioni sul territorio di Licata (AG) in epoca romana: contributo per l'identificazione della stazione di Plintis nell'Itinerarium per maritima loca." In *Atlante tematico di topografia antica: Roma, strade e infrastrutture, città e monumenti*, 165–178. Rome: Bretschneider.

———. 2017. *Finziade e la bassa valle dell'Himera 1: la Montagna di Licata.* Catania, Sicily: CNR.

Toscano Raffa, A., et al. 2015. "Nuovi dati dall'abitato ellenistico-romano di Finziade sul Monte S. Angelo di Licata (AG): gli scavi dei settori H (2012–2013), F (2014) e J (2014)." *QuadA* 5:63–82.

Tribulato, O. 2012. "*Siculi bilingues*? Latin in the Inscriptions of Early Roman Sicily." In *Language and Linguistic Contact in Ancient Sicily*, ed. O. Tribulato, 291–325. Cambridge: Cambridge University Press.

Trojani, M. 2005. "Il c.d. ginnasio romano di Siracusa." In *Μεγαλαι νησοι: studi dedicati a Giovanni Rizza per il suo ottantesimo compleanno*, ed. R. Gigli, vol. 2, 177–186. Catania, Sicily: CNR.

Tsakirgis, B. 1984. "The Domestic Architecture of Morgantina in the Hellenistic and Roman Periods." PhD diss., Princeton University.

Tusa, V. 1966. "Aree sacrificali a Selinunte e a Solunto." In *Mozia rapporto preliminare II*, 143–153. Studi Semitici 19. Rome: Centro di Studi Semitici.

———. 1968. "Il teatro di Solunto." *SicA* 1.3:5–11.

Uggeri, G. 2004. *La viabilità della Sicilia in età romana.* Lecce, Italy: Congedo.

———. 2015. *Camarina: storia e topografia di una colonia greca di Sicilia e del suo territorio.* Galatina, Italy: Congedo.

Vaccaro, E. 2013. "Re-Evaluating a Forgotten Town Using Intra-Site Surveys and the GIS Analysis of Surface Ceramics: Philosophiana-Sofiana (Sicily) in the Longue Durée." In *Archaeological Survey and the City*, ed. P. Johnson and M. Millett, 104–145. Oxford: Oxbow.

Valente, I., and B. Bechtold. 1992. "Recenti scavi nella necropoli punica di Lilibeo: problemi e considerazioni." In *Giornate Internazionali di Studi sull'Area Elima*, 687–701. Pisa: SNS.

Vallarino, G. 2017. "L'epigrafe dall'area del Tempio ellenistico-romano." In *Agrigento: nuove ricerche sull'area pubblica centrale*, ed. L. M. Caliò et al., 123–126. Rome: Quasar.

Vallet, G., F. Villard, and P. Auberson. 1983. *Mégara Hyblaea 3: guide des fouilles.* Rome: EFR.

Vandermersch, C. 1994. *Vins et amphores de Grande Grèce et de Sicile (IVe–IIIe s. avant J.-C.).* Naples: Centre Jean Bérard.

Venuti, M. 2015. "Le apparecchiature laterizie del teatro di Taormina: una proposta per le fasi edilizie." *QuadA* 5:33–59.

Vera, D. 1996. "Augusto, Plinio il Vecchio e la Sicilia in età imperiale: a proposito di recenti scoperte epigraphiche e archeologiche ad Agrigento." *Kokalos* 42:31–58.

Voza, G. 1980–1981. "L'attività della Soprintendenza alle antichità della Sicilia orientale, 1." *Kokalos* 26–27:674–693.

———. 1999. *Nel segno dell'antico: archeologia nel territorio di Siracusa.* Palermo, Sicily: A. Lombardi.

Wallace-Hadrill, A. 2008. *Rome's Cultural Revolution.* Cambridge: Cambridge University Press.

Walthall, A., R. Souza, and J. Benton. 2016. "Preliminary Report on the 2014 Field Season of the American Excavations at Morgantina: Contrada Agnese Project (CAP)." *Journal of Fasti Online*, no. 364. http://www.fastionline.org/docs/FOLDER-it-2016-364.pdf.

Walthall, A., R. Souza, J. Benton, and J. Huemoeller. 2014. "Preliminary Report on the 2013 Field Season of the American Excavations at Morgantina: Contrada Agnese Project (CAP)." *Journal of Fasti Online*, no. 322. www.fastionline.org/docs/FOLDER-it-2014-322.pdf.

Walthall, D. A. 2011. "Magistrate Stamps on Grain Measures in Early Hellenistic Sicily." *ZPE* 179:159–169.

———. 2013. "A Hoard Containing Late Republican Denarii from Morgantina (Sicily)." *AmJNum* 25:171–177.

Ward-Perkins, B. 1996. "Urban Continuity?" In *Towns in Transition: Urban Evolution in Late Antiquity and the Early Middle Ages*, ed. N. Christie and S. T. Loseby, 4–17. Aldershot, UK: Scolar.

Wickham, C. 2005. *Framing the Early Middle Ages: Europe and the Mediterranean 400–800.* Oxford: Oxford University Press.

Wilson, R. J. A. 1980. "On the Date of the Roman Amphitheatre at Syracuse." In *Φιλίας χάριν: miscellanea di studi classici in onore di Eugenio Manni*, 2217–2230. Rome: Bretschneider.

———. 1981. "The Hinterland of Heraclea Minoa (Sicily) in Classical Antiquity." In *Archaeology and Italian Society: Prehistoric, Roman and Medieval Studies*, ed. G. W. Barker and R. Hodges, 249–260. Oxford: BAR.

———. 1985. "Changes in the Pattern of Urban Settlement in Roman, Byzantine and Arab Sicily." In *Papers in Italian Archaeology 4, Part 1: The Human Landscape*, ed. C. Malone and S. Stoddart, 313–344. Oxford: BAR.

———. 1988. "Towns of Sicily during the Roman Empire." *ANRW* II.11.1:90–206.

———. 1990. *Sicily under the Roman Empire: The Archaeology of a Roman Province, 36 BC–AD 535.* Warminster, UK: Aris and Phillips.

———. 1996. "La topografia della Catania romana: problemi e prospettive." In *Catania antica*, ed. B. Gentili, 149–173. Pisa: IEPI.

———. 2003. "A Group of Roman House-Tombs at Tauromenium (Taormina)." In *Studi classici in onore di Luigi Bernabo Brea*, ed. G. M. Bacci and M. C. Martinelli, 247–274. Palermo, Sicily: Regione Siciliana.

———. 2011. "The Fourth-Century Villa at Piazza Armerina (Sicily) in Its Wider Imperial Context: A Review of Some Aspects of Recent Research." In *Bruckneudorf und Gamzigrad: Spätantike Paläste und Grossvillen im Donau-Balkan-Raum*, ed. G. von Bülow and H. Zabehlicky, 55–87. Bonn: Habelt.

———. 2012. "*Agorai* and *Fora* in Hellenistic and Roman Sicily: An Overview of the Current *Status Quaestionis*." In *Agora greca e agorai di Sicilia*, ed. C. Ampolo, 245–267. Pisa: SNS.

———. 2016. *Caddeddi on the Tellaro: A Late Roman Villa in Sicily and Its Mosaics*. Leuven, Belgium: Peeters.

Wilson, R. J. A., and A. Leonard, Jr. 1980. "Field Survey at Heraclea Minoa (Agrigento), Sicily." *JFA* 7:219–239.

Wolf, M. 2003. *Die Häuser von Solunt*. Mainz: P. von Zabern.

———. 2012. "Nuove ricerche nell'*agora* di Solunto." In *Agora greca e agorai di Sicilia*, ed. C. Ampolo, 223–228. Pisa: SNS.

———. 2014. *Die Agora von Solunt: Öffentliche Gebäude und öffentliche Räume des Hellenismus im griechischen Westen*. Wiesbaden: Reichert.

Woolf, G. 1998. *Becoming Roman: The Origins of Provincial Civilization in Gaul*. Cambridge: Cambridge University Press.

Zambito, L. 2007. "Intervento statale e attività urbanistica: sul ruolo dei curatores reipublicae in due epigrafi da Tindari." *MinEpigrP* 12:103–110.

———. 2014. "La produzione dello zolfo in Sicilia in età romana: primi dati da una ricerca." *Journal of Ancient Topography* 24:137–156.

Zoumbaki, S. B. 2010. "Elean Relations with Rome and the Achaean Koinon and the Role of Olympia." In *Roman Peloponnese III: Society, Economy and Culture under the Roman Empire*, ed. A. D. Rizakis and Cl. E. Lepenioti, 111–127. Athens: NHRF.

INDEX